THE DISPUTED ISLANDS

ORDINARY LIFE IN EXTRAORDINARY TIMES
THE SAN JUANS, 1850 - 1874

Boyd C. Pratt

Mulno Cove Publishing
FRIDAY HARBOR

*The beauty that we see in the vernacular landscape
is the image of our common humanity:
hard work, stubborn hope, and mutual
forbearance striving to be love.*
—John Brinckerhoff Jackson

THE DISPUTED ISLANDS
ORDINARY LIFE IN EXTRAORDINARY TIMES
THE SAN JUANS, 1850-1874

by Boyd C. Pratt

Copyright © 2024 Boyd C. Pratt
All rights reserved

No part of this publication may be reproduced or transmitted in English or in other languages, in any form or by any means, electronic or mechanical, including photocopying, digital scanning, recording, or any other informational storage or retrieval system, without the written permission of the author.

ISBN: 978-1-7342351-5-9

Layout & graphic assistance by WBC Design

Published and Distributed by Mulno Cove Publishing
Printed in the United States of America

TABLE OF CONTENTS

How to Read This Book.. 1

Introduction: The View from Valley Cemetery 7

What About the Pig? 13

Identity
    "Indians" 21
    "British".. 29
    "Americans".. 35
    Cross-Cultural Families... 39
    Changing Cultural Attitudes Towards Ethnicity 47
    Identity... 60

Place
    Physical Features... 63
    Climate... 70
    Indigenous Places 73
    European and American Exploration..................... 79
    Dividing up the Land 89
    Changes in the Land... 103
    Place 114

Dwelling
    Dwellings 115
    Indigenous People's Villages and Camps............... 119
    Hudson's Bay Company Posts 127
    Military Camps.. 136
    Cross-Cultural Settlements 147
    Homesteads 152
    Barns and Outbuildings... 162
    Improvements 165
    Dwelling.. 171

Work
- Working 173
- Indigenous Seasons 175
- Gathering 177
- Hunting and Trapping 185
- Fishing 190
- Farming 203
- Limemaking 214
- Logging 227
- Trades 233
- Laboring 235
- Slavery 240
- Work 241

Intercourse
- Boats and Shipping 243
- Trails and Roads 260
- Mail, Newspapers, and Telegraph 271
- Commerce 273
- Merchandizing 278
- Financing 285
- Customs and Smuggling 289
- Intercourse 293

Society & Governance
- Marriages 295
- Burials and Cemeteries 303
- Festivities, Political Meetings, and Celebrations 305
- Religious Observances and Churches 309
- Education and Schools 311
- Fraternities 315
- Towns 316
- Friday Harbor 320
- Government 322
- Taxes 331
- Judicial Courts 332
- Society & Governance 340

Epilogue: The Disputed Islands 341

Appendices

Islanders 368
Charles Griffin to Governor James Douglas,
    June 15, 1859 407
Lyman Cutlar to Paul K. Hubbs, Jr., June 23, 1859 408
Lyman Cutlar Affidavit September 7, 1859 409
Alexander Grant Dallas to General Harney,
    May 10, 1860 411
Indigenous People Listed in Censuses 412
List of Petitioners for Naturalization, January 13, 1873 ... 426
William Warner, Description of a Passage between
    Spencer Spit and Frost Island off the East Shore
    of Lopez Island 427
North West Boundary Survey Storm Account 428
Salish Villages 429
Reef Net Locations 430
Joseph Banks' Orders to Archibald Menzies 431
Charles Wilkes' Description of Navy Archipelago 431
James S. Lawson, Description of Survey Methods 432
George Davidson's Description of the San Juan Islands ... 433
North West Boundary Survey Descriptions of
    Agricultural Lands 433
W. F. Tolmie, Letter on Hudson's Bay Company
    Claims on San Juan Island 434
Homestead Implements 438
Lila Hannah Firth, San Juan Island Range Wars 438
An Act to Regulate Sheep Running at Large in
    San Juan County 439
Tools and Building Materials 440
Homestead Houses 441
Homestead Furnishings 443
Homestead Improvements 443
Edible Marine Invertebrates 446
Edible Plants 446
Fishes and Other Marine Seafood 448
Homestead Livestock 449

Appraisal of Property, Augustin Hibbard Probate 449
List of Property of William F. Taylor Sold at Sheriff's
   Sale, January 28, 1874 451
Inventory of Goods, J. K. Bowken Store,
   San Juan Town 452
Mortgages and Loans 453
Petition of Samuel H. Gross for Insolvency 453
Samuel H. Gross, Exhibit One, Account of Sales 456
Creditors of Samuel H. Gross 457
The Excursion to San Juan 457
School House No. 1 Minutes 458
Subscribers to Portland Fair Schoolhouse 459
Assessment of Property on San Juan Island
   Henry R. Crosbie, Whatcom County Assessor,
   1859 460

Acknowledgements 461
Illustration Credits 462

LIST OF ILLUSTRATIONS

Cover
San Juan Valley Looking Northwest

Title Page
View of San JuanValley from Bailer Hill

Introduction
San Juan Island, 1859 Map of The Disputed Islands.....6

What About the Pig?
San Juan or Haro Archipelago, A. Peterman, 1872.......12
Belle Vue Sheep Farm Post Journal, June 15, 1859......15
Lt. James W. Forsyth, Tracing of 1860 Map of South End of San Juan Island...15

Identity
Map of the Indian Tribes and Lands Ceded by Treaty, George Gibbs, 1855 22
States of Origin in 1860 Census....................................36
Population Pyramid of 1860 Census............................38
Population Pyramid of 1870 Census............................39
Map of Dispersal of the Children of Catherine Delaunais..44
Delaunais Family Tree 44
Children of Catherine Delaunais LePlante 45
Detailed Map of Na-ME-At-Cha Indian Homestead...51
Countries of Origin in 1870 Census.............................59
Countries of Origin in 1880 Census.............................59

Place

San Juan Islands Place Names 62
Bathymetry of the San Juan Islands 68
U.S. Coast Survey of West Side of San Juan
    Island, 1854 76
Reef Net Locations in the San Juan Islands 78
Names of the San Juan Islands 83
Captain G. H. Richards Survey of Roche Harbor
    and Its Approaches 87
Robert Frazer Land Claim 92
Township and Range Survey Diagram 95
Sections in Township Diagram 96
Subdivisions of Sections Diagram 97
Homestead Claims in San Juan Valley 98
Homestead Applications in the San Juan Islands,
    1877-1923 100
Louis Cayou with His Yoke of Oxen 106

Dwelling

James Madison Alden, Sketch of Belle Vue
    Sheep Farm 116
Long House Construction 120
Reef Net Camp 123
Plan of Fort Simpson, British Columbia 129
Belle Vue Sheep Farm, Photo by North West
    Boundary Survey, ca. 1859 130-131
Belle Vue Sheep Farm Structure with *Piece sur Piece*
    Construction 133
Fort Nisqually Granary 135
Sibley Tents at American Camp 137
English Camp with Garden and Tents, 1860 138
American Camp from the Redoubt 139
Lt. Fred H. W. Ebstein, Belle Vue Sheep Farm and
    American Camp, 1873 143

Brig. Gen. Nathaniel Michler, Map of
  English Camp 144
"Indian Camp at Kanaka Bay," U.S. Coast and
  Geodetic Survey (1892) 148-149
Kanaka Bay Camp ca. 1873 150
Map of Brown's [Grindstone] Bay, Orcas Island 151
Log Cabin Construction with Notching Types 154
Log v. Frame Houses 159
Section and Plan of Center-Drive Pole Barn 163
Fences at Firth Farm (Belle Vue Sheep
  Farm/American Camp) 166

Work

Salish Woman Digging Bulbs 181
Paul Kane, "Clal-lum Women Weaving a Blanket,"
  Showing a Woolly Dog 184
Squamish Woman Spinning Wool 185
"Four Remarkable, Supported Poles, in Port
  Townsend," Captain George Vancouver 187
"Sketch Map Showing Approximate Route of
  the Sockeye Salmon…" 192
Diagram of a Reef Net 195
Graignic Family in the *City of Paris* 203
Period Illustration of a Berkshire Boar 207
Orchards in Eastsound, Orcas Island, ca. 1900 212
San Juan Lime Company (Lime Kiln) 215
San Juan Lime Company Chart of Ownership,
  1860-1876 216
Lime Kiln and Quarry Crew, Cowell's,
  San Juan Island 218
North Kiln and Boarding House, Lime Kiln,
  San Juan Island 220

Diagram of a Lime Kiln 222
Coopers Displaying the Tools of Their Trade, Roche
    Harbor, San Juan Island 223
Hauling Cordwood, San Juan Island 230
Woodcutters with Spring Boards and a Misery
    Whip 232

Intercourse
Washington Dugout Canoe 244
Northwest Dugout Canoe Types 246
Reef Netters off Stuart Island 249
Canoes and Columbia River Salmon Boats at
    Kanaka Bay 252
Indigenous Fishers Bringing Their Catch to Sell 253
Sloops 255
Hudson's Bay Company "Beaver" 258
Advertisement for *Eliza Anderson* 259
Sheep Station on North End of San Juan Island 261
Township and Range Survey Map of San Juan
    Valley, San Juan Island 263
Sketch of County Road, Keddy [Cady] Mountain to
    Friday Harbor 264-265
Map of 1887 Road Dispute in San Juan Valley 266
Masthead of *The British Colonist* 271
Telegraph Line on 1874 Township and
    Range Survey 272
Israel Katz Invoice for Samuel H. Gross 282

Society & Governance
    Alfred and Annie Burke and Family, Shaw Island 294
    Catholic and Presbyterian Churches, San Juan
        Valley 310
    No. 1 Schoolhouse, Portland Fair, San Juan Island ...313
    James Madison Alden, View of Griffin Bay and San
        Juan Town 316
    Map of Friday Harbor, 1895 320
    Earliest Photo of Friday Harbor..................................321
    Changes in Washington Territory Counties that
        Include the San Juan Islands...............................323
    Washington Territory Civil Cases Compared to
        Population 333
    Washington Territory Criminal Cases Compared to
        Population 334
    Witness Transportation Costs.....................................338

Epilogue
    Jessie Douglas, Pioneer Cabin, San Juan
        County Fairgrounds 342

*Let us acknowledge that we reside on
the ancestral lands and waters of
the Coast Salish people,
who have called this place home
since time immemorial,
and let us honor and protect
inherent, aboriginal, and treaty rights
that have been passed down from
generation to generation.*

HOW TO READ THIS BOOK

This book discusses ordinary life in the San Juan Islands during extraordinary times: the run-up to the Pig War, the War itself, and subsequent joint military occupation until the settlement of the boundary dispute. To do so, I have delved deeply into the details of people's lives and environment. I understand that this may not be of interest for every reader; if that is your case, I suggest you read the Introduction, What about the Pig, the first and last paragraphs of each chapter, and the Epilogue. Then, if you want to explore a specific theme or topic, go for it.

After introducing and discussing the pig incident itself (What about the Pig?), I have arranged the chapters of this book into general categories: Identity, Place, Dwelling, Work, Intercourse [intentionally, despite modern day connotations], and Society & Governance, in order to examine the context and repercussions of that event through several critical lenses. However, because this divides up a continuous history arbitrarily into themes, there is bound to be repetition. For instance, one cannot discuss Indigenous identity without talking about the treatment of "Indians" as a political category resulting from the boundary dispute. Many islanders transported goods and people across Haro Strait to Victoria: should they be mentioned in "Work" or "Intercourse"? What about homesteaders, who came from a wide variety of ethnic and national backgrounds, settled and 'proved up' their land, worked multiple jobs, marketed their crops, sent their children to schools and were active members of churches and fraternities, and often held political office. So, in which chapter should they be discussed?

It has been my intent to present, wherever possible, the original sources from which I have subsequently drawn conclusions about this history. These come from many places and take many forms: writings, such as diaries and journals, invoices, newspaper articles, and contemporary historical accounts; visual documents such as photographs and maps; and material evidence such as archaeological sites and standing historical structures, objects, and landscapes—what we can still see 'in the field.' My purpose for doing this is threefold: it allows the people and things to speak for themselves; it provides an opportunity to reveal the basis for my method of approach and analysis; and it allows the reader to come to their own conclusions regarding the history of the period.

To view local history in this way, I have had to examine primary sources as much as possible, trying to understand what the participants saw and experienced in their time. These sources encompass reports of exploring and surveying parties; governmental censuses; property records such as homestead 'proving up' papers and land deeds; journals and correspondence of Charles John Griffin, Post Trader of Hudson's Bay Company Belle Vue Sheep Farm, and farmers such as James Fleming; court cases ranging from claims, crimes, and misdemeanors to tribal treaty rights recognition by the federal government (such as *Duwamish et al v. United States of America*); birth, marriage, and death certificates and probates and wills; newspaper and magazine articles; reminiscences in anthologies such as *Lummi Elders Speak* and *Told by the Pioneers*; and governmental records such as county commission journals, property taxes, school records, and road surveys and projects. And then there is that jungle of genealogical information, at times contradictory and misleading but always fascinating. I am particularly appreciative of those who shared their family histories with me in this way.

As with my other books on the history of the islands, I have tried to incorporate the "voices" of various actors in history in order to represent the very real polyphony of the polyglot society that constituted The Disputed Islands. These quotes, along with the illustrations, are meant to have equal weight with the narrative. At times this inquiry revealed statements that are distasteful or offensive to us in the context of the current era: the rigid racial categorization of the federal censuses; and James Francis Tulloch's rants about his neighbors the "Squaw Men," an example of the predominate Euro-American attitude toward "Indians," to list a couple of the more egregious examples. My overarching propensity has been to let the people speak for themselves, even when I find that offensive. That does not mean uncritical acceptance; but it does mean trying to understand the context within which these quotes occur. As Jennifer Raff says in *Origin: A Genetic History of the Americas*, "...as you read this genetic chronicle, please do not lose sight of the dignity of the human beings who live this history and the rich complexity of individual existences that are lost in the telling."

I am grateful for the many secondary sources that have been written about the islands. Without the paths forged by David Richardson (*Magic Islands* and *Pig War Islands*), Jo Bailey Cummings and Al Cummings (*The Powder Keg Islands*), and Lucille McDonald (*Making History: The People Who Shaped the San Juan Islands* and numerous articles), I could not have even begun this book. Equally essential is the work of Wayne Suttles, particularly his dissertation *Economic Life of the Coast Salish of Haro and Rosario Straits*, Daniel Boxberger, *San Juan Island Cultural Affiliation Study*, and Dave Elliott, Sr., *Saltwater People* In addition, there were several signal islands histories: Fred John Splitstone, *Orcas...Gem of the San Juans*; Dorothy Powell and Fran Hilen, *Shaw Island: Earliest Known History to 1994*; James Bergquist, *The History of Stuart Island*; and Charles Ludwig, "A Brief History of Waldron Island." Karen Jones-Lamb's *Native American Wives of San Juan Settlers* provided an inspiration for the exploration of cross-cultural families in the Islands. I am also indebted to several of my historically minded contemporaries: Robin Jacobson, genealogist extraordinaire, who is greatly missed; Mike Vouri, whose work on the Pig War, with all its ramifications, has been essential; Lynn Weber/Roochvarg, whose meticulous research has resulted in numerous essays for *HistoryLink*; and Candace Wellman, whose books and correspondence have opened my eyes to the complexity of Northwest cross-cultural marriages. They have led me to explore sources that I had not considered and to reexamine what has been considered to be established truth.

A final note on terminology: several terms used in this book require explanation. As a general rule, the term "Indigenous peoples" refers to the inhabitants of the region prior to the arrival of Europeans, Euro-Americans, and their descendants. In the Salish Sea, this term refers to the Coast Salish—an anthropological term for groups of people who spoke similar languages—with the specific descriptive "Straits Salish" referring to the Coast Salish in the Salish Sea, related not only in their language but also in many cultural practices, such as reef netting. This group includes the Lummi, Saanich, Samish, Semiahmoo, Songhees, and Sooke, with mutually intelligible dialects, as well as the S'Klallam of the Olympic Peninsula, a different language group.

The arrival of Europeans and Euro-Americans complicated the designation of Indigenous peoples. Not only did the Spanish, English, and Americans overlay their own names on places in the Salish Sea, they assigned various peoples to various groupings that did not necessarily reflect how those peoples described themselves. When another system of control—government—was imposed, Indigenous groups were defined by recognition through treaties. In the newly formed Territory of Washington (1853), Governor Isaac Stevens negotiated 13 treaties with "Native Nations"; the Treaty of Point Elliott (1855) included "Tribes" of the Salish Sea. On Vancouver Island, James Douglas of the Hudson's Bay Company purchased, at the request of the British Crown, 14 parcels of Indigenous land (now known as the "Douglas Treaties") in the period from 1850–1854. With the establishment of the international boundary, the Canadian government officially refers to Indigenous peoples as "First Nations," the American counterparts "Native Americans." "Tribes" and "First Nations" then became "recognized" or "unrecognized" (i.e., defined by their political status in relation to the United States or Canadian governments).

The terms "European" and "Euro-American" are used to define any non-Indigenous peoples. They include such ethnically diverse groups as English, Irish, Scots, and Welsh historically subsumed by the designation "English" and all sorts of immigrants classified as "Americans." Furthermore, the Hudson's Bay Company—at the forefront of European settlement in the region—employed, in addition to "Englishmen," a wide variety of ethnicities, including French Canadians, Hawaiians (Kanakas), Iroquois, Norwegians, and Métis (people of mixed French Canadian and upper Midwestern tribes). This terminology is compounded by the use of "Euro-American" to describe ethnic groups such as the Chinese—clearly neither "European" nor "American" at the time.

As a result, in this book I have tried to use (and explain the use of) the terms as they are found in original sources. For instance, the prevailing term for Hawaiians in the Pacific Northwest was "Kanakas," a designation that was considered pejorative in the past but has recently been re-engaged by contemporary Hawaiians as a source of prideful identity: *Kanaka Maoli*. There are exceptions. Euro-American men who married Indigenous women were often derogatively called "squaw men." A more palliative term at the time was "Métis," originating from cross-cultural marriages in the upper Midwest and Canada; today the Métis Nation is a group of self-defining people. I have chosen to use the more neutral and generic term "cross-cultural" to refer to these unions in the islands.

Wherever possible, I have included Indigenous group or place names in specific variations of Straits Salish. These are rendered in Americanist Phonetic Notation or North American Phonetic Alphabet (NAPA), originally developed by European and American anthropologists for the phonetic transcription of Indigenous languages of North America. Sometimes transcriptions are given in English. For those who would like to hear how some of these names are spoken, I recommend the Samish Indian Nation's StoryMap "Coast Salish Place Names of the San Juan Islands," which includes links to recordings of the words being spoken. *https://storymaps.arcgis.com/stories/9b0f86b51e-054ba78b83ab39c4d0b1a6?fbclid=IwAR0vZrxyvm8EUOHFv-jHmTARQD-JtMAD_TI0L4wCfJOvyJVGkMzukE1pljqs*

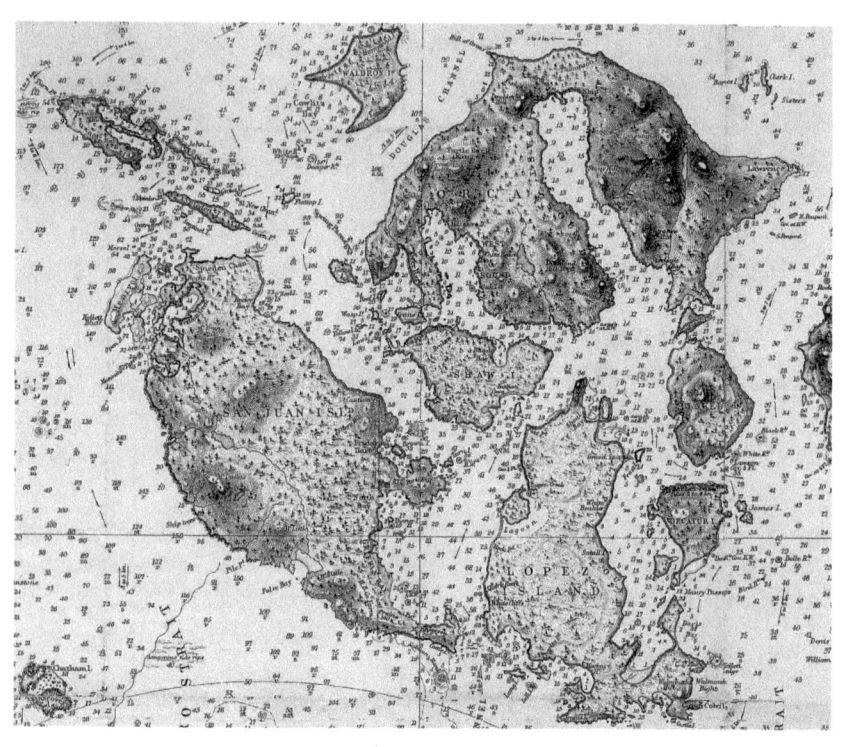

*1859 Chart of The Disputed Islands
(courtesy of San Juan Island National Historical Park)*

INTRODUCTION
THE VIEW FROM VALLEY CEMETERY

It is a venture that I have mulled these past years of my becoming less headlong and more aware that I dwell in a community of time as well as of people. That I should know more than I do about this other mysterious citizenship, how far it goes, where it touches.

—Ivan Doig, *Winter Brothers: A Season at the Edge of America* (1980)[1]

From Valley Cemetery, among the gravesites of those who have lived and died on San Juan Island, the view leads toward the south, across the gentle expanse of the valley that slopes down toward False Bay, the Strait of Juan de Fuca, and the Olympic Mountains beyond. One can see the grassy areas where the Coast Salish once harvested camas and burned the prairie to keep it free of shrubbery and bushes so that the bulbs could flower freely and the deer graze. One can see the Garry oaks, named for Hudson's Bay Company Chief Deputy Governor Nicholas Garry, ringing the valley in patches, ideal grazing ground for flocks of Company sheep, such that they named it Oak Prairie. And one can see the pattern of fenced fields that delineated the homesteads of the Euro-American settlers who turned the valley into some of the richest farmland in the islands.

This, in a way, is the very soul of San Juan Island. It is where early Euro-American settlers gave portions of their homesteads for both the Catholic and Protestant churches and their respective graveyards. And it is where I want to be buried when I die.

It wasn't always so. I was born on another island, Oahu, in the then Territory of Hawaii. My first encounter with the San Juan Islands was as a ten-year-old boy, when my parents bought part of the old Mulno/Ackerly Farm—then owned by the Halseys—and built a Pan-Abode log 'cabin' there as a summer place. We would come from our other island home to Friday Harbor in the summers, soon after school got out, and then head back a week or so before classes started again in the fall. My brother and I spent most of our time outdoors, exploring the woods and the fields, Mulno Cove and Griffin Bay. Being "Summer People," we experienced great enjoyment of the place, but not so much the people—we knew and worked with our neighbors, and we had acquaintances on the island, but not much beyond that. Eventually, my parents retired here; I would still visit, but not for long.

All that changed after my father died in 1990, and my wife Lovel and I decided to move here in order to be with my mother. We farmed, raised our children, and built a home, and in the process, we became truly part of the island community, getting to know island families, old and new. And it was through farming and farmers that I met that I became curious about the history of the place: why did the land look the way it did, who grew what where, and how did they farm?

It all started with The Pig. In researching the history of agriculture in the islands, I was led to ask questions about the single and signal victim of the so-called Pig War: What kind of pig was this? Why did the Hudson's Bay Company value it so highly, and the man who shot it so lowly? What was it doing in Cutlar's potato patch, and, for that matter, what was he doing raising potatoes there? One day, thinking about all this while weeding our potato patch, I reached down to uncover a stone projectile point, possibly thousands of years old. That got me thinking about the deep history of the islands, starting with an Indigenous presence and continuing with the intermarriage of Coast Salish women with Euro-American men in the years following contact—associations that were rich in helping the newcomers settle and subsist. And I realized that in fact Cutlar's potato patch was in all probability his Indigenous wife's, given the history of Coast Salish matrilineal cultivation of camas beds and adoption of the potato soon after the Hudson's Bay Company arrived in the region. All of these questions and speculations, as well as the many others this incident raised, led me beyond an examination of early farming in the islands, to an investigation of ordinary life in the San Juans from 1850—the year of the first Euro-American 'settlement' on San Juan island—to 1874, two years after the decision settling the boundary dispute, a year after the establishment of San Juan

County, and the year that the township and range survey was begun in earnest.

My intent is to examine the early environment and history of the pre- and post-contact San Juans to understand why the islands are the way they are today, and in order to dwell here in a better way. My approach is a vernacular one, developed over years of professional practice. I was born in Hawaii, at Kapiolani Hospital, the same maternity ward where Barack Obama would enter the world eight years later. There amid Hawaii's rich mix of diverse cultures and ethnicities, I encountered a geographical dyslexion: the East was west of us and the West was east of us, and the two—no, the way more than two—certainly met in the "Crossroads of the Pacific."

I left Hawaii to attend St. John's College in Santa Fe, where I learned to read the Western Classics critically, with the help of robust seminars and tutorials. After I received my Master of Architecture degree and worked in an architectural firm for several years, I went to work for the New Mexico State Historic Preservation Office. In the mid-1980s, I struck out on my own, as a consultant, and fell in with a group of fellow scholars in the Vernacular Architecture Forum. Writing from a viewpoint of "history from the bottom up," and influenced by Ferdnand Braudel and others of the French Annales School, as well as W. G. Hoskins in England and J. B. Jackson in America, I began to look at historic architecture and landscape from a vernacular point of view. New Mexico, with its long, complex, and conflicted history, offered an intriguing place to study the interactions of cultures with the landscape and among themselves. Rather than the traditional "Three [Indian, Spanish, Anglo] Cultures" approach, I was interested in the many more "cultures" that resulted from this mix, or *mestizaje*, broadened from notions of race or ethnicity to culture itself. When we came to live in the San Juans, I, born and raised into the melting pot of the "Paradise of the Pacific" and schooled in the *mestizaje* of the "Land of Enchantment," applied this approach to the very local history of the islands.

As Edward Gibbon, the author of *The Decline and Fall of the Roman Empire* and certainly not one to shy away from asserting his own point of view, stated, "Every man of genius who writes history infuses into it, perhaps unconsciously, the character of his own spirit."[2] No man of genius, coming from a position of privilege, a person of white descent firmly established in the social and economic hierarchy of the Hawaiian Islands, I have found my encounter with the "Other" of heterogenous, cross-cultural society in the history and living landscape of the San Juan Islands to be enriching. The often-times painful process of realizing my biases has been enlightened by looking at those areas that first appear marginal, peripheral, or borderland that come to be central to vernacular history. In a biological metaphor, these ecotones or liminal areas, where one ecozone melds with another, prove to be where biological diversity is at its greatest. And, in a dialectical process, these areas of mixing or mingling in turn demand a reexamination of the original, "pure" categories that meet there; for example, the context of cross-cultural marriages in the islands leads one to question elements of the cultures that are 'crossing'—"American" or "English," locally "Indian" or from elsewhere.

During the Covid pandemic, I gave two Zoom presentations, one on "Island Neighbors Helping Neighbors" and the other on "The Kanakas of San Juan Island." Both were the outcome of my research into the history of the islands but informed by recent Black Lives Matter demonstrations that spurred a growing awareness of issues of race, gender, diversity, and ethnicity. At the time I ran across among my mother's things a postcard of a "Hawaiian Surf-Rider" from the Field Museum in Chicago. I recall my mother telling me a story about my godfather, David Pilnoi Kahanamoku (1895-1967), who had taught my mother how to board surf at Waikiki Beach. David, the younger brother of the more famous Duke Kahanamoku, was chosen by Malvina Hoffman, the sculptor who created the Hawaiian Surf-Rider, as the model for a typical Polynesian. He related how Hoffman made a plaster cast of his full body; he had to pose in that surfing position for hours while the plaster hardened, with only two straws to his nostrils for breathing. Hoffman's method was to then take the casting and remodel it so as to accentuate the "typological" features of the "race" that it represented. The finished bronze sculpture was featured in the Hall of the Races of Mankind Exhibit when it opened in 1933, and is still among the Museum's holdings, albeit reinterpreted via a 2016 retrospective exhibit,

"Looking at Ourselves: Rethinking the Sculptures of Malvina Hoffman." The back of the postcard reads: "This man is typical of the Polynesians, who are tall in stature, have straight or wavy hair and light-brown skin. Polynesians are a mixture of White, Mongoloid, and Negro stocks, and are scattered over many of the Pacific islands." It is challenging to enumerate how many things are wrong about this statement, but one could start with the awful project of stereotyping "The Races of Man" in a disturbing era of white supremacy, racial purity, and eugenics.

There are, of course, fundamental differences between visiting a place, dwelling there, and growing there as a home. In many ways I have been an "outsider" in all the places I have lived: while I was born and grew up in Hawaii as a *kamaaina*, I am not Hawaiian and indeed descended from the missionaries who both radically altered and shaped Hawaiian culture; my twenty years in New Mexico, all be they blessed by wonderful experiences of the place and its history, were as an "Anglo" in (what was then) a predominantly Hispanic-Indigenous society; and now I live in the islands not as an "old-timer"—I'd have to be from a family who had lived here for several generations to be that—but as a citizen who has been here long enough and invested in local society deeply enough to call this place my home. In many ways, the sentiment of Leslie P. Hartley's "the past is a foreign country; they do things differently there" is at work here; by approaching this place as an "outsider," I hope to offer a different perspective. In this way, I can only hope that this endeavor is a reflection of the transition from being a visitor to a resident, embracing the islands as home.

We shall not cease from exploration
And the end of all our exploring
Will be to arrive where we started
And know the place for the first time.

—T. S. Eliot, *Little Gidding*
(*The Four Quartets*)

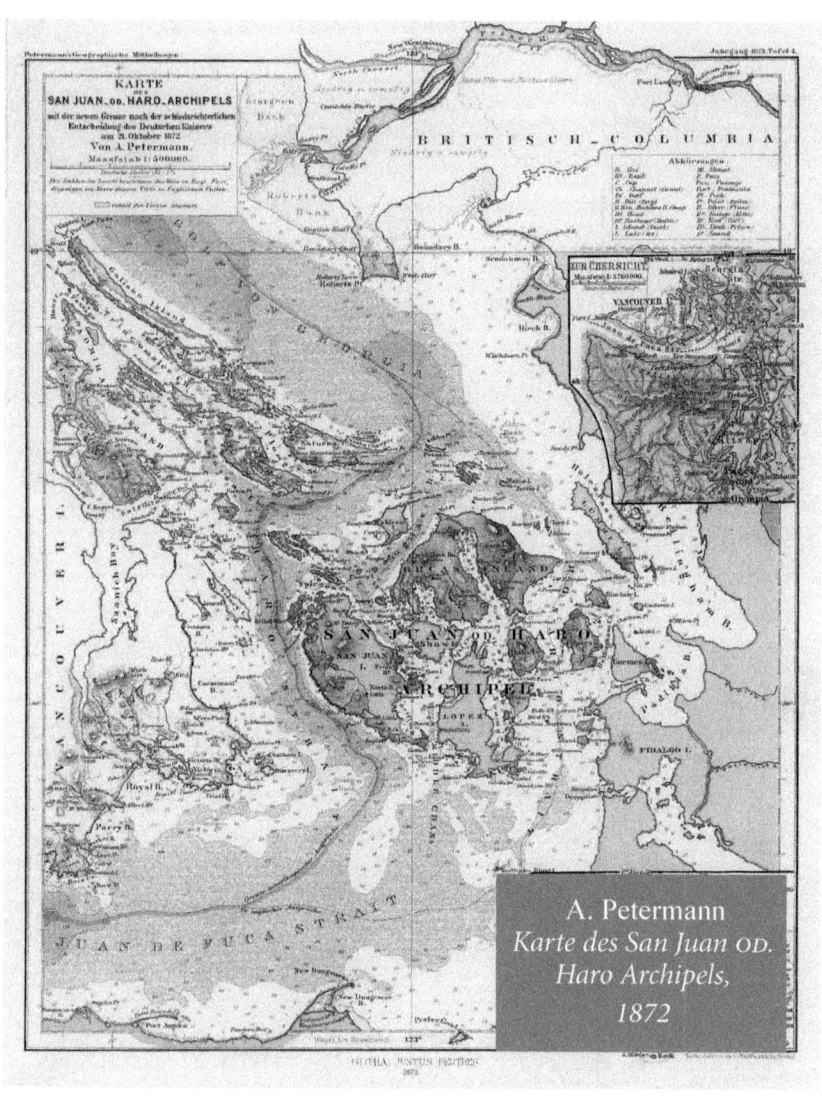

A. Petermann, "Chart of the San Juan or Haro Archipelago" (courtesy of San Juan Island National Historical Park)

WHAT ABOUT THE PIG?

One of the great eye-openers of the twentieth century is the realization that the use of humble everyday objects is not habitual—which is to say that we cannot do without them—but that these things are "ordinary" in the earliest and fullest sense of the word also: they embody our mostly unspoken assumptions, and they both order our culture and determine its direction.

—Margaret Visser,
Much Depends on Dinner (1986)[1]

The Disputed Islands is the name that American government officials used to refer to the San Juans, an archipelago of about 418 islands in the Pacific Northwest. The "Dispute" had to do with national possession: were they part of Oregon (and then Washington) Territory—and thus the United States of America, or were they part of the Colony of Vancouver Island (and then the Province of British Columbia)—thus part of Great Britain? This diagreement was the result of the vague language of the Treaty of 1846:

> *[the boundary] shall be continued westward along the said forty-ninth parallel of north latitude to the middle of the channel which separates the continent from Vancouver's Island; and thence southerly through the middle of the said channel, and of Fuca's Straits to the Pacific Ocean.*

It focused on the islands themselves in an increasingly conflicted course of events that climaxed in the Pig War, so called because of a very specific dispute over an American's shooting of a British pig. These events eventually led to a dozen-year joint occupation of San Juan Island by British and American troops and ended with the findings of an International Boundary Commission, presided over by Kaiser Wilhelm of Germany, settling possession of the islands upon the United States in 1872.

It is not my intention to revisit the military and political events of the Pig War, which has been well researched by my colleague and friend Mike Vouri, among others.[2] What I will address are the other ways in which the islands were, indeed, disputed. Specifically, I want to explore how ordinary people lived their everyday lives in what developed into an extraordinary situation. These people not only came from different cultures: Coast Salish and Northern "Indians," "English" (including Irish, Scots, and Welsh), Hawaiian Islanders, French Canadians, Iroquois, Métis, and "Americans" (who came from regions as diverse as New England, the Midwest, the South, and California). They all had to adapt both to the physical environment of the islands and the other cultures who co-inhabited them.

Let's begin by looking at the Incident of the Pig. On June 15th, 1859, Lyman Cutlar shot a pig he caught rooting in his potato patch.[3] In the ensuing altercation, first American, then British, military were called upon to defend the rights and possessions of their respective citizens and countries. The first record of the event appeared in the Belle Vue Sheep Farm *Post Journal*, written by Charles Griffin, the Hudson's Bay Company (hereinafter referred to as the "Company") Post Trader, in his standard 'shorthand' description of an otherwise 'typical' day:

Wednesday 15th
Heavy rain during the night & showery all day, light wind. —
Shepherds packing wool, finished shearing
Ignace's flock last eve.g. —Jacob & Lamane hauling logs.
Robillard & George sawing oak for hay carts, cradles
&c. —Ind^s weeding &c. —
Napoleon left for Victoria to have his account settled. —
An American shot one of my pigs for trespassing!!!—
Beaver arrived w^h Messrs Dallas, Fraser & Dr Tolmie. —[4]

By the end of the day, Griffin dashed off a letter to his superior, Chief Factor James Douglas, and sent it the 14 miles across Haro Strait to Fort Victoria by canoe (see Appendix: *Charles Griffin to James Douglas, June 15, 1859*).[5] What began as a simple dispute

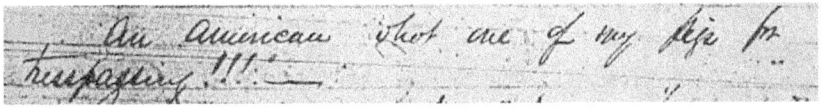

*Belle Vue Sheep Farm, Post Journal, June 15, 1859
(courtesy of San Juan Island National Historical Park)*

over the value of remuneration for the shooting of the pig soon escalated into an international incident: the value of the boar, the presence of Cutlar in the 'centre' of the best grazing land, the personal threat to Griffin and his livestock, the general threat to Griffin's herdsmen, the growth in American "squatting," and ultimately the international dispute over possession of the island itself.

But on second look, there are some more mundane questions that I want to ask. What was Cutlar doing on San Juan Island in the first place? Why had he chosen what the Hudson's Bay Company considered to be the "centre of the most valuable sheep run"? Why did the Americans, such as Cutlar, take up claims and make improvements with "a log cabin and a potatoe patch"? What, for that matter, were Griffin and his "Herdsmen" doing there? What kind of pig was it, and why was it running loose?

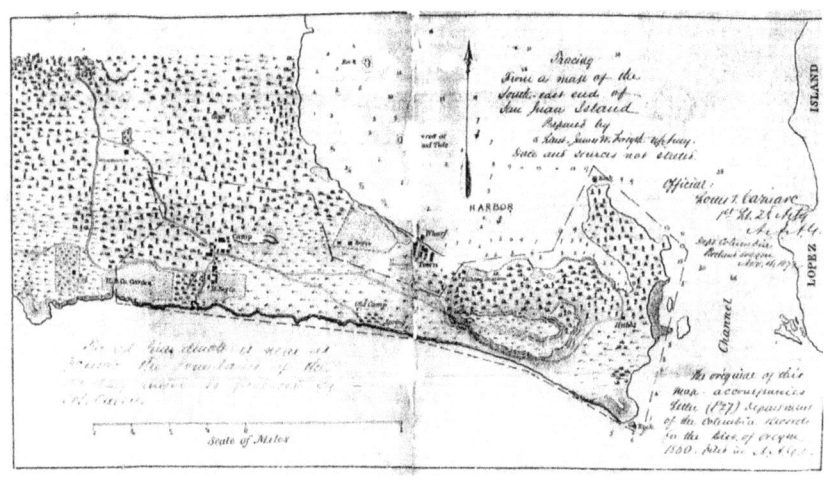

*Lt. James W. Forsyth, Tracing of 1860 Map of the South End of San Juan Island [Cutlar's Potato Patch is in the upper left.]
(courtesy of San Juan Island National Historical Park)*

Upon further examination, the situation becomes more complex. Cutlar gave his version of events in a letter dated June 23rd to Paul K. Hubbs, Jr., the American customs agent on the island (see Appendix: *Lyman Cutlar to Paul K. Hubbs, Jr., June 23, 1859*)[6]. This was followed by an affidavit, written on September 7th and enclosed with a letter dated the next day (September 8, 1859) from Hubbs to U.S. Secretary of the Treasury Howell Cobb; it tells a slightly different story (see Appendix: *Cutlar Affidavit September 7, 1859*).[7] Based on these documents, another review of the situation leads to a further set of questions and observations, such as why did Griffin consider his pig a "very valuable Boar," while Cutlar thought that it was worth no more than ten dollars, and tradable either with a pig of his own or one from "up sound"? One of the incitements that Cutlar gave for shooting the pig was that his attention was called to the animal's trespass by "one of the Hudson Bay Co servants," Jacob, who was riding by and allegedly laughed at the situation of the pig "at his old game" in the potato patch; according to this account, Cutlar "enraged by the independence of the negro knowing as he did my previous loss…upon the impulse of the moment seized my rifle and shot the hog." Although called a "collard man," a "negro," and a "niggar," Jacob was probably a native Hawaiian—"Sandwich Islander," "Owahee," or "Kanaka" (as they were commonly referred to at the time), one of a polyglot culture of Hudson's Bay Company employees that included Englishmen, Scots, Norwegians, French Canadians, Metis, Iroquois, and local and regional Indigenous groups, including Nuxalt (Bella Coolas), S'Klallams, Haidas, Lummis, Samish, W̱SÁNEĆ (Saanich), Skagits, Songhees, and Tsimshians. Did Cutlar's response have something to do with his own origins, which were in Kentucky or Ohio, during a time of growing friction over the issue of slavery in the United States?

Cutlar proffered a method of resolution: "they could select three men, and whatever valuation they might place on the animal he would at once pay." On first reading, this seems clearly to his advantage—after all, most of his neighbors would, of course, be Americans and take his side—but on further reading we realize that it reflects the differing social and political solutions to conflicting issues. Griffin, a "servant" of the Company, reported and complained to his superior, James Douglas, whose associates (also Company men) apparently pushed for civil action within the British juridical system (which, in Victoria, capitol of newly formed British Columbia, was closely interwoven with the Company), while Cutlar called for a typically American frontier solution: the judgment of one's peers.

A fourth document—the rebuttal of Alexander Dallas, a Chief Factor of the Company (as well as the son-in-law of Chief Factor and Governor James Douglas), to charges of threatening Cutlar with forceful removal to Victoria for trial in the British court system—provides further insight into the dispute (see Appendix: *Alexander Grant Dallas to General Harney, May 10, 1860*).[8] Dallas amplifies Griffin's initial description of Cutlar's claim—"one third of an acre in which he planted potatoes & partly & very imperfectly enclosed"—with the observation that "what has been dignified by the name of his "farm" consisted of a very small patch of potatoes, partially fenced on three sides, and entirely open on the fourth." This statement sheds more light on the significance of Cutlar's place to the British; in their eyes the farm itself was of small value but was placed in a very valuable location, causing inconvenience and irritation to the Hudson's Bay Company. From the documents, we can glean that, in addition to being in the "centre of the most valuable sheep run," it was located about a mile and a half from the Company's Establishment (Belle Vue Sheep Farm), near the edge of the forest (where the pig was apparently shot—not in the garden), and alongside a road (upon which Jacob was travelling). Focusing upon this particular pattern of settlement—in the midst of open prairie land but close to a forest and a road—changes the point of view from a general dispute over territory to the differing specific acts of claiming land, and, in particular, how the land was used.

Finally, there is the overarching theme of the potato patch. Why potatoes? One of the traditional uses of the islands was by Indigenous groups to harvest camas, a lilaceous plant that produces edible bulbs. Coast Salish women maintained camas—both the small, or purple, and great varieties—in cultivated beds—where use rights were through matrilineal lines. In the islands, camas bulbs are found naturally in areas of well-drained loam, such as island prairies, meadows, and grassy bluffs, as well as rock outcroppings with pockets of soil. The women used fieldstones to delineate the beds, which were weeded of grass and death, or poison, camas, and then planted with smaller bulbs and seeds. They harvested the bulbs in the spring (April or May), when they could be distinguished by their purple blossoms from that of death camas with white flowers. The Coast Salish burned the savannah-like areas of prairie grass and Garry oaks to keep them open for cultivation of camas and other lilaceous bulbs as well as for ease of hunting game such as deer. These were the very "prairies" that the Company sought for their sheep runs, and which Americans like Cutlar settled on in order to farm. Because it was easier to cultivate, the Coast Salish rapidly adopted the potato when it was introduced into the region via Euro-American trading posts in the early nineteenth century (via Fort Astoria, est. 1811, and Fort Langley, est. 1827)—or possibly earlier through indirect trade with California or Mexico. Coast Salish women continued as the main cultivators of root crops, using delineated beds, digging stick cultivation, and harvesting techniques similar to camas production.

Cutlar lived on his farm with a Coast Salish wife, and it was probably her potato patch the boar had rooted through. The post-shooting description of the potato patch as being "partly & very imperfectly enclosed" and "partially fenced on three sides, and entirely open on the fourth" matches historic descriptions of traditional Coast Salish women's camas—and later potato—plots. Although Cutlar later claimed that he had rowed to the nearest American settlement—Port Townsend—to get his seed potatoes, his wife could have just as easily gotten them from her nearby Coast Salish relations; Charles Griffin, for instance, had obtained his potato stock from Cowichans on nearby Vancouver Island. That Cutlar's claim occurred in the midst of a Hudson's Bay Company sheep run, which had been appropriated from the Coast Salish's camas harvesting, highlights an earlier, fundamental 'dispute' in the islands.

The San Juans, from the very time of Euro-American "discovery" to the present day, have been disputed in many ways. The purpose of this book is to examine the ways in which the islands were disputed during the period from the first Euro-American "settlement" (ca. 1850) to the 1874 'resolution' of the boundary dispute (although the overall years covered extend well into the past and approach the present). This period—just shy of a quarter of a century—offers a narrow window into some of the disputes over this place at that time, and how they were manifested on the ground.

This study takes as its main method the examination of how various extraordinary historical events played out upon a general field or background of ordinary history. Included in this larger historical background is the transitional use and settlement of the islands by different groups—historically referred to as "Indian," "English," and "American"—all of whom are themselves complexly composite when examined closely. This study explores their various methods of using and settling the land—varying from seasonal fishing, hunting, and gathering to establishment of isolated family-scale farming homesteads to large agricultural and industrial enterprises. However, as with the monolithically labeled ethnic groups—Indian, English, and American—it also explores and analyzes the intermixing and transitional varieties of land use and settlement.

History can be divided into so many seemingly arbitrary categories. In homage to the Victorians, whose era within the Western cultural tradition overarches the period under discussion, this study approaches general subjects under idealized categories—Identity, Place, Dwelling, Work, Intercourse, Society, and Governance—much as the Victorians talked and wrote about Family, Faith, Honor, Loyalty, etc. The irony in using these capitalized appellations is intentional: under the seemingly placid surface of each Idea there teems a myriad of typological varieties, just as the Victorian ideal of "Love" (romantic attachment between a man and a woman of equal social stature consummated in marriage and resulting in a nuclear family) has been shown to contain a myriad of actual historical manifestations (socially misaligned marriages, extramarital affairs, homosexual relationships, prostitution, etc.). This categorization offers one way of viewing the same place during a specific period through different lenses, as opposed to the more conventional approach to history of a strictly chronological narrative.

Normally, I would have begun a book on local history with a description of place—the islands that make up the San Juan Archipelago. But in this case, I found it important to examine the people of these islands first. With this emphasis, this study explores several themes: the different ethnic groups that peopled the islands and how they perceived themselves and others; how some of these groups "discovered" this place; how islanders perceived the islands differently; how some had originated from the islands and how some settled on the land; the various ways in which they 'made a living'; and finally, how they interacted among themselves, ranging from getting around by boat, foot, horse, mule, and cart, to communication through various media and the materialization of various social constructs such as education, religion, and politics.

IDENTITY

When Lyman Cutlar shot the pig, it was within a milieu of peoples from several different cultural backgrounds: Cutlar himself, from the American South; his Coast Salish wife, whose name we do not know; Jacob, possibly a Kanaka (native Hawaiian); and Charles John Griffin, from "Lower Canada" (French-speaking Montreal), as well as other members of the Hudson's Bay Company who were English, Scots, and Métis (from families of Indigenous and Euro-American peoples). Add to this mix the diverse ethnicity of the Belle Vue Sheep Farm shepherds—Indigenous peoples from outside of the region (Iroquois), Northern tribes (Bella Coola, Haida, and Tsimshian), and regional groups (S'Klallam, Saanich, Songhees, Cowichan, and Lummi); Métis from the upper Mid-West and local cross-cultural families (Kanakas and Coast Salish); French-Canadians; and men from the Isle of Lewis and Orkney Islands. The result is a multi-ethnic, polyglot society in the Disputed Islands. This chapter examines who they were and how they came to be in the San Juan Islands.

Indians

Indigenous peoples have been living in the San Juan Islands for millennia. One way of identifying these peoples is by language. Scholars grouped the Coast Salish by their common Salishan languages; local regional speakers have been called Northern Straits Salish and are grouped with the speakers of Clallam, Nooksack, Halkomelem, and Squamish as Central Coast Salish. At least three Northern Straits Salish groups had winter villages in the San Juans: the Klalákamish on northern San Juan Island and the Alaleng at West Sound and the Swallah at East Sound on Orcas Island. A fourth group, possibly with the name "Lummi," were associated with northern Lopez Island, and a fifth, the Samish, probably had winter villages at the present location of Richardson and near Mud Bay. The *Lhaq'temish* (Lummi), W̱SÁNEĆ (Saanich), Samish, and *Lekwungen* (Songish or Songhees) claim that Open Bay (*Lhuh-lhee-ng'kwulh*) on Henry

Island and Garrison (*Pe'pi'ow'elh*) and Mitchell (*Pqwéy7elwelh*) Bays on San Juan Island (*Lháqemesh*) are the places of origin of their peoples through their earliest ancestor, *sweh-tuhn*. Wayne Suttles relates a traditional story that "when the Klalákamish had become nearly extinct, the last man of them gave his house to a man that owned a house that stood on Flat Point on Lopez Island; the latter now having two houses but not enough space to [put] them up, put the new one at a right angle to the old one to make a L-shaped structure...called x^{w}láləməs (facing each other, and from this comes the name x^{w}lə'mi (Lummi)."[1]

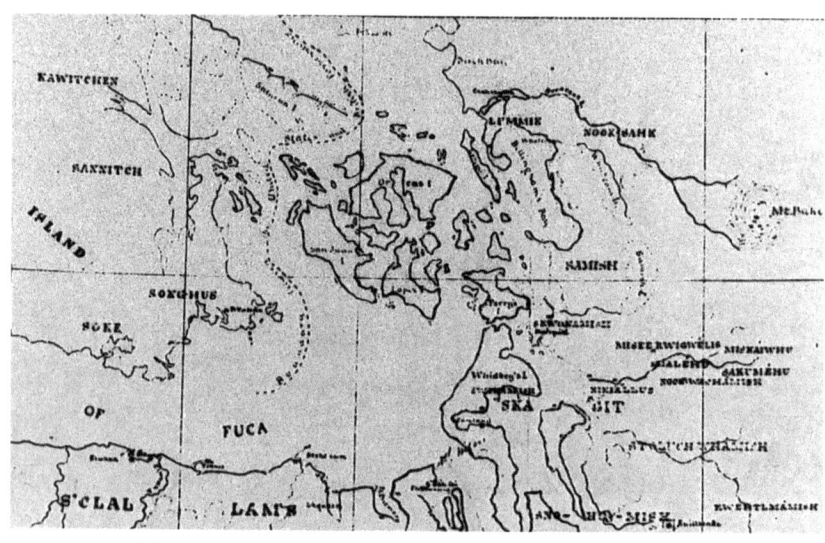

Map of the Indian Tribes and Lands Ceded by Treaty
(George Gibbs 1855)

At the time of Euro-American arrival in the islands, Northern Straits groups mostly lived in winter villages on the mainland and Vancouver Island in a large area surrounding the islands, although there is some evidence of permanent, year-round occupation by small communities. These included the Semiahmoo, to the north around Boundary Bay, Birch Bay, and Drayton Harbor; the *Lhaq'temish* (Lummi), near Bellingham Bay to the northeast; the Samish, near Anacortes and on Fidalgo Island; the *S'Klallam*, on the Olympic Peninsula from Point Discovery to the Hoko River; the *T'Sou-ke* (Sooke), near the inlet bearing their name on the south tip of Vancouver Island; the Lək^{w}əŋən (Songhees), to the southeast near present-day Victoria and its nearby islands; and the *WASANEC* (Saanich), on the peninsula to the west bearing their name as well as the Gulf Islands to the north. According to Wayne Suttles, after they had moved to their settlements at Gooseberry Point and the Portage on the mainland, the Lummi considered their territory to comprise, "all of Orcas and the smaller islands around it, Shaw, the north-western half of Lopez, and the northeastern half of San Juan Island."[2] The groups on Vancouver Island—the Sooke, Songhees, and Saanich—claimed as traditional use areas Henry and Stuart Islands and the western portion of San Juan Island (as well as the southern Gulf Islands in present day Canada). The S'Klallam used the southern and western portions of San Juan Island, and the Samish the southeastern region of the archipelago, including southern Lopez and Decatur Island.

Historians are always limited by their sources, along with their cultural biases; this is perhaps even more the case for our modern-day perception of these historic peoples. Many of these traditional groups were in cultural and locational flux because of the changes wrought by European contact. These changes involved several factors, two of which were population decline due to introduced diseases and the introduction of trade systems with subsequent disruption to traditional local subsistence economies.

Population decline from disease devastated Indigenous life in the Northwest. The initial contact of Europeans and Euro-Americans with Northwest Indigenous peoples brought massive epidemics of diseases new to the Indigenous peoples: dysentery, influenza, malaria, measles, smallpox, typhus, typhoid fever, and whooping cough. Smallpox, first introduced in the 1770s, was a particularly virulent killer. Subsequent outbreaks in 1801, possibly 1824-25, 1853, and 1862 resulted from the epidemiology of the disease, which is based on new introduction to a group of non-immunes, usually a generation apart. The last-mentioned smallpox recurrence is well recorded: the arrival of the steamer *Brother Jonathan* from San Francisco on March 13, 1862, in Victoria Harbor became a point of origin of a vector that quickly spread among visiting northern groups such as Haida, Tsimshian, Kwakwaka'wakw, and Stikine Tlingit. The local Songhees, who had been largely immunized, did not suffer as severely. They did, however, flee to San Juan Island, where the name for Smallpox Bay may have originated. Banned from Victoria by the government, the Northern tribes headed home, leaving corpses strewn along the way, and thus spreading the disease throughout the islands including the San Juans and into northern British Columbia. An estimated 19,000 Indigenous peoples died from smallpox during 1862-1863 on the Northwest Coast.[3]

Robert Boyd estimates that the overall Indigenous Northwest population fell from 188,344 in 1770 to fewer than 35,000 by the mid-1860s.[4] Focusing on the Northern Straits Salish, there are only estimates of the losses, in part because of the varying definitions of groups. In 1849, R. M. Martin, quoting from a "Census of the Indian Tribes in the Oregon Territory from latitude 42^0 to latitude 54^0, derived from the trading lists of the Hudson's Bay Company…," gave a total population of 4,895 for those tribes situated in the "Straits of St. Juan de Fuca and Vancouver's Island."[5] Boyd estimated that this Northern Straits Salish population, prior to the epidemics, was probably around 4,500.[6] Based on information from Hudson's Bay Company Chief Factor James Douglas and North West Boundary Survey member and ethnologist George Gibbs, Wayne Suttles estimated that that number had dropped to about 1,800—almost two thirds—by the 1850s.[7]

The disruption to traditional Indigenous lifeways was exacerbated by the introduction of new trade systems and the subsequent disruption of traditional subsistence and trade economies. Russians and Americans originally introduced the sea otter trade to the Pacific Northwest; the Hudson's Bay Company (the "Company") joined the competition in 1825. The establishment of Fort Victoria on the southern tip of Vancouver Island in 1843, in anticipation of the loss of the British claim to the land north of the Columbia River, accelerated visitation and trading by groups of northern Indigenous peoples.

Although the Laich-kwil-tach (or Ligwilda'xw), the southernmost of the Kwakwaka'wakw tribe, raided the Coast Salish as early as the 1820s, it was probably not until the late 1840s that groups such as the Haida launched war parties to the south.[8] Despite being commonly referred to as Haida, because they generally travelled in the seagoing canoes produced by that group, northern raiders could also have been Kwakwaka'wakw from northern Vancouver Island, Tlingit from the Stikene River, or Tsimshian from the Fort Simpson region. Raiding by northern Indigenous peoples led to the establishment of American forts in the region, particularly Forts Bellingham and Townsend (both in 1856), as well as the passage of a Territorial law prohibiting trade with the Northern tribes. Protection of American citizens from attack was offered as an excuse for the establishment of Pickett's troops on San Juan Island during the Pig War.[9]

In addition to the cultural change precipitated by depopulation, disease, and trade, the definition of various groups presents a problem. Groups formed through recognition of general cultural and specific linguistic similarities. Although there seems to have been a large degree of intermarriage among different Salish groups, extended family groups affiliated at the local level with their occupation of a shared longhouse within a village. The term 'tribe' developed from the American and Canadian governments' need to define Indigenous groups legally and politically in the nineteenth and twentieth centuries, and does not necessarily represent the way that they perceived themselves either historically or at present.[10] The problem of dislocation and definition, already experienced regionally during this period, was further exacerbated locally by the introduction of various Euro-American groups to the islands, particularly the "English" and "Americans."

The Hudson's Bay Company had a long history of hiring local Indigenous peoples as workers. Chief Factor John McLouglin began hiring local "Indians" at Fort Vancouver as early as 1841, and they proved to be particularly useful to the Company after the labor shortage resulting from men leaving for the California Gold Rush of 1849. Belle Vue Sheep Farm employed local groups from its initial establishment. An important source of information is the *Post Journals*, where Charles Griffin named these employees after their cultural group, such as "Chimsiams" (Tsimshian), "Cowitchins" (Cowichan), "Hyders" (Haida), "Klalams" (S'Klallam), "Skatchets" (Skagit), "Sneehomish" (Snohomish) and "Songis" (Songhees). (See Appendix: *Indians Employed by Belle Vue Sheep Farm*.) He also designated Indigenous peoples after the Company fort or trading post nearest their place of origin, such as Burbank Bay, "Millbank" (probably Bella Bella, from Fort McLoughlin on Campbell Island near Milbanke Sound), and Fort Hope (probably Upriver Halkomelem on the Upper Fraser where the fort was located). Specific references to these men occur frequently, both collectively (the "Cowitchins" who built "Cowitchin Road") as well as individuals, such as Johnny Chimsiam, Klalam Charley, Hyder Jim, and Skatchet Charlie. Furthermore, the *Post Journals* mention several groups and at least one individual not directly employed by the company. For instance, Griffin refers to a group of Songhees, with their chief "Freizie," who came to collect camas and fish for salmon.[11]

In general, relations between Euro-Americans and groups of visiting Indigenous peoples were peaceful. In the standard Chinook trade jargon of the time, the Indians referred to the English as "King George-Men" or "Georgemen" and the Americans as "Bostons" or "Boston-Men" (originating from the 1803 attack of the American trading ship *Boston* at Nootka). In general, "Indians" were either associated or affiliated themselves with the English; when the local Indian King George asked about his name, he said "Me King George Indian."[12] On several occasions, Griffin traded blankets for fish caught by local Straits Salish, and certainly the S'Klallam and Songhees returned to their traditional use areas for fishing, gathering, and hunting. In addition, large groups of Indigenous peoples from the North travelled through the area to Fort Victoria and Puget Sound, often encamping in "rancheries" (temporary settlements) on the shores of San Juan Island. Sometimes it is hard to distinguish these groups from others consisting of predominantly Northern Indigenous women who Euro-American traders brought in for the purposes of either "selling" for marriage or prostitution.

The introduction of alcohol clearly exacerbated the disruption of the traditional Indigenous way of life and tensions among natives and between natives and Euro-Americans. Consumption of "spirits" precipitated or aggravated many of the more violent events recorded by Griffin, as well as American and British military authorities. On several occasions drunken bouts led to fighting among and ultimately death within Indian communities. In addition, traditional rivalries among various Indigenous groups continued. Hudson's Bay Company officials, military authori-

> *October 10th, 1854...Last night about 8 PM a Hyder woman – who has hitherto been stopping with McLeod, but left him when he last went to the Fort – started from here late in the evening – for the purpose of going to McLeod – the night was so dark that the Millbank Indian who watches the sheep out there – did not recognize her as she approached near the Park —& fancying it was a wolf or some other animal fired —& wounding this woman severely – his gun was loaded with a Ball & several grains of shot – the ball struck her on the left groin & passed thro' & came out behind the hip bone – a flesh wound – all the shot, but one grain, likewise passed thro' her flesh – one grain is still lodged deep in her side – she seems considering loss of blood & pain to be doing well – I had her brought home in the ox sledge this afternoon –*
>
> *October 16th, 1854 – two Millbanks, "Capn blue"[?] & McLeod's watchman deserted last night – since the latter accidentally shot & wounded this Hyder woman they have been too much afraid to remain here...*
>
> —Charles Griffin, Belle Vue Sheep Farm Post Journals

ties, and others duly noted whenever northern tribes—referred to by contemporary Euro-Americans as "Vikings" of the Northwest—passed through. Raids by northern tribes occurred more frequently during this time period due to disruptions in cultural life caused by shrinking population from disease and from the fur trade. Time that might have been spent fishing, gathering, and hunting in the traditional economy was instead taken up by fur trapping; when there was a shortage of food, raids were more likely to occur.

Local Indigenous groups particularly feared Haidas from the north. On two occasions in 1859—in May and again in June—Haidas raided Hudson's Bay Company station shepherded by Friday. A signal example of the tension present at the time occurred in 1860 when a Haida man was shot dead and left to lie in the muddy street of San Juan Village. The commander of American Camp, George Pickett, who had lived with and fathered a son with a northern Indian woman in Bellingham, was well-aware of the potential ramifications of revenge by the dead man's relatives.[13] He managed to avert retaliation through gifts to the widow and her family. Incidents such as this always presented the danger of escalating into a larger conflict. When James "Harry" Dwyer and his wife Selina Jane were found murdered in 1873, one of the early rumors was that the relatives of Ellen, the Haida woman that Dwyer had cast off in order to marry Selina, had sought retribution against him (see "Kanakas" later).

> *We are in receipt of a letter from a citizen of Lopez Island, detailing the depredations by roaming bands of British Columbia Indians. Mr. Hutchinson is reported to have lost some 80 head of sheep, the Davis estate over 50 head, C. A. Swift over 40, and other losses of 50 or more. The settlers and precinct officers appear to be powerless to render themselves adequate protection, and the military at Fort Townsend ought to lend a hand. As these depredations are committed by foreign Indians the U.S. Government should take cognizance and order the military to render our citizens the necessary protection.*
>
> —The Daily Intelligencer *September 2, 1879*

The 1880 census enumerated 41 adults on San Juan Island who were designated as being "Indian." Of these, two were wives or widows of Euro-Americans; the others were either single male Indians or couples who were both Indian. One of the difficulties with the census information is the transcription of full names or just first names (this shortcoming was not limited to Coast Salish and other Indigenous peoples, but applied to all ethnic groups). For instance, in the Mitchell Bay area of San Juan Island this census records these "Indians" from British Columbia (BC) or Washington Territory (WT): John (WT) and his wife Susan (WT); Thomas Man Nacha (WT) and his wife Mary (BC); Selpannt (WT); Semore (BC) and wife Sequat (BC); Charley Senakin (WT) and wife Jennie (BC); Statta'Mish (BC), and wife

Susan (BC); Suke (WT); and Thomas (WT), Laborer, and his wife Caquade (BC). (See Appendix: *Indigenous People Listed in Censuses*).

"English"

Some of the earliest sources describing the peoples who occupied the region stem from the operation of Belle Vue Sheep Farm, the Hudson's Bay Company trading outpost on San Juan Island first established in 1853. When James Douglas, in his dual capacity as Governor of the Crown Colony of Vancouver Island and Chief Factor of the Hudson's Bay Company, enumerated the island's population two years later, the 29 "white" inhabitants of the island consisted of 16 men, 3 women, and 10 children (all under 10 years of age). George Gibbs, a member of the North West Boundary Survey, noted that the outpost consisted of "one Englishman, four Frenchman, one Canadian, one Scotchman, two half breeds and a Kanaka. Besides these there are employed in herding sheep and farming, 5 Kanakas, 1 Scotchman and 6 or 8 Chinese and Inds."[14] In Chief Trader Charles Griffin's *Post Journals*, he commonly uses the phrase "Men & Ind^s variously employed." That he distinguished the two groups as such reflects both the cultural prejudices of the time and the Company's hiring practices regarding Indigenous groups. "Men" seems to refer to a wide-ranging group of employees of European origin: Scots, Englishmen, French Canadians, and Norwegians.

The Company had absorbed both Scots and French-Canadian employees when it merged with the North West Company in 1821. Among these men were James Douglas, Charles John Griffin, and other members of the Company hierarchy ("Gentlemen") such as Alexander Dallas and Dr. William Tolmie. Born in 1803 in British Guinea to a Scottish father and African-Caribbean mother, James Douglas first joined the North West Company and then, after the merger, gradually rose through the ranks of the Hudson's Bay Company, serving as assistant to Chief Factor John McLoughlin at Fort Vancouver and then appointed Chief Factor at Fort Victoria, which he helped establish in 1843.

Griffin was born in Montreal, then called "lower Canada", and was likely part French Canadian; he served at Stuart's Lake in New Caledonia (near the Fraser River) and Fort Rupert (at the north end of Vancouver Island) prior to coming to San Juan

Island as a Clerk. R. M. Ballantyne remarked in his 1848 book *Hudson's Bay* that three quarters of the servants, as the Company called its employees, came from the Scotch Highlands and Orkney.[15] Robert Firth, who succeeded Griffin as manager of Belle Vue Sheep Farm, was born on Pomona (Mainland), the central Orkney Island. In 1857 he journeyed back there to marry Jessie Grant, and upon his return to San Juan Island managed the farm until 1873. He was then naturalized and applied for a homestead at the former Hudson's Bay Company headquarters. Several of the Belle Vue shepherds came from the Western Hebrides; the name Murdo McLeod, shared by both a father and son who worked at the farm, was common on the Isle of Lewis. (Dugald MacTavish said that their terms of employment were: "Laboring people engaged in the Orkney Islands or the Island of Lewis, five years and free passage").[16]

It is possible that Griffin's term "Men" also referred to Métis (translated from the French as "mixed" or "half-breeds") and Indigenous peoples from farther east (e.g., Iroquois). The Métis and Iroquois came from Hudson's Bay and the North West Company's territory around the Great Lakes and the Red River Valley of Manitoba.[17] The Métis were an ethnically distinct group formed from the union of French Canadians and Indigenous peoples. The Company actively encouraged marriages of employees with local Indian groups, and their offspring were often hired by the Company as servants (employees).[18] At Belle Vue Sheep Farm, several of the employees that the Company used for their special skills were probably Métis. For instance, many of the men who had French names—Antoine (Banne), Baptiste (Bohn?), Chapuis, Francois, George (Barishe?), Ignace, Napoleon (Dease?), and (Joseph?) Robillard—were primarily engaged in more skilled jobs, such as construction of the intricate "Red River style" buildings.

Belle Vue Sheep Farm, like other Company outposts in the Northwest, employed "Kanakas" from the Sandwich Islands, the English name for Hawaii at that time. Hawaiians first arrived in significant numbers in the Northwest in 1811, when they were recruited to work at the North West Company's Fort Astoria. In 1831, the Company established an agency in the Sandwich Islands, and actively recruited Hawaiian laborers—valued for their skilled paddling, diving, and swimming—for the Northwest fur trade. By 1842, it is estimated that there were 500 Kanakas employed by the Company. In Hawaiian, the term "Kanaka," although literally meaning "human being," "man," or "person," had the pejorative connotation of a lower-class laborer for hire.[19]

One of the earliest known persons of Kanaka descent is "King Freezy" (?-1864), also known as Chea-clach, Chee-althluc, Jeeatthuck, Tsilathack, and Tshiaschac. He was possibly the "Chea-clach," head chief of the "Clal-lums," sketched by Paul Kane in 1847, but later references say that he was chief of the Songhees from the 1840s to 1864. According to James Robert Anderson's reminiscence, he "was nicknamed 'Freezy' in adaptation of the French word "frizer" to curl, in reference to his mop of closely frizzled hair, and inheritance of his Kanaka progenitor."[20] This may have been the same person that Charles Griffin referred to in his April 4th, 1854, entry in the *Post Journals*: "Freizie and several Inds arrived from Lummey [sic]…" With many connections throughout the region, Freezy was the grandfather of Jennie Wynn of Bellingham, whose connections through marriage to the Euro-American community was influential in cross-cultural relations.[21]

The Company names for Hawaiians working on Belle Vue Sheep Farm reflect the variety of nicknames and orthographies used to "name" these men: John Bull, Friday, Kahahopa, Kahaliopua, Kamaka, Kaukana, La Laima, Lamane, Nahua, Pakee, Wahouree, and even just plain Kanaka. The case of the man named "L'Gamine" (French for "kid") by Griffin is illustrative, for he was also called Lacamin, Lackaman, Legamin, Lickamean, and Lucamene, as well as William Naukana, Nowkin, Noukin, and even Manton.[22] Many of these men formed the nucleus of a small settlement at Kanaka Bay on the west side of San Juan Island. The 1870 Federal Census recorded a group of them and their Indigenous wives and children: Kion Handy, William Warno, Keopool, Cahoona, Kon Baalow, Kami Kam, William Kiarni, Louis(?) Kamalika, Alum Kioni, and Kioplitz.[23]

Among this dozen or so Kanakas employed at Belle Vue Sheep Farm was Friday, whose residence as a shepherd on the east side of San Juan eventually led to the place name of Friday Harbor. Friday, whose Hawaiian name was written as "Poalie" but was most probably "Poalima" (which means Friday in Hawaiian). In 1841 at the age of twelve Friday came to work for the

Company at Cowlitz Farm (on the west bank of the Cowlitz River, near present-day Toledo, Washington). By the time he arrived at Belle Vue Sheep Farm on San Juan, he brought along a ten-year old son (Joe), probably the offspring of a Cowlitz woman. As was common with many Kanakas, he married a local Straits Salish woman, Mary Saaptenar of the Songhees, a daughter of Chief Jim Skomiax, at St. Andrew's Cathedral, Victoria, in 1870. In becoming a Catholic, Friday received the Christian name Pierre (Peter). Mary and Peter eventually had three children—Lassel, John, and Emma—and lived for a while on the farm that Joe homesteaded in San Juan Valley. Peter died in 1894 in Victoria; Joe drowned off the coast of Alaska the following year in a gale and snowstorm that capsized the *Walter A. Earle*, a schooner in the Victoria Sealing Fleet; Joe was the cook.[24]

> Walking along the country road, which passes through a series of beautiful fir, oak and maple glades, opening out into natural prairies, between Friday harbor and the Presbyterian church on San Juan Island, recently, there appeared before us at a sudden turn in the road, the vision of an aged Kanaka on horseback, which halted by us, and arrested our attention by a most respectful obeisance. "That is old man Friday, after whom Friday harbor was named by the English coast survey people, a great many years ago," whispered our companion, a resident of the island. The old man's chocolate-colored skin and his moss-grizzled hair and beard, carried us back in one minute to the time—how changed!—when the Hudson Bay Company's stations… were the only English-speaking settlements on this coast. Date, about 1840: A herd of sheep belonging to the Hudson Bay Company, grazing peacefully on the grassy hills west of the harbor, and this Kanaka herder, the only inhabitant of the island that was encountered by the sailors. The next minute we were brought back again, for old man Friday we learned was a farmer, the father of a numerous half-breed family, and a good neighbor, having sustained the character of an excellent citizen of the United States from time immemorial.
> —Northwest Enterprise June 3, 1882

Another well-known Kanaka, John Bull, married Fu-huewut Mary Skqulap in 1849; her father was Lummi and her mother was S'Klallam. They came to the island in 1854. Upon his death around 1860 she married John Kahana (also called John Hallum Kahano, Kahanan, or Alum Kioni). John Bull and Mary's daughter, Catherine Bull, married an American settler in the Bellingham area, Joseph Emmerling, age 38, when she was 16, Joseph must have died in 1873, for in 1876, Catherine Emmerling, left out of his probate, secured through the homestead process her father's claim in San Juan Valley, made while he was still a Company employee. As the only eligible member of the Bull family, she applied first for a preemption claim but then changed it to a homestead application. She married John Vermouth in 1880. After their ownership was certified, she sold their property to John Sweeney in 1886 and joined her brother Joseph and sister-in-law Mary in Crow Valley on Orcas Island. There they were part of a community of cross-cultural families, including many French Canadian and Indigenous peoples, such as the Bodines, Frechettes, Iottes, and LaPlantes. Later, Catherine sold that property and moved to the mainland.

In addition to Alum Kioni [John Kahana—see above] and Mary, the 1880 federal census lists four other Kanakas with Indigenous wives, all on San Juan Island: Cahoona and Sally; Kion [Keon] (Jim) Handy (also called William Naukana) and Cecilia; William Kamo [William Newanna or Nuana, also known as Cahoona] and Mary, a Songhee (enumerated in the 1870 census with half breed children but apparently widowed); and William Keaini and Mary. Jacob Low(e) is another possible Kanaka, although he may have been African American or Canadian. (He may have been the same Jacob, who, as a Company employee, laughed at the pig rooting in Lyman Cutlar's potato patch; Cutlar called him a "collard [colored] man," and later "negro" and "nigger.") In the 1870 census Jacob Low is enumerated as married to an Indian woman, Amelia (from BC), with several children; at that time, he was farming on the north end of San Juan Island.

An indication of the complexity of identifying Kanakas from the Hudson's Bay Company, Victoria, and San Juan Island records is the instance of the December 19, 1870, marriage of a

Kanaka, Lonalem Grego to Mary, a Songhees woman, in Victoria. It was witnessed by Cahoona (William Newanna) and Lagamin (William Naukana). This was the same day and at the same place that Friday was married to Mary Saaptenar and Kam Kamai was married to Mary Ann Skomiax. It is hard to sort out who is who, with all the different names and nicknames.

Probably the most notorious of the local Kanakas was Joe Nuana, also known as Kanaka Joe. It is possible that Joe was the son of Mary Teseleachei and Joseph Tahouney Cahoona, who was also called William Kamo, Newanna, or Nuana (Nuanna). Lila Hannah Firth speaks of an "old Kanaka…named Nuanna, his wife was an Indian, they had a family. The 2 older we came to know quite well. The eldest was named Jo, the second Kye [probably Kai, Hawaiian for water]." Joe borrowed a gun from the Hannahs and used it to kill a young couple who were homesteading on the island, James "Harry" and Selina Jane Dwyer; the murder was particularly heinous because Selina, who was pregnant, had been shot and mutilated. The new county sheriff, Stephen Boyce, searched the murder scene and then went to Kanaka Bay. This visit became the occasion for one of the earliest photographs of the settlement, where both he and the Victoria police searched for the murderers. The photo shows a group of men, women, and children lined up in front of several buildings; some hold Straits Salish style canoe paddles, several hold guns, and one has on the distinctive "Bobby" hat of a British constable. Kanaka Joe was eventually found in Kanaka Row in Victoria, along with evidence, and transported to Port Townsend for trial; after being found guilty, he was hanged on March 6, 1874. Some family members have conjectured that one of the reasons that the names Cahoona and Tahouney were later used by the family was to disassociate themselves from the name Nuana.

This incidence sent a frisson of fear throughout the San Juan Island community and probably influenced later opinions towards Kanakas. Lila Hannah Firth, whose family was so close to the Nuanas, recalled: "One thing that frightened me though, was, now and then, we would meet a big kinkey haired blackfaced Kanaka, seemed to me the woods were quite full of them going and coming, hither & thither, through the little trails in the woods."

"Americans"

Americans came to the islands for a variety of reasons. Some of these were political: they disputed, either officially through the establishment of a customs office or unofficially by making preemptive claims on the land, the assumption on the part of the Hudson's Bay Company and other Englishmen that it was British territory. Many were attracted for the same reasons that others had settled around Fort Vancouver and the nearby Willamette Valley in Oregon Territory previously: the islands offered rich, open farmland in a beautiful setting with a relatively mild and sunny climate. The means by which they came varied, although word of mouth generated by prospective miners who followed the Fraser River Gold Rush of 1858/1859 was a large factor. Reports by Griffin and his superiors to the management of the Hudson's Bay Company show that the number of Americans on San Juan grew from a handful prior to the Gold Rush to several dozen at the time of the shooting of the pig. The establishment of American Camp, which brought American soldiers to the island, also increased the civilian population by attracting merchants and others who catered to Army needs, as well as soldiers who mustered out to start life as farmers on the island.

> *The island of San Juan, that so lately brought to the mind images of war, is rapidly becoming a peaceful Arcadia. There are about 60 settlers, all of whom, we believe, are Americans, opening farms and engaging in industrial pursuits. Lime manufacturing is carried on to a considerable extent, the most of it being exported. The British and American troops are still in camp on the island. The most friendly intercourse subsists between them.*
>
> —Olympia Pioneer and Democrat, January 25, 1861

The "First Federal Census of Washington Territory" in 1860 enumerated 56 adults—50 men and 6 women—and 11 children on San Juan Island. Although several of these people came from the British Isles—England (5), Ireland (4), and Scotland (1)—and a handful from the European continent—Germany (2) and France (2), most of the men (72%) were from (although not necessarily born in) the United States. There were settlers from Tennessee (8), Massachusetts (5) and Virginia (4), followed by Pennsylvania, New York, and Maine (3 each), Connecticut and New Jersey (2 each), and Alabama, New Hampshire, Ohio and Missouri with one each. A full third of the men were New Englanders, with a significant minority—a quarter—being Southerners. The women were evenly split between American and British—two from New York and one from Ohio; two from Ireland and one from England. Interestingly, most (8) of the children were born in California (suggesting a possible connection with the 1849 Gold Rush there), with two from Washington Territory itself and one from Pennsylvania.

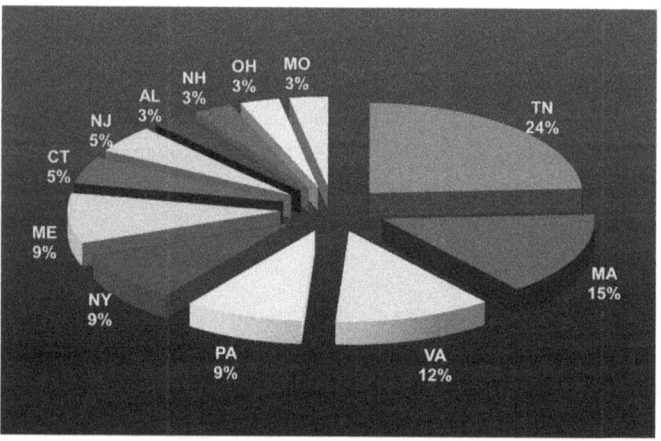

States of Origin in 1860 census.

Another vector for Americans settling in the islands from New England, and Maine in particular, was the establishment of the Pope and Talbot works at Port Gamble in 1853. Alexander Jackson Pope and Captain William Talbot, both from families who owned sawmills in Maine, first founded the Pope & Talbot Company in San Francisco in 1849. Because the main source of lumber was the Northwest and shipping was a major cost, they soon founded the Puget Mill Company at Port Gamble. Many lumber men crossed the country from Maine to work at one of what would eventually become several mills owned by the company: several at Port Gamble, expanding to Utsalady in 1877 and Port Ludlow in 1878. Several applicants for homesteads in the San Juans listed part time work at Port Gamble as a reason for their frequent absences and it can be conjectured that word of the islands' bounty must have spread among the workers.[25]

Notable among the Euro-American immigrant groups who settled the San Juans were the Irish. Irish immigration to the United States had risen from 151,000 in the 1820s to 2,314,000 in the 1850s, largely due to the potato famine resulting from the blight of 1845. This period of massive starvation reduced a population of 8 million in Ireland by 6 million, half through death and half through emigration to England and the United States. Many young Irish men joined the United States Army: in a survey taken of 5,000 recruits during 1850-51, 3,516 were immigrants, of whom 2,113 were Irish. Pickett's Company that landed on San Juan Island in 1859 was certainly no exception to this trend: of the 73 enlisted men, 65 were foreign born—43 Irish and 14 German. A decade later, in Haskell's Company, two thirds (61 of 93) of the enlisted men were foreign born, and of these, over half (33) were Irish. There were enough Irishmen, whether mustered out of the Army or coming to the islands via major emigration locales such as New Brunswick, to form a small Irish 'colony' in San Juan Valley: Patrick Beigin, Patrick Gorman, and the brothers Daniel and Patrick Madden, among others, formed the backbone of the Catholic Church parish there.

When the boundary decision was finally made in 1872, many settlers of foreign descent rushed to declare their intention to become American citizens, a process called "naturalization." On January 13, 1873, thirty-nine men applied *en masse* for citizenship at Port Townsend (see Appendix: *List of Petitioners for Naturalization, January 13, 1873*). The majority (32) of them renounced their political allegiance to Great Britain and Ireland. Of these, most were former employees of or associated with the Hudson's Bay Company: French Canadians such as the brothers Jacques Cyprien and John Louis Archambault, Peter Frechette, and Fermin Iotte; Irish such as Thomas McCarthy; Englishmen such as William Bell, John Crook, Stafford Merrifield, and Hugo Park; Scots such as Robert Firth; and Kanakas (who, although coming from the Hawaiian Kingdom, were assumed to be subjects of Great Britain) such as Joseph Bull and Joseph Friday. The rest of those who renounced their allegiance to Great Britain and Ireland had come to the islands through other channels. Scots came both because of the imposition of the Inclosure Acts (the first of which was passed in 1773 but intensified by those starting in 1845 and continuing through the decades thereafter), which consolidated individual farmsteads in the Highlands and the Hebrides: Alexander and Donald Ross. The rest consisted of two from Germany—Fred Jones and Anton Gesselman; two from Denmark—Peter Nelson and Peter Peterson; two from Norway and Sweden—John Gibson and Thomas Smith; and one from Austria—A. Ofner. Although there was not another mass event, naturalization occurred at a steady pace throughout the 1870s, 1880s, and 1890s.

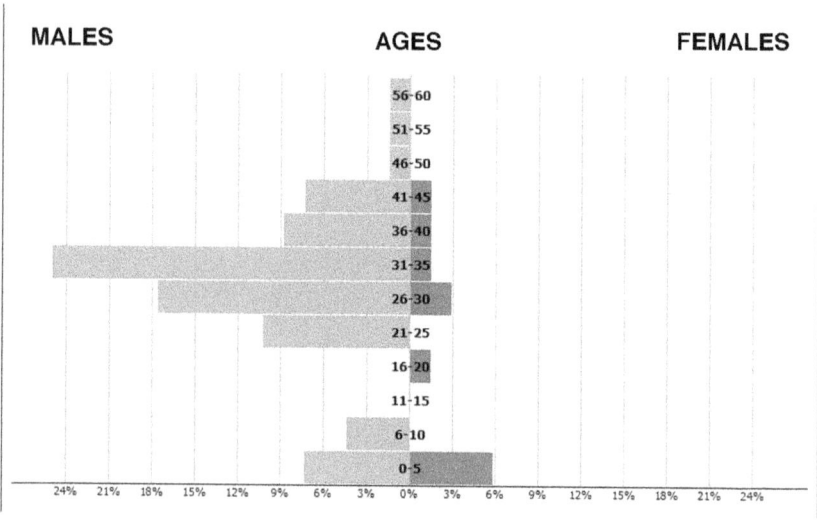

Population Pyramid of 1860 Census

Cross-Cultural Families

Although the 1860 Census of San Juan Island did not record any "Indians" (Indigenous peoples), the "White" (Euro-American) people it did record—56 adult males as opposed to 6 adult females, and only 11 children—indicated a "frontier" situation in which single "White" males far outnumbered marriageable "White" women and fostered a climate of intermarriage with Indigenous peoples. The 1870 Census of the "Disputed Islands," which included not only San Juan but also Orcas, Lopez, Decatur, and Blakely Islands, was the first to record "Indians" as well as "Whites." By that time, there were 189 adult men, 83 adult women, and 185 children. On San Juan Island, married men ranged in age from 21 to 60 with an average of 37.8, whereas married women ranged from 17 to 56 years of age and averaged 29.5. Of the 32 married women, 17 were "Indian" and 15 "White." The "Indian" wives, however, ranged in age from 17-38, averaging 26.6. On the other islands—Orcas, Lopez, Decatur, and Blakely—

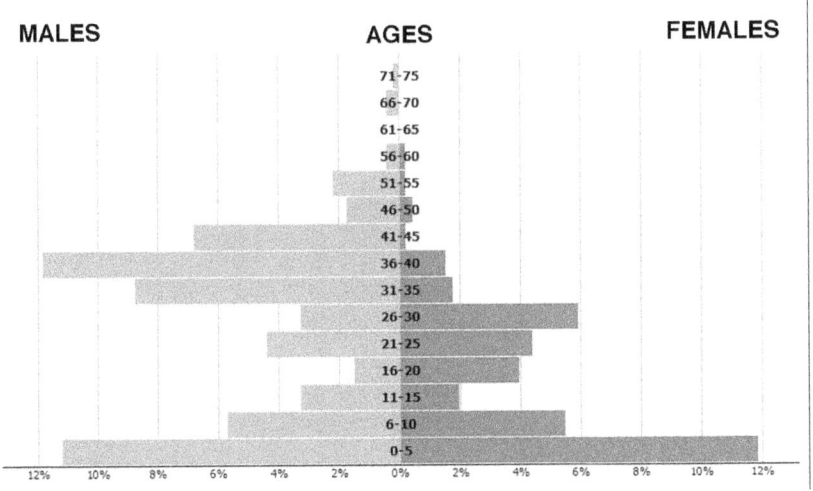

Population Pyramid of 1870 Census

all of the wives were "Indian" except one. The 25 "Indian" wives on Orcas ranged from 16-35 years of age, with an average of 24. On Lopez, the 7 women varied from 24-30 years of age, with an average of 27. The other two islands had one couple each: on Decatur, 21-year-old Mary from British Columbia was married to 42-year-old John T. Reed from Pennsylvania, and on Blakely 41-year-old Paul Hubbs from Maryland was married to 24-year-old Susan from Washington Territory. Although the overall sizes of these samples are small, one can conclude that most wives were younger than their husbands, and Indigenous brides were even more so; on average, about 10 years younger.

Cross-cultural marriages occurred among several groups with benefits to both spouses. Husbands were employees of the Hudson's Bay Company, American settlers, or various nationalities that came to the islands. The Company employees were encouraged to marry local Indigenous women in order to secure peaceful relations with the Indigenous populations and foster trade connections. Several of the Company's British Governors or Chief Traders married Native Americans or First Peoples. Chief Trader at Fort Vancouver and later Governor of Vancouver Island and then British Columbia James Douglas married Amelia, the daughter of Chief Factor William Connolly and Miyo Nipiy, a Cree. Chief Trader John Tod, who retired at Fort Victoria, first had a "country wife" (married according to the Indigenous custom)—Catherine Birstone in the York Factory area. After the death of his second wife, in 1863 he formally married Sophia Lolo at Thompson's River Post, after they had had seven children. One of their sons was John Tod, Jr., who, together with John Bowker, formed the firm of Bowker and Tod and ran sheep throughout the Victoria/San Juan Islands region. Americans who came to settle in the islands gained a significant helpmate in marrying an Indigenous woman; Coast Salish wives introduced them to family trade ties as well as taught them how to live in this place.

From the wife's point of view in a cross-cultural marriage, Euro-American husbands were a good alliance, one that conferred social status. The economies of most Coast Salish societies were based on an elaborate trade system. Marriage to a Hudson's Bay Company employee strengthened ties with the Company and its posts in the region. Union with an American or English settler in the islands helped secure traditional ties to the land and broaden trade networks. As Candace Wellman has shown in her publications (*Peace Weavers: Uniting the Salish Coast through Cross-Cultural Marriages* [2017] and *Interwoven Lives: Indigenous Mothers of Salish Coast Communities* [2019]), well-placed marriages also resulted in political alliances between indigenous groups and the emergent military and civil governments.[26]

Many of the women who married settlers in the islands were from the Mitchell Bay area on San Juan Island, a group that would later be designated the Mitchell Bay Band or Tribe. They were most likely the descendants of the Klalákamash of Garrison and Mitchell Bays on San Juan Island and Open Bay on Henry Island. Because there was an extensive kinship among members of regional groups, the "Mitchell Bay Band" included the Sooke, Songish, Saanich, and Cowichan on Vancouver Island, the Semiahmoo, Lummi, Samish and Skagit to the north and east, and the S'Klallam on the Olympic Peninsula. Furthermore, as is common with other Indigenous groups, there were frequent cases of members of Northern groups such as those from Haida Gwaii and the Stikene River being adopted as children into the Mitchell Bay Band. Some groups from the North visited the islands, often staying in temporary encampments or "rancheries," to escape fighting, to seek better economic conditions, or to sell girls and women as slaves. Women from these groups include Anna Pike (Tsimshian), who married Christopher Rosler; Tacee Little Bird (Tlingit), who married John P. Reed; Lucinda (Stikine) who married Arthur "Billy" Barlow; Mary Jane K-naugh "Conna" (Tsimshian) who married Charles Brown; and Ginny Kahlan (Haida) who married John Gottlieb Viereck. Another example is Mary Elizabeth "Lizzie" O'Clain, a Tsimshian from Lax Kwalams (Port Simpson), who married English naval officer Richard Davis of Nova Scotia, on August 22, 1864, in Victoria B.C.; they came to Lopez Island and settled at Shoal Bay on Port Stanley Road.

In addition to French Canadian and Métis employees of the Hudson's Bay Company, men who contracted with the Company often married Indigenous women and settled down to farm or fish. In Deer Harbor on Orcas Island there was a small community of English and French-Canadian men who worked for or with the Company and married local women: Louis Cayou married twice, first to an unnamed and culturally unidentified Indigenous woman, who was apparently abducted by raiders from the north, and then to Mary Anne Sulwham (Toochley) (Celia Ukitoff). James Bradshaw married the daughter of Catherine Delaunais LaPlant, Idel.

Americans began arriving in the islands in the early 1850s, but the Fraser River gold rush of 1858 precipitated settlement in the San Juans by men travelling south from the gold fields in British Columbia to what is now American territory. (Many American miners ran out of funds before they were able to realize profits and felt oppressed by governmental oversight by James Douglas, setting the stage for resentment against him and the Hudson's Bay Company.) Samuel H. Gross came to San Juan Island in the early 1860s and married Mitchell Bay Jane Jennie Quinalt Satart by Indian custom in 1862, and then, through a minister, married civilly in either 1869-1870 (or in the winter of 1872-1873). Gross filed for a homestead in the Mitchell Bay area in the 1870s and received a patent in 1882. Neighbor John Wesley Briggs, a shoe/bootmaker, married Mitchell Bay Band Mary Jones Seamtenitt [Seamtnott] either in Whatcom or on San Juan Island in 1869; he also filed for a homestead in the Mitchell Bay area in the 1870s and received a patent in 1883. Julian Laurence [Lawrence] (1837-1905) came from the Fraser River gold rush to Shaw Island to hunt game for railroad crews on the mainland and met Theresa [Teresa or Terice] Seymour (1849-1950), who was living there with her father Thomas Seymour and mother Sarah Tomsemu, both part of the Chemainus group of Cowichans. Theresa's older sister Sarah (1843-1913) married William Moore (1827-1897), originally from South Carolina but who possibly came to the islands from the Gold Rush, at Olga on Orcas Island around 1866. After the 1872 settlement of the boundary and their parents moved back to Vancouver Island, Julian and Theresa and their growing family lived near Blind Bay and William and Sarah stayed at Olga.

Then there were men who were passing through or somehow heard about the islands, married Indigenous women, and settled down. Examples from Lopez Island include Hiram Hutchinson, who married Marion Bones (likely Indigenous, from Hell's Gate area on the Fraser River), and Sampson Chadwick, who married Adelia Bradshaw, daughter of Judge Charles Bradshaw and a (unnamed) S'Klallam woman. Edouard Graignic and Louis LaPorte, two Frenchmen who jumped ship in Victoria, met two sisters from the Swinomish Tribe—Lena and Louisa Thompson—and ended up living on Waldron. Charles A. McKay, a friend of Lyman Cutlar who was involved in the Pig War, married Mary Josephine Innis, who was probably a Mitchell Bay Indian but whose birthplace was listed as British Columbia.[27]

Soldiers from both American and English Camps settled in the islands in the 1860s after being discharged ("mustering out"). Patrick Beigin, born in Ireland, had enlisted in the U.S. Army around 1851 and eventually arrived at American Camp in 1859 with Captain Pickett. He mustered out of the Army the following year, and, according to family history, traded some goods for an Indian dugout canoe he used to transport cargo between San Juan Island and Victoria. In Victoria, Beigin, then about thirty years old, met Lucy Morris, the thirteen-year-old daughter of a chief of the Howcan Tribe from Sitka. Although Morris wanted to marry Beigin, when she returned to her village her father forbade it, so she stowed away on a canoe going back to Victoria and eloped with Beigin. They married in 1864. Christopher Rosler was born in Hessen-Kessel, Germany, emigrated to New York in 1854, and joined the U.S. Army in California a year later. He served under Pickett at American Camp, mustered out in 1860, and settled on land just north of the Military Reservation. The following year he met Anna Pike, then only fifteen years old, a Tsimshian originally from Lax Kw'alaams (Fort Simpson, British Columbia), who had moved with her family to the south end of the island. They were married in an Indian ceremony, and then later—with several of their children in attendance—by a Catholic priest. They had nine children, four boys and five girls. Former Royal Marine Robert Smith, who was stationed at English Camp on San Juan Island, married Lucy Ontanna Jack after he had mustered out; upon his death she married John Jack "Henry" Balam, another Englishman (but not a Royal Marine).

Catherine LaPlante
(1850-1923)
m. Peter Frechette

Idele LaPlante
(1855-1928)
m. James Bradshaw

Peter L. LaPlante
(1852-1925)
m. Idele Iotte

Catherine Delaunais
(1836-1902)
Lezim Verrier

Adeline Verrier
(1864-1942)
m. James F. King

Idele LaPlante
m. Martin Nichols

Victoria Frances LaPlante
(1857-1943)
m. John Taylor

Map of Diaspora of the Children of Catherine Delaunais

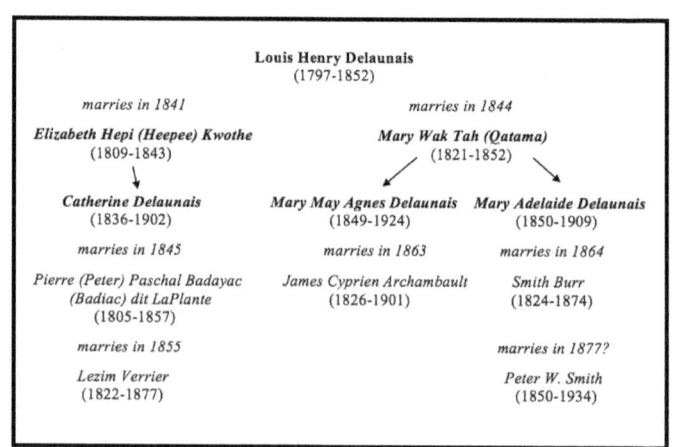

Louis Henry Delaunais
(1797-1852)

marries in 1841 — Elizabeth Hepi (Heepee) Kwothe (1809-1843)

marries in 1844 — Mary Wak Tah (Qatama) (1821-1852)

Catherine Delaunais (1836-1902)
marries in 1845
Pierre (Peter) Paschal Badayac (Badiac) dit LaPlante (1805-1857)
marries in 1855
Lezim Verrier (1822-1877)

Mary May Agnes Delaunais (1849-1924)
marries in 1863
James Cyprien Archambault (1826-1901)

Mary Adelaide Delaunais (1850-1909)
marries in 1864
Smith Burr (1824-1874)
marries in 1877?
Peter W. Smith (1850-1934)

Delaunais Family Tree

*Children of Catherine Delaunais Laplante
L to R, Idel, Catherine, Victoria, and Peter
(courtesy of Orcas Island Historical Museum)*

Cross-cultural marriages often led to interconnected families throughout the islands. A well-documented example is of the Delaunais family. In Cowlitz Prairie, Washington (now the Lewis County area) where the Hudson's Bay Company had a major grain producing post, French-Canadian Louis Delaunais first married Indigenous Cowlitz Hepi [or Heepee] (Elizabeth) Kwoithe, with Catherine Delaunais as offspring; then, upon Hepi's death, he married Mary Qatama, Cowlitz daughter of Elias Qatama and Schookpie, who gave birth to Mary Agnes and Adelaide. Catherine first married Pierre [Peter] Paschal dit LaPlante and then, after he died, Lezim Verrier. Catherine and Lezim ("Catharine and Liginet Varrier") homesteaded on the north end of San Juan Island. After Lezim died, Catherine moved to Deer Harbor on Orcas Island. Five of her children played a large part in San Juan Islands history: Catherine LaPlante married Peter Frechette; Peter LaPlante married Idele Iotte and farmed in the Deer Harbor area; Idel LaPlante first married James Bradshaw at Deer Harbor and then, upon Bradshaw's death in 1873, married Martin Nichols and moved with him to Friday Harbor where they platted the Nichols Addition to the town; Victoria Frances LaPlante married John Taylor and settled near Friday Harbor; and Adeline Verrier married James F. King, who homesteaded the west side of Friday Harbor.

Mary Agnes Delaunais married Jacques Cyprien Archambault and had 15 children. James Adams McKay, son of Charles A. McKay and Mary Josephine Innis, married their daughter Lucretia Archambault. Their son Peter was the first husband of Mary Jane "Jennie" Berdillon (Jones), the daughter of Mitchell Bay born Ellen Thloynnock Yackship; Jennie later married Frederick Alfred Jones, who homesteaded on Mitchell Bay.

Adelaide Delaunais married Smith Burr and they had eight children; after Burr's death, she married Peter W. Smith, and they had six children. Several of Adelaide's offspring married into other cross-cultural families: Joseph Mantiville Burr married Mary Alice Woodworth and his brother John Burr married Mary Alice's sister Margaret "Maggie" Ann Woodworth, who had formerly been married to Lincoln A. McKay. Adelaide's daughter with Peter W. Smith, Agnes Smith married Ben Briggs, and her son Peter Henry Smith married Harriet "Hattie" Matilda Briggs. James Adams McKay, son of Charles A. McKay and Mary Josephine Innis, married Lucretia Archambault, daughter of Jacques Cyprien Archambault and Mary Delaunais, and their son James Floyd McKay married Agnes Phyllis Burr, daughter of Adelaide Delaunais and Smith Burr.

Some Indigenous women had truly remarkable lives, having multiple husbands and children and forming important community ties wherever they settled. Jane "Cecilia" Chanique, also known as Higlolucolus and Sluequlite, was Semiahmoo; she first married Dr. C. B. R. Kinnerly of the U.S. North West Boundary Survey when she was 15 or 16 years old and they had one child, George Kinley. After Kinnerly left her, she married John Brown, and they had one child, Mary Jane Brown. When Brown died in 1880, she married William "Billy" Clark on Orcas Island, and they had two children. Finally, she moved to Lummi and married Quiach-tun Joseph (Yel-Chent) Toby and they had three children. She died at the Lummi Reservation in 1924. Another remarkable woman was Isabel Ladebauche. The daughter of Peter Ladebauche and Mary Spencer, she married Thomas Dixon, a hunter and trapper on Orcas Island in 1875, when she was 16 years old. They homesteaded in Crow Valley and had four children. After Dixon's death in 1898, she married John Taylor Kittles at Deer Harbor. Upon his death in 1907, she married George Shattuck, the son of Charles Shattuck who had homesteaded at Eastsound, and settled in Bellingham. All of these indicate the interconnectedness and significant influence of cross-cultural families in the islands.

Changing Cultural Attitudes Towards Ethnicity

As the islands became increasingly populated by families of Euro-American origin, attitudes toward Indigenous peoples and cross-cultural families became more negative. Husbands were called pejoratively "squaw men." (The term itself—squaw man, defined as "a white or other non-Indian man married to a North American Indian woman," has its own cultural baggage, stemming from the use of the term "squaw," an Algonquian term for an Indian female, usually a wife, that was translated from the northern territories of Canada to wherever Americans encountered Indigenous groups.) In the 1870s James Francis Tulloch, who had decidedly strong prejudices, described the situation on Orcas Island, which had the highest number of Euro-American male/Indigenous female marriages: "Among the French Canadian squaw men were Yoots [Iottes], the Cayous, the Largins, the Berries, etc.; and a number of their married half-breed children such as the LaPlantes, the Freshettes [Frechettes], the Bulls, etc. Among the squaw men were Shattuck, Stevens, Adams, "Col." May, Truesworthy, Brown, Clark, Moore, Vierick, Smith, Guthrie, Hitchens, Legbandt, Robinson, Boos, Bratton, Bridges, etc."[28] Even when whites were 'accepting,' their language was prejudiced; Lilla Hannah Firth reminisced that "So many oldtimers married Indian women, & had very large familys [sic], so you may know our schools were overflowing with half-breed children, some of whom made very bright pupils though."[29] And the obituary for Jennie Viereck, in the April 21, 1898, edition of *The San Juan Islander*, while laudatory, was also ambivalent: "There, amid the hardships of pioneer life she dedicated herself to her family and God. She was an Indian, but that she had a heart as kindly beats in any woman's breast no person who knew her could doubt for a moment."[30]

> *After hinting at the advantage of my getting a half-breed wife who he said would be such a help in opening up a farm, the old wretch by the way was something of a marriage broker in the half-breed market. I heard him through and then said "Mr. May I suppose it's no man's business who you marry, Red, Black or White, but it's every man's business that you (do) marry, not for your sake, for we care nothing about you, but for the poor wretched children that you have brought into the world."*
> —The Diary of James Francis Tulloch (1970)

The legacy of prejudice and shame associated with Indigenous heritage lingered into modern times. When Benjamin Franklin (Frank) Shattuck, son of Charles Shattuck and his Indigenous wife, Jeannie, wrote a family history for the local newspaper in 1944, he included everyone except his mother.[31] Asked by Jacilee Wray about other children in school with Indigenous heritage, Babe Jewett, granddaughter of Patrick Beigin and Lucy Morris, recalled:

> *They didn't show their Indian blood too much either and they wouldn't admit that they had Indian blood in them. So most of the kids in my class didn't know that there were three or four kids in my class that had more Indian blood in them than I had. And they used to call me a Sayawash and all of that stuff. So actually it sort of ruined my life for close friendships.*[32]

These attitudes persisted into the 1970s, when growing awareness of Indigenous heritage culminating in the legal recognition of treaty rights by the Boldt Decision (1974) brought recognition and sometimes respect for cross-cultural marriages.

With Euro-American settlement, the identity of "Indians" became increasingly significant politically because of acknowledgement and treatment of Indigenous peoples by both the American and Canadian governments. With the initial settlement in the 1840s of indigenously populated areas of what was to become British Columbia, the British government, represented by James Douglas, negotiated the "Douglas Treaties" with a half dozen Coast Salish groups on southern Vancouver Island. These treaties, in exchange for access to First Nations lands, guaranteed them the right to hunt, fish, and forage "as formerly," which clearly included traditional fishing methods, catches, and areas. In the Territory of Washington, Governor Isaac Stevens negotiated a series of thirteen treaties with Indigenous groups; among these was the Treaty of Point Elliott (1855), which was signed by Indigenous groups in the Salish Sea region. The Treaty did not acknowledge ownership or reservations for Indigenous peoples in the San Juan Islands, which were attributed to the Lummi, despite the acknowledgement by the Secretary to the treaty commission, George Gibbs, at least graphically on an 1856 map, that the northwest part of San Juan was used by the Saanich and the southwest by the Songhees. After the ratification of the Treaty in 1859, the Lummi were to remove to their reservation on Lummi Island and nearby mainland and the Samish to Guemes Island. Under the Treaty of Point-No-Point the Clallam were supposed to go to the Skokomish Reservation on Hood Canal, but they remained in their traditional villages along the Strait of Juan de Fuca.

Indigenous claims to occupation and use of the islands were generally ignored by both the English and American governments, but not without protest—particularly regarding the use of traditional fishing areas. The Victoria *Colonist* of August 15, 1859, reported that "Another claimant is found to San Juan, in the Cowichin Indians, fishing at the north end of the island. They deny the right of the 'Bostons' to occupy the island till they pay them for it. We learn the American authorities intend to buy them out."[33] The *Victoria Daily Colonist*, in an August 28, 1863, article on local salmon fishing, reported that "The Indians are naturally jealous of the encroachments of fishermen with their nets on their fishing grounds, and recently some Italians who had made a good haul opposite a rancherie on San Juan Island, were attacked by the whole camp including men women and children and had to seek protection in a precipitate skedaddle." Although the Straits Salish did not have a system of land ownership in the sense that Euro-Americans did, family groups did lay claim to the use of traditional resource areas, including camas beds and plant gathering places as well as fishing sites. Many reef net locations were 'owned' by families and passed down through the generations. During the post contact period, with the cross-cultural marriage of the Coast Salish with Euro-Americans, many of these locations were handed down to mixed heritage progeny of these unions.

After the settlement of the international boundary and the establishment of the United States public land system in the San Juans, Euro-American settlers (some with cross-cultural families) began to claim lands formerly occupied by Indigenous peoples. Because the system did not acknowledge prior use and settlement of land—all now being public land of the United States of America—prior Indigenous claims were either assimilated through marriage relations or simply ignored and abused. During the twentieth century, this was exacerbated by efforts of American officials to disassociate Indigenous peoples from their traditional use areas. Pauline Hilaire recalls that Lummi Tribal leaders Joe Hilaire and Eddie Jefferson were hired by local Bureau of Indian Affairs officials with promises to pay them $18,000 to burn down longhouses on Orcas and San Juan Islands in the 1920s or 1930s.[34]

> *They had a nice, great big campground. Good camping place for the Lummi people. Canadian people and everybody were all mixed there. They had a nice big smokehouse built there; we call it a longhouse. There was about three of them, I guess. Then they had small camping houses that they stayed in. Made out of shakes and one thing or another, but they were nice. This at Mitchell Bay on both sides of the bay… A white fellow moved in there. They homesteaded the whole thing. They just plain homesteaded it wrong and everything. Then on the other side of the bay, what there was left, the Lummis moved across, just a stone's throw across the bay; they had two great big houses there. Then they had some more small houses, cabin-like, too. White people came and homesteaded the darn place and never even left their ground for the Lummis.*
>
> —Herman Olsen, quoted in Ann Nugent, Lummi Elders Speak (1980)

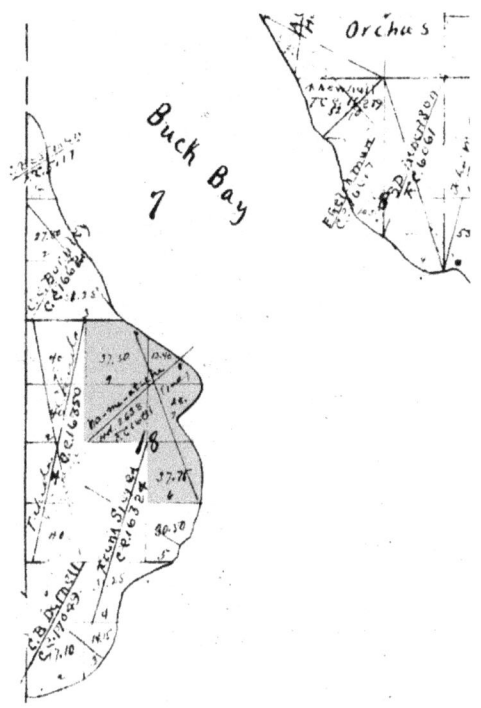

Detailed Map of Na-ME-At-Cha Indian Homestead ["Buck Bay" is East Sound]
(General Land Office, Bureau of Land Management)

Prior to 1884, "Indians" were not allowed to apply and receive a patent for public lands because they were not recognized as United States citizens. This changed under the provisions of the Indian Trust Homestead Act (in the Revised Statutes of the United States, Chapter 5, Title Thirty-Two, supplemented by a July 4, 1884, Act of Congress entitled "An Act make appropriations for the current and contingent expenses of the Indian Department"). As a result of this legislation, four "Indian Homestead" claims were filed in San Juan County: on San Juan Island, She-Kla-Malt obtained title to land near Lonesome Cove and Mary Littleman near Eagle Point; on Orcas Island, Na-ME-At-Cha received title to land near Eastsound and Sit-Sa-Lum on the west shore of East Sound (called Buck Bay on the map).

Thomas Suclamito (She-Kla-Malt Tom), who claimed Lummi descent, filed a claim for the site at Lonesome Cove on April 15, 1884, although he may have occupied this place as early as 1860. The site was one of four traditional Lummi and/or Saanich villages (the other three were at Garrison, Mitchell, and Westcott Bays) on San Juan Island. She-Kla-Malt, who reef netted at Reid Harbor, Stuart Island, died in 1900 and his grave, marked by an obelisk, stands in the cemetery still located on the property. She-Kla-Malt married Mary Yakship Sluckhachwa and they had three children: John "Johnny"; Margaret "Maggie" S. Playwhilloot, and Emma Marie. Maggie married Charles Mason Fitzhugh and had Pearl, who married William Little. Pearl, a great reef netter like her grandfather, lived on the homestead, which became known as the "Pearl Little" place.

Mary Littleman's claim (filed March 7, 1892) was allegedly located near a traditional reef net site. She was a widow at the time: her husband George (John) Littleman died after their filing for the homestead. In 1907, San Juan County issued a certificate of delinquency of payment of property taxes to S. V. Boyce; this was cancelled because they recognized that it was actually part of Mary Littleman's allotment and that she still held title thereto. George's ancestors were mixed Clallam and Cowichan, and some of their offspring lived at or near Clallam reservations.[35]

Sit-Sa-Lum was known by several names, including Siscilam (in the 1880 census), Boston Tom, Indian Tom, and Chechitem, according to his granddaughter Lena Daniels. He resided on land at North Beach on Orcas Island, which he received as an Indian Homestead Trust; this was probably the site of a Samish village called *Chulxwesing*, where there was a longhouse of some 800 feet in length. Chechitem was the last leader. He and his relatives reef netted off Point Doughty, at what would become "Orcas Nos. 1 & 2," an area codified under the State Law. Sit-Sa-Lum was married to Whee-wel-so (Walwhets) and they had 6 children: David Tom; Julia Tom; Jasiss Tom; Cecila (Secil); Peter Tom; and Joseph Tom. Apparently, Sit-Sa-Lum contracted pneumonia in 1912 and died on October 19. His probate was administered by J. T. Whitely; the inventory consisted of his patent, which was valued at $4,350, and the two reef net sites off what was then called Coal Point, valued at $500. His children, David and Peter Tom and Cecila Steel, agreed to the sale of the real estate in 1914, and it was subsequently mortgaged and sold; by that time, the children had all moved to Vancouver Island.

George Na-ME-At-Cha was the brother of She-Kla-Malt. His Indian Homestead was on the west side of East Sound; the significance of this site is not known. Na-ME-At-Cha married Mary Nani Dadh-rah and they had four children who lived with them at the homestead (in the custom of the time, Christian names of Indigenous peoples were often given as their surnames—thence Name-atcha George was the last name of each of the children): Patrick Chad-Que-Bulh; Louisa (Luisea); Lewis (Louis) Sea-yam-ton; and Cecilia (Se Sil).

In 1887, the United States Congress passed the General Allotment Act, also known as the Dawes Severability Act, which enacted a system whereby Indians could receive individual properties from reservation lands—a policy that would have a devasting effect through the privatization of tribal lands. Only members of officially recognized tribes qualified. After a survey of the large Quinault Reservation was conducted in 1904, in 1911 the Secretary of the Interior directed that allotments be assigned on the reservation to Quinault tribal members as well as those "who are affiliated with the Quinaielt[sic] and Quilleute tribes in the treaty and who may elect to take allotment on the Quinaielt[sic] Reservation rather than on the reservations set aside for these tribes." Many non-Quinault Indians applied to be adopted by the Tribe; however, the Office of Indian Affairs revoked this rule in 1912. In response, Thomas G. Bishop organized a meeting of over 50 delegates from various recognized and non-recognized tribes at Tacoma in 1914; as a result, the Northwest Federation of American Indians was formed to represent both groups, particularly when it came to applications under the General Allotment Act.

As part of his effort to locate Indians who were not living on reservations, Bishop travelled to the San Juan Islands and encouraged many Indians to submit affidavits of their tribal affiliation and applications for adoption by the Quinault Tribe so they could apply for allotments of land on the Quinault Reservation. He provided a standard affidavit format and many Mitchell Bay as well as other self-identified tribal families submitted these applications. These forms affirmed the applicant's Indian blood, their parentage with tribal affiliation and ancestry, and their siblings and offspring, including married names; all finalized forms were signed by three witnesses or witnessed and notarized by Bishop himself or his representative. In 1915, Bishop travelled to Washington, DC to present over 1,000 affidavits to the Secretary of the Interior. The Secretary recognized that there were many non-federally recognized Indians in Western Washington and appointed Charles E. Roblin of the Office of Indian Affairs to get more detailed information.

From 1916-1919, Roblin tried to contact applicants and get a more detailed understanding of their family history and tribal affiliation, as is evidenced by his detailed notes filed under the heading of each family name. He finished his work and submitted the *Roblin Report and Roll of Unenrolled Indians of Western Washington* on January 31, 1919. Roblin's Report is of signal importance to the identification of the Mitchell Bay Band and San Juan (Island) Tribe of Indians. Roblin was the first to use the terms "Mitchell Bay Tribe" and "San Juan Island Tribe" and recognized that they were composed of a mix of individuals from regional groups now in the United States (Clallam, Lummi, Samish, and Swinomish) and Canada (Saanich, Songhees, and Sooke), as well as from further north (Bella Coola, Haida, and Tsimshian [which he called "Alaskan Tribes"]).

> *On the islands of San Juan County, Washington, there are a number of mixed blood Indians, and a few full-bloods, who claim membership in the "Mitchell" Tribe of Indians. Mitchell Bay is a harbor on San Juan Island, the largest of the group. These Indians are inextricable with the Indians of British Columbia, (Vancouver Island), and from Alaska. The bands and tribes of the inland waters of the coast have mingled for centuries; but those who are still on the Washington side of the international boundary should be classed as one band. They call themselves the Mitchell Bay Indians, and I have scheduled them as such.*
>
> —Charles H. Roblin, "Mitchell Bay Tribe,"
> Roblin Report and Roll of Unenrolled Indians of Western WA,
> January 31, 1919

The roll is broken down by tribe, both federally recognized (Clallam, Cowlitz, Lummi, Skagit, Skokomish, and Swinomish) and not (Mitchell Bay, Samish, and San Juan Island). Roblin identified 12 Mitchell Bay Tribe families and 2 San Juan Island Tribe families. Although there is a considerable amount of cross-tribal marriage among the families, it appears that Roblin assigned the family files to the applicant's choice of affiliation; for instance, although there are many Mitchell Bay families that could have claimed Clallam or Lummi affiliation, they chose Mitchell Bay, and, contrariwise, there are families filed under Clallam, Lummi, and other tribes that could just as well have been listed as Mitchell Bay.

Bishop presented these findings to President Warren G. Harding in 1921 but the situation went unheeded until Congress passed a law on February 12, 1925 (43 Stat. 886, Ch. 214) allowing Puget Sound Indians to bring claims in the federal Court of Claims. Duwamish, Lummi, Whidbey Island Skagit, Skagit, Upper Skagit, Swinomish, Kikiallus, Snohomish, Snoqualmie, Stillaguamish, Suquamish, Samish, Puyallup, Squaxin, Skokomish, Upper Chehalis, Muckleshoot, Nooksack, Chinook, and San Juan Islands Tribes of Indians v. the United States (*Duwamish et al v. United States*) was filed in 1926 but not decided until 1934 (No. F-275). Witnesses for the plaintiff included thirteen from the "San Juan Islands Tribe of Indians," whose depositions were taken on March 14, 1927, at Friday Harbor. These included several members of families that Roblin had identified as belonging to the Mitchell Bay or San Juan Island Tribes: Alice G. Lightheart, Catherine Mason, William Rosler, John Dougherty, Johnny Tom, Stephen B. Gross, William H. Viereck, Ben Briggs, Jim Walker, and Cecilia Knowlsen. Their testimony includes description of indigenous and transitory settlements in the islands; resources such as game (bear, deer, elk, fish, and wildfowl); and cultivation, fishing, gathering, and hunting. One of the depositions, by Catherine Mason, secretary of the San Juan Tribe of Indians (when Mr. Iotte was president), claimed that there were 318 members enrolled at that time. Although testimony in *Duwamish et al v. United States* made a strong case for traditional occupation and use of the San Juan Islands by specific Indian groups, the Court of Appeals decided that the claim was without merit.

In the 1950s several tribes, including the "San Juan Tribe of Indians," filed cases before the Indian Claims Commission. Because all of these groups—Lummi, S'Klallam, and Samish—involved members of the Mitchell Bay Band and San Juan Tribe of Indians, their dockets (arguments presented before the Commission and their finding) are germane. The Lummi (Docket 110) case was based, to a large extent, on research presented by Wayne

Suttles about the areas of the San Juans that were not covered by the terms of the Treaty of Point Elliott, to which the Lummi were signatories. The Commission offered a settlement, which was refused by the Lummi as too low. The S'Klallam (Docket 134) did not involve claims to San Juan Island, even though some families—many of whom considered themselves Mitchell Bay Band—clearly constituted part of the Indigenous peoples there. The Samish (Docket 261) claimed traditional use of areas of San Juan and Cypress Islands but were rejected because the Commission considered these "free-use" areas. Finally, the San Juan Tribe (Docket 214) was dismissed with the reasoning that they were a subsection of the Lummi and Samish Tribes.

In 1973, thirteen western Washington tribes brought suit against the State of Washington to ensure recognition of treaty rights, particularly in regard to resources. In February 1974 federal district court judge George Boldt decided that the wording of the Indian treaties guaranteed to the tribes an allocation of salmon, which he set as fifty percent. In the period from 1974 to 1978, the Boldt Decision was challenged in court 35 times. After lackadaisical enforcement by the State of Washington, in July of 1978 Judge Boldt stepped in and assumed jurisdiction over the fishery. Finally, in 1979, the United States Supreme Court reversed its 1976 decision not to hear an appeal and on July 2nd of that year upheld the Boldt Decision, with some modifications, such as including ceremonial and subsistence catches in the 50% allocation and reducing the tribal share if they did not use it. The State of Washington, which was charged with managing the resource, had to comply. During the 1970s and 1980s, members of the Mitchell Bay Band continued to seek federal recognition, in order to fall under the jurisdiction resulting from the Boldt Decision. Members of the Chevalier family, who were connected to the Mitchell Bay Band through their ancestor Lucy Jack Ontonna and to the Swinomish Tribe through their ancestor Lena Thomas, were invited by the Swinomish Tribe, as part of the "Mitchell Bay band of the Swinomish Aboriginal Tribe," to fish with the Tribe under their treaty rights.

In their effort to gain federal recognition, members of the Mitchell Bay Indian Tribe met on June 5, 1976, to formally organize the Tribe. Some of the records from this period are available, including a Tribal Constitution, petition for federal recognition, and various meeting notices and minutes, bank documents, and related newspaper clippings. The Constitution and By-Laws of the Mitchell Bay Tribe of the San Juan Islands and Adjacent Areas begins with a preamble: "WE THE PEOPLE of the Mitchell Bay Tribe, of the San Juan Islands, in the State of Washington, and adjacent areas, in order to establish our tribal organization, keep our identity, develop our community resources, administer justice and promote economic and social welfare of ourselves and our descendants, do hereby establish this constitution and by-laws." The first article defined the territory of the Tribe: "The jurisdiction of the Mitchell Bay Tribe shall include all lands once held by the aboriginal, native Indian people of the San Juan Island area and adjacent territorial waters. However, nothing in this article shall be construed as restricting the hunting and fishing rights of members, including the right to hunt and fish in the usual and accustomed places." Membership in the Tribe was defined as:

a. *All members that appear on the 1919 census recorded with the Bureau of Indian Affairs of the Mitchell Bay Tribe, taken by Special Indian Agent Charles E. Rowgran*[sic, should be Roblin], *submitted January 1, 1919.*

b. *Or any other Indian people of the San Juan Island area that were enrolled with the San Juan Tribe prior to 1945.*

c. *Membership shall also include any children born to any member on the 1919 Mitchell Bay enrollment list or any children born to any member of the San Juan Tribe enrollment list, prior to 1945.*

d. *Membership shall also include any person of Mitchell Bay Indian blood or San Juan Island blood, who has applied for adoption and are approved for membership by the Mitchell Bay Indian Council.*

The Council, elected by qualified Tribal voters, was composed of a chairman, vice-chairman, secretary, treasurer, and a councilman. The initial council consisted of W. P. Chevalier, Chair; Charles Chevalier, Spokesman or Chair Pro-Tem; Caroline Mills, Vice-Chair (with Bill "E.W." Chevalier as Alternate and Sherman Thompson as 2nd Vice Chairman); Renee Chevalier Higbee, Secretary; Betty Nash, Treasurer; and Dennis Gerlt, Legal Council. Ten members enrolled and paid $10 each.

In *Are You Listening Neighbor? A Report of the Indian Affairs Task Force* and *The People Speak Will You Listen?* (State of Washington 1978), under the Mitchell Bay Indian Tribe, an author (probably Charles Chevalier) described the history of the group. Claiming that "Currently more than 100 persons are listed on tribal enrolment," he went on to report:

> *Like many Indian Tribes today, the Mitchell Bay Indians find themselves in the political dilemma of being landless and without federal acknowledgement of their rightful status as an Indian Tribe. Despite numerous problems stemming from their non-status, the Mitchell Bay People have continued through the years to function as an Indian Tribe without the benefit of federal assistance. At times their numbers have dwindled and the Tribe lacked a sophisticated government. Today, however, the Tribe has a constitution and operates under the leadership of a five member Tribal Council. The Mitchell Bay Tribe will continue to seek federal recognition of its fishing rights as well as other benefits for its members.*

The struggle for recognition of the Mitchell Bay Band continues today. There are records of a Mitchell Bay Indian Tribe meeting in February of 2004. When the Port of Friday Harbor commissioned Coast Salish House Posts, carved by Susan A. Point, for the waterfront Fairweather Park, they invited members of indigenous groups to participate in the March 20th, 2004, dedication ceremonies; many members attended, including at least a dozen members of the Mitchell Bay Tribe.

In 2021, the San Juan County Charter Review Commission recommended the following addition to the charter for adoption by the citizens:

ACKNOWLEDGEMENT

Let us acknowledge we reside on the ancestral lands and waters of the Coast Salish people who have called this place home since time immemorial and let us honor inherent, aboriginal and treaty rights that have been passed down from generation to generation.

Charter Amendment Proposition No. 1 was put to a vote, and passed, but with a mere 1% margin: 50.51% to 49.49%.

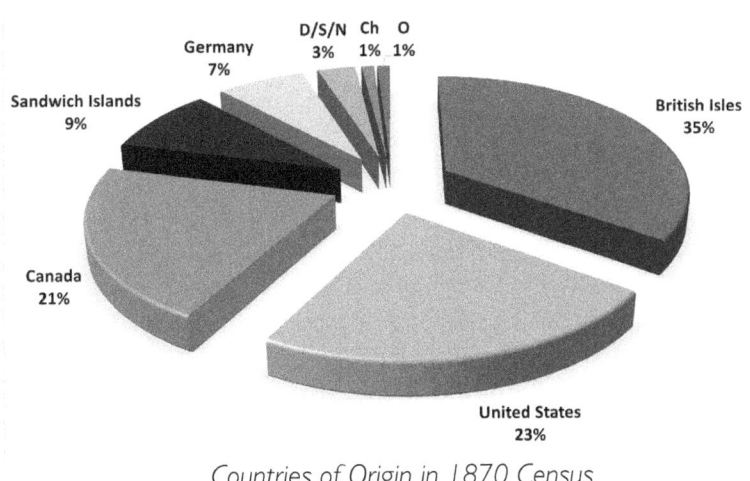

Countries of Origin in 1870 Census

Countries of Origin in 1880 Census

Identity

The inhabitants of San Juan Island during Pig War period were a varied mix of ethnicities: Indigenous peoples who had lived and used the islands for millennia; Northern tribes that came to trade and raid; English, Irish, Scots and Welsh, as well as French Canadians, Métis, and Kanakas, all of whom were called "English"; and Americans who came to the Disputed Islands from a variety of states and territories. All these groups intermarried, to the extent that a significant and influential portion of the population was composed of cross-cultural families. This period was a time of flux, when cultural attitudes towards each other and among themselves changed significantly.

Comparison of two censuses—the 1870 federal census of the "Disputed Islands" and the 1887 territorial census conducted on the brink of Washington statehood—shows a marked change in cultural groups. In both, the categories regarding "race" were rigid: enumerators categorized residents as White (W), Indian (I), Sandwich Islands (SI) [i.e., Hawaiian or Kanaka], Black (B), and Chinese (C), or a combination, such as "½ I" [half Indian]. In 1870, San Juan Island had the largest White population (194), a small number of Indians (19, all married women), at least 10 Kanaka men with their Indian wives and their 15 mixed children, one Black man with his Indian wife and their six mixed children, and two Chinese. The other islands had only Whites and Indians and their progeny, with Orcas showing the highest ratio of White men (60) to Indian women (25). Of the 102 "heads of household" on San Juan Island in 1870, 35% were from British Isles (England, Ireland, Scotland, and Cornwall), 23% from the United States, and 21% from Canada. Among other ethnicities, the largest minority were Hawaiians ("Sandwich Islands") at 9%, Germans at 7%, and then a smattering of Danes, Swedes, Norwegians, and Chinese.

In 1887, with 134 heads of household, 25% were from the British Isles, 45% American, and 12% Canadian, again with significant minorities of Danes, Germans, and Norwegians, and a few French, Finns, and Swedes. Although there were no Hawaiians recorded, the examples of the Bull and Friday families indicate that some families remained. This shift from a multi-cultural milieu to one of increasing Euro-American dominance, accelerated in the succeeding decades, leading to the physical, social, and cultural dominance of Whites in the San Juans and suppression of recognition and acknowledgement of the rich heritage of the early period.

San Juan Islands Place Names

PLACE

When Lyman Cutlar shot the boar and precipitated the Pig War, he did so near his potato garden located in an open area—variously described as a prairie, pasture, and sheep run—near the edge of the woods. Was this description of a portion of San Juan Island typical of the landscape, and if so, how did it get that way? Furthermore, how did the Coast Salish and Hudson's Bay Company's use of these 'natural' prairies change them? This chapter examines the geology and geography of the islands, which, together with climate, determined the physical basis of occupation of the archipelago. The location and situation of Indigenous places came first, then the European exploration of the islands, and eventually the various systems—English colonial and American public land—that were applied to land. The changes that occurred in the natural landscapes of the islands, through controlled burning, cultivation, introduction of new animals and plants, and suppression or extirpation of others, exacerbated the 'disputes' of occupation and use of the place that we called the San Juan Islands.

Physical Features

The San Juan Islands lie within a recently (2009) designated region, the Salish Sea, which consists of Puget Sound, the Strait of Juan de Fuca, and the Strait of Georgia. It can also be defined as the body of water surrounded by the landmasses of the Olympic Peninsula to the south, Vancouver Island to the west, and the Canadian and United States mainland to the north and east. The Salish Sea comprises a water surface of 6,535 square miles and a coastline that is 4,642 miles long, and contains 419 islands, with a combined land area of 1,413 square miles. Located in the northwest corner of Washington State, the San Juan Islands are bounded by Haro Strait to the west and northwest, the Strait of Georgia to the north and northeast, Rosario Strait to the east, and the Strait of Juan de Fuca and Puget Sound to the south. San Juan County—which encompasses most of the San Juan Archipelago and consists of over 128 named islands, reefs, and rocks at high tide—has more than 400 miles of marine shoreline and approximately 172 square miles of land area, with the three largest islands (comprising about 80 percent of the overall land mass) being Orcas (57 square miles or 36,432 acres), San Juan (55 square miles or 35,448 acres), and Lopez (29 square miles or 18,847 acres), and Shaw, Blakely, Waldron, Decatur, Stuart, and Henry (in order of size) each being less than 10,000 acres.[1]

Comprising the highest points of a submerged mountain range, the islands consist of older base rock associated with the surrounding Cascade and Olympic ranges. This bedrock, according to Bates McKee,[2] consists of "an old, crystalline basement rock; a late Paleozoic and Early Mesozoic eugeosynclinal sequence of marine volcanic and sedimentary rocks; thrust faults of Cretaceous age; and Lower Tertiary sandstones and shales." What would turn into one of the most important economic assets in the islands' history is the limestone contained in this bedrock. Lime (CaO) is produced from limestone, a sedimentary rock composed primarily of calcite, or calcium carbonate ($CaCO_3$), in the form of marble made of aragonite. Limestone deposits in the San Juan Islands extend from the northeastern portion of Orcas, across the island to the northern and western portions of San Juan and the smaller islands in between such as Crane, Jones, and Shaw.

The geology of the San Juans is extremely complex, but local limestone is predominately from two terranes. (A terrane is a discrete fault-bounded layer of rock that typically formed in one location and was transported by tectonic movement to another.) The older Turtleback/Eastsound Terrane dates from 415 to 260 million years ago; it is found on the west coast of Orcas. The Deadman Bay/Orcas Terrane, dating from 280 to 190 million years ago, is the primary source of limestone in the San Juan Islands and found at Lime Kiln, Roche Harbor, and other locations on northern San Juan Island and throughout much of Orcas Island. Both consist of basalt inter-fingered by thin beds, or lenses, of limestone, which is what is quarried. Their formation is like the atoll island system of the tropical Pacific, where lava erupts, cools in the ocean, and is subsequently covered by limey mud—calcium that was dissolved in seawater combined with carbon dioxide to form the solid calcite—and reefs formed from organisms that absorbed calcium to form shells and skeletons and then died. Neither terrane, though, formed near its present location; eastward movement of the Farallon Plate under the Pacific Ocean carried the basalts and limestones of the Deadman Bay/Orcas Terrane and accreted, or attached, them to the North American Plate over 100 million years ago. (Evidence of their age and origin comes from single-celled invertebrate fossils in the limestones, known as fusilinids, which formed in the Tethys Sea near ancestral southeast China.) In contrast, geochemical analysis of the Turtleback/Eastsound Terrane suggests that it formed as an island volcanic arc initially near the North Atlantic. It subsequently migrated along the northern edge of the North American continent where limestone reefs developed along its ancient volcanos before it was accreted to the West Coast.

> *The limestones of western Washington were originally formed as horizontal or nearly horizontal layers, mounds, and lenses on the sea floor. They have since been lifted above the sea and tilted, complexly folded, squeezed into irregular shapes, and broken by faulting.*
>
> —Wilbert R. Danner
> Limestone Resources of Western Washington (1966)[3]

During the Pleistocene Era, a series of three great glaciations occurred, with the ice reaching as far south as modern-day Olympia, filling the depression known as the Puget Trough and leaving only the surrounding mountain ranges uncovered. As they receded, the glaciers not only scraped the existing rocky areas, but also left behind glacial till, as well as the large boulders, called erratics, that can be seen standing unmoved in the middle of farm fields and pastures.

After the release of the weight of the glacial ice, the islands gradually rose in a process called isostatic rebound. During the same period, however, the melting of the receding glaciers also caused a gradual rise in sea level, so that the result of these forces led to a series of shorelines that have differed from the current ones. In all probability, all or most of Center Valley, Mud Bay, and Swift Bay on Lopez Island; Deer Harbor, Crow Valley, Eastsound, and Olga on Orcas Island; and Beaverton, San Juan, and West valleys and other lower areas on San Juan Island were under the ocean at one time. This submersion, together with glacial action, resulted in the current general soil Bellingham-Coveland-Bow association of low-sloped, poorly drained soils interspersed with small outcrops or 'islands' of Roche-Rock complex. These soils usually have a profile of 18-30 inches above a relatively impermeable clay subsoil that is locally referred to as 'hardpan.' The other soil association—Roche-San Juan—occurs in the uplands and other rocky settings, with better drainage.[4]

The islands exhibit a wide degree of relief. There are numerous rocky knobs, including 15 mountains that rise 1,000 feet or more above sea level, with Mount Constitution on Orcas being the highest at 2,407 feet in elevation. The glacial scourings of the islands led to areas of low relief, such as glacial plains and gently rolling and basin-like areas, exemplified by San Juan Valley on San Juan, Crow Valley on Orcas, and Center Valley and several other parts of Lopez. Drainage mainly occurs by means of short, intermittent streams; only a few streams were probably capable of bearing fish spawning. Some estuarine tidal systems also occur, such as Fish Trap Creek, which drains into Cayou Lagoon near Deer Harbor on Orcas Island. The watersheds that recently or currently support marine fish such as salmonids are Davis Bay on Lopez (which has a tide gate); False Bay and Garrison Creeks on San Juan Island; and Bayhead/Victoria, Fish Trap, Cascade, Crow Valley (West Sound), Doe Bay, and West Beach Creeks on Orcas Island.

After the glaciations, the landscape of the islands evolved from open, savannah-like prairies to forested areas of cedar, Douglas fir (*Pseudotsuga menziesii*), and their respective plant communities arrived only 3-4,000 years ago. The more extensive prairies contain well-drained black soil with scattered Garry or white oak (*Quercus garryana*), while the forested communities are largely composed of Douglas fir, mixed with western hemlock (*Tsuga heterophylla*), white fir (*Abies grandis*), and Sitka spruce (*Picea sitchensis*). Deciduous trees such as red alder (*Alnus rubra*) and bigleaf maple (*Acer macropyllum*) are also present, particularly in disturbed areas. Lower elevations contain stands of Douglas firs mixed with lodgepole pine (*P. contorta*). Wetter soils support the growth of western red cedar (*Thuja plicata*), while some of the drier areas have scattered growth of madrona (*Arbutus menziesii*). The islands are noted for open rocky outcrops, in the form of rocky knolls, stony slopes, and gravelly prairies. These feature pockets of shallow soil where grasses and herbs, and sometimes drought-tolerant bushes and trees, can grow.

The coastlines of the San Juan Islands are deeply indented with many sheltered coves and inlets, including several, such as East and West Sounds on Orcas, which resemble fjords. These rugged and irregular shorelines are generally elevated and rocky, although there are stretches of gravelly and sandy beaches. The same physical forces that formed the exposed land also formed the sea bottom or ocean floor. The channels between the islands are generally narrow and U-shaped from glacial action and range from 16 to 100 fathoms deep. The large amount of water moving to and from the Strait of Juan de Fuca and the Strait of Georgia through the islands causes heavy riptides and eddies (see Appendix: *William Warner, Description of a Passage between Spencer Spit and Frost Island off the East Shore of Lopez Island*).

> *The archipelago occupies an important position in its relation to the other parts of this region. Lying just north of the eastern end of the Straits of Fuca, through which the currents of Puget Sound, and perhaps also of the Gulf of Georgia, flow during the rise and fall of the tides, it obstructs the currents flowing to and from the Gulf of Georgia, giving them various courses of deflection, and often producing, in many places, tide-rips sufficiently extensive to endanger small craft.*
>
> *The islands are separated by narrow but very deep channels, so deep indeed that the largest class vessels can pass through almost any of them. This is the character of almost every narrow channel separating islands lying between the continent and Vancouver's Island, and has led many a sailor to compare these waters to the Straits of Magellan, where it is often difficult to find anchorage.*
>
> —Geographical Memoir of the Islands between the Continent and Vancouver's Island in the Vicinity of the Forty Ninth Parallel of North Latitude *(1860)*

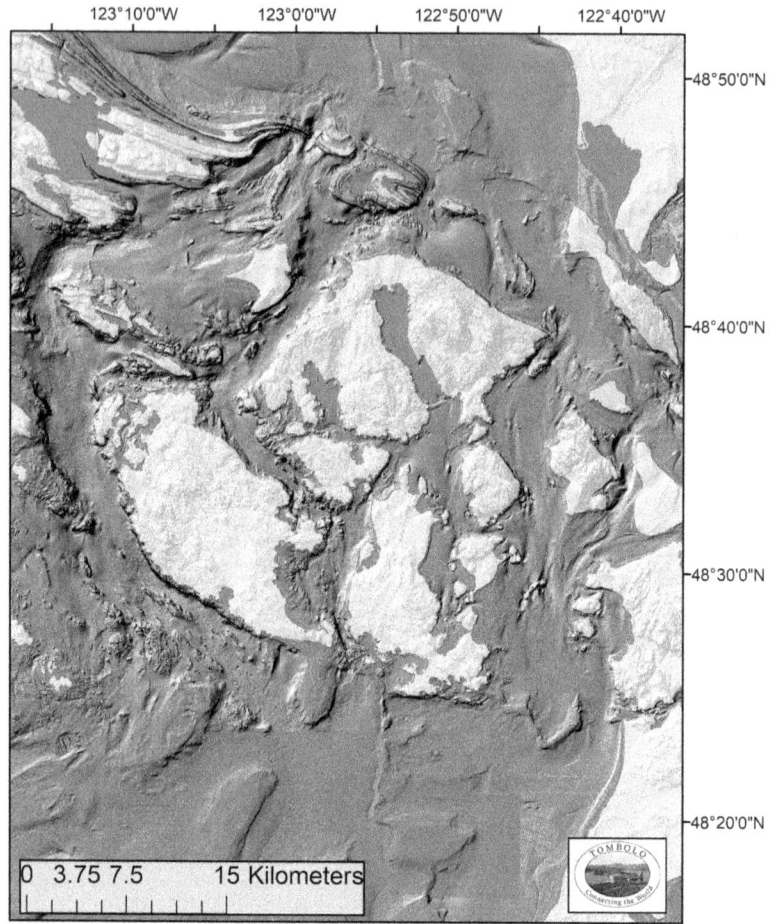

Map Developed by John Aschoff and Gary Greene
San Juan Archipelago in Central Salish Sea

Bathymetry of the San Juan Islands
(courtesy of Tombolo Mapping Lab, Moss Landing Marine Labs Center
for Habitat Studies, Geologic Survey Canada, and NOAA)

The situation of the islands also lends itself to several distinct marine habitats. Sheltered by Vancouver Island and the Olympic Peninsula from the direct waters of the Pacific Ocean, the Salish Sea has a wider range of salinity and temperature, which in turn requires a greater degree of tolerance by sea organisms. Average

Salish Sea water temperatures vary from 45°F in the winter to 52°F in the summer. Water currents course through the islands with two ebb and two flood tides each day. Because of all the obstructions and constrictions in the inland waters, there is a large difference in tides: for instance, Victoria, on the southern tip of Vancouver Island, has tidal shifts 5 hours and 35 minutes later than Tofino, located on the west (Pacific) side of Vancouver Island. Tides in the islands can range up to 14 feet, with an extreme low of -4 feet and an extreme high of over 10 feet.

The overall system of circulation in the Salish Sea is complex and influenced by many variables. Because of the height of Coast, Olympic, and Cascade Ranges, moisture-laden air coming in from the Pacific Ocean encounters the cool mountainous air and sheds most of its water, in the form of fog, rain, and snow, on the western slopes of the mountains. (An exception is the region defined by Victoria to the west, the Gulf Islands to the north, and Sequim on the Olympic Peninsula to the south, with the San Juans in the middle—the "Blue Hole," which, lying in a rain shadow, experiences drier, sunnier weather.) This precipitation feeds the rivers—mainly through the melting of the snow in late summer—and they in turn discharge their freshwater, laden with sediments, nutrients, and other organic matter, into the Salish Sea. Since freshwater is less dense than saltwater, it flows from the river's mouth and, in the case of the Fraser River, the main source, toward the Strait of Juan de Fuca and the Pacific Ocean, while the denser saltwater flows in from the ocean toward the islands and Strait of Georgia. Winds in the region, which are northerly in the winter, push the surface water off the coasts, which cause an upwelling of nutrient-rich but oxygen-poor water. These waters—outgoing estuarine surface water and incoming nutrient-rich ocean water—get mixed when the currents encounter the sills of underwater mountains. Furthermore, tidal currents flow past protruding parts of land and cause eddies to the lee side of the land, bearing nutrients and microorganisms such as plankton to nearshore marine communities. This overall exchange of nutrients and other factors sustain the many unique habitats of the Salish Sea.[5]

Climate

From regular, consistent observations that extend back over one hundred years, the climate in the islands in the recent past is known. But what was it like before that, particularly in that period when Euro-Americans first began to settle here? Perhaps the only ways to tell are to study what the scientific observations indicate is the general trend in recent times, as well as to examine the few glimpses at the climate in the historical records prior to that time and glean from Indigenous oral traditions of events in the past.

Located in the rain shadow produced by the Cascades to the east and the Olympics to the south, the San Juans currently have an average rainfall of 29 inches per year (based on the recording station at Olga on Orcas Island, 1890 to present). However, being an average, various parts of the archipelago tend to differ from other parts, with the general rule being wetter in the north and drier in the south. On San Juan Island, for instance, precipitation ranges from a low of 19 inches at Cattle Point to the south to 29 at Roche Harbor to the north, with San Juan Valley in between, averaging 25. Elevation, of course, also makes a difference: the lowest lying lands on Lopez average 19, while 2407-foot-high Mt. Constitution on Orcas has been known to get 45. During the historic record, however, average annual precipitation has varied from almost 38 inches in the wettest year, 1917, to 15 inches during the driest year of 1929. On average, the thirty-year period from 1891-1921 was wetter (31.04) than the succeeding twenty-four years, 1921-1945 (26.33). The period following World War II indicated a trend toward wetter and cooler years. Because most precipitation occurs during the winter months (70% from October through March), the islands usually experience drought conditions during the summer, favoring either agricultural crops that need little water, farming in water-retentive soils, or irrigation.[6]

> Some portions [of prairie land], those lying on the south west side of the island [San Juan], are so exposed to the sweep of the southern gales that no grain or fruit could be grown there. The violence of these gales is sufficiently shown by the appearance of the trees, whose tops are bent almost at right angles to the remainder of the trunk.
>
> —Henry Custer, North West Boundary Survey (1859)

The climate in the San Juans is generally mild, tempered by the surrounding sea waters and southwesterly and westerly winds. Due to the rain shadow, the number of days of sunshine is high compared to the surrounding region. Temperatures range from an average of 40 degrees F in the winter to 59 in the summer. San Juan Island has an historic average of 226 frost-free days (the "growing season"), although low-lying pockets have been known to experience freezing in July. Violent storms or gales are not uncommon in the San Juans during the winter; in fact, when I first wrote this (Winter of 2006-2007), a series of strong southeast storms with high winds (clocked at 100mph on the south end of Lopez) and heavy rains had lashed the islands, causing the uprooting of trees and extensive branch fall. Extraordinary weather was noted by several other observers during the historic period. For instance, Hudson's Bay Company Post Trader Charles Griffin reported the daily weather in his *Post Journals*, particularly noting extreme conditions. In December 1858, he wrote that the winter was as harsh as the one he had experienced in 1853. In the summer of 1859, during the time of the Pig Incident, the weather was "oppressively hot", while on December 10, 1860, he woke up to ice a half inch thick. Thunder and lightning storms, a relative rarity in the San Juans today, were remarked upon at least annually (see Appendix: *North West Boundary Survey Storm Account, January 21, 1859*).

> Orcas Island was visited nearly every winter by one or more terrific snowstorms from the Northeast, which drifted the snow so deep that the roads were impassible and though it rarely went below freezing, still, in that moist climate we felt the cold worse than the same degree in the drier climates of the East. Fortunately these blizzards only lasted a few days at a time. The islands, owing to their exposed condition, are always very windy, which makes the catarrh problem very common.
> —The Diary of James Francis Tulloch (1970)

The winter of 1861-1862 was particularly harsh in the Pacific Northwest. Arthur Denny recorded a temperature of 2° below zero in Seattle, and Lake Union froze to a depth of six inches.[7] According to Hudson's Bay Company records, the farm at Fort Nisqually lost about nine-tenths (4,500) of their sheep due to severe weather conditions.[8] New settlers on Salt Spring Island, in the nearby Gulf Islands, also lost much of their livestock, resulting in eventual departure of about a third of the population.[9] Undoubtedly the San Juans suffered the same conditions.

The local atmosphere was altered by Indigenous and Euro-American peoples' practice of burning prairies and forests to clear land. The Coast Salish burned the open, savannah-like areas of prairie grass and Garry oaks to keep them open for camas lily growth and game like deer. Euro-Americans burned standing trees, as well as stumps and slash, to clear the land for farming

> Generally in that region, in breezeless days of August smoke from burning forests falls, and envelops all the world of land and water. In such strange chaos, voyaging without a compass is impossible. Canoes are often detained for days, waiting for the smoke to lift.
> —Theodore Winthrop, The Canoe and the Saddle (1862)[12]

acreage. On June 12, 1858, Charles Griffin records in the *Post Journals* sighting "dense smoke from fires all over the country," and ten years later Thomas Fleming noted in his *Journal* on September 18-19, 1868, "grate[sic] smoke all over the Island" probably from fires lit by Indigenous peoples.[10] As a pioneer from nearby Skagit County recalled, "In 1868 the smoke from the forest fires throughout the county became so dense that navigators could not see a boat's length ahead and birds were suffocated by the thick black smoke clouds of the upper air, fell onto the decks of the boats and into the water, dead."[11] There are numerous references to Indigenous peoples burning fields in the surrounding region.

Indigenous Places

Wayne Suttles, in his 1951 dissertation *Economic Life of the Coast Salish of Haro and Rosario Straits*, identified four village sites on or near San Juan Island associated with the "*Kla-la-ka-mish*": *pqwi'E'kwət* (Mitchell Bay); *tatinkwat* (Open Bay, Henry Island); *sma'ya* (Garrison and Westcott Bays); and *xwl̓e'lqt* ("The Fitzhugh place" on the north shore of San Juan Island, facing Spieden Island).[13] According to his various interviewees, one or several of these sites were claimed by the Saanich to belong to a separate tribe with their principal village at Garrison Bay. In *Saltwater People*, Saanich elder Dave Elliot, Sr., called Mitchell Bay PLÁYELWEŁ "place of ancient wood."[14] A Songish interviewee claimed the origin of the modern day Songhees from this cultural group; and the Lummi, who claimed Garrison Bay as their point of origin, associate all four sites with their ancestors (see Appendix: *Salish Villages*).

Suttles also described at least four permanent villages on Orcas: *E'le'lay* ("Houses") West Sound, believed to have stood at the site of the present town of West Sound; *Calxwe's?y*, East Sound, at or near the present town (possibly Madrona Point); *Makwa'lnic*, Rosario; and *Xwt',.ct*, Olga. He goes on to explain:

> The name Swe"lax was given to Mount Constitution and the people of the last three villages were called swe"lax people. This is the name "Swa;;ah" or "Swallash" occasionally met with. Eliza's map of 1792 shows three squares, presumably for "rancherias," on the southeastern tip of Orcas Island, but it is difficult to tell their precise location. Gibbs identifies "Hu-tat-ch'l" as the "site of an Indian Village on the S.E. of Orcas Island." He does not identify the other former village sites in the islands as "villages"; therefore, this one may still have been occupied at the time he wrote, about 1860.[15]

On June 19th, 1792, Archibald Menzies landed on one of the islands in the San Juans and described a settlement there near a swamp. Newcombe conjectures that the site was probably on the north shore of Orcas opposite East Sound, where such a swamp existed.[16]

There were several villages on Lopez, where both the Lummi and the Samish and their forbears and relations had village sites. (On the Samish Indian Nation's Coast Salish Place Names of the San Juan Islands, Lopez is called "Sx'wálech," "Bottom of Reef Netting," either something to do with the shape or bottom of a reef net, or because this island is the furthest south and the end or "bottom" of the areas that were reef netted; the Sencoten Language Dictionary name for Lopez is listed as WTISEĆEN, "Land of the pegged earth").[17] The principal Lummi one was TLA W ALAMES (shortened to Tlawalmes) or "Kalka'nip/X̱alX̱a'lnip" a winter village site at Flat or Sandy Point. According to Bernhard Stern this was the site of an unusual L-shaped longhouse ("Wulalemus" meaning "facing each other") which was moved to Gooseberry Point on the mainland when the Lummi migrated there.[18] Lopez Village was apparently sited on an Indigenous village, and several places served as fishing camps: Agate Beach, Mud Bay, Richardson, Spencer Spit, Sperry Peninsula, and Watmough Bay (when Sampson Chadwick settled nearby there were fish drying racks still present). (Also of note are the remains of Indigenous defensive trenches near MacKaye Harbor.)

Place names bear witness not only to the presence of Indigenous peoples in the islands but also the importance of resources in their Salish Sea economy. According to Lucille McDonald, local Lummi place names include "the place of deepwater fishing" for Waldron; "where the native oyster is found" for Patos, and "mussels on the rocks" for Sucia.[19] The Samish Indian Nation's website Coast Salish Place Names of the San Juan Islands notes Blakely Island (*X'emx'emílhch*, place of horsetail plants); Cherry Point (*Nuxws7áx'wom*, place to always get butter clams) and Dakota Creek (*Kw'ol7óxwem*, place to get dog salmon) on the mainland; Decatur Island (*Sx'eméne7*, place of ratfish); Deepwater Point on Samish Island (*Xwtl'échqs*, Troll for spring salmon here); Deer Harbor, Orcas Island (*Tqá7ech*, place of aerial ducknet hunting); Lopez Island (*Sx'wálech*, bottom of reef netting); Matia Island (*Penáxweng*, place of harvesting camas); Orcas Island (*Sx'wálex'*, scattered reef netting); Patos Island (*Tl'x'óy7ten*, place of harvesting oysters); Sucia Island (*Lhéwqemeng*, place of harvesting mussels); Waldron Island (*Ch'x'ení*, place of seaweed); and White Rock on the mainland (*Q'imeqweng*, place of catching octopus).[20]

Records of early Euro-American exploration and surveys in the region document the presence of Indigenous peoples in this area. For instance, a chart of the west side of San Juan Island produced by the 1854 U.S. Coast Survey indicates four locations marked "Village" on the coast, including one that appears to be on the north shore of Mitchell Bay.[21] Charles Griffin in his *Post Journals* has several references to villages on the west coast of San Juan, including a large one that was abandoned, where he sent his men to "collect shells from the middens there in order to make lime" (September 25, 1854).[22] Griffin also mentions trading salmon with Indians fishing off the west coast of San Juan Island, as well as his unsuccessful attempts to imitate their fishing methods.

After the settlement of the boundary dispute in 1872, the United States government authorized a Township and Range Survey of the islands, starting in 1874. The survey field notes, as

1854 U.S. Coast Survey Westside of San Juan Island. (courtesy of San Juan Island National Historical Park)

well as the maps of each section, have several references to both Indigenous and Euro-American settlement in the Mitchell Bay/ Garrison Bay/Westcott Bay area: on the shoreline, in Section 35, at 12 chains they noted "several Indian Huts;" farther on (376.2 links), there were "Several Indian Huts on Beach." At 165.0, they noted "To wharf & fishery of Peter Lawe [Lami] House 150 lks." In this same description of the shoreline meander, in Section 24 (past English Camp), they noted "Smith Burrs house bears S.760 W." and further on "Jacob Lowe's house brs. East 200 lks."[23]

Several of the elders who gave depositions in the petition *Duwamish et al v. United States* (1927) testified as to the location of both permanent and temporary settlements in the islands. F.

D. Sexton noted villages at the Larson [Lawson?] place and Kanaka Bay, as well as a fishing village at Griffin Bay, all on San Juan Island. Alice G. Lightheart mentioned "Mitchells Bay, that was a regular village there; they had big houses all along, and of course, a lot of Indians there," as well Kanaka Bay. Jane Williams mentioned villages at Roche Harbor, with at least ten buildings, and one near Griffin Bay. Caroline Ewing enumerated "a big reservation up here at Hobbs Point, and one at the fort, in early times, and one below Peter Lawson, and one below our place, Jimmy Fleming's place, and one at Roche Harbor, and scattered all along the beach that way, villages all through." John Dougherty mentioned a settlement at Mitchell Bay and two to three at the south end of San Juan Island. Johnny Tom mentioned a village at West Sound, including a longhouse, three houses at East Sound, and "removable houses" scattered about Orcas Island. On Shaw, he noted that "it was only where the fishing villages and temporary houses, where they used to cure fish." Tom also mentioned that parts of Lopez had been settled with longhouses. In addition to the settlement at Kanaka Bay (with "one big large house") on San Juan Island, Jim Walker mentioned a longhouse at Argyle, "until the whites settled there, they clear out, of course."[24]

According to an April 19, 1900, article in the *San Juan Islander*, an Indian man, allegedly named "Captain George" (after Captain George Pickett), and his wife were living in one of three dwellings ("huts") called a "rancherie" on the sandy hill above the water near American Camp and Belle Vue Sheep Farm.[25] Several charts and maps indicate these structures were located above current Grandma's Cove: the 1858 Richards Chart with the designation "Indian Village"; the 1873 Ebstein Map with the term "Indian Hut"; and the 1897 U.S. Coast and Geodetic Survey map that indicates three structures, labeled "Indian Houses."[26] Paul K. Hubbs claimed to have first encountered Captain George and his wife dwelling there in 1855. Two of the three "rough shacks" were abandoned, but the writer does describe the occupied one as a "rude habitation from which the smoke of an open fire within was curling through a hole in the roof." "Captain George" allegedly was born in 1830 on San Juan Island to a Clallam father and a Samish mother. This site may be related to the one occupied by the Clallams when they came seasonally for fishing and camas gathering.

The Coast Salish who first inhabited the islands all year long and later used them for seasonal fishing, hunting, and gathering already had an intimate knowledge of the islands that comes from centuries of traditional habitation and use of resources. The surviving record of Indigenous place names reveals this knowledge, in particular, the importance of fishing and marine gathering in Salish Sea economy: Cherry Point (*Nuxws7áx'wom*, place to always get butter clams) and Dakota Creek (*Kw'ol7óxwem*, place to get dog salmon) on the mainland; Decatur Island (*Sx'eméne7*, place of ratfish); Lopez Island (*Sx'wálech*, bottom of reef netting); Orcas Island (*Sx'wálex'*, scattered reef netting); Pa-

Reef Net Locations in the San Juan Islands

tos Island (*Tl'x'óy7ten*, place of harvesting oysters); Sucia Island (*Lhéwqemeng*, place of harvesting mussels); and Waldron Island (*Ch'x'ení*, place of seaweed).[27]

Many of these settlements were associated with reef netting (see Appendix: *Reef Net Locations*). According to tradition, Straits Salish groups reef netted at ten locations along the west shore of San Juan Island: (in modern place names) Eagle Point; the headland southeast of Kanaka Bay; the west point of Kanaka Bay; Pile Point; two sites northwest of Pile Point; Lime Kiln, off the point north of the light house; on north side of Low Island in Andrews Bay; Sunset Point; two sites at Mosquito Pass; and Open Bay on Henry Island. There were also two reef net locations near Reid Harbor and four locations off the southeast headland of Stuart Island and two locations off John's Island.[28] On Lopez, fishers reef netted at Flat Point; Fisherman's Bay with seven locations; Shark Reef; Iceberg Point; Aleck Bay with three locations; and Kellett Ledge. Orcas Island had two areas: Point Doughty with two locations and West Beach with eight. Shaw Island had several locations: Neck Point, Lutz Bay with five locations and Squaw Bay [currently called Reef Net Bay] with nine locations. At Decatur Head there were two locations; Waldron Island had one, Cowlitz Bay; and Yellow Island also had one.

European and American Exploration

To live on an island is to be constantly aware of the water that surrounds it. A more proper viewpoint might be that of putting the emphasis on the water, with the islands as a series of 'non-water' between them. The early experience of the traveler in the Salish Sea in general and among the San Juan Islands was from the viewpoint of the water, not the land. This was knowledge that the ancient Greeks called the *periplous*: literally "a voyage around," the word was used to refer to a narrative of a voyage among and around islands. It is not off the subject to speak of the Ancient Greeks and the Greek Isles in this regard, for the classical paradigm that was established for most Europeans and Americans was that of the Greek classics and the Mediterranean world.

To the Europeans who first arrived in the 1790s, this was literally a "New World." Originally seeking a Northwest Passage

> *To describe the beauties of this region will on some future occasion, be a very grateful task to the pen of a skillful panegyrist. The serenity of the climate, the innumerable pleasing landscapes, and the abundant fertility that unassisted nature puts forth, require only to be enriched by the industry of man with villages, mansions, cottages, and other buildings, to render it the most lovely country that can be imagined; whilst the labour of the inhabitants would be amply rewarded, in the bounties which nature seems ready to bestow on cultivation.*
>
> —George Vancouver, A Voyage of Discovery to the North Pacific Ocean around the World (1984) [29]

from the Atlantic to the Pacific Ocean, their goal was to determine how to get around and through the islands. For the members of the United States North West Boundary Survey, for instance, the navigability of the "Haro Archipelago" was of paramount importance. The relation of the islands to the rest of the region, and Puget Sound in particular, was one of the first concerns of early explorers and chart makers. Mapmakers charted a region as they travelled through it, and because travel was by boat, the terminology of discovery and description was experiential. Travelers referred to the "right" or "left" bank of a river or stream oriented to the flow downstream; in the case of Puget Sound, one moved "up sound" or "down sound" depending upon its outlet. We moderns have become so used to taking the orientation of maps for granted that a common reading of region's geography is that North is "up," and South is "down." It's not uncommon to hear people talk about the southern portion of Puget Sound as "down sound," whereas historically it was "up sound." Mrs. Ebey, in her *Journal*, for instance, consistently mentions the ships that pass to and fro within sight of her vantage point on Whidbey Island and is careful to distinguish those going "up sound" from those proceeding "down sound."[30]

The Spanish explored the Strait of Juan de Fuca, the San Juan Islands, and Haro and Rosario Straits, as all of these names imply. In 1790, the sloop *Princesas Real*, under the command of Ensign Manuel Quimper and Pilot Gonzalo Lopez de Haro, first journeyed from Nootka on the west coast of Vancouver Island south and east, entering the Strait of Juan de Fuca, proceeding as far as present-day Victoria. After a long boat was sent ahead to discover and name Haro Strait, the *Princesas Real* moved across the Juan de Fuca to Dungeness, and discovered Rosario Strait, again with a long boat. Hearing of these discoveries, Spanish explorer Francisco Eliza resolved to explore the area the next year and sent First Pilot Juan Pantoja y Arriaga, commanding the schooner *Santa Saturnina*, in June of 1791. They proceeded north through Haro Strait as far as Saturna Island (a corruption of the ship's name) and Georgia Strait then southeast to Patos (named for the ducks they saw there), Sucia ("dirty," for the bad weather, and Matia (a corruption of *Mal Abrigado* [Poor Shelter]) to Lummi. They named the new strait they encountered the *Gran Canal de Nuestra Señora del Rosario la Marinera* ("Grand Canal of Our Lady of the Seaman's Rosary")—shortened to Rosario. Their trip long overextended, they made their way back to the main ship *San Carlos*.[31]

In 1792, Captain George Vancouver, also looking for the Northwest Passage, had entered Admiralty Inlet with his boats the *Discovery* and *Chatham*, an armed tender. Vancouver ordered his lieutenant, William Broughton, to reconnoiter the islands while he explored what he came to name Puget Sound. Broughton sailed between San Juan and Lopez, exploring both Upright and San Juan Channels. He then proceeded through Harney (recently renamed Cayou) Channel, exploring the islands, and then eventually travelled through Obstruction Pass to Rosario Strait. Crossing to Cypress Island, he stopped to gather strawberries at the eponymous bay (Strawberry Bay), and then sailed south to meet Vancouver near Alki Point. The Spanish ships *Sutil* and *Mexicana*, under the command of Lieutenants Dionisio Galiano and Cayetano Valdez, respectively, set out to explore Rosario Strait. The English and the Spanish met near present day Vancouver and agreed to explore Georgia and Queen Charlotte Straits to the Pacific Ocean together.[32]

Aside from naming islands and bodies of water, the two expeditions did not leave specific descriptions of land or water for posterity. Archibald Menzies, botanist for Vancouver's expedition (the madrona [*Arbutus menziesii*] is one of several plants named for him), and Vancouver as well as several others in the expedition, were impressed by the Puget Sound region and its potential for settlement (see Appendix: *Joseph Bank's Orders to Archibald Menzies*).

> On ascending the bank to the summit of the island, a rich lawn beautified with nature's luxuriant bounties burst at once on our view and impressed us with no less pleasure than novelty—it was abundantly cropped with a variety of grass, clover, and wild flowers, here and there adorned by aged pines with widespreading horizontal boughs and well sheltered by a slip [sic] of them densely copsed with underwood stretching along the summit of the steep sandy cliff, the whole seeming as it had been laid out from the premeditated plan of a judicious designer.
>
> —Archibald Menzies, Journal of Vancouver's Voyage (1792)[33]

Charles Wilkes, Captain of the *U.S.S. Vincennes*, who commanded the "Great United States Exploring Expedition" (abbreviated to the "U.S. Ex. Ex."), turned to the Northwest Coast after his explorations in the mid-Pacific, in part because of the looming international conflict over the fate of the Oregon Territory, jointly held by Great Britain and the United States. Wilkes, who realized during his explorations that the bar at the mouth of the Columbia prevented it from being a useful port, turned his focus on the more navigable waters of Puget Sound, and then proceeded to explore the San Juans because of their proximity to an American-proposed international boundary at the 49th parallel (see Appendix: *Charles Wilkes' Description of Navy Archipelago*). Although he and his crew spent only a brief time there (three days in late July 1841), one of Wilkes' principal legacies was the naming of literally hundreds of places in the region, including the renaming of many of the San Juan Islands. Because he chose the

Current Name	Indigenous	Spanish	English	U.S. (Wilkes)
Henry			Henry	Henry
Lopez	Sx'wálech	*[Lopez]	Lopez	Chaunceys
Orcas	Sx'wálex'	*[Orcas]	Orcas	Hulls
San Juan	Lháqemesh	Isla de San Juan	Belle Vue	Rodgers
Shaw			Shaw's	Shaw
Waldron	Ch'x'ení	Lemos	Waldron	Waldron

Names of the San Juan Islands
[*presumed by English surveyors)

names of either naval officers or battle sites associated with the War of 1812 (with Great Britain), many of these names proved to be an affront to the British surveyors.[34]

> *Our work for the Canal de Haro was commenced at the S.E. part of the Gulf of Georgia. The Astronomical Station was on a low point on N.E. side of Lummi Id., in Hal's Passage, and the base line located on Sandy Pt. at the mouth of the Lummi River. From this base the triangulation was carried between the Matia, Sucia, and Patos groups of islands on the North and Orcas and Waldron Ids. on the South, to the Canal, and thence between the islands forming its boundaries. As our time was brief, our work was necessarily rapid; I went ahead erecting signals. Mr. Davidson followed with the theodolite, the Active and her boats taking the soundings. The work was carried to between Henry and Sydney Ids.*
>
> —Autobiography of James S. Lawson (1879)[35]

One of the next surveyors of the islands was James Alden, Lieutenant Commander U.S. Navy, who served as Assistant to the U.S. Coast Survey (see Appendix: *James S. Lawson, Description of Survey Methods*). Alden had served as a lieutenant on board the *Vincennes* under the command of Capt. Wilkes of the U.S. Ex. Ex., and therefore was already familiar with the islands. Commanding the *U.S. Surveying Steamer Active* during the years 1852-1860, he started work in the fall of 1853 in the Gulf of Georgia and on the adjoining coast, linking up with the British survey of Captain Prevost of the *Plumper* and the land survey of Assistant George

> *From all the observations made of the soil, productions etc of these islands and vicinity I am satisfied that the land in Washington Territory is far inferior to that of California. Good crops of potatoes are raised, but it is too cold for Indian corn. The climate in winter is not at all severe, nor does the snow remain on the ground for any length of time. +++ The timber is good and abundant. It consists of Pine and some white Cedar and Alder. We found coal on almost every island we visited. Salmon abound in great quantities at certain seasons of the year, when the water in every direction seems to be filled with them. We caught large quantities of red fish averaging 12 pounds each, some Cod, closely resembling those on the Atlantic side and a few fine Halibut.*
>
> —James Alden, Lieut. Com. U.S. Navy, to Prof. A. D. Bache, Superintendent of the U.S. Coast Survey, October 31, 1853[38]

Davidson. (Alden recruited his nephew, James Madison Alden, as survey artist; several of the latter's watercolors reveal important historical details about the San Juans and their region.)[36] In 1855 Davidson wrote a dismissive assessment of the potential of the San Juans for settlement: "I consider the islands between Canal de Haro and Rosario strait as fitted only for limited settlement, there being little arable land and a great scarcity of fresh water. They can be used as fishing depots, and coal, perhaps, exists on some of them."[37] (See Appendix: *George Davidson's Description of the San Juan Islands*.) Alden himself came to a similar conclusion about the region in general; however, it should be kept in mind that as a superb sailor, he was principally concerned with the survey of the waters among the islands, so that perhaps his judgment should be taken with a grain of sea salt.

The only Euro-American resident of the islands that Alden encountered during his survey, other than the Hudson's Bay Company fishing station on San Juan, was an American, R. W. Cussans. Although Cussans asked Alden for counsel and aid in his claim for logging on Lopez Island, the latter was unable to assist him due to his position and instructions. (See the "Logging" section of *Work*.)

The naming of the islands continued to be a matter of confusion and contention for some years. Both the British and the Americans recognized that the honor of naming 'discovered' places lay with the 'discoverer'; the dispute arose over the understanding of who was there first. (Neither of the parties bothered to ask the Coast Salish their names for their homeland.) As a result, what appears on charts and maps today is an amalgam of the various European and Euro-American explorers' names. A good example is San Juan Island itself. It was first named San Juan (as was the whole archipelago) by Lieutenant Francisco Eliza on June 24, 1791—the feast day of San Juan Bautista (St. John the Baptist). The British servants (employees) of the Hudson's Bay Company, who were of French-Canadian origin, named it Belle Vue Island; Wilkes named it Rodger's Island (after Captain John Rodgers). On the island itself, there is a mixture of names of prominent officers of Hudson's Bay Company—Mts. Dallas and Finlayson; English naval officers—Roche Harbor; Kanaka shepherds—Friday Harbor and Kanaka Bay; and even some corruptions of early names—Portland Fair from Port L'Enfer. The name of Griffin Bay, as it eventually was called, changed quite a bit. It was first called "Grande Bay" by Griffin and his fellow servants of the Company; "Ontario Roads" by Wilkes and subsequent American officers and members of the Boundary Survey; and finally renamed "Griffin Bay" in honor of its significant resident.

From 1857 to 1861, Captain G. H. Richards, commander of the British *H.M.S. Plumper*, and his crew surveyed the islands as part of the general effort to chart the west coast of Canada. The *Plumper* was a 484-ton, three-masted steam screw sloop, and had already served in several regions of the world—most notably the West Indies and west coast of Africa—prior to her being stationed out of Esquimalt for the Royal Navy's Hydrographic Survey in the Northwest. The legacy of the ship's work can be read in the various places in the Gulf Islands named for the *Plumper*, as well as Richards and members of the ship's crew including lieutenants Richard Charles Mayne, Daniel P. Pender, and Edward P. Bedwell.[39]

Richards and his crew surveyed Roche Harbor just prior to the end of 1857, and then Friday Harbor in February of the following year. In 1859 they surveyed Haro and Rosario Straits as well as the area around Victoria. After they moved north, Charles Griffin's *Post Journal* at Belle Vue Sheep Farm has several references to the *Plumper*, on duty transferring Royal Marines to San Juan Island, as well as the pinnace *Shark*, which was used to survey closer to shore. For instance, on June 19, 1860, Griffin noted: "H:M:S: "Plumpers" boat "Shark" arrived last eve.g from Esquimalt to discover a rock off the entrance of Harbor w$^\text{h}$ the "Massachusetts" lately struck on. They found it this morning & returned to Esquimalt." The British survey of the islands resulted in a set of very accurate hydrographic charts of San Juan Island and Lower Vancouver Island, with Haro Strait between. Some of the more detailed surveys also indicated land features.

The British land survey was headed by Col. John Hawkins of the Royal Engineers, with Lt. Charles William Wilson, also of the Royal Engineers, acting as secretary and transport officer. They were accompanied by Lt. Charles John Darrah, astronomer, Dr. David Lyall, medical officer (and botanist), John Keast Lord, naturalist and veterinary surgeon, and Hilary Bauerman, geologist. Begun in 1858, their work consisted mainly of surveying on the mainland, but their contributions to the understanding of the natural history of the region were substantial. Lyall collected specimens on Lopez, Orcas, and San Juan Islands that formed part of an extensive herbarium that was eventually classified and housed at Kew. Lord, writing in *The Naturalist in Vancouver Island and British Columbia* (1866), described several species, including herring and salmon.[40]

The United States Commission, on the other hand, spent two substantial sojourns in the islands, in addition to their work along the 49$^\text{th}$ parallel on the mainland. Archibald Campbell was appointed head by President Franklin Pierce on February 14, 1856, with Lt. John Grubb Parke of the U.S. Army Corps of Topographical Engineers as chief astronomer-surveyor. Campbell recruited George Clinton Gardner to oversee the field party of fourteen, which included William J. Warren, secretary; George Gibbs, a linguist as well as geologist and ethnologist; Joseph Smith Har-

Captain G. H. Richards Survey of Roche Harbor and Its Approaches (courtesy of San Juan Island National Historical Park)

ris, assistant surgeon and naturalist; Henry Custer, topographer; and Dr. Caleb B. R. Kennerly, a surgeon and naturalist. Arriving in Victoria in June of 1857, the party proceeded to Semiahmoo Bay, near present-day White Rock, BC, just northwest of the 49th parallel, and established camp complete with a semi-permanent observatory for their zenith telescope. From this base, they not only explored and mapped the 49th parallel, but also made two expeditions through the archipelago: a survey of San Juan Island by Kennerly in December of 1857, and an overall reconnaissance of the islands in February of 1859 by Curtis, Gibbs, and Kennerly (see Appendix: *North West Boundary Survey Descriptions of Agricultural Lands*).

To explore the islands, the Survey used whale boats, which they rowed and sailed. The organizers had purchased a dozen "conical" tents for $1,046 (approximately $87 each) and another dozen "reconnaissance" tents for $402 (or $33.50 each) for its survey of the San Juans and the surrounding region. In a short expedition through the islands in January 1860, both Dr. Kennerly, commander, and Warren, secretary, slept in a wall tent, while the other five members of the crew spent their nights in a conical tent.[41]

The purpose of the North West Boundary Survey was not only to establish the actual boundary along the 49th parallel on the mainland and its probable course through the islands, but also to scope out the geography of the region in light of its strategic and economic potential for settlement by United States citizens. These tasks included analyses of its agricultural, timber, and mineral resources.

> *Next to Orcas, San Juan contains a greater area than any other island in the Archipelago; but is second to none in its amount of agricultural land. Extensive prairies exist upon it in several localities, which when subjected to cultivation will doubtless reward the husband man with abundant crop, and from the south end of the island to within a short distance of its northern extremity flocks may feed on green grass almost throughout the year. In addition to the emphasis on agricultural potential, others reported on coal, limestone, potential sources of waterpower from island streams.*
>
> —Dr. C. B. R. Kennerly,
> *Report of a Reconnaissance of the Haro Archipelago* (1860)[42]

The surveyors made note of the condition and extent of arable lands on San Juan, Orcas, and Lopez Islands. They noted the poor quality of island timber in comparison with that on the mainland, but praised the fish stock in the islands, particularly on Salmon Bank and off the southern tip of Lopez Island. Finally, while noting the presence of coal in a few locations, they excitedly described the discovery and subsequent testing of limestone, particularly on the west side of San Juan Island, and went on to remark that it was the largest known quantity on the West Coast other than California. (A summary of the results of the Survey by Archibald Campbell was published as the *Geographical Memoir of the Islands between the Continent and Vancouver's Island in the Vicinity of the Forty Ninth Parallel of North Latitude*, part of the record of the 40th Congress [1860].)

Dividing up the Land

> ...From the point on the forty-ninth parallel of north latitude, where the boundary laid down in existing treaties and conventions between the United States and Great Britain terminates, the line of boundary between the territories of the United States and those of her Britannic Majesty shall be continued westward along the said forty-ninth parallel of north latitude, to the middle of the channel which separates the continent from Vancouver's island, and thence southerly through the middle of said channel, and of Fuca's Straits, to the Pacific Ocean: Provided, however, that the navigation of the whole of the said channel and straits, south of the forty-ninth parallel of north latitude, remain free and open to both parties.
> —Article 1, Oregon Treaty of June 15, 1846[43]

Prior to the settlement of the boundary dispute between Great Britain and the United States, both sides presumed that their separate means of dividing and settling the land were legal. The 1846 Treaty of Oregon, which established the 49th parallel as the international boundary, while specific on the mainland and Vancouver Island, was more ambiguous about the islands that lay between. Unfortunately, what would soon become obvious was that there were at least two major channels—Rosario to the east, and Haro to the west—as well as a third, minor channel that ran among the San Juan islands, all of which could be the referenced channel, but which would include the islands on one side or other of the boundary.

> [San Juan Island]...was in the first place taken possession of by the Agents of the Hudson's Bay Company, in the month of July 1845, and a notice to that effect engraved on a wooden Tablet, was erected on an eminence [Mt. Finlayson] near the South east point of the Island, a record which is still [1855] in existence, but there was no real occupation of the island until the year 1850, when a fishing station was established by the Hudson's Bay Company.
>
> —James Douglas to Sir William Molesworth, Colonial Secretary, December 13, 1855[44]

On January 13, 1849, the British government awarded to the Hudson's Bay Company a Charter of Grant of the Colony of Vancouver's Island, which Chief Factor (and later Governor of the Colony of British Columbia) James Douglas and others took to include the San Juan Islands. One of the provisions of the 1849 Charter was the establishment of a resident settlement of British subjects by January 13, 1854. The Company's prospectus of January 24, 1849 ("Colonization of Vancouver Island") stipulated that the land, divided into parcels of no less than 20 acres, would cost £1/acre, and that purchasers of lots of 100 acres or more had to "take out with them five single men, or three married couples, for every hundred acres."[45] This presumed the so-called Wakefield model of colonization, which assumed that sufficiently large arable areas of land would be settled in a manner replicating the landed gentry of the homeland, Britain. On Vancouver Island, while the Company endeavored to colonize the island through this landed estate system in the country and town lots in Victoria itself, the £1/acre price for land of mixed agricultural potential proved to be too steep, particularly considering the American alternative of either donation or pre-emption across the border in Oregon Territory.[46]

On San Juan Island the Company, through their local outpost, Belle Vue Sheep Farm (established in December 1853, barely a month prior to the deadline of the five-year charter), claimed most of the land as part of their farm operations. However, Chief Trader Charles Griffin alludes in his *Post Journal* to the fact that some distinct claims had been given to several of the employees to work as their own, but there are no official records of these claims. North West Boundary surveyor George Gibbs mentions that "[a] Scotchman and 2 Kanakas are said also to have taken claims for preemption," probably referring to these claims by Company servants. One claim may have been that taken by John Bull in San Juan Valley. He died around 1860; after the international boundary was established in 1872, Bull's daughter Catherine, then named Emmerling, claimed the land, first as a preemption and later as a homestead—one of the few women to do so in San Juan County. In Charles Roblin's notes of an interview with her in 1917, he recorded that "Father [John Bull] was a Hudson Bay employee and took care of sheep for Co. When he died the Co. put son in possession of property." By that time, Catherine's mother had remarried, her brother Joseph had already taken up a homestead on Orcas, and her sister Theresa was not old enough, so she was the remaining family member eligible to claim the property. Catherine had been left out of her husband Joseph Emmerling's probate in Bellingham, so she was probably motivated to establish the claim on San Juan Island.

As early as 1859 Governor Douglas was petitioned by Vancouver Island farmers who wished to settle in the Cowichan region—which included Salt Spring Island—to be able to gain title to the land through improving the property: constructing residences and farm structures and cultivating the land. Colonial Surveyor Joseph Pemberton responded by authorizing the first pre-emption system, predating the American homestead act by three years: a single man could take up to 160 acres of unsurveyed land if he occupied and improved it, in addition to paying ten shillings upon survey and obtaining title. In 1860 Douglas, as Governor of the Colony of British Columbia, codified this by enacting the Land Proclamation Act (subsequently amended by the Land Ordinance Act in 1870). This Act provided for any British male subject eighteen years or older to be eligible to pre-empt 160 acres of Crown Land, by dwelling on his claim for a period of four years and improving it by at least $2.50 per acre. He could get legal title for $1.00 per acre. There is no evidence of this pre-emption in the San Juan Islands other than an 1863 petition by Robert Frazer to the Colonial Office in Victoria for recording a land claim. After the boundary decision, Frazer filed a U.S. homestead claim on the same piece of land, which was granted on May 5, 1883.

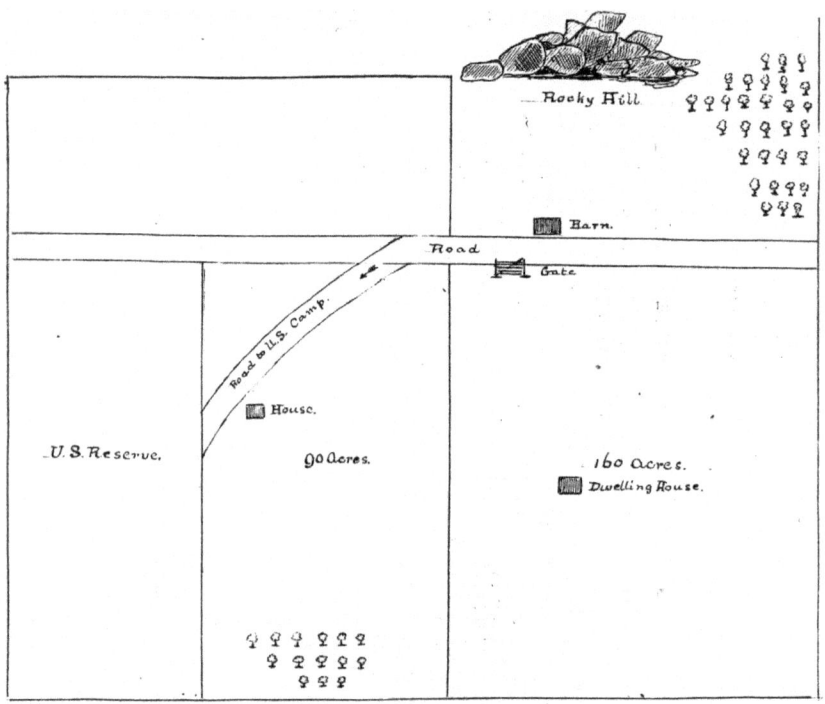

Robert Frazer Land Claim
(Royal British Columbia Museum and Archives)

In the meantime, Americans were trying to establish an alternatative claim to the land. Concern about this was articulated by James Douglas when he wrote to Sir E. Lytton on February 19, 1859, "There has been for the last ten days parties over here from Victoria Surveying & laying out land, as far as I can hear they have been sent by a number of Americans residing in Victoria, their obstensible [sic] purpose is evidently to make a few improvements on these respective sites at present & in the event of the Island falling into the hands of the United States holding these claims as pre empted land."[47] Charles Griffin, in a letter to Douglas, went on to say that "These people leave here for Victoria tomorrow, one of them is a Mr. Denman formerly in Mr. Pemberton's office, the other a Mr. Gillette. I heard them say they were going over to hire a vessel, a scow I suppose, to bring over lumber, Provisions etc…Mr. Denman intends buying Nebbers [Webber's] House & finishing it, & holding that as his own."[48] In North West Boundary Survey Member George Gibbs' 1859 notes for the *Geographical Memoir* he described this exploratory survey as mere speculation:

> *Mr. Capt. Denman who was staying here came from Victoria with a Mr. Eillet [Elliott] to survey preemption claims on the island. He stated that they were employed by Americans hiring them, among whom was a lawyer named Sabatt, to make these surveys, and that the agreement was that they should be paid only for those that were taken up. He added that Mr. Nugent had encouraged the undertaking in the strength of advices secured from Washington. They had survey 26 claims of a quarter section each, leaving 27 [?] quarter sections (4000 [?] acres) to the H. B. C. around the Bellevue Station. New or more [Few or none?] of these claimants intended to settle, as far as I could judge, and the whole seemed to be a matter of bare speculation.*[49]

After the settlement of the boundary dispute when the San Juans were designated as American, the U.S. government looked into British claims in the islands. When the Washington University State Historical Society unveiled monuments in 1904 at each of the joint occupation military camps, General Hazzard Stevens, son of the first territorial governor, in sending his regrets, reminisced:

> I had the last act in the San Juan controversy. In 1874 President Grant appointed me commissioner on the claims of British subjects on the San Juan archipelago. Having given notice at every postoffice on the islands of my appointment and opportunity to present claims, I proceeded to the islands with a revenue cutter, secretary and inspector, and visited every settlement and made diligent search for claims. It appeared, however that there were none, all former British subjects having become American citizens and taken their lands under American land laws.

What Stevens did not mention was the claims of the Hudson's Bay Company, which requested compensation for their holdings on San Juan Island in 1867 and continued to do so long after the settlement in 1872 (see Appendix: *W. F. Tolmie 1867 Letter on Hudson's Bay Company Claims on San Juan Island*).[50]

Despite the semi-official attempt in 1859 at establishing preemption claims for current and future American settlers on the islands, the official survey and apportionment of the land was not accomplished until after the settlement of the boundary dispute. The United States Land Ordinance of 1785, which was first applied to the old "Northwest" (present-day Ohio), established the rectangular cadastral survey system subsequently used for most of the public lands in the central and western United States. This involved the establishment of a beginning point defined by north/south and east/west base lines. In the Pacific Northwest, because the center of settlement in the Oregon Territory originated near the Hudson's Bay Company's Fort Vancouver, the principal Willamette Meridian, running north-south, and an east-west baseline were established near the confluence of the Columbia and Willamette Rivers in Oregon. From these lines, at six-mile intervals surveyors platted east-west township lines and north-south range lines. The San Juan Islands fell west of the principal meridian and north of the baseline; hence the townships enumerated from the intersections of these lines were designated "Township x North" and "Range y West", where x and y equaled the number of miles from the Willamette Meridian and east-west baseline. These townships were in turn subdivided into 36 sections (or squares consisting of one mile on each side) of 640 acres each. These sections could then be subdivided into half sections of 320 acres, quarter sections of 160 acres, eighth sections of 80 acres, and so on. Because the principal lines ran north-south and east-west, subdivisions were designated as quarters of successively larger squares: for instance, the southeast quarter of the northwest quarter of the northeast quarter of Section 17 of Township 35 North Range 3 West (abbreviated as SE¼NW¼NE¼ Sec. 17 T35N R3W).

Township and Range Survey Diagram
(Manual of Surveying Instructions for the Survey of Public Lands)

**THEORETICAL
TOWNSHIP DIAGRAM**
SHOWING
**METHOD OF NUMBERING SECTIONS
WITH ADJOINING SECTIONS**

36 80Ch.	31	32	33 6 Miles —	34 480 Chains	35	36 80Ch.	31 80Ch.
1	1 Mile 6	5	4	3	2	80Ch. 1	6
12	7	8	9	10	11	12	7
13	18	17	16	15	14	13	18
24	19	20	21	22	23	24	19
25	30	29	28	27	26	25	30
36	31	32	33	34	35	36	31
1	6	5	4	3	2	1	6

Sections in Township Diagram
(Manual of Surveying Instructions for the Survey of Public Lands)

Because ownership of the land was tied up in the boundary dispute until 1872, it was not until 1874 that the islands were surveyed and divided into townships and sections. The General Land Office hired three surveyors, T. M. Reed, James Tilton Sheets, and John M. Whitworth, who began work in the autumn of 1874. Reed covered central San Juan, Sentinel, and Cactus Islands in September, and then Henry, Pearl, and north and west San Juan Islands in October. Sheets did mostly Orcas Island, starting at Olga on the east end in mid-September and ending in the West Sound area in October, and then moved on to Shaw Island in late October/early November. Whitworth, after completing the south end of San Juan Island in August, then did Spieden, Flat Top, and Jones Islands in September; James, Cemetery, George, and Stuart Islands in October; and finally, Long, Turn, and south and north Lopez Islands, including the Turn Point area of San Juan

Island, in November. Reed returned in the October of 1875 to survey the smaller islands such as Blakely, Center, Trump, Frost, Decatur, and James. (In 1878, Reed completed Guss Island and Sheets did Waldron Island; E. Vongohren surveyed Crane Island in 1884, F. G. Betts Sucia Island in 1924-25, and last, but certainly not least—for his descriptions are very detailed—H. L. Coffin did Cliff, Sheep, and then Bell and Double Islands in 1928.)

By means of a solar compass and a 100-link, 66-foot-long surveyors' chain, the survey team established each township and monumented section corners. In their field notes, they also commented on prominent features (trees marked to indicate survey points and boundaries, rock formations, etc.). Wherever there were signs of human habitation—roads, fields, fences, dwellings, outbuildings, etc.—these were also noted, with the location recorded in number of chains along the section line. In addition to the specific descriptions of the landmarks, natural and cultural, encountered along each section line, the surveyors summarized each township in terms of both terrain and either current or potential use. Many of these descriptions confirmed the findings of

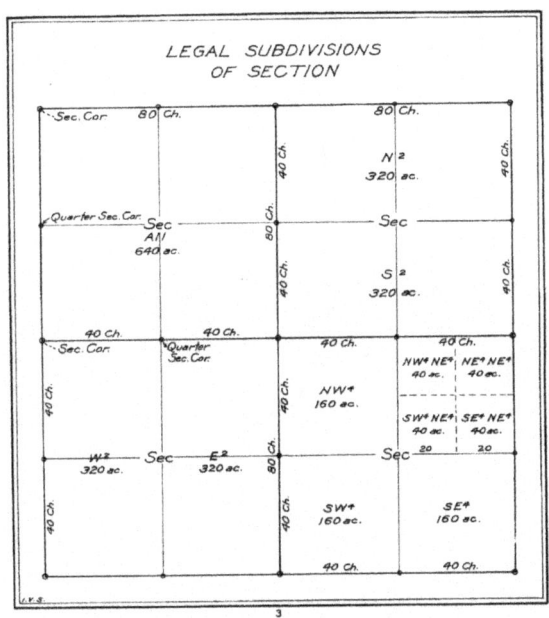

Subdivisions of Sections Diagram
(Manual of Surveying Instructions for the Survey of Public Lands)

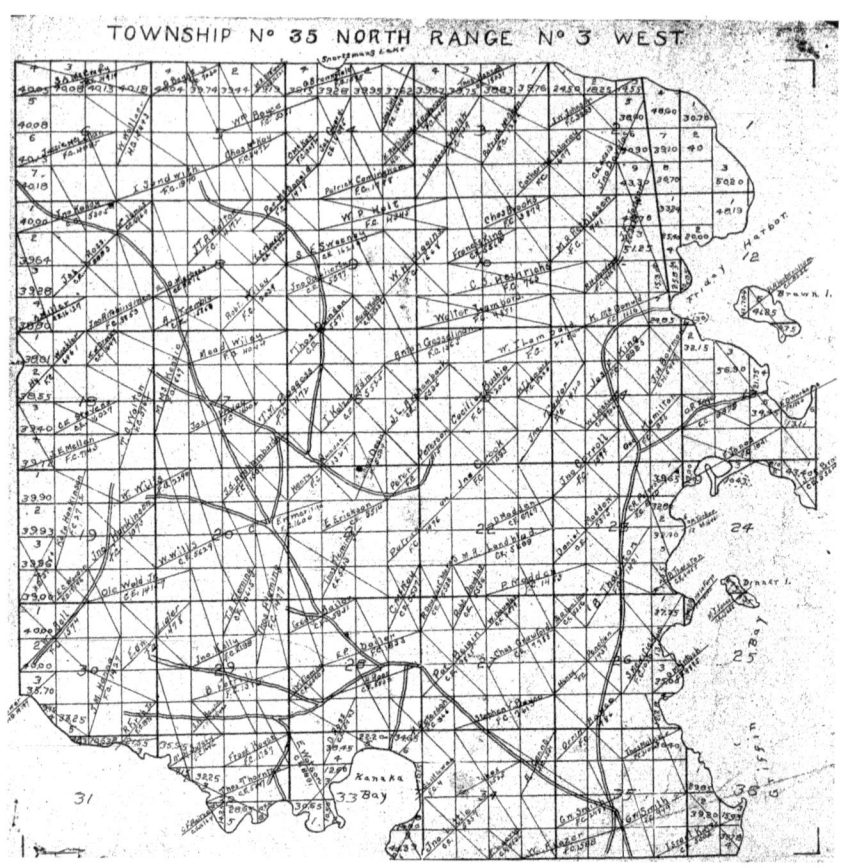

Homestead Claims in San Juan Valley
(C.M. Anderson Engineering Co., Township Plats of San Juan County)
[False Bay is Incorrectly Called Kanaka Bay]

the Boundary Survey: the most cultivatable lands were on San Juan (San Juan Valley), Orcas (Crow Valley and East Sound), and Lopez (scattered areas), while the more hilly and mountainous areas were good for sheep and other livestock grazing. Whitworth noted that James, John, and Stuart Islands were all being used as sheep pasture by John Tod, and Reed noted that Ed Heland had "upwards of 200 sheep" on James Island. Furthermore, Sheets noted on June 12, 1878, on what is presumably Guss Island in Garrison Bay on San Juan Island, "the underbrush and timber has all been cleared off and the island is cultivated for garden purposes, on which large quantities of vegetables are raised." The only industries noted were limekilns on the west side of San Juan—Lime Kiln—and the east shore of Buck Bay (East Sound)—Port Langdon. San Juan Town, on Griffin Bay on the south end of San Juan Island was the only village called out as such. Whitworth noted that Cemetery Island was used as a burial ground by the Indians.

Public domain in the San Juan Islands was "alienated"—deeded into private ownership—through two principal land claim processes: preemption and homesteading. After the establishment of Oregon Territory in 1848, the United States Congress passed the Donation Act of 1850, which allowed any white or "half-breed" settler over 18 years of age to claim 320 acres of land if they had arrived in the Territory before 1850. This law was later amended to provide that only males of 21 years or older could claim 160 acres if they settled between December 1, 1850, and December 1, 1855; if married, their wives were entitled to an equal amount. These provisions were extended by Congress to Washington Territory upon its formation in 1853.[51] The only person to file under the Donation Act of 1850 on San Juan Island was Henry Webber, who claimed 160 acres around Belle Vue Sheep Farm/American Camp; he was issued title on February 18, 1879.

In 1830, Congress passed a second Preemption Land Act, which was superseded in 1841. This was extended to the Territory of Washington in 1854. This law permitted every white male squatter over 21 years of age to claim 160 acres. In order to do so, the claimant had to secure a certificate from the land office as a declaration to "prove up" with a dwelling and evidence of six months residence. In addition, he had to pay $1.25 per acre in cash in order to secure title to the land. (In 1891, Preemption laws were repealed, and a commutation provision allowed homesteaders to purchase their land for $1.25 an acre under the Homestead Act.) The Homestead Act of 1862, which came into effect on January 1, 1863, allowed any head of household or single individual (including single, independent women) over twenty-one years of age to file for a quarter section or 160 acres of land. After filing a declaration of intent (an "entry"), the claimant had up to six months to occupy the land. If after 14 months of settlement and cultivation of the land the claimant wished to do so, they could purchase the property for a minimum price. However, if they chose to go a free route, within seven years of the date of entry, the claimant had to submit certified proof of residence and cultivation for a minimum of five years after the date of entry.[52]

Several other public land laws affected the disposal of public domain in the San Juans. The Timber and Stone Act of 1878 allowed private individuals to purchase 160 acres of land "unfit for farming" for $2.50 per acre. The purpose of the act was to develop timber and mining claims, and in San Juan County there were several claims made. These included James McCurdy at Lime Kiln on the west side of San Juan Island for limestone for his operations at the San Juan Lime Company and Frank Mason near Broken Point on the north part of Shaw, who described his land as "high...and rocky, very gravelly and full of narrow ravines and between the ravines are ridges of solid rock."[53]

From 1875, when the survey of the islands was finally completed and claims could be entered, until the 1940s, when there was no more public land available, some 749 preemptions and homesteads were filed in the San Juan Islands, with the majority occurring between 1890 and 1894. The areas of greatest potential—around American Camp and San Juan, Beaverton, and West Valleys on San Juan Island; Deer Harbor, Crow Valley, East Sound, Olga, and Doe Bay on Orcas Island; and Center Valley on Lopez Island—were the earliest to be claimed; gradually the other, less fertile lands were occupied.

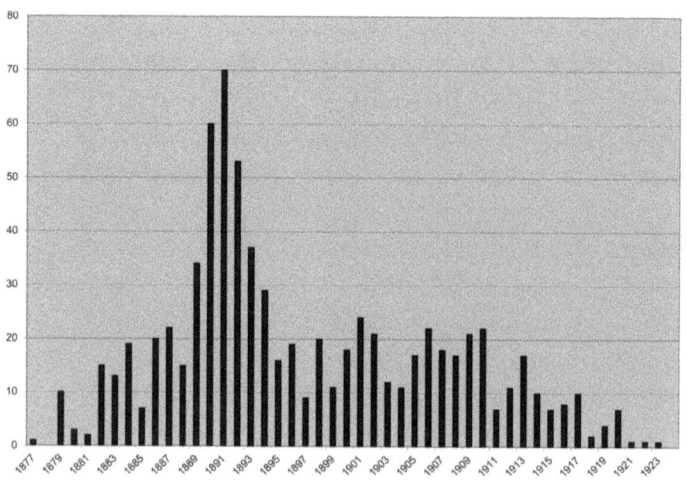

Homestead Applications in the San Juan Islands, 1877-1923

Because land in San Juan County was not surveyed until 1874, preemption and homestead claims were not processed until the late 1870s, the earliest being in 1877, or five years after the settlement of the boundary dispute. However, many of these were for lands that had been located and 'claimed' as early as the 1860s by Hudson's Bay Company employees and soldiers who had mustered out of the U.S. Army or the Royal Marines. Several homestead applications indicated that there was a prior occupant on the land. Some claimants recorded paying what was the equivalent of a "finder's fee" to brokers such as Israel Katz, John Sweeney, or Edward Warbass, while others indicated that they bought a dwelling that had already been erected on the land. In yet other cases, applicants witnessed (in response to the question about whether they had made another claim) that they had previously tried to claim another property but had abandoned the effort. For instance, Henry Struve, a fisherman who homesteaded on Mitchell Bay in the 1880s, said that he had filed earlier for a pre-emption on John's Island but had either lost it or given it up. In his papers he indicated that he had only cultivated one acre of ground on a claim that was largely wooded and rocky, adding "I have a sloop & fishing outfit or tackle that I keep anchored near claim"—clearly suggesting that his location near fishing grounds was more important than the land itself.

Several cases involved disputes over claiming land. For example, in an 1879 case of land in San Juan Valley, both Robert Douglas and Charles McKay applied to purchase 80 acres of land between their two cash entry claims; the land office decided to award title to them jointly. In another, more complicated case, William Crook applied for and occupied a homestead where English Camp had been, but it soon became clear that he was not entitled to the remaining military structures. This became an issue after all 15 buildings were auctioned by the Office of the Chief Quartermaster of the Department of the Columbia; both the Captain's and the Subaltern's Houses were purchased by John Izett for Henry Webster (both of whom were U.S. customs agents). In a subsequent civil case that came before the District Court in 1879, Major E. W. Blake stated that he had "aided Mr. Crook in getting there to English Camp and showed him the place, and I had intended to take the place myself as a homestead, but I gave way and permitted him and his family to take the place," going on to say that he understood he was to "have the Captain's and Lieutenant's quarters and the hill on which there were situated… about five acres was mentioned and estimated as the area to be included."[54] While Crook acknowledged that he had indeed made an agreement, he denied that there was any land in the transaction—only the buildings. The records of the auction are not extant, but Crook did indeed obtain the homestead and occupied the remaining buildings with his family.

The homestead application process involved a substantial amount of paperwork: filing forms and entry fees, proving citizenship, and then proving that the applicant had improved the land, requiring the testimony of at least three witnesses in addition to the applicant's own, as well numerous notices of publication of claims, non-mineral affidavits, and final payment. This was particularly onerous because the nearest filing office was in Olympia, requiring significant travel from the islands. County officials, especially the county clerk, supported this process and would sign affidavits allowing for the claimants to apply without appearing in person. This in part explains why there were periods of greater than five years after an initial claim before title was actually awarded, through a certificate signed by the President of the United States.

> Homes for the homeless can be had on Government land of 160 acres & The productions of the soil are various and when properly cultivated, yield immense crops & Nimrods can hunt to their hearts' content and sit down every morning of the year to venison beef steak. The water surrounding the island is very productive & Ducks and geese are plentiful & The healthfulness of the climate cannot be surpassed & Thousands that are eking out their worthless lives in cities and towns, can find a happy home in this Lower Sound, either on the island or on the mainland, as there is still thousands of acres of good land awaiting the hardy tiller of the soil.
>
> —Letter Published in the Portland West Shore (1876)[55]

Just as there was boosterism among the various American groups in the 1850s regarding promoting and facilitating the division and settlement of land in the San Juan Islands, this continued apace after the settlement of the boundary dispute and survey of the islands. A certain amount of land speculation may have been occurring. For instance, in an 1877 court case involving some land near Roche Harbor that contained limestone deposits, Edward Warbass "represented himself as an agent for the sale and purchase of real estate on San Juan Island," while another person involved in the deal, Israel Katz, is known to have invested in several properties as well as 'facilitated' the filing of homesteads.[56] Later land transactions were aided by men who helped certify homesteads and then acquired and resold them, essentially acting as a real estate agent; Joseph Sweeny, the owner of a mercantile store in Friday Harbor, is a prominent example.

Changes in the Land

One of the first acts of most homesteaders was clearing the land and preparing it for crops through cultivation. Early Euro-American settlers intent upon farming crops chose land that was already clear of large trees; witness that Cutlar planted his potato patch in one of the Belle Vue Sheep Farm's prime prairies used for sheep pasture. The November 25, 1859, *Sacramento Daily Union*, quoting a reporter for the *Alta* on the "disputed territory," noted that "The soil is a mixture of clay, sand and gravel, and is said to be great in the production of potatoes."[57] Descriptions of 'raw' land come mostly from answers to questions posed in the 'proving-up' documents submitted by homestead and pre-emption claimants: "Ques.9—What is the character of the land? Is it timber, mountainous, prairie, grazing, or ordinary agricultural land? State its kind and quality, and for what purpose it is most valuable." According to his neighbor and witness George W. Smith, Thomas Mulno's land on San Juan was "Alder bottom and Fir land Clay subsoil where not Cleared, covered with Fir, Alder and Willow." On Shaw, August Bjork described his land as "some black sandy loam [bottom land] part [high and] rocky," with some "scrubly timber." Many described the better farming land as low areas that consisted of clay subsoil and black sandy loam covered with alder and willow, whereas the upper, rocky areas or forests of fir and pine were better for grazing. In response to "Question 11—If the land is timber land, state the kind, quality, and amount of timber thereon…" applicants noted that the existing trees were "not valuable for timber" and "cut only for clearing," as expressed in the words of Shaw homesteader Hans Christensen.[58]

Preparing this 'raw' land involved clearing all trees and brush, removing stumps, and plowing the soil. One of the early mortgages on land in the San Juans specified that the lessee was to "grub, stump, and clear and make the said lot of land thoroughly fit for cultivation."[59] If the land was wooded, then a far heavier task was posed: either cutting or burning down the trees. Cutting was done by means of either axes or two-man crosscut ("bow") saws. Most homesteaders mention possessing one if not several axes, as well as mauls and wedges, and several list crosscut saws among their tools. Burning involved drilling two holes—one at an approximately 50° angle into the trunk, and another straight in to meet the first hole. Live coals were then dropped into the angled hole and fanned through a bellows applied to the second hole. Once the tree caught fire, it would burn for several days and then collapse.

> Dad and the boys worked hard with axe, saw, and auger, working the hard way, but they soon clear the logs from around the house. They felled trees, bored holes on both sides of the tree, kindled a fire in the holes. The holes measured rail length. When they burned through, they were split in rail lengths for fencing.
>
> —Marie Wallace,
> daughter of early settlers on Salt Spring Island[60]

Sometimes the stump and roots also burned; most often these had to be hauled out through oxen or later, blown out with dynamite or left to rot.[61] Antoni Marino, in applying for his homestead on Shaw, described the lot as "Ordinary agricultural land with lots of heavy stumps, it is black sandy soil but it is very hard to clear," while James Ross stated in his application that "No use can be made fit until the stumps rot out."[62]

The laborious process of grubbing would then begin. Grubbing involved the process of removing brush and ferns from the area to be cultivated, which could either be accomplished through heavy plowing with teams of oxen or slashing and burning the brush, or a combination of both.[63] Teams of oxen, worked in pairs (a "yoke"), pulled plows that would break up the prairie grass or fern cover and dig up any roots that were present. In addition, homesteaders list, among other tools, brush hooks, plows, harrows, mattocks, rakes, and hoes (see Appendix: *Homestead Implements*).

Early homestead records often mention that a certain area of land (20 acres, 40 acres) had been cultivated by the claimant and "planted in timothy." Timothy was the most common pasture grass used by early pioneers in the Northwest. It was first introduced into the area by the Hudson's Bay Company at their Fort Vancouver outpost, where pastures were often planted in timothy and clover.[64] Timothy grows better in clayey loams than in sandy soils, and is well adapted to cool, humid climates such as the Northeast (where it was first used as a pasture crop) and the coastal regions of the Northwest. The plant grows to about 20 to 40 inches high and is topped by a distinctive furry seed head of 2 to 3 inches. Although it is often too rough to be eaten in its growing state, timothy dries well and makes excellent hay. It can be seeded in the fall or the spring; less seed (about 3 to 5 pounds per acre) is required at the former time than the latter (10 pounds). On Shaw Island, the 1885 probate of Hugh Park's estate listed among his personal property "about 800 lbs of Timothy seed in sacks" and "about 2000 lbs in chaff" stored.[65]

The gradual replacement of prairies of native bunch grasses and wooded areas of either lowland alder and willow or forests of fir and pine with pastures of timothy and other hay and pasture crops represented a major change to the islands' ecosystem. Native prairie systems, which were originally dominated by perennial grasses such as Idaho fescue, California oatgrass, and junegrass, were soon transformed to a mixture of introduced perennials—redtop, velvet grass, and Kentucky bluegrass—and annuals—silver and early hairgrass, cheatgrass, and other brome grasses. Furthermore, the cessation of uncontrolled wildfires or

*Louis Cayou with his Yoke of Oxen
(courtesy of Orcas Island Historical Museum)*

controlled burns deliberately set by Indigenous peoples, along with the introduction of domesticated animals such as cattle, hogs, and sheep led to the gradual disappearance of savannah land with its occasional Garry oaks and Rocky Mountain junipers, as well as the succession from Douglas fir forest to hemlock and spruce.[66]

In addition to the intrinsic difficulties associated with raising crops and livestock, the islands' Euro-American farmers also had to contend with natural challenges in the form of both native and introduced flora and fauna. It is assumed that cultural conditions help define how the environment and its components are viewed: one culture's resource may be another's weed. The nettle, for instance, was a significant resource plant for the Coast

Salish, used for medicines and dyes as well as string and chord making, while it was considered a weed by Euro-Americans. Furthermore, along with introduced 'beneficial' species came weeds, pests, and predators. The simple act of introducing grain crops to the islands brought along a host of weeds inadvertently included with the seed.

Charles Pickering, who wrote the chapter on "Introduced Animals and Plants of America" in Volume IX of the Reports of the United States Exploratory Expedition, noted two weeds already abundant near Chinook villages in Oregon: prostrate knotweed and common lambsquarters, and mentions that a Mr. Brackenridge encountered another—buckhorn plaintain—near Gray's Harbor. He goes on to mention several other weeds (in addition to cultivated crops) associated with Hudson's Bay Company posts (Forts Colville, Nisqually, and Vancouver, as well as the farms at Cowlitz and Willamette): *Polyganum nigrum*, mayweed, pigweed, shepherdspurse, annual sowthistle, and low speargrass.[67] In his research on Island County, Richard White noted the introduction of European foxtails, American black nightshade, and dock or sorrel. Perhaps the introduction with the greatest effect was the Canada thistle. Thistle spreads both through seeds (the "down") and roots, the latter particularly when they are cut up and spread through plowing. White noted that it probably reached Whidbey Island by 1856.[68] The spread to the San Juans most likely came soon thereafter. Two plants that were introduced as ornamentals—Scotch broom and common hawthorn (as opposed to the native black hawthorn)—were first introduced by Englishmen as ornamentals, the former in Victoria in 1850 and the latter (allegedly) by Alfred Douglas to San Juan Valley for hedgerows in the 1890s. The Second Edition of Atkinson and Sharpe's *Wild Plants of the San Juan Islands* (1993) reports that of the 970 vascular taxa reported in San Juan County, 350, or approximately one third, mostly of European origin, were introduced.[69]

Not all "weeds" or noxious plants were introduced. Death camas, native to the San Juans, is quite toxic to both men and other animals. Apparently when pigs were first introduced at Fort Vancouver, they died from ingesting the bulbs, but they soon learned to distinguish between the species.[70] In August of 1854, several dozen Hudson's Bay Company sheep died as a result of poisoning, which Charles Griffin conjectured was from the consumption of some herb located in a swamp near First Prairie. He lost another dozen in the same spot a few weeks later and recorded other poisonings later in the year. Although Griffin carefully performed necropsies on all his animals that were not deliberately slaughtered to determine cause of death—and his anatomical descriptions are both graphic and precise, he does not seem to have determined the source of the toxin. The herb may have been Douglas' water-hemlock, an extremely poisonous member of the carrot family that lives in marshes and swamps.[71] The Company was not alone in experiencing losses through animals encountering their new environment: one of the many misfortunes that Samuel Gross enumerated as leading to his filing for bankruptcy was the loss of fifty sheep during a two-day period from "eating poisonous weeds in a swamp near by."[72]

Early on, wolves were a continuing menace, and although eventually extirpated from the island through trapping, they were killing sheep on San Juan Island as late as December of 1859 (on Lopez Island the last wolves were wiped out in the 1880s).[73] Both Company employees and other settlers tried to kill as many as possible, and Thomas Fleming claims that the last wolf on San Juan was killed by the Company servant John Bull, a Kanaka.[74] In the October 10, 1860, entry to his *Diary*, visiting Anglican Bishop George Hills described a wolf trap on San Juan Island,

> *... formed by a horseshoe of stakes firmly driven into the ground, the front open. On the top of a huge block, below, the bait of a piece of sheep. The wolf comes in, begins to eat, moves a prop & brings down the stone which crushes him.*[75]

In the *Geographical Memoirs*, the surveying party related how they used strychnine-baited meat in an attempt to kill wolves on Lopez; this same poison was used at Fort Nisqually and probably Fort Vancouver.[76] There seems to have been no evidence of cougars (called "panthers" by settlers) that were so prevalent on the islands closer to Vancouver Island, such as Salt Spring.

> *Upon this island alone of the entire group did we find any positive evidence of the existence of beasts of prey. Wolves are numerous and of the larger species known to exist on our continent. Why they should be found here and not on Orcas and the other islands of the archipelago is a mystery which must for the present remain unsolved. Formerly there were a few of these animals found on San Juan, but in a very short time after its occupation by white men they almost entire disappeared, and are now no longer any annoyance whatever to flocks. So it will be on Lopez after a few persons have taken up their abode upon it*
>
> —Dr. C. B. R. Kennerly, U.S. North West Boundary Survey (1859)[77]

Homesteader Theodore Tharald mentioned that he lost his chickens to mink.[78] Former British Royal Marine turned farmer Charles Whitlock was more descriptive: "Dear sister I must describe the mink to you the mink is a small animal like a stoat or a pole cat ferret but a little larger they get in the fowele[sic] houses at night and they will kill every one if they are not disturbed they only suck the blood and then leave them I had sixty killed in one night I lay wait for him and shot him…"[79] Although bears were mentioned as being present on several of the islands, they were not necessarily considered a threat, although they were hunted and eventually extirpated.

Deer were not only a source of meat but proved to be a pest for the homesteaders' orchards. James Tulloch resorted to several methods of discouraging them: still hunting, hunting with a fire jack, setting guns, and setting stakes. The first two methods involved hunting with guns—either waiting quietly near trails or dazing them at night with an iron basket full of lit pitch wood carried on a pole over the shoulder. Setting either guns (with a trip line tied to the trigger) or stakes (sharpened and set in the ground pointed toward where the deer would jump over the fence) was far more dangerous, because one was as likely to hurt or kill a person as a deer. Early orchardists also built fences to keep out the deer. "Whispering Pete" Serry, ironically named because of his booming voice obtained from working in a sawmill, built a ten-foot-high cedar rail 'snake' fence around his orchard on Waldron.[80] Early photographs show both Friday Harbor and Eastsound surrounded by extensive orchards, which are enclosed within tall (8 feet or more) picket fences. Judging by extant examples, these pickets were probably made from cedar that was split or riven and sharpened at one end.

Deer were not the only animals that had to be controlled. The first fences of San Juan County were built to also keep open-range livestock out of gardens and orchards. As the infamous event that precipitated the Pig War made apparent, it was expected that anyone trying to establish crops would set up a sturdy fence to keep out free ranging animals. Since 1853, the Hudson's Bay Company's Belle Vue Sheep Farm used most of San Juan Island as pasture for its sheep, hogs, horses, and cattle. Americans settling (or, according to the Company, squatting) on the island in the late 1850s chose those spots that were the most fertile and easiest to cultivate: the open prairies that the Company used for pasturage. Lyman Cutlar, for example, established his potato garden on choice Company land—what Farm Manager Charles Griffin called "First Prairie." According to one version of the varied testimony in the case, Cutlar had built a rough fence on three sides, which proved to be little challenge for Belle Vue Sheep Farm's Berkshire hog.

Although the British may have been on disputed ground regarding the boundary question, the Company was not unique in assuming the prerogative of open range. It was a common presumption, as well as legally correct, that a farmer had to fence free-ranging livestock out of his crops, and there was little he could do about it if the animals broke in. In a February 14th, 1869, letter to his sister, Charles Whitlock, a former Royal Marine who had been stationed on San Juan during the joint occupation and had then established a farm "in the thick woods About one mile from the British camp," wrote, "I am sorry to tell you that I had a verry bad misfortune since you last heard from mee it nearly broke mee down the cattle broke my fence and destroyed all my oates and wheat and turnips and carrots and about 10 tons of potatoes..."[81] Murder was even committed over the issue of animals and fences. On May 15, 1882, for instance, John Kay, a Norwegian immigrant, killed John Anderson, a Swedish immigrant, in a dispute over his cow wandering during a low tide around the fence separating the two men's farms on Lopez.[82]

One of the most important ways of securing livestock ownership was through the process of marks and brands. On January 31, 1855, the Legislative Assembly of the Territory of Washington had established *An Act Relative to Marks and Brands*:

> *That it is hereby made the duty of the county auditor of each county in this territory, on application of any person residing in his county, to record a description of the marks or brands which said person may be desirous of marking or branding his horses, cattle, sheep and hogs, but the same description shall not be recorded for more than one resident of the same county.*[83]

One of the earliest tasks in newly formed San Juan County was for the auditor, Edward D. Warbass, to record these proprietary markings for cattle, sheep, hogs, and horses. His first entry, dated December 17, 1873, noted, "James M. Fleming claims as his sheep mark Letter (Z) size about one square inch formed[?] on the side of the face with a Brand made of Iron Right Ear Cropt and a small hole through it and left ear split." There follows a long list of filers with their distinguishing marks—crops and half crops, swallow tails, underbits, splits, holes, and even one "cut to a point like a Bull Dog"—and brands (mostly the first letter of the owner's last name), described in writing, illustrated through drawings, and even, in one case, by means of a life-size cut-out. To illustrate the significance of open-range stock raising during this period, consider the numbers of recorded marks and brands: beginning with 3 entries in 1873 (only begun in December), thereafter the pages are filled with 37 in 1874; followed by 13 in 1875; 16 in 1876; and 13 in 1877. (Only 4 or so a year were recorded thereafter.)[84]

Not that this regulation was always obeyed. Open range was often a disputed commodity in the islands (see Appendix: *Lila Hannah Firth on San Juan Island Range Wars*). James Tulloch notes in his *Diary*,

> "Orcas Island being quite mountainous was largely devoted to sheep raising by the early settlers who each claimed certain portions of the island as their range. Sheep thief was quite a common term to fling at each other. But local stealings were small compared to the exploits of certain enterprising citizens of Victoria who often made forays and with the aid of trained sheep dogs rounded up whole boat loads on moonlight nights."[85]

One of the ways to control sheep was by using the unique geography of the archipelago, *i.e.* the use of small islands for sequestering rams. There are several examples of either "Sheep Island" or "Ram Island" (located between Lopez and Decatur), stemming from their exclusive use. The surveyors of the 1874 Township and Range Survey wrote in their field notes of several that were used exclusively for sheep: Dinner Island ("It is claimed by Fred Jones, who makes use of it for pasturage for 'Rams' for which it is well adapted, as it is covered with rank growth of bunch grass") and Brown Island ("The island is made use of as a pasture for rams"), both off San Juan. The main flocks of ewes

> There was a custom among the squaw men who had sheep in the early days of cutting off the tails of all lambs at round up time each spring. Anyone who had sheep on the range had the right to kill any longtailed sheep at any time. So Charlie Basford, a neighbor of ours who had bought a half dozen weathers and turned them loose boasted that he lived off the increase. I don't believe he overstated his case judging by the number of sheepskins I have seen on the mountainside from time to time. We were glad when the vexing sheep problem was settled, and every man had his just allotment of sheep.
>
> —*The Diary of James Francis Tulloch (1970)*

and wethers (castrated male lambs that were not kept as rams) were pastured on larger islands, and the rams rowed over during breeding season. The Coast Salish peoples used the same strategy for sequestering woolly dogs; to keep their animals' lines pure, women would keep their packs on smaller islands, canoeing out to feed them every day.[86] (See the section on "Farming" in *Work*.)

Open range was a common legal situation in most Western states and territories. Those who had animals on the range took precedence over farmers who were trying to establish crops, and it was a major change when laws were established to require fencing animals in.[87] James Tulloch in his reminiscences claimed that he was instrumental in passing such legislation for Washington Territory:

> *The great herds of sheep naturally became a nuisance after the island was surveyed and homesteaded by white families and the old range claims were at once denied. So we called a meeting and raising the necessary funds sent one of our number to Olympia to lay the matter before the legislature. The result was a stock law requiring all sheep to be enclosed and as soon as the law came into effect we proceeded to enforce it.*"[88]

It is not clear from Tulloch's memoir when this occurred, nor the law he specifically referred to. It may have been *An Act to Regulate the Running of Sheep at Large in San Juan County*, which was approved on November 12, 1875 (see Appendix: *An Act to Regulate the Running of Sheep at large in San Juan County*). Stock raisers appeared before the County Commissioners as early as the February 7th, 1876, meeting of the Board. The first protest was the "Petition of James Peers and J. Anderson residents of San Juan County praying for a permit to run sheep at large in San Juan County. The parties having shown that they have complied with the Naturalization Laws of the States, it is hereby ordered the Auditor issue a permit for the same in pursuance of the Act passed by the Legislative Assembly in regard to running sheep in San Juan County."[89] Peers and Anderson were soon followed by James M. Fleming, Robert Douglas, John Kay, Peter Lawson, Louis Cayou, G. W. Smith, P. Madden, and D. Brookman. An attempt was made to repeal this law during the next, 1877, session, but range laws continued on the books.

As early as January 29, 1855 the Legislative Assembly of the Territory of Washington enacted *An Act in Relation to Fences and Fence Viewers* specifying what constituted a "legal and sufficient" fence and then "If any domestic animal or animals break into an enclosure the persons so injured thereby, shall recover of the owner of said animal or animals, the amount of damage, if it shall appear that the fence through which animal or animals broke was lawful; but not other wise."[90] In the next few decades, the Legislature enacted several fencing laws. In *An Act Concerning Fences* passed by the Legislature in 1869, for instance, three basic types of fences were considered as lawful in Territory of Washington: post and rail (with either planks or rails); worm; and ditch and pole, or board or rail.[91] What these, and other laws that followed, meant was the end of the use of land as an open range and the legitimization and growth of the private homestead.

Place

Geologically and geographically, the San Juan Islands offered a rich environment for millennia-long Coast Salish marine harvesting, plant gathering, hunting, and agriculture. This was based on a system of traditionally passed-down resources, such as the matrilineal 'ownerships' of camas beds and family-held reef net sites. Europeans and Euro-Americans 'discovered' the islands in waves: first Spanish, then English and American sailing expeditions explored and named the San Juans, gradually refining the location and description of the archipelago, situating it in a scientific world view that corresponded with an abstract Cartesian grid superimposed upon the sky and the earth. Upon the settlement of the boundary dispute, the islands were then surveyed with another Cartesian system of township and range lines, which allowed for the systematic alienation of the (then U.S.) public domain ignoring Coast Salish habitation. Settlers used various methods to then claim the land, through clearing and cultivation, fencing, and other delineation of private property. Their methods of land use in turn led to significant changes in the plant and animal ecosystems.

DWELLING

When Lyman Cutlar decided to settle on San Juan Island, he chose to do so in a natural meadow or prairie that was clear of trees resulting from Coast Salish selective burns to facilitate the cultivation of camas and then Belle Vue Sheep Farm's pasturing practices. Yet he also located his dwelling and garden at the edge of a forest. In the narrative reports of the Hudson's Bay Company officials that visited Cutlar's place after the shooting, they derisively described his place ("What has been dignified by the name of his 'farm'") and variously described his dwelling as a "log cabin" and "hut or tent." In the Disputed Islands, there were, indeed, myriad ways of dwelling, stemming from the background culture of the various groups that inhabited the San Juan Islands. The Coast Salish built large longhouses that housed several families as well as temporary shelters for fishing, hunting, and gathering. The Hudson's Bay Company had its own method of establishing a trading post, with its distinctive "Hudon's Bay Company Style" of construction. Later the U.S. Army and Royal Marines built camps that reflected military structure. Euro-American homesteaders built cabins on their claims. In some local communities, the cross-cultural nature of the families was reflected in the architecture of the settlements, blending several different building traditions. Lyman Cutlar's dwelling represented one of many approaches to living in the islands.

Dwellings

As various groups settled in the islands, they employed different strategies for the selection of sites and placement of structures, as well as construction techniques. However, there were some common elements to all cultures' approach to these areas. One important aspect for all those who dwelt in the Islands was visual control over their environment; most settlements were designed to clearly see others approaching from afar. Because early transportation was via the water, location on a landing or harbor, sheltered from summer and winter storms, was also important. Another commonality was the availability of natural materials, such as timber for lumber. However, the various building traditions differed in the use of wood, ranging from the Coast Salish post-and-beam structures sheathed in riven cedar boards to the various types of Euro-American log and frame structures.

The location of most of the permanent and seasonal Coast Salish villages in the islands was on sheltered bays or inlets with sloping beaches for their canoes, which were drawn up with their prows toward the water, both to break the waves and for rapid launching. Seasonal fishing villages were arranged in a U-shape open to the shore, with the headman's dwelling at the uppermost position, facing the water, fish processing equipment in front of his house, and other shelters arrayed on either side. Permanent villages were sited on the banks above the high tide line, paralleling the shore with the higher walls of the shed-roofed longhouses facing the water. This situated them in the sometimes-narrow zone between the water and the forest, sources for fishing, hunting, and gathering. It also helped in terms of surveillance and defense from raids by hostile Indigenous groups from the North.

James Madison Alden Sketch of Belle Vue Sheep Farm (courtesy of San Juan Island National Historical Park)

In the case of the Hudson's Bay Company Belle Vue Sheep Farm, the site of the "Establishment" or main post was chosen on the open prairie on the south end of the San Juan Island, where the farm manager enjoyed full visual command of the Straits of Juan de Fuca as well as Fort Victoria on the southern tip of Vancouver Island, across Haro Strait. Indeed, in order to enhance this vista ("Belle Vue"—French for "Good View"), Charles Griffin had all the intervening trees cut down.

> *A canoe of Mill Banks arrived from Fort bring news of the Millbanks up north having been attacked the Rupert & other Inds—so my fellows are all going in the morning.— Employed them to day cutting down all the large trees which obstruct the view between my Ho:-[House] & Fort.*
>
> —*Belle Vue Sheep Farm Post Journal*
> May 18, 1854

Even the layout of the compound was designed for Griffin to be able to see all comers. According to comparable historic records and archaeological evidence of the Hudson's Bay Company establishment, the factor or chief trader's residence was located either at the 'head' or upper short side of the U-shaped compound, or on the prominent downslope corner, where he could observe any approach to as well as the activities within the compound itself. All ships and boats observed were duly noted in the *Post Journal*, and there was hardly a week that went by without the sighting of some vessel in the straits.

Visual surveillance also played a dominant role in the locations of both American Camp and English Camp. The Americans moved camp three times before they settled on the ridge overlooking both Haro Strait and "Ontario Roads" (later named Griffin Bay). The siting and construction of "Robert's Redoubt"—the earthen work fortification with gun emplacements—was critical to the artillery command of the approach of British war ships. Historic photographs indicate the siting of the camp against the edge of the forest, with temporary shelter provided by tents among the trees.

After the agreement to the joint military occupation of the islands, the British went on a scouting expedition around the island to choose likely sites for an encampment, using as their criteria sheltered anchorage and access to the shore; availability of water and grass; and a relatively level site for structures and parade ground. In a manner similar to Griffin's at Belle Vue Sheep Farm, upon choosing the site on Garrison Bay, the commanding officer ordered the removal of trees from Bazalgette Point that were obstructing the view outwards towards Haro Strait,

Later Euro-American farmers also chose house sites on knolls or slopes at the edge of the forest with panoramas of their surroundings. These locations were often untillable—they were literally 'outcroppings'—but they also afforded a visual command of their surrounding fields. In the case of Christopher Rosler, to whom we were introduced previously as an American soldier who married an Indigenous woman after he mustered out, his farmstead was located on a rise above the crop and sheep fields that originally constituted Belle Vue Sheep Farm's "First Prairie." In the trial of Kanaka Joe for the murder of James "Harry" Dwyer and his wife Selina Jane, witnesses testified that Dwyer was found still attached to the reins of his ox team in the field below, while Selina Jane was discovered inside their house located on the rise above. According to Lila Hannah Firth,

> *the place that Dwyer bought consisted mostly of swamp land, that is, all that was under cultivation was this meadow land, on a knoll above this meadow, sat his house, Barn, & outhouses, from his house, or, front porch one could see all over his field, which was a very pretty setting from the house. Out back of his house was some very heavy timber land, ranging up toward the mountain.*

Clearly there were several reasons for choosing such a site: use of non-tillable land; visual command of the fields ('survey of all the domain'); and aesthetic considerations.

Indigenous People's Villages and Camps

Nowadays, there are no intact Indigenous village structures or remains in the San Juan Islands. Although there were few large Coast Salish winter villages in the San Juans at the time of Euro-American arrival, there were certainly the remains of longhouses, used by Indigenous groups arriving during the spring and summer for fishing, hunting, and gathering activities. On February 7, 1860, William J. Warren of the North West Boundary Survey wrote:

> *About 8 o'clock a.m. broke camp and proceeded down the western shore of San Juan Id. Camped on the site of an old Indian village on the shore of a deep inlet or bay opposite the lower end of Henry Id. Portions of the old lodge were still remaining. It had been about 500 or 600 feet in length, by about 50 or 60 feet in width, and must have accommodated over a thousand Indians. As usual at such localities there were immense quantities of clam shells on the shore.*[1]

Julie K. Stein notes that the Royal Marines setting up their camp at Garrison Bay on San Juan Island dismantled existing structures and modified the shell midden.[2] Excavations at English Camp on San Juan Island did reveal the remains of what may have been a house structure, as recorded in editors Amanda K. Taylor and Stein's research report, *Is It a House?* (2011).[3]

The style of house structure varied somewhat among the various subgroups of the Coast Salish, but standard patterns do emerge from the areas surrounding the San Juans; in particular, the excavations at the Makah whaling village of Ozette have revealed intact houses and their structural elements, as recorded in editor Stephen R. Samuels' *House Structure and Floor Midden*, Volume I of the Ozette Archaeological Project Reports (1991). Most villages were arrayed close to a smooth beach for landing canoes, and the structures were aligned parallel to the shoreline. Wayne Suttles says that the Lummi favored orientation that pro-

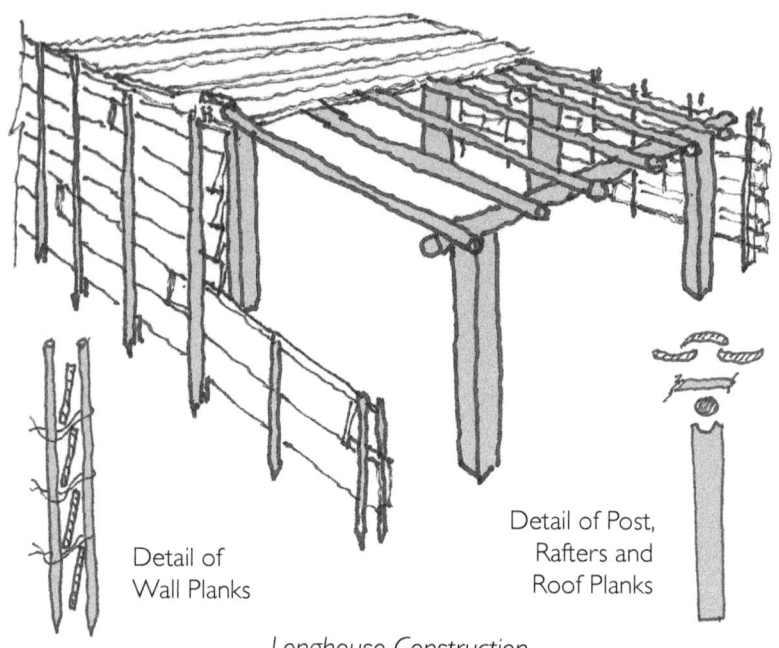

Longhouse Construction
(adapted from: R. G. Matson, "The Coast Salish House" 2002)

tected them from the cold north winds as well as the rain-bearing southwesterly storms. Coast Salish men married wives outside of their kin group, and family units usually consisted of offspring as well as relatives of the husband. Family units often occupied the longhouse according to kin—the same as the seating arrangement in their canoes. These dwellings were called "longhouses" because this basic unit could be repeated for upwards of 500-600 feet.

Longhouses, either shed or gable roofed, were constructed of large rectangular (2-3 feet wide by 5-8 inches thick) posts that bore long round beams, which in turn bore rafters and riven cedar boards that acted like long shingles or roof tiles. The dimensions of the living space were determined by the length of the major roof beams (ca. 36-60 feet), while the vertical space was set by the height of tallest post—usually around 10-16 feet high. In the shed roof form, the taller posts would run along one side of the structure, and the roof would slope down to the beams on the lower post at the other side; in the gable roofed building, the tallest posts would run down the middle, and the roof sloped down to both sides. Walls were usually constructed of light riven cedar boards lashed horizontally with cedar-withe ropes to thin poles leaning against the side beams. Some structures had boards placed vertically on the sides.

In the winter the walls of the longhouse were often lined on the interior with woven reed or rush mats. Each family 'unit' shared a space defined by the posts of the structure (usually around 15 feet apart), divided off from others by vertically hung mats. A bench, which was used for sleeping and storage, ran along the inside wall; it was constructed of heavy cedar planks about 6 feet wide on supports 2-3 feet high. Shelves located on the walls above the bench also served for storage. Firepits were located towards the center of the space, and the roof boards were moved aside to allow the smoke to rise unobstructed. Doors were often at the end of the dwelling, either centered in the gable or near a corner. The doorways sometimes had plank walls that extended into the interior space for protection from winter cold and uninvited guests.[4]

> *Here they landed to dine near a large deserted Village capable of containing at least 4 or 500 inhabitants, tho it was now in perfect ruins—nothing but the skeletons of the houses remained, these however were sufficient to shew their general form structure and position. Each house appeared distinct and capacious of the form of an oblong square, and they were arranged in three separate rows of considerable length; the Beams consisted of huge long pieces of Timber placed in Notches on the top of supporters 14 feet from the ground, but by what mechanical power the Natives had raised these bulky beams to that height they could not conjecture. Three supporters stood at each end for the longitudinal beams, and an equal number were arranged on each side for the support of smaller cross beams in each house.*
>
> —Archibald Menzies, *Journal of Vancouver's Voyage (1923)*[5]

As Wayne Suttles has summarized, "The shed-roof house provided flexible space for a multifamily household...the most important social group in Coast Salish society."[6] But it was not only used as shelter, "The winter house was more than a dwelling; it was a workshop and a factory for the preservation of food." Women wove tules (a form of bulrush) and other plant materials into mats and men fashioned halibut hooks as well as bows and arrows. Fall salmon catches were smoked and other food was preserved through cooking and drying.[7] Because the permanent, or fixed, part of the longhouse was the post and beam structure, when the roof and wall boards were removed for transport to a winter village site, the seasonal settlement seemed deserted. Since early Europeans and Euro-Americans visited in February, the villages that they visited may have been temporarily vacated for the winter but would soon be reoccupied come spring.

> And they had shelters where they made their equipment, like lumber, rope, fishing equipment. Near where they built their canoes, their mutual fishing locations were well known. Each family had their reef netting location. Each location had a name. It dates way back. They just didn't go and step on somebody's toes.
>
> —Al Charles, quoted in Ann Nugent, Lummi Elders Speak (1982)

Fishing camps were established near reef net sites throughout the islands in the mid to late summer. They were located on a southeast- or southwest-facing promontory, either directly on shore or across the bay from a net site. Because the camp was used for drying the fish, exposure to both sun and wind was important—hence the south-facing directions. The camp itself consisted of a U-shaped arrangement of structures, open to the shore where the canoes were pulled up on the beach. Franz Boas, in explaining the reef-netting methods of the Songish, also offered this description of an encampment, together with an illustration:

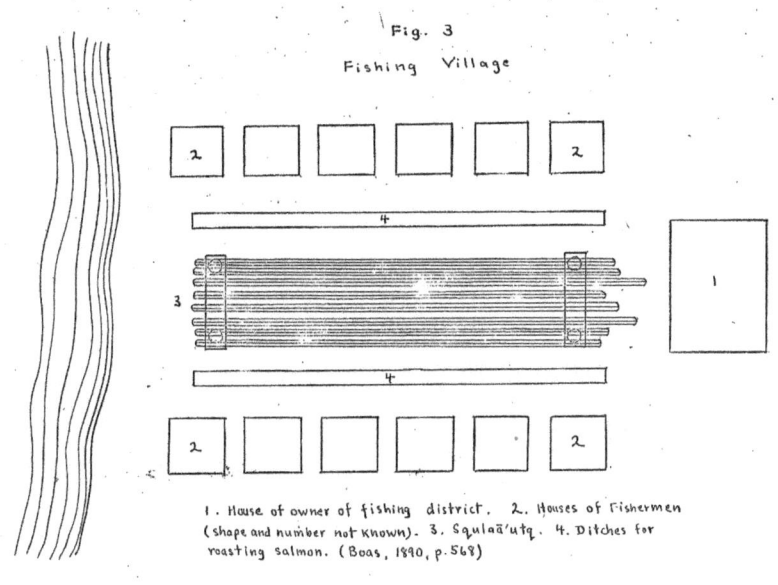

Reef Net Camp
(after Franz Boas, in Wayne Suttles, Economic Life of the Coast Salish of Haro and Rosario Straits / 951)

The fishing village is arranged in the following way. The centre is formed by the scaffold for drying salmon (squlaā'utq). It consists of two pairs of uprights carrying a cross-beam each, which support the long heavy beams on which the salmon are dried. These are cut off close to their supports nearest the sea, while at the other end their length is different according to the size of trees which were used in the construction. The house of the owner of the fishing-ground stands behind the scaffold. On both sides of the latter there are a number of huts. The crew of one boat lives on one side, that of the other on the other side.[8]

Suttles notes that the name that Boas recorded for the scaffold—*Squlaā'utq*—is the same as one of his interviewees used for the whole camp—*sx^{w}alaq'utx^w*—which literally means "reef-net house." The owner's house could be of regular longhouse construction, with the posts and beams left for the winter and then either walled with planks or mats taken from the winter villages, or it could be a more impermanent structure of posts and beams with mat walls. Just as the spatial arrangement of family members within the longhouse reflected the paddling order in their canoe, so also did the spatial arrangement of the fishing camp reflect the order of owner/captain and two canoes crews.[9] Caroline Ewing, one of the elders who gave depositions in the 1927 petition *Duwamish et al vs. United States*, described "a big place where they dry their fish, and split cedar and put the posts up like that, and they have long cedar posts, and they have that all filled up with fish, all kinds of salmon."[10]

There were other, less permanent structures that were constructed by the Coast Salish while temporarily inhabiting the islands in the fishing, hunting, and gathering seasons. These seem to have been post-and-beam structures with two types of covering: bark and mats. Archibald Menzies observed both. On June 19th, 1792, he landed on one of the islands in the San Juans. "We had not gone far when the appearance of smoke issuing from a part of the wood on an Island before us induced us to land at a place where we found four or five families of the Natives variously occupied in a few temporary huts formd in the slightest & most careless manner by fastening together some rough sticks & throwing over them some pieces of Mats of Bark of Trees so partially as to form but a very indifferent shelter from the inclemency of the weather."[11] He went on to say:

> *...afterward walkd for some distance along the Sea side where we passd a low extensive Morass well cropd with Bullrushes of which large patches had been pluckd by the Natives & were now laid neatly out upon the Beach to season them for making their Mats, & it is probably that the conveniency of procuring a good supply of this Plant so necessary to their domestic comforts induced these few families to fix their temporary residence in the vicinity."*[12]

The bulrushes to which Menzies referred were no doubt tules (*Scirpus occidentalis*).

Bark huts, as described by Wayne Suttles, were constructed of four light poles forming a shed roof, covered by large pieces of cedar bark taken from either a living tree in the spring or a dead one in the winter. When the Hudson's Bay Company established a fishing station on a "small sheltered bay" on San Juan Island in 1850 or 1851, William John MacDonald said he and his men erected "a very primitive rough shelter—four posts stuck in the ground with a cedar bark roof on" for sleeping.[13] (Later his four workmen built a more permanent, Euro-American house "of round logs with bedstead and table of the same".)

Mat houses were constructed of a framework of poles forming a gable roof, which was then covered with ordinary house mats. Aurelia Balch Celestine in *Lummi Elders Speak* noted how

> *They used the cattail to make mats out of. …*
> *And whenever they'd go any place, like camping*
> *out, they'd take mats along and use them for their*
> *shelter. They used the cattail for the roof because*
> *it doesn't leak. The tules they used that for the*
> *sides. Tules soak easily so they don't use them for*
> *the roof. They'd gather them and they'd dry them.*
> *They'd make long needles out of hardwood. Oh, the*
> *needles must have been about three feet. Some of*
> *them are long and some of them are short. But the*
> *longer it is, the better, I guess. They used the finer*
> *parts from the cattail and they put that together*
> *and they twisted it. They made string out of that*
> *and they used that to put those tules together. They*
> *didn't use strings. If they used strings, it would cut,*
> *you know. It's a lot of work.*[14]

During the Euro-American settlement period, Hannah Sandwith Jensen recollected that Indians would land their canoes in Garrison Bay near their homestead and hike to a place several miles distant called "Grassy Swamp," where they would gather "broad reeds" for basket making.[15]

Several of the elders who gave depositions in the petition *Duwamish et al vs. United States* (1927)[16] described smaller houses (at Kanaka Bay) made of "split cedar and bark." They also described the actual dimensions of several of the longhouses, including ones that were larger than the building in which they were testifying (35 feet by 60 feet), and ranging from 50 feet wide by 150-160 feet long to 60 feet wide by 200-250 feet long. Smaller ones ranged from 30 to 40 feet in length. There are also historic descriptions of several split cedar dwellings, including a longhouse, as well as a bath house located near a spring well on the south side of Mitchell Bay.[17]

Several sources have described more temporary settlements throughout the islands. When Johnny Tom in his testimony for *Duwamish et al v. United States* noted "removable houses" on Orcas, in contrast to the more permanent settlements with longhouses. There were several mentions of "rancheries," or temporary settlements of migratory Indians. (The term probably originated in California from *rancheria*, the residential area of a *rancho* inhabited by Indigenous groups there, and applied to the collective habitations such as shacks, huts, or cabins of Indigenous peoples.) Several of these were of concern to American military officials, who objected to them as being locations for prostitution. One of these settlements, described as a "rancherie" and located somewhere on Griffin Bay, was the temporary home of the family of Anna Pike, who married the American soldier Christopher Rosler.

In the transition to Euro-American material culture, the older construction techniques of the longhouse were abandoned, but newer dwellings were constructed with a similar form. They had gable roofs and vertical wall planks in a board-and batten style, with cedar shakes for roofs.[18] Examples can be seen in historic photographs of the Kanaka Bay settlement and the Samish settlement on Guemes Island.

Mrs. Julius Charles described to Wayne Suttles a house that

> ...was not made of native materials; the walls were of milled lumber and the gable roof of shakes. As in the other big houses, the floor was just the earth under it. The ridge-pole was held up by a post at each end with perhaps one in the centre. These and the posts along the walls were neither painted nor carved. Around the walls ran a bed-platform about the width of a modern double bed and at about the same height. Around the walls overhead ran a storage-shelf. Mats lined the walls, and mats could be used to construct partitions between family sections.[19]

A significant example is the longhouse of Jim Eldridge, the last of four described in an 1870s report on Old Lummi Village on the mainland. According to informants, seven families lived in the house, each with its own section and firepit. The section in the corner to the left of the door in the north end was Jim Eldrdge's; this, the "first," was succeeded by the "second," "third," and so on going in a clockwise direction. With the six adult males each having a wife and their children, there were from 40-45 people in the house.[20] Otherwise, as in the San Juans, on the Lummi Reservation the new pattern of settlement was noted by a visiting commissioner in 1871: "They dress as white men and live in wooden houses, which are scattered over the reservation on their small farms."[21]

Hudson's Bay Company Posts

In December 1853, Charles Griffin and James Douglas established Belle Vue Sheep Farm on a prairie on the south end of San Juan Island. There are no surviving structures at the site of what they called "the Establishment." Despite written descriptions and historic maps and photographs of the buildings, as well as archaeological investigations at the site, there is still a lot to understand in terms of the layout of the compound and its nearby outbuildings. However, given the historical and archaeological material available, combined with comparisons with the descriptions of other Company forts and farms, a general idea of the layout, design, and construction of the buildings at Belle Vue can be formulated.

By the time Belle Vue Sheep Farm was settled in 1853, the Hudson's Bay Company had developed a template for the establishment of its trading posts in the Northwest. Typically, the Company chose open land, usually the savannah/Garry oak habitat that could be found extending from Fort Vancouver and nearby Willamette Valley to the south to the Nisqually settlement on Puget Sound and nearby Fort Victoria. When the Company faced the potential loss of Fort Vancouver due to boundary negotiations with the United States, in 1843 Chief Factor Douglas ordered Captain McNeil to locate a new base of operations near the tip of Vancouver Island, which would eventually become Fort Victoria: "You are to find a well-protected harbor, fertile soil and stands of timber." These, together with a source of fresh water, were the essential components to the successful operation of a post: a safe anchorage and landing place; cleared land for pasture and tillage; and woods for lumber and firewood.

The layout of Company forts had also become standardized by the 1850s. These were large compounds surrounded by tall (8' high) picket fences, with bastions in opposing corners. The chief factor or trader's house occupied a position of prominence, usually facing the main gate to the fortress (to the south or principal approach by road or water), with the kitchen nearby. The servants' (Hudson's Bay Company's employees') dwellings occupied the east side of the compound, while more utilitarian structures, such as workshops, were to the west. (Unfortunately, descriptions of smaller outposts are not as extensive as those of the larger Pacific Northwest forts such as Nisqually, Vancouver, and Victoria.)[22]

In the case of Belle Vue Sheep Farm, the compound was formed by eight or so structures arranged around an open rectangle and separated from each other as a precaution against fire, as in other Company establishments.[23] Griffin's house—the residence and office of the Clerk and later Chief Trader—probably

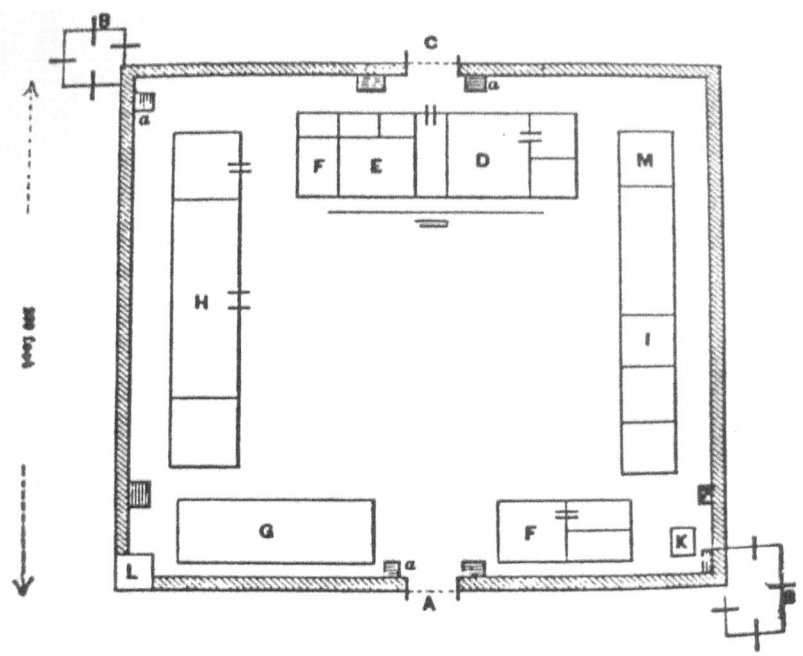

GROUND PLAN OF FORT SIMPSON, BRITISH COLUMBIA, 1859-66; AFTER A SKETCH BY P. N. COMPTON, VICTORIA, 1878.

A, Front Entrance.
B, B, Bastions, 4 guns.
C, Back Entrance.
D, Commanding Officer's Quarters.
E, Mess Room.
F, F, Officers' Quarters.
G, Trade Shop.
H, Warehouse.
I, Men's Houses.
K, Blacksmith Shop.
L, Carpenter Shop.
M, Kitchen.

a, a, a, a, Gallery along the inside of the picket wall, reached by staircases, affording separate entrance to upper story of bastions.

*Plan of Fort Simpson, British Columbia
(from David H. Chance,* Fort Colville, *1972)*

occupied either the south side or the northeast corner—the most prominent, uphill site. Archaeological evidence indicates that a triplex was located in the middle of the east side. This fits a type—three unconnected rooms in a line—that was common among various Company posts. In the more important locations, these rooms were used for "officer's barracks" housing "officers, clerks, and transient visitors of officer or clerk rank." Although Belle Vue was visited by numerous higher-ranking Company officials, this structure might have been used as a "men's house," i.e., for laborers.[24] The kitchen, which was identified by means of its large (6½ by 4¾ feet), centrally located chimney, was situated directly to the south of the triplex. Both buildings had counterparts at Forts Colville and Nisqually, among others.[25] The buildings forming the west and north sides of the compound were probably either men's houses or storage structures.

In general, the dimensions of the buildings ranged from 18-22 feet by 20-29 feet, and their area averaged around 400 square feet, which compares favorably with evidence from other Company posts. The well, which was lined with squared posts, was located in the center of the compound, while a flagpole with the Union Jack was erected some 100 feet or so to the south.[26] By the time the structures of the farm were enumerated in a census prepared in 1855 by James Douglas, in his dual capacity as Governor of the Crown Colony of Vancouver Island and Chief Factor of the Hudson's Bay Company, the establishment included 9 dwelling houses, 1 store or shop, and 5 "out-houses" (houses outside the area of the Establishment, not outhouses or privies).

Most of the routine landings from Fort Victoria occurred at what is now named Grandma's Cove (also known as Granny's or Grannies Cove), so a shed for Griffin's canoe was probably located there, as well as one or several Indian structures sited above the slope. To the east of the compound was the main farm building complex, consisting of one or two barns, a sheep shed, and

Photograph of Belle Vue Sheep Farm Taken by North west Boundary Survey (1859)

a granary. Written records indicate the construction of a barn around 1856, which James Douglas recommended to Charles Griffin in a letter dated November 12, 1856:

> *A barn of 70 or 80 feet will certainly be required, and I would recommend your getting the wood squared and hauled and as opportunities offer and I will serve you aid from this place to get it created, and also a few Indians to make shingles on the spot for roofing it.*[27]

Based on data from other Company posts, it was probably 18-21 feet wide. There were seven barns at Mill Plain at Fort Vancouver, for instance, all of which were 18-21 feet wide except one (32 feet); at Cowlitz, there were 13 barns of 20 by 105 feet and one "close barn" of 25 by 80 feet.[28] A historic photograph reveals that it had an English plan, i.e. side-entrance drive-through. Typically, in this plan there was a hay mow to one side of the drive and an open area to the other—forming, together with the drive, a square area to turn the teams around on the threshing floor—with grain bins beyond.[29] Probably located in the fields themselves were at least two cellars or "pits" (also called "root houses") for storage of root crops such as carrots, potatoes, and turnips.

(courtesy of San Juan Island National Historical Park)

In addition to these buildings, there were other structures described in the *Post Journals* that are less easily located. These include a shed for shearing, hen house, dairy, pigsty, and horse stable—all probably located in the farm complex near the barn—and Griffin's privy (although there is no specific mention of others). At each of the "stations" located in the various "parks" or outlying grazing ranges ("prairies"), the men built a house and dug a well, as well as constructing a "standing park" (fenced enclosure) for the livestock. The old fishery house was located somewhere on the west coast of the island; in 1858, a road from "Prairie" to the fishery was constructed and a "stage" for shipping sheep was erected there. The same year, a temporary "slip" or wharf was built at the "Harbor"; this would later be expanded to form the wharf on Griffin Bay. Finally, there were several road structures including at least four bridges (one at the "washing place" [also known as Holland's Bridge]; one across the "Riviere Castor"; one "above" Holland's Bridge; and one across the swamp in Norwegian Road) and a section of corduroy road, consisting of logs laid side-by-side over damp or wet ground, in a corner of the large field used for growing crops near the Establishment.

Probably the earliest structures to be used in the Company's settlement on the island were tents.[30] They were relatively inexpensive, featured rapid assembly, and offered shelter until the servants could erect more permanent dwellings. The Company *voyageurs* and other servants employed two types of tents: wedge and tipi. The former was described by Alexander Henry the Younger as

> ...*a large leather tent...of a triangle [tripod] set up with three poles in each end to support a ridgepole extending her length; small poles being there laid from the ridge to the gunnels, and the tent stretched over all.*"[31]

Two modified forms of this were a simple diamond fly tent (a square sheet over a ridge pole, with the two ends left uncovered) and a wedge tent with a bell, or rounded space at one end. The tipi design came from the Indigenous peoples of the North American Plains. According to a description by David Thompson,

The tent poles were now cut, and placed to form a circular area of about 12 to 14 feet diameter and 12 feet in height; the door poles are the strongest, about these poles we wrapped our tents, the fire place is in the centre, and our beds of pine branches, with a log next to the fire."[32]

The *Post Journals* indicate that tents were used by the Company shepherds at least in the early years of settlement on San Juan Island; they were most probably of the wedge design.

It was not long before Griffin and his Métis servants trained in standard Company construction methods began building more permanent structures on the island. The Company brought with them the men and building techniques that they had acquired when working around Hudson's Bay and the Red River Valley. The general French-Canadian term for horizontal log construction was *pièce sur pièce* (simplified from *pièces de bois sur*

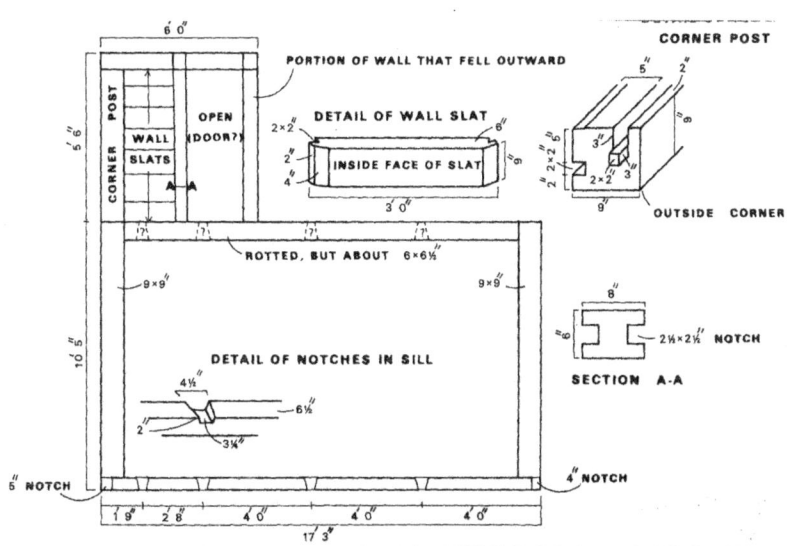

**FLOOR PLAN OF RUINS OF HBC STRUCTURE AT BELLEVUE FARM
COPIED FROM FIELD DRAWING BY SUPERINTENDENT CARL STODDARD**

*Belle Vue Sheep Farm Structure with Piece Sur Piece Construction
(from Erwin N. Thompson,* Historic Resource Study *1972)*

pièces de bois—"pieces of wood on pieces of wood"). More specifically, structures that consisted of vertically grooved posts filled with planks or squared logs was called *poteaux et pièce collisante* ("posts and sliding piece"), and the posts themselves were placed on sills (*poteaux sur sole*), as opposed to when the posts were set in the ground (*poteaux en terre*). With its dissemination into the Red River Valley by French Canadian *voyageurs*, *pièce sur pièce poteaux et pièce collisante* took on the name of Red River Style. After the absorption of the Red River-based North West Company by the Hudson's Bay Company, the style soon became known as "Hudson's Bay Company frame" where it was used throughout the West, so much so that it is also commonly referred to as the "Canadian" style.[33]

The logs used in this style of construction were hewn to 6- or 7-inches square before use. A sill (*sole*) was either placed upon the ground or supported by rocks or cedar stumps. Fitted into this by means of mortise and tenon were corner and intermediary squared posts, which had a mortise of about 2" wide and 3-4" deep running their full lengths. Into these grooves, shorter logs with ends formed into tenons or tongues were slipped down horizontally from above, forming solid wall panels, and then capped with a mortised plate. Openings such as doorways were framed by vertical posts on either side. On the middle of the gable ends of the structures, a vertical post would rise to the full height of the gable, to carry the ridge beam, from which rafters were sloped to a plate on top of the side wall panels and posts. The gables themselves were filled with planking, and the roofs covered with cedar shingles. Cracks between the logs were chinked with cotton, moss, or mud. Floors usually consisted of either smaller logs hewn flat or planks. Doors were constructed of planks or slabs and windows, where glass was available, consisted of sash with 8"- to 9"-square panes. Chimneys were constructed of brick hearths and stone flues, mortared with mud as well as lime manufactured from clamshells. Finally, Company tradition and numerous references indicate that the buildings were periodically whitewashed with lime.[34]

Entries of Griffin's *Post Journal* during spring and summer of 1858 offer a specific local example of this type of construction: the erection of a granary. In April, Robillard, George, and Ler-

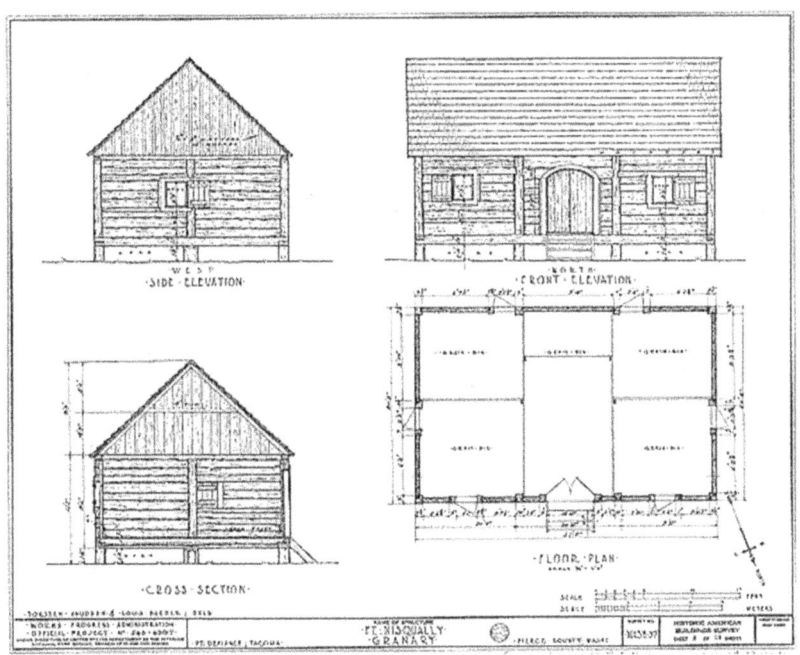

Fort Nisqually Granary
(Historic American Building Survey)

oux—all Métis—began cutting and laying "sole blocks" for framing. They continued with cutting and squaring the sills and then grooving the posts. In May, the men started cutting and squaring the "filling-up" logs, i.e. the horizontal panel pieces. By early June they had begun work on the loft and doors. They were only able to complete a temporary roof that summer. In April of the next year, they began re-roofing, and in May they put ½" cedar boards to the gable ends. In August, steps were added. (By comparison, it took two months for the granary at Fort Nisqually to be built by three experienced carpenters, probably assisted by several other men. It measured 20 by 31 feet and was 10 feet high.)[35]

Other buildings, such as sheep sheds, would have simpler forms and different construction. The root houses, which were also called "pits," were dug into the ground, with a log roof covered with dirt or turf. More time and expense were spent on other buildings, such as Griffin's house, which received a front and back gallery or porch—typical of the house of the Chief Factor or Trader ("The Big House"), as at Forts Nisqually and Vancouver.

Efforts were made to make the houses as hospitable as possible, at least for those who counted. In 1859, John de Courcy, the British Magistrate on San Juan Island, wrote to the Colonial Secretary of Vancouver Island William A. G. Young: "Will you also kindly give me your advice, as to whether I had better make this hut of mine wind[?] tight. The cold makes itself felt in these huts with[?] their longitudinal holes."[36] Griffin responded by assigning men to put cotton and paper in his room. In contrast, one of the complaints of two shepherds—"Old Man" Page and Murdoch McLeod—was that "their House was not fit to live in," although Griffin protested that he had done "all my power at present to make them comfortable & could do no more."[37] Maintenance and repair of many of the houses and farm buildings was ongoing. For instance, at one point the 'filling-in' logs in the side of the barn had shrunk so much as to need replacing.

Military Camps

After the initial encampment by the American forces, first near the Hudson's Bay Company wharf and later at the springs near South Beach, Lieutenant Colonel Silas Casey settled on the ridge overlooking both Griffin Bay (originally called by the Americans "Ontario Roads," after Wilkes's designation) and Haro Straits and reported to Captain Alfred Pleasonton: "… I have taken up a position near the Hudson's Bay establishment, and shall put my heavy guns in position to bear on the harbor, and also on vessels which might take a position on the other side."[38] A visitor reported in the August 23rd, 1859, Victoria *Gazette* that it was located

> *… immediately inland from the HBC's sheep farm … in a little valley, and … selected with a view to protection against the cold and disagreeable winds to which the camp had hitherto been exposed. It is hard to conceive a more romantic spot; the white tents peeping up and out from among the green foliage … the glittering arms of the sentinels … and the line of artillery which faces upon a small, clear, sward-covered square."*[39]

Sibley Tents at American Camp
(courtesy of San Juan Island National Historical Park)

Historic photographs from this area indicate that several different types of tents were used by the soldiers and their officers for temporary housing, among them tipi (conical) shapes as well as wedge and wall forms.

A modified design of the tipi, employing modern materials, was patented by Major Henry Hopkins Sibley in 1856, and subsequently issued by the U.S. Army as the "Sibley Tent." (Despite some 43,958 being used during the Civil War, Sibley, who sided with the Confederacy, received no royalties.) Eighteen feet in diameter and twelve feet tall, it was made of canvas, unlike the leather of the original, and supported by a pole stabilized by an iron tripod. Iron stoves were even designed specifically for the tent, with the stovepipe extending through a twelve-inch diameter hole at the apex. The Sibley tent was sometimes raised on a 4'-high stockade, but because the tent weighed up to 73 pounds, it was very cumbersome and therefore only used in permanent encampments. Designed to sleep twelve men, the tents sometimes held up to twenty soldiers, and Army regulations specified that all sleep with their feet toward the center, while 'spooning' each other.[40] Sibley tents appear in the earliest photographs of Amer-

*English Camp with Garden and Tents, 1860
(courtesy of San Juan Island National Historical Park)*

ican Camp. The British had a similar design called a "bell tent," which can be seen in historic photographs of early English Camp.

Several other types of tents can be seen in these early photographs. The oldest type used by the U.S. Army was the wedge or "A" tent, which consisted of canvas stretched over a 6-foot-long ridgepole supported by two 6-foot-high poles. Designed to sleep four men, these tents often accommodated as many as six, allowing about 7 square feet per person. A "wall" or "hospital" tent had four upright sides or 'walls', often with a fly added to the front. Being roomier, they were used for officers, or, in a larger version (14 by 14 feet, with 11 feet at the apex and 4'6" at the wall), as hospitals. Hospital tents, each of which could accommodate 8 patients, were often joined together to form larger spaces. All of these tents were relatively large and cumbersome; in response, personnel designed smaller, lighter shelter tents, also known as "dog" or "pup" tents, because they were "only fit for a dog." Two soldiers each carried half of the tent (originally 5'2" by 4'8" wide; by 1864, 5'6" by 5'5"), which were then buttoned together and hung over a rope stretched between poles or trees, or, in some exceptional cases, the trigger guards of two muskets with bayonets thrust into the ground. Called the *tente d'abri* by French troops in the Crimea during the 1850s, it was adopted in the United States late in 1861 or early 1862; there were 1,500,000 used in the Civil War alone.

While still in tents, one of the first major tasks of the American troops was the construction of a redoubt (technically, a "lunette"), with emplacements for five 32-pound guns removed from the *Massachusetts*, under the direction of Lieutenant Henry M. Robert.[41] Work commenced around September 11th and lasted forty-five days until the visit of General Scott shut down the operation in accordance with the negotiations that resulted in the joint military occupation. When historian Hubert Howe Bancroft visited the site, he described the redoubt.

> *The earthworks extended on the west water-front 350 feet, on the southeast 100, on the east 100, and on the northeast 150 feet, the north side being left open, with the garrison ground in its rear. The embankment had a base of twenty-five feet, and a width at top of eight feet. Inside of the redoubt were five gun-platforms of earth, reaching to within two feet of the level of the parapet, each twelve by eighteen feet, two of them being at corners of the redoubt. The parapet was seven feet above the interior, and the slope of the interior twelve to fifteen feet, the exterior slope being twenty-five to forty feet, with a ditch at the bottom from three to five feet across.*[42]

American Camp from the Redoubt
(courtesy of San Juan Island National Historical Park)

Within a year after abandonment, it was derogatorily known as "Robert's Gopher Hole."[43]

When joint occupation of the island with the British was mandated, the American troops began erecting more permanent structures to form the Camp. To a large extent, the Camp was modeled on the place where the troops came from—Fort Bellingham—which in turn had been modeled after Hudson's Bay Company trading posts. This included the guardhouse, which according to an 1878 description by Bellingham pioneer and sawmiller Henry Roeder, was:

> *...built of sawn logs, 8 inches thick dovetailed. The difference between the blockhouse & a regular log house was that we had sawn timbers in the blockhouse with port holes cut through them. It was 20 X 30 feet, two stories. The upper story projected over.*

Because it occupied such a commanding site, it was not deemed necessary for American Camp to have a full palisade wall surrounding it as was the case at Fort Bellingham.

Roeder explained the design of the camp:

> *We built it on the plan of the Hudson Bay Company in their forts. The stockade we had must have been over 100 feet square. That consisted of posts set upright in the ground. They were about 12 feet high; & we would set them about 3 feet in the ground, tight together. We pinned strips on them on the inside about 3 feet from the top. On the two opposite corners diagonally we place bastions up so as to protect the two sides nearest to each. We had steps leading up into them from the inside of the stockade. The bastions were built the same as the blockhouse of square timber. The upper story projected over the lower about 2 feet on each side. The lower story was about 8 feet square, & the upper story about 12 feet. It rested on the ground.*[44]

The standard form of a fort was used here: a large (approximately 425 feet on the side) parade ground, aligned northeast-southwest and faced by enlisted men's quarters (barracks, mess hall, and wash house) on the northeast side and officers' quarters on the opposite, southwest side, along with auxiliary structures such as the hospital and laundress's quarters. This central square was surrounded by a white picket fence, with a blockhouse (guardhouse) near the arched gateway to the southeast, service entrances to the northwest and northeast, and a prominent flagpole with the Stars and Stripes in the center. Because the garrison was commanded to supply its own vegetables, a garden was located near the Hudson's Bay Company's fields, and a barn for the draft and riding animals was erected.[45]

Most of the building materials were reused from structures barged over from Fort Bellingham. Many of these were made of one of the simplest types of lumber construction called "vertical plank" or "box," because it resembled the construction of boxes or crates. A platform foundation, laid on field stones or cedar rounds, was constructed with hewn girders and hewn or milled joists; to this were nailed vertically 1-2-inch-thick boards, ranging from 12-20 inches wide, and a ledger was nailed along their upper edge. Then, either the gaps between boards were covered by thin lumber strips called battens, or another layer of vertical boards ("two-ply" or "double wall construction") was applied, or the first layer was covered with horizontal clapboard or shiplap (weatherboard) siding.[46] An extant example of vertical plank construction is the Officers' Quarters at American Camp. The wood of the vertical planks has the same saw markings as the Pickett House in Bellingham, indicating that the lumber probably came from the Roeder Mill, which operated at Whatcom from 1853 to 1873.[47] One of the new officer's quarters constructed in the building campaign of 1867-1868 was in fact reconstructed from Fort Bellingham: "This building was taken down with great care, and can be put up at a small cost, the material required being what is absolutely necessary to render it habitable."[48] Later structures were built with imported lumber.

One of the few structural plans that has been saved is that of the Enlisted Men's Barracks, indicating a long (54 feet), narrow

(20 feet wide) main section for quarters and the orderly room, with a shorter (44 feet), narrower (16 feet wide) section for the mess room and kitchen. The document specifies that the ceiling height was eight feet, with another six feet for the roof, and brick chimneys were specified in the barracks and kitchen. Facing south, the building had a shallow porch along the front (parade ground) facade. Commanding Officer Captain Hunt wrote in 1860:

> *My men are all comfortably housed and I am established in as neat and snug a cottage as you wish to see. It is built of hewn logs, closely fitting and lined within, a piazza in front, the columns of which are decidedly rustic, being cut from the forest, peeled and the knobs left some inches long.*[49]

Several structures were constructed with trees felled near the site, as testified to by William Warren of the North West Boundary Survey: "the men were at work cutting down the large trees in the vicinity of the Camp and finishing the Erection of log houses for quarters."[50] Judging from historic photographs of structures at Fort Bellingham, the logs were hewn both inside and out, and joined with full dovetail joints.

Because no one had anticipated that the joint military occupation of the island would last a dozen years, the camp was not constructed for longevity and soon began falling apart. In 1867-1868, a major building program began, with the construction of two sets of officers' quarters, an adjutant's office, non-commissioned officers' mess house, set of laundresses' quarters, new hospital, quartermaster storehouse, commissary storehouse, blacksmith shop, two-story barn and stable, granary (attached to the barn), additions to the reading room-orderly room building, and general mess. Buildings and materials were again scavenged from Fort Bellingham, which had been abandoned, and lumber was again produced from the surrounding forests. In addition to the troops themselves, a civilian construction team consisting of three carpenters, a mason, and a blacksmith were employed for the work. Most of the buildings were whitewashed, with the front of the officers' quarters painted with white lead.[51]

The old barracks, however, were not renovated, and, despite periodic pleas from camp commanders, continued to deteriorate until 1871. In the fall of that year, General E. R. S. Canby visited the camp and authorized the purchase of 8,000 bricks, 23,500 shingles, and 700 pounds of nails for repairs. However, little work was done to the camp prior to its abandonment in 1874.[52] In 1874, Major Nathaniel Michler prepared a map of the southeast portion of the island including numbered and labeled structures both within and outside of the fence that surrounded the main part of the camp. Aside from the more general maps produced by Lieutenant Colonel Silas Casey in 1860 and Lieutenant James Forsyth in 1860 (retraced in 1872), the Michler map and inventory of buildings provide the best description of American Camp from that period.

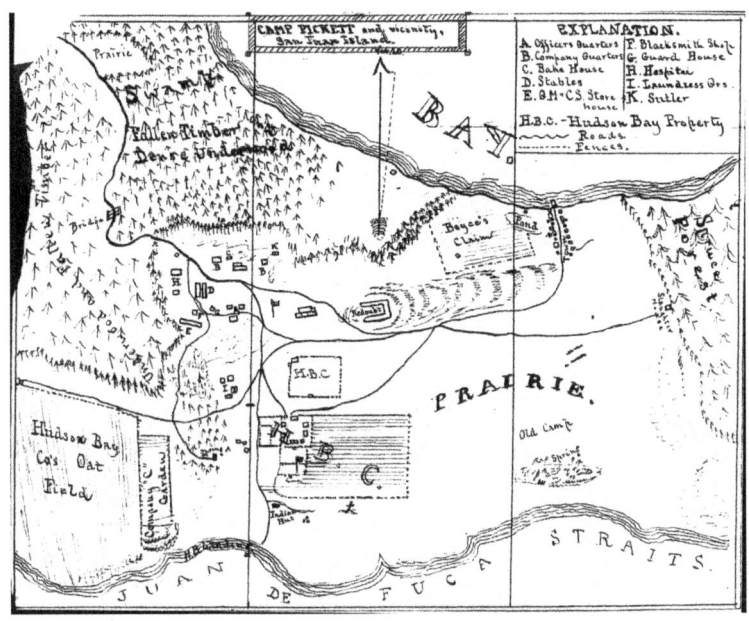

Lt. Fred H. W. Ebstein,
Belle Vue Sheep Farm and American Camp, 1873
(courtesy of San Juan Island National Historical Park)

On the north end of the island, the British responded to the terms of the joint military occupation in kind with a camp of their own. Captain James Charles Prevost had circumnavigated the island, choosing from at least eleven sites, including the future location of the town of Friday Harbor (which was initially considered the best). Prevost reappraised the choices and settled on a site on what is appropriately known today as Garrison Bay.

> *About three quarters of a mile in a SSE direction there is a large patch of water, half lake, half swamp, on the northern shore of which is a situation admirably adapted for an encampment. It slopes gently to the S.W., is well sheltered, has a good supply of water and grass, and is capable of affording maneuvering ground for any number of men that are likely to be required in that locality, there being a large extent of Prairie land, interspersed with some very fine oak Timber.*[53]

There the British troops, under the command of Captain George Bazalgette, first camped in tents, like their Americans counterparts, and then built frame structures. The British encampment differed in one way from that of the Americans: after some initial construction by the Royal Marines, the subsequent buildings

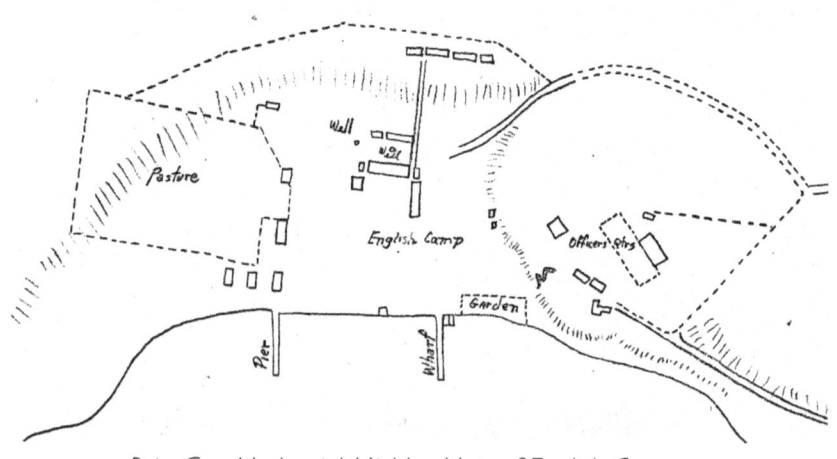

Brig. Gen. Nathaniel Michler, *Map of English Camp*
(courtesy of San Juan Island National Historical Park)

were constructed by the colonial government, and the work was often contracted out to civilians from Victoria. Both the list of tools and supplies requisitioned from Vancouver Island and extant samples of specifications are revealing of standard building techniques (see Appendix: *English Camp Tools and Building Materials*).

The basic layout of the camp consisted of a large parade ground—formed by leveling the extensive shell middens of the former Coast Salish village at that site, surrounded by the blockhouse, store houses, and wharf on the south (water) side; barracks to the north and west; and miscellaneous support buildings including kitchens and mess rooms, hospital, and stables. Ranged along the slope to the north were a blacksmith and shoemaker's shop; company mess; school, library, and reading room; and carpenter shop with sawpit. In comparison with American Camp, where the spatial hierarchy of command was expressed by the horizontal separation of the officers' quarters from that of the enlisted men by a parade ground, at English Camp it is articulated vertically, with the subalterns (both married and single subaltern as well as the company surgeon) and the Commanding Officer's quarters located on terraces in the slope rising above the barracks, parade ground, and, later, a formal garden below.

After the initial site work of leveling the ground and clearing trees surrounding the site, the Royal Marines also constructed a storehouse, a "cooking house," a barn, and a vegetable garden encircled by a lattice work fence. They then built a blockhouse, which, like its counterpart at American Camp, was a two-story log structure, with the second story placed obliquely atop the first. The barracks were put out for bid, with the firm of Elford & Mann, Victoria, winning with an offer of £690. This building, along with a small officers' quarters, was finished by October of 1860. Like the buildings at American Camp, most were whitewashed, probably with lime burned at a small kiln that Bazalgette had had established near Roche Harbor in October of 1860.[54]

Just as the Americans came to the realization in the mid-1860s that the period of joint occupation may be an extended stay, so too the British concluded that their original structures at the camp were inadequate for the long run and set about a rebuilding campaign in 1867. In part this was prompted by the replacement of Capt. Bazalgette as Commanding Officer with Captain William Delacombe, who, with his wife and three children, required a new residence. Delacombe chose a site upon a terrace on the slope above the parade grounds, barracks, and the old officers' quarters, and the contract was awarded to John King and James Syme for $2,010. The frame "Cottage dwelling house," with five rooms flanked by two wings of two rooms each, measured 42 by 33 feet for the main section and 12½ by 31½ feet for each wing. In addition to a chimney with double fireplace, the complex included a bath house, pantry, and woodshed. A solicitation of bids for preparation of plans and specifications for "a small Cottage for the married Subaltern of Royal Marines" was also let at this time and awarded to James Grahamslaw of Victoria.[55]

The specifications for "the erection and completion" of the commanding officer's quarters reveal a lot about contemporary construction methods. The foundation, as with many frame structures built during that period, consisted of cedar logs, "not less than 12 inches in diameter placed not more than 7 feet centre to centre," although in this case they were to be buried 3 feet into the ground, with 2 feet projecting, as opposed to the more common method of just placing rounds directly on the surface of the ground. The sills were 4"x6", the floor joists 2"x6" at 24" on center, and the flooring 1" tongue-and-groove. Wall studs were to be 3"x4" at 16" on center, braced with 1"x6" boards on angle. Partitions had 2"x4" sills and 3"x4" studs and plates, with 4"x4" door studs. Rafters were 2"x6" at 30" on center, covered with rough 1"x6" planks and shingled with split cedar with five inches "to the weather" (i.e., exposed). The windows were to be constructed of 10" by 16" lites "to be of the best description of glass, both top and bottom sashes to be hung with all the necessary weights pulleys and patent sash lined with good brass window fastenings on the meeting rail," and the "double moulded four panel" doors were 30" wide by 80" tall.

During the same period, several of the older structures, including the single subaltern's quarters, the enlisted men's barracks, and the noncommissioned officers' quarters, were repaired or renovated in 1875. Recommendations for repairs to the barracks included:

> *The three fireplaces and hearths should be reset with fire brick and the floors, having settled in several places in consequence of the ground cill [sic] and floor joists having rotted away—must be taken up, new timbers laid down where necessary, so much of the present planking relaid as may be found sound—and some new flooring supplied.*[56]

The estimated cost for these repairs was $50.00 for the fireplaces and $350.00 for the floors of the barracks, storehouse, and guard house, bringing the total cost of improvements and new construction to some $5,541.63. Otherwise, there were little to no major additions, alterations, or repairs until relinquishment of the camp upon the settlement of the boundary dispute in 1872.[57] In 1874, several years after the abandonment of the post by the British, the camp was surveyed by Major Nathaniel Michler, who prepared a map and list of buildings.

Cross-Cultural Settlements

Several early settlements in the islands were established by cross-cultural families that might have included Americans, employees of the Hudson's Bay Company, or members of local Coast Salish groups. Although there is little documentary evidence of the physical layout and composition of these settlements, there is some indication that hybrid building forms may have been adapted in the process of mixing the cultural traditions. One of the earliest known locations was Kanaka Bay. Lila Hannah Firth recollected:

> *Another old Kanaka with his family, & a number of his friends, moved out to a point near our home, I would guess about 1½ miles of our place [the Hannah farm]. There was a great long point of land that went out into the Strait of Juan de Fuca. After this colony settled in there, the settlers named it Kanaka Point. Out near the end of this Point on the north side there was quite a sheltered*

> Bay where boats could lie at anchor in any kind of bad storms, which are quite severe on the Strait at times, that was also named, Kanaka Bay.[58]

Historical records indicate that the Kanaka Bay area had been the site for at least one longhouse, as well as several smaller fishing huts. During the Belle Vue Sheep Farm period Kanakas employed as shepherds by the Company married Songhees and Mitchell Bay women and settled on land under the provisions of the colonial system used by the British government on Vancouver Island. Among these were Legamine (William Naukana), Kama Kamai, and Alexander Kane.[59] Evidence of the various structures at Kanaka Bay comes from several historical photographs. They indicate at least five structures, all of which are rectangular in plan with gable roofs. The materials include regular

"Indian Camp in Kanaka Bay"

cedar shingles and board-and-batten exterior wood walls; several have a door flanked symmetrically by two windows with nine lites each. None seems to have a chimney structure. What is intriguing is that the largest of the structures, on the left side of the photographs, has irregular shingle patterns, wood siding, and ridge and purlin poles that seem to indicate a longhouse style of construction, although the roof is gabled, unlike the traditional local Coast Salish shed form.

In one of the photos, which encompasses more of the foreground including the bay, there are several types of small craft. These include at least two types of canoes—the older Coast Salish type and the Nootka or West Coast variety—as well as several Columbia River sloops. In the other men are lined up in front of structures, with some women and children standing to the side and sitting in the middle. The men are holding both rifles and

U.S. Coast and Geodetic Survey. (1892)

Kanaka Bay Camp ca. 1873
(courtesy of San Juan Historical Museum)

Coast Salish canoe paddles. All of this is possible material evidence for the cultural 'mixing' that had occurred in the marriages between Kanaka men and Coast Salish women.

Orcas Island had a larger share of cross-cultural families than the other islands, and that was possibly reflected in the physical layout and construction of several settlements there. In his typical fashion, James Tulloch recalled:

> 'Col.' May had returned to the island [from Whatcom] before my arrival and had located on a claim near North Beach where he had a band of the worst Indian characters always camped under the leadership of an outlaw Indian know as Old Tom to whose credit more than one murder was attributed. Here May posed as the King of Squaw Men, declaring that it was their last ditch (stand) and that he would fight to prevent the settlement of the island by white families...[60]

Ignoring the blatant prejudice and racism, it is clear that there was an extensive settlement of cross-cultural families on and around North Beach. The settlement at Grindstone Bay on Orcas Island may also have exhibited a mixture of Indigenous and Euro-American building techniques. Paul Hubbs had settled there in the 1860s, and apparently engaged in active trade with the growing number of settlers on Orcas and other nearby islands, in part because of his possession of the only grindstone in the area (hence the name of the bay). In the 1882 records of the trial of Lars Brown for the murder of Yves Jaffrett, a map of Brown's Bay (which Grindstone Bay was called at the time), entered as evidence, indicated several "Indian houses" and Brown's blacksmith shop and house, as well as a handful of other settlers' houses. The names of witnesses who testified included several what are assumed to be Indigenous people—Indian John and Indian Tom (who, by the way, were witnesses on opposite "sides" of the trial)—as well as some of the "squaw men" Tulloch enumerated— Enoch May and James Guthrie, as well as the defendant, Lars Brown, and the victim, Yves Jaffrett. Again, it is not clear whether the architecture reflected the mixed status of its residents.

Louis Cayou and three other men—Guard (whose first

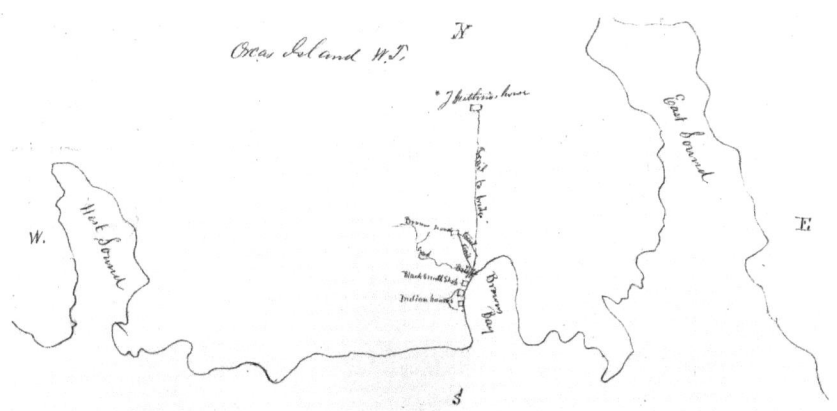

Map of Browns [Grindstone] Bay, Orcas Island (Northwest Regional Branch, Washington State Archives)

name is unknown), James Bradshaw, and William (Billy) Moore—moved to Deer Harbor on Orcas Island in 1858 and supplied English Camp with venison. Of the group, both Cayou and Bradshaw married Indigenous women. Cayou married Mary Anne Sulwham, who was born at Mitchell Bay on San Juan to parents of English, American, Lummi, and possibly Saanitch heritage, and Bradshaw married Idel LaPlante, the daughter of Catherine Delaunais. A historic photograph of the Cayous' first home site shows structures of mixed style. Their son Henry is shown standing in front of a shingle gable roofed building with lapped vertical boards or shingles used as siding and to the side of this are some horizontal log structures. Perhaps Cayou, Bradshaw, and others who married Indigenous women formed a mixed settlement with buildings reflecting their cross-cultural heritage.

Homesteads

The process of "proving up," discussed in the previous chapter (*Place*), focused on establishing residence on the claim and preparing it for cultivation. In addition to clearing land in preparation for crops, one of the first requisites was shelter, and this was achieved by means of structures that could be erected quickly. As the land was developed and the homesteaders' families arrived and grew, a succession of house structures followed. Many homesteaders arrived as either single or married men without their families until they could provide sufficient housing. The first structure in many cases was probably a tent, which provided shelter until a small log cabin was constructed. Then, either additions were made to the cabin, in the form of an ell or a lean-to, or a new, larger structure was built. This three-staged approach to dwelling—first a temporary shelter, then an improved transitional structure, and finally a permanent house—has been documented in frontier situations as diverse as the Willamette Valley[61] and the plains of Alberta.[62] The San Juans certainly fit this pattern.

There is some, although scant, evidence that early settlers used tents as their first shelter upon settling in the islands. Because many of the men who either squatted or homesteaded in the islands had come from West Coast gold rushes, they were used to dwelling in tents. Lyman Cutlar's dwelling was described by a contemporary witness as a "hut or tent." Charles W. Shattuck, who had been active in both the California and Fraser River gold rushes, first lived in a tent at the head of East Sound before he built a house of frame lumber, which he had shipped in.[63] Harvey Hudson, in his 1883 application for a homestead on Shaw

Island, stated that he had first lived in a tent while he slashed, cut a trail, and built a house.⁶⁴

There are not many extant structures in the San Juans dating from the period under discussion, and tents were certainly too ephemeral to last. But written records and the few early photographs and drawings that are available indicate that the earliest permanent homestead structures were log cabins. Royal Marine Sergeant Charles Whitlock, writing to his sister on February 14, 1869, said

> ...in the country places they [the houses] are chiefly built with logs joined together at the corners (of wood) and no up stairs to them a man that want a house hear just look for a place he can till some land and then he will take his axe and go to the woods and cut his timber and build his house in about a week.⁶⁵

These structures were erected rather quickly: a good axe man could cut and square ten logs per day. If the logs were about 7" in diameter, there would be about 90 logs per cabin, so the structure could be built in little over a week. In *Told by the Pioneers* Annie Ebey recalled her mother, Mrs. Phoebe Judson, telling her about homesteading in nearby Whatcom County:

> Mr. Judson at once began to fell the fir trees and hew them to build our habitation, the dimensions of which were sixteen by eighteen feet, surmounted by a shake roof, and floor of the style called puncheon. The shakes, puncheon, doors, bedstead, table and stools were made from lumber split from a green cedar tree.⁶⁶

This description by Mrs. Rebecca E. [Tarte] Jeffcott of a cabin in the Nooksack Valley indicates the similarity in the use and working of cedar to that of the Coast Salish:

This home was constructed entirely of timber found on the site. First they cut and split cedar logs twenty-four feet long. These they hewed down to five inches thick to form the walls. For ceiling, floors, and doors, they selected straight-grained timber, which they split into inch boards, some of which were as long as twenty feet. Every bit of the building...was built from trees on the ground; we bought nothing but the nails, window glass, locks and hinges...[67]

Much of the materials came from the trees at hand, and there was an added benefit of clearing land for tilling in the process.

These homestead log structures differed considerably from the *pièce sur pièce poteaux et pièce collisante* structures of the Hud-

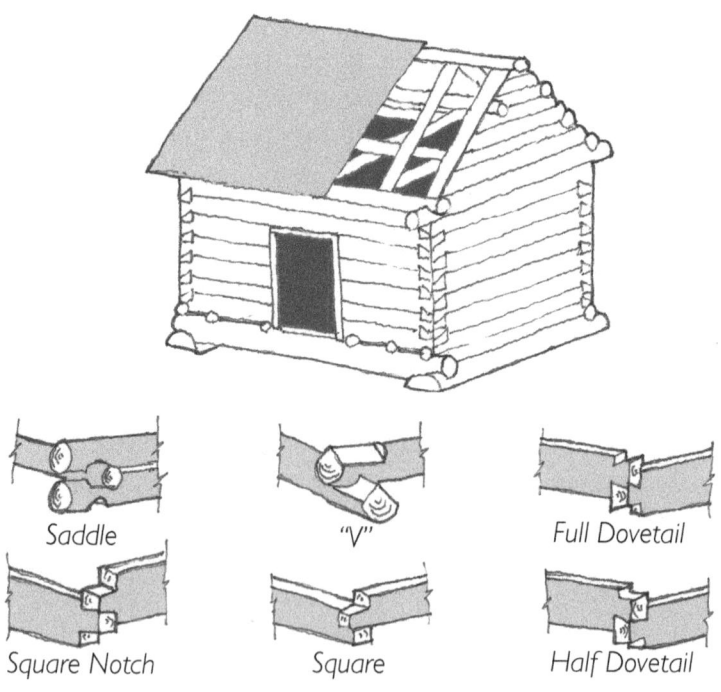

Log Cabin Construction with Notching Types
(adapted from: Mary Wilson, "Log Cabin Technology and Typology" 1984)

son's Bay Company. They consisted of hewn cedar or Douglas fir logs that were laid on top of each other horizontally and notched at the corners. The principal types of notching were full or half dovetail and square, although some "V" and saddle (also called "round" or "scribed") notching was used in outbuildings. In one documented case, the upper parts of the logs were left with their bark and moss intact, while the lower parts were hollowed out to fit onto the curved outer surface of the log below, in a style that has been termed "Fenno-Scandinavian" from its region of origin.[68] In other cases, the interstices between the logs were caulked with mud, moss, or rags, a process called chinking. Sometimes their outer surfaces were plastered or whitewashed with lime.

Most cabins had gable roofs, with the gable ends covered with split or sawn planks. Roofs were covered with shakes that had been split from short sections of cedar logs ("bolts") and planed flat; it was only later, in the 1880s, that milled shingles were available. Fireplaces and chimneys were located on the outside of the log structure and constructed of either stonework or sticks mortared and plastered with clay.[69] Later, iron cookstoves were introduced into the house interiors, often attached by a metal stove pipe to a brick chimney in a wall dividing the cabin into two rooms.

When saddle notches were used, the logs were generally left rounded; for dovetail and similar notching, logs were squared. Nearly all the descriptions in the homestead applications indicate that most island cabins had logs that were hewn and not left round. Some witnesses even took the pains to emphasize "split cedar log" and "hewed inside." Only rarely were the ends of the logs left protruding from the exterior walls; this was generally considered sloppy workmanship.[70]

There is some evidence from surrounding areas on the mainland that other types of cabins were constructed in the islands as initial, temporary dwellings. In *Told by the Pioneers*, Charley Nelson, whose father settled in Skagit County, recalled that their house was "Rough boards standing on end, formed the walls, the sills were of hewed lumber, the rafters were of cedar poles and the roof was of split cedar." (He added that there was also a stone fireplace and a chimney of poles and mud.)[71] Rosa Ellen Flynn, in Clark County, said that "The first houses I recall were little box houses made of lumber and battened. Most of them were unpainted."⁷²

Most of these houses were small, ranging from 10 to 18 feet wide to 12 to 24 feet long—due to a large part upon the length and manageability of the logs themselves—and either one or one-and-a-half story in height. Many were about 12 feet by 14 feet, and had only one door and one window, although larger structures had upward of 3 doors and as many as 5 windows. Floors were of dirt or, when floored, hewn or planed logs as well as tongue-and-grooved boards. Orpha Higgins Sutton said in *Told by the Pioneers* "I was born in a log cabin that had floors, but I remember that some had swept dirt floors."⁷³ Ceilings ("ceiled inside and out") are mentioned in several homestead documents and recollections of 1875 (see Appendix: *Homestead Houses*).

The number of rooms also varied, from one to three or more. A common plan was two rooms on the main floor—a hall (used for cooking, eating, and socializing) and parlor (a more private space, often used for sleeping)—with additional sleeping quarters up in the loft. In *Told by the Pioneers* Mary Jane Fraser recollected that her father's home, which was a log house, "was larger than the usual one, with three rooms and a kitchen downstairs, a fireplace in the kitchen, and two rooms upstairs."⁷⁴ Lizzie Lawson, describing the home her parents (Peter Lawson and Fannie Dearden) built, recalled:

> *There were two bedrooms, a parlor, living room and a small kitchen. The only closet was in the parlor against the fireplace and bedroom wall and had a home made door."⁷⁵*

Several structures had porches. However, most houses were small and used for temporary shelter until a more substantial, frame structure was built.

Not only were these dwellings small, but homesteaders also did not have many goods to fill them. As Orpha Higgins Sutton recollected:

> *Our sleeping facilities were somewhat different than those of the present day, at least in our family. We slept five in a bed. The bed was pushed back to the wall during the day and out into the middle of the room at night. The cabin was one of two rooms. My mother made the quilts real long, so that they could be tucked in around the sleepers.*[76]

Lizzie Lawson said that after her parents moved into their house,

> *…the furnishings were very simple: a Dutch oven to cook on in the fireplace, which was a double fireplace back-to-back. The long table was made of two boards, each board was over two feet wide. The legs were bought in Port Townsend and were nailed to the table top and frame around the table. We also had a long bench used for seating people at the table.*[77]

A settler on the South Fork of the Nooksack in nearby Whatcom County recalled:

> *We had made our beds, table, stools and benches and a lamp stand. Also the few packing boxes were utilized for dish cupboards. A wide shelf was built across one corner with a curtain, and made a very good place to hang our clothes. We kept some of our things in trunks which could be left in the shed or on the porch. Our little cookstove also answered for a heater, and stood in one corner, our bed in another. The table and cupboards were on one side near the window, and the sewing machine at the foot of the bed. There was room for Aunt Mary's rocking chair too.*[78]

All of this, in "one room, 12 feet square," indicates how space was at a premium.

Applications for homesteads indicate typical furnishings of the period. In 1883, Bert Tift listed the set of furnishings for his homestead on Shaw: "Cooking stove & utensils 2 tables and tableware 12 chairs 2 stands Cubbard 4 beds & bedding 3 clocks 4 lamps." Most homesteaders had a cook stove, described as either "complete" or with "fixtures" or "utensils," although in *Told by the Pioneers* Mary Jane Fraser remembered her mother using only "reflectors to cook before the fire, and a dutch oven on occasion."[79] Settings for meals varied: although most mentioned tables, chairs ranged in number from one to twelve, and stools were also used; one homesteader even lists a rocking chair and a "lounge." Storage also varied: several mention cupboards (invariably spelled "cubbard"); one mentions some trunks. Beside the "only closet" in her parent's house, Lizzie Lawson says that "We had the trunk my mother brought with her from England for storing linens."[80] Beds and bedding were common, and several have "stands," but clocks, looking glasses (mirrors), and lamps were called out by a few, the latter being the most common (see Appendix: *Homestead Furnishings*).

> In the early days family cooking was done over an open fire. The family used Dutch ovens to bake bread, biscuits, pies and cake. They were also used to roast meat and potatoes. There were rods over the fire on which were hung iron kettles. When the bread was raised it was placed in the oven and when it had risen again it was placed in the Dutch oven, put over hot coals on the hearth, the lid put on and covered with coals. This Dutch oven had legs on it about four inches long. A good housewife knew just the required number of coals to use in baking. A long handle fire shovel was used for handling the coals.
>
> —Mary L. Iotte, "Freeman Iotte Walked to the West in 1849; Lived, Worked on Orcas Is.," Orcas Islander 1966

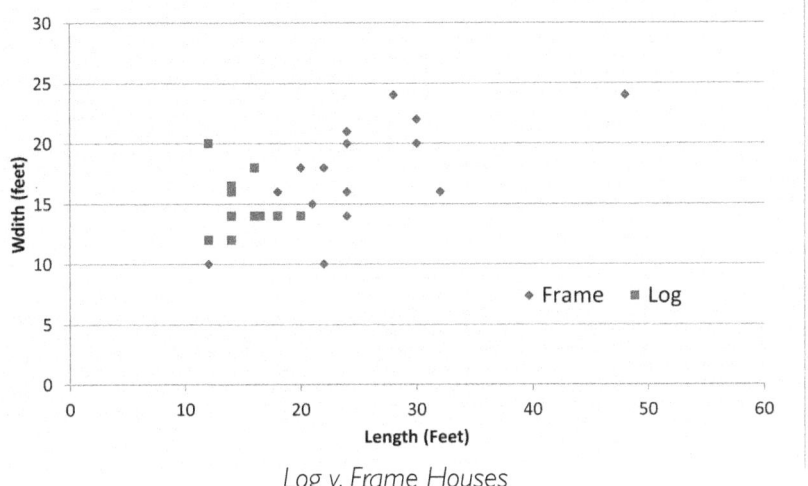

Log v. Frame Houses
(Logs Restricted by Length; Frame Unrestricted)

Homesteaders eventually either added to their existing cabins or built newer, larger houses to accommodate their families. In either case, the construction was apt to be frame, because of the growing availability of sawn lumber and nails and the increasing ability of the settlers to afford them. Some of these additions or new structures were constructed of "box" or "vertical plank" construction. This offered a relatively quick, cheap, and easy method of erecting a structure, but had the drawback of not providing as sturdy and weatherproof a structure as a log cabin or frame construction.

Frame construction was often called either "stick" or "balloon frame," because the lumber used is so light compared to the wood members used in either log or timber frame construction. Frame lumber, sawn in standard 2x4s, 2x6s, 2x8s, and 2x10s (at that time an actual 2" by 4", not the "nominal" 1½" by 3½" of today), along with mass-produced machine-cut (and later wire) nails, helped the spread of "lumber" houses and other structures throughout the San Juans. After the initial establishment of a sawmill at Budd's Inlet near Olympia by Colonel M. S. Simmons in 1850, followed the next year by the Hudson's Bay Company's Vancouver's Island Steam Sawing Mill Company near Cadboro Bay, commercial sawmills developed rapidly in the Puget Sound region, so that by 1856 James Alden of the U.S. Coast Survey could note that there were establishments in Olympia (4), Henderson's Inlet (1), Hammersley's Inlet (1), Nisqually (2), Steilacoom (1), Puyallup (1), Seattle (1), Port Orchard (1), Port Gamble (1), Port Ludlow (2), and Bellingham Bay (probably Roeder's Mill, whose lumber was used to construct many of the box frame structures moved to American Camp). In his *Post Journals*, Griffin noted the delivery of several shipments of lumber (for instance, February 1, 1858: "hauling with oxen 2000 feet lumber brought by the "Beaver""), and, as we have seen, both American and English Camps had frame structures. The concurrent spread of machine-cut nails, which rapidly replaced those that were hand-forged, is witnessed by inventory records of the Hudson's Bay Company store at Fort Vancouver, as well as records from the archaeological excavations at English and American camps.[81]

Frame construction consisted of standard pieces of lumber that were nailed together in a frame, consisting of floors of joists usually at 24" on center (o.c.), diagonal subflooring, and finished floor; walls of 2x4 or 2x6 studs at 16" or 24" o.c. sided with either clapboard or shiplap; and gabled, hipped, or pyramidal roofs of 2x4 or 2x6 joists at 16" or 24" o.c. covered with 1x4 nailers and either hand-split shakes or, when milling was more widespread, shingles. If the structure had a second story, the floor structure was usually "hung" or nailed onto the wall studs. The spacing of these light members at regular intervals eventually led to the use of standardized building materials, based on multiples of 12, 18, or 26 inches—hence the importance of centering the framing pieces. Standard manufactured doors, windows, and molding also became available through planning mills, established in the region soon after sawmills.

An example of an early frame homestead house is that of Jennie Hellen, who was widowed at the age of 20 upon the death of her husband John M. Hellen in 1889. She described it as "A lumber house about 28 x 24 ft 1½ story 5 rooms 4 doors 9 windows, floor ceiled."[82] One of the largest early frame houses in the San Juans was that of Archibald Rader, who homesteaded his property on Shaw Island in 1881. His neighbor Jeremiah Griswell described him as a farmer principally "but before his eyes got bad he sometimes made small boats at home," and his list of implements included a "full chest of carpenters tools." Rader described his dwelling as "A lumber house L shape 24 x 48 feet. 7 rooms and shed. 7 doors & 8 windows Wood shingled roof Good floor val. $500"; Griswell added that it was weatherboarded and "well finished for the country."[83]

Although not a homestead structure *per se*, a signal example of balloon frame construction is the structure that served as a boarding house, store, manager's dwelling, and kitchen for the San Juan Lime Company. This structure, roughly 33 feet by 36 feet, sat upon a hillside that slopes down to the water from east to west. It consisted of two parts: a one-story, shed-roofed section to its north and a two-story, gable-roofed section to the south. The shed-roofed section contained three rooms: a 12- by 14-foot kitchen to the northeast, and two rooms of unknown use—a 9½- by 12-foot space in the north central area and a 11½ by 19½ foot space in the northwest, overlapping into the second story section. The ground floor of the second story section consisted of a 19½- by 24-foot dining hall to the southeast and a 19½- by 11½ foot room of unknown use—possibly a stove—to the southwest. The second story contained three rooms of approximately 12 by 19½ feet each; presumably these were all used as a dormitory or sleeping quarters. The building was constructed with wood balloon framing. Cedar logs placed vertically on the ground supported 6x6 girders, which in turn supported 2x6 joists at 24" on center. The exterior walls are constructed of 5"-wide ¾"-shiplap nailed to 2x4 studs at 24" on center. The second floor (2x10) joists are supported by a 1x6 board that is mortised into the 2x4 walls. The roof is constructed of 2x4 joists at 24" on center, with 1x8 nailers spaced with a 4" gap in between and covered with wood shakes with 5-6" lap. All lumber dimensions are real, and machine-cut nails were used throughout. Simple manufactured windows and doors were used to cover the openings. Although larger than most homestead houses, this was essentially the same type of construction.

Barns and Outbuildings

> 1 dwelling, 30 by 32', four rooms, constructed mostly of drift material
> 1 good square-log barn, 32 by 32', double floor
> 1 stable, 16 by 30', shake building
> 1 woodshed, 12 by 14', shake building
> 1 wagon shed, 20 by 20', shake building
> 1 dairy, 12 by 12', shake building
> 1 root house, 12 by 18', shake building
> 1 poultry house, 10 by 12', shake building
> 25 acres under cultivation, partly timothy
> 14,565 rails in fencing (the captain thought 10,000 more accurate)
> A few 6-year-old fruit trees
> Value of improvements—$1,800
>
> —Captain G. Burton, Inventory of George Jakle's Homestead, 1876

In addition to dwellings, the homesteads of the early Euro-American settlers contained several structures that were specialized for their use on the farm in 1875 (see Appendix 23: *Homestead Improvements*). The most significant structure, both in terms of size and relative importance, was the barn. Often barns were built before families erected a more permanent home (i.e. were still living in log cabins). Many of these barns were constructed with timber frame systems, which consisted of large (8"x10" to 12"x16") posts and beams joined together with either lapping or mortise-and-tenon joints. In traditional timber frame construction, individual sections of the structure, composed of sills, posts, girts, and braces, were framed together to form "bents," which were then placed at regular intervals to form bays. Joists, collars, and rafters were then added to form the roof structure. In early island structures, however, posts were often placed in the ground, and then joined and braced to girts to form the bays of the barn. If the girts were not long enough, particularly for the spans that covered the middle bays forming the threshing areas, they were lapped. Queen posts were then mortised and tenoned and braced at approximately third spans to support the purlins, which in turn supported the roof rafters. This created a large open space for hay storage and grain processing: bays ranged from 12 to 15 feet on the side and heights of 15-18 feet to the girt, and open above all the way to the rafters.

On Blind Bay on Shaw Island is an intriguing example of what appears to be a cross-cultural barn that utilizes several building traditions. The farmstead was the original site of a settlement of a family of Cowichan Indians. The French-Canadian hunter Julien Lawrence married Terice Seymour, a daughter of the family, and settled and farmed there.[84] Hans Christensen, who applied for a homestead there in 1882, noted on the application a "cedar post barn 57 x 60, good cedar shake roof $150." The existing barn, which probably dates from Julien and Terice's tenure, is 25 by 60 feet, oriented east-west lengthwise, with 16-foot sheds on the two (north and south) long sides, thus forming an overall width of 57 feet. The structure consists of 12"-diameter poles that have been barked and burnt; four of these support a beam-with-timber frame, braced king posts, which, together with the 20-foot-high gable end posts, support the ridge beam. The plan is that of an "English" barn, with a 12-foot-wide side-entry drive-through. To the west of this was probably the mow, where the hay was stored, while to the east was an indent that, together with the drive,

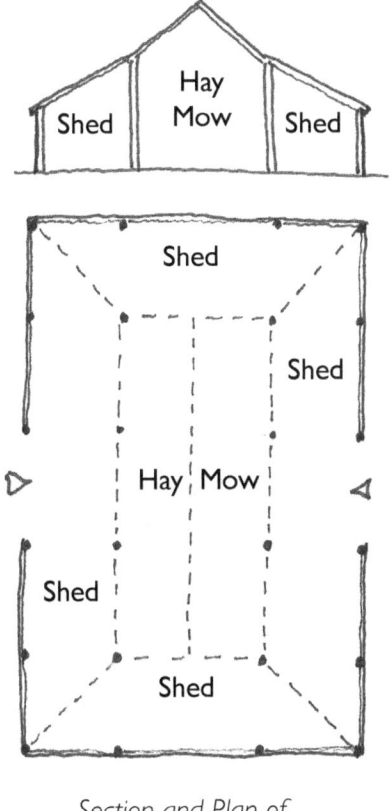

Section and Plan of Center Drive Pole Barn

formed an area approximately 21 by 25 feet for threshing. To the east of this may have been grain storage bins. The exterior siding consists of 8-12"-wide riven cedar planks, nailed vertically to the girts with hand-forged nails. Overall, what this suggests is the plan and form of an English barn with the construction materials and methods of a Coast Salish longhouse.

Other homestead barns were less grand, and probably of a standard "pole" construction. This meant that the structure was post and beam, consisting of tall, barked and charred cedar posts that carried the beams that supported the roof. In contrast to later, lofted barns, the hay was loosely piled on the ground at one end of the barn, while the other areas were kept free for threshing or animals. In the historical records, there are a handful of dimensions, indicating relatively small structures: 16 by 24 feet; 18 by 21 feet; 20 by 36 feet; and 24 by 30 feet. A few are described as "cedar log," "cedar post," or "post barn with sheds." The latter indicates a common feature: adding lean-to sheds to one or several of the sides of the barn for both more area and structural stability.

An important structure on the farm was the root house for storing root crops such as carrots, potatoes, and turnips. As noted earlier, Belle Vue Sheep Farm had at least two cellars or "pits" (also called "root houses"). Most likely located in the fields themselves, these structures were dug into the ground, lined with logs, and had a log roof covered with dirt or turf placed on top. One homestead application mentions a "root house & cellar," another a "cedar log root house 9 x12 feet," and a third a "root house 14 x 16 feet."

Although it is not clear as to when the Norway or brown rat (*Mus decumanus*) arrived in the islands, farmers certainly needed buildings to secure their grain from rats, mice, and other vermin. Early granaries were constructed of logs—either in the *pièce sur pièce poteaux et pièce collisante* style used by the Hudson's Bay Company or Scandinavian-derived horizontal construction with corner notching. Lila Hannah Firth described the building where they stored grain as "… a good rat proof granary made of hand hewn logs, plastered well inside."[85] Later granaries were constructed of frame lumber. Whether log or frame, the form of the building was universal: rectangular in plan with a gable roof, a lack of windows or other openings, and the distinctive feature of being raised on wood piers, usually cedar or fir rounds, often several feet high.

Other important outbuildings and sheds included dairies, hog houses, poultry houses, storehouses, smokehouses, stables, woodsheds, and workshops. Most outbuildings were constructed of either log or frame construction, but their form varied little in relation to use. Both stables and woodsheds could be more open, of course, but the others would be enclosed. Poultry houses were mainly used for chickens, although it is possible that other birds were kept there. Belle Vue Sheep Farm had a hen house located somewhere in the complex of farm structures near the Establishment compound. Many homesteaders mentioned one or several chicken houses on their homesteads; Elihu Fowler (1888, Shaw) had four. In general, poultry houses ranged in size from 10 by 10 feet to 12 by 16 feet.

One structure that was undoubtedly on every homestead, but rarely mentioned in the records, is the privy or outhouse. The witness for one homestead application mentions a "hewed cedar log…privy." We can assume that most of these structures were small: examples from a later period (1890s) are frame and measure approximately 4¼ by 6½ feet by 8 foot 3 inches tall for a 'two-holer.'

Improvements

Besides structures, homesteaders also improved the land through clearing, ditching, fencing, and planting. The task of clearing has been described in the chapter on *Place*. The homestead was generally divided into two cultivated spaces: a kitchen garden and orchard located near the dwelling, and fields that were cleared and planted in a grass seed such as Timothy and clover. The former was used to produce subsistence crops—regular vegetables and staples such as potatoes and turnips—and fruit as a cash crop, while the latter was used to pasture livestock such as cattle, hogs, and sheep.

Many areas were either bottomland or marshy areas, which had rich, productive soils that first needed to be drained to produce. Homesteaders dug ditches to drain off these areas, and several accounts record the number of rods of ditching, usually around 30-40 rods long (a rod is 5½ yards or 16½ feet) or 500-

660 feet long. Homesteader Hiram Hutchinson hired an Indigenous man called "Siwash Charley" to dig a ditch on his property that would later encompass present-day Lopez Village. Claus Sax Hinrichs and Matthias Paul Rethlefsen each dug ditches during the 1870s in Beaverton Valley on San Juan Island; on the proving up papers they were both described as seventy-one (271) rods [4,472 feet] in length.[86] San Juan County Commissioners did not establish formal districts for the purposes of financing ditches until the 1890s.

One of the most important elements of the farmstead were fences. Edward Todd, in his *Young Farmer's Manual* of 1860, gave the advice, "Wherever a farm may be located, or whatever may be its production, fence, fence, fence, is the first, the intermediate, and the last consideration in the whole routine of the operations of the farm." The farmstead as it developed in the islands followed the evolution of many farms in the western United States, where different fence types were used for different applications. Often this resulted in what Philip Dole has been referred to as a "trinity" of fenced spaces: closest to the house, a yard with surrounding wood picket fence; beyond that, barn yards and paddocks

Fences at Firth Farm (Belle Vue Sheep Farm/American Camp) (courtesy of San Juan Island National Historical Park)

with post-and-board fences for the close confining of livestock; and then the ubiquitous worm fence surrounding the fields. As we have seen in the chapter on *Place*, "An Act Concerning Fences," enacted by the Legislature in 1869, specified three basic types of fences as lawful in the Territory of Washington: post and rail (with either planks or rails); worm, and ditch and pole; or board or rail.[87] Apparently, picket fences, used to enclose smaller areas of land, were not considered.[88]

The first type of fence built on San Juan Island consisted of split cedar rails alternately stacked in a zig-zag pattern that earned the nickname "worm" or "snake" fence. Local wood was plentiful and needed to be cleared to create cropland. Cedar was chosen for fence rails because of its durability—it has a high resistance to rot—as well as the ease with which it can be split. Split rail fences were usually constructed ten rails high, with two "stakes" or rails driven into the ground at an angle to secure the corners; top rails, called "riders," were then laid upon these stakes. If the fence bed were five feet wide, and each panel of rails 10 feet long, then the actual linear distance covered would be eight feet.[89] According to 1855 Territorial of Washington law, worm fences:

> *...shall have not less than four feet worm to rails of ten feet in length (and if greater length, in that proportion,) shall be four feet high, well staked and ridered upon that, according to practice. Below the third rail from the ground, no crack or space of more than five inches shall intervene, and below two feet in height, there shall be no crack or intervening space more than seven inches, and the whole height of said fence shall not be less than five feet.*[90]

The 1869 Law adopted basically the same proscription, except that the two lower spaces could not be more than 4 inches, and that the top space between the riders could not be more than 16 inches.[91] It took about two miles of zig-zag fence to enclose 160 acres, the standard farm allotment under the Homestead Act of 1862. This would comprise approximately 15,000 rails consisting of 10 rails per 10-foot section or panel. A two-person crew could build about 100 panels per day, in contrast to four people completing 35-40 sections of post-and-rail fence.[92]

Before the availability of sawmills, farmers would spend winter months splitting logs into manageably sized and weighted fence-building material. According to mid-nineteenth century sources, splitting 100 rails was a good day's work, while "a strong farmer" could split 200 a day. Diaries and journals of island farmers provide clear testimony to the many hours of labor spent on fences. For example, San Juan Valley farmer Thomas Fleming recorded in the month of January 1869, "Wether [sic] has been fine some rain so as we could work all the mounth[sic] I have split 1,100 rails and helped James with his fencing." On January 12th of the next year he noted only 176 split, but in the month of February ("wether blustrey, some fine days, little snow"), 1873, he split some 900 rails.[93] At an average of 200/day, it would take 75 days to enclose 160 acres, so fencing took up a major portion of a farmer's time and labor.

Perhaps one of the most telling documents concerning split rail fences consists of an inventory taken in 1876 by a U.S. Army Captain from American Camp. The captain, frustrated with what he considered to be the trespass of a homestead claimant on the military reserve, decided to itemize all of the improvements and then make a settlement. He and his lieutenant recorded some 14,565 rails in fencing (although the captain thought 10,000 more accurate).[94] According to the 15,000-rail figure supplied above, this would almost enclose 160 acres if it were laid out in a square.

When sawmills became more prevalent, sawn lumber was used along with cedar fence posts for fencing. Often the imperfect boards (with rough corners and/or some bark left intact) were used in fencing, while the best boards were reserved for building construction. The 1869 Law specified:

> *...post and rail, or plank fences, five feet high, made of sound posts, five inches in diameter, set substantially in the ground, not more than ten feet apart, with four planks not less than one inch thick and six inches wide, securely fastened by nails or otherwise; said planks not more than nine inches apart.*

According to this law, post and rail fences "with posts not more than ten feet apart, and rails not less than four inches wide, (five of them)," were specified as "made in all other respects the same."[95] This type of fencing was most often used for paddocks and other types of livestock holding areas. To make a stronger fence that could hold livestock in, such as paddocks and other types of holding areas, split cedar rails could also be nailed to cedar fence posts.

Rough, riven cedar or fir pickets were used for the taller fences surrounding orchards. These fences kept deer as well as livestock out. The pickets were usually attached to top and bottom rails nailed to cedar posts. Picket fences were costlier: for instance, in his application for a homestead in 1888, Theodore Tharald noted under improvements "75 rods Picket Fence $100," as compared to "150 rods rail fence $140." Lila Hannah Firth, in her reminiscences "Early Life on San Juan Island," described how her father built a picket fence surrounding their house in response to her mother complaining about unexpected guests (particularly Indians) showing up in their house uninvited:

> *He found a cedar tree, with good splitting qualities in it, down it came with the help of a well ground ax & was sawed into 4 foot lengths, split in strips, & rived into pickets. Posts of that fence were also split out of that tree, & in a very short time it seemed to me, Father had a picket fence all around our house, a foot board around the bottom of the fence, which when finished made the fence 5 feet high.*[96]

James Hannah also made gates for the fence, and then bought a bulldog so that anyone not known to the family would not dare enter the enclosure. This was probably the same style of fence that Patrick Beigin built around his house and orchard, as related later in the *Society and Governance* chapter. Griffin had noted in his *Post Journals* that he had his men cut willows to put around his garden fence to keep hens and other poultry out—a technique that was derived from the older English wattle or woven fence consisting of pales driven into the ground and interwoven with branches or twigs.[97]

Fancier, sawn lumber pickets (often with the tops cut specially diamond, lozenge, and other fancy shapes) were used later to keep livestock out of residential yards. Use of these depended upon the availability of milled lumber, as well as the extra funds needed to purchase it. Although associated with yards in front of houses on town lots, where they also served to keep out livestock roaming in the streets, they can be seen in historic photographs adorning rural yards as well.

A final important improvement was a well for people, livestock, and crops. Most homestead records mention at least one well, and some several. In a letter to his relatives 'back East,' homesteader Wesley Warner described the water situation on Lopez:

> *The "running streams" are not so plentiful as we expected, but there is good water on all parts of the island; but for the house they depend on cistern water mostly and this is how they make cisterns here: They dig a hole in the ground, and it needs no boarding or walling up at all, and will fill up in the winter, and none of it will leak out, and it is soft and good as any water you ever drank. There is plenty of water for stock all over the island.*[98]

Early wells were hand-dug, some as much as 20-30 feet deep. The aim was to dig down until one reached either a clay bed or bedrock, where the water would (hopefully) be pure and plentiful.

At Mr. Griswold's house [at Blind Bay on Shaw Island], he had a few years ago, a well some 10 or 12 feet deep, which running dry, he decided to deepen. After going down a few feet a subterranean stream was tapped which filled the well so rapidly that the man digging hastily escaped, leaving his tools. The well filled to the brim and overflowed, and has run a good stream ever since. The water has a mineral taste but is quite healthful. This well is on low ground; it is 16 ft. deep, which would bring the bottom about to the level of high tide, and it is only about 80 feet back from the beach.

—J. J. Gilbert, U.S. Coast and Geodetic Survey
Descriptive Report Sheet No. 2230 (1895)

Hand-dug wells were wide, ranging from about 3 feet in diameter (room enough for a man to do the digging) up to 8 feet. Depending on the time and effort put into the homestead, they were sometimes lined with squared logs or mortared field stone, cobblestones, or brick (and later concrete), and often fenced with rails to keep the livestock from falling in. Some wells were covered with log or frame structures ("well or pump houses"), and there are a few rare instances of dwelling structures constructed over wells. Other sources of water were springs or seeps in hillsides, which were widened and lined with masonry to form cisterns; later, pipes were led from these to nearby dwellings.[99]

Dwelling

The way in which people dwell on the land and water often reflects their cultural usage. Coast Salish villages and fishing camps occupied that liminal area where the land meets the sea, with canoes beached and ready for use; villages offered kin-based communal living and working spaces while fishing camps reflected the organization of the reef netting operations. The Hudson's Bay Company had its own rules for their "Establishments," occupying strategic locations near to important resources such as pasture and adequate fresh water. Strategic location was also a defining factor in locating military encampments, which in turn reflected the hierarchy of command. The encounter of Indigenous peoples with Euro-Americans and others often led to hybrid communities based on the cross-cultural families that established them. With the imposition of a public land system that supported individual farms as a means of "improving" their claims, residences and farm structures provided the spaces to support a subsistence economy based on agriculture.

WORK

When Lyman Cutlar established his farm in the midst of a Belle Vue Sheep Farm pasture, he was surrounded by people employed in various ways of 'making a living.' He farmed, as no doubt did his wife, who was probably the one who tended the potato garden. Cutlar must have relied upon her to gather both terrestrial and marine food for their sustenance, as well as "keep house." He chose to locate on a prairie that had been kept cleared by Coast Salish cultivators of camas and then by the Hudson's Bay Company for sheep pasture. No doubt he was directly affected by the joint military occupation of the island by American and British troops. Later, Cutlar joined two others in developing the first site of the lime industry in the islands, the San Juan Lime Company. These and other occupations formed the basis for living in the islands.

Working

In order to survive in the San Juan Islands, the various groups who lived, visited, or settled there had to 'make a living' of some sort. However, as is still the case today, not all worked at a single specific job or occupation. Indigenous peoples, for instance, performed several food-related tasks while in the islands during the summer season—hunting, gathering, and fishing. Even the later, Euro-American settlers worked at several occupations: the employees at Belle Vue Sheep Farm raised sheep, grew other crops, fished, and harvested timber. American settlers did a variety of jobs: farming, hiring out to other farmers, and transporting goods and men by boat. Given this situation, when one talks about commerce in the islands, the proper approach should be to examine aspects of work, rather than actual occupations.

It is interesting to examine the United States censuses of 1860 and 1870 in regard to the category "Occupation" as well as the Manufacturing Schedule for 1870. In 1860, the census, which was limited to San Juan Island, enumerated 50 adult males and

7 adult females (and 8 male and 3 female children). Their occupations were listed as 26 farmers; 4 carpenters; 3 laborers; 2 lime burners; 2 barkeeps; and 1 gambler[!], post sutler, bookkeeper, baker, restauranteur, engineer, blacksmith, merchant, prisoner, U.S. customs, fisherman, hunter, laundress, and clerk. In addition, there were 72 military personnel, all at American Camp.

The 1870 census, which included all the "Disputed Islands," enumerated 100 adult males and 47 adult females (as well as their 135 children). They were listed as 105 farmers, 4 farm laborers, 7 shepherds, 1 sheep grower, and 1 stock raiser; two lime burning operations (one each on San Juan and Orcas) which listed between them 5 lime manufacturers, 7 quarrymen, 1 miner, 10 coopers, 3 carpenters, 5 choppers, 1 teamster, and 3 cooks, as well as at least 12 of the 19 total laborers listed; 4 fishermen; 3 merchants and 2 store clerks; 2 schoolteachers; and 1 each timber worker, sawyer, seaman, ship carpenter, and telegraph operator. Most adult women were listed as married (or single with children) and "keeping house," although one was listed as "widow; farmer" and another (married) as a laundress. Several did not have an occupation listed. Of the 68 U.S. military, 2 were officers, 1 a surgeon, and 63 were just listed as "men," although the census actually lists 93 [with 1 transfer, 3 deserted, and 1 "attached for muster pay"]. The English garrison had 102 total: 3 officers, 1 surgeon, 92 men, 4 women, and 2 children.

Before discussing each of these individual occupations, it is important to state that the most basic economic unit was the household, and that therefore there is a 'hidden' element of domestic work as well as various occupations undertaken by women and children. This was particularly the case for those households that consisted of Indigenous wives, who brought with them much of the knowledge and many of the skills for utilizing the natural resources of the islands. Many early settlers commented on the rich marine abundance especially, adopting the Coast Salish phrases "dinner awaited at one's feet at a low tide" or "when the tide is out the table is set." As Edward T. Coleman, passing through in 1869, noted: "Thus the necessities of life are easily gained; in fact, no man need starve in Washington Territory. Many of these settlers live with Indian women, and find a charm in this free and independent life which reconciles them to the discomforts of roughing it in a new country."[1] Women in particular—predominantly Indigenous, but some Euro-American—provided essential services in maintaining households, gathering native plants and seafood, fishing and hunting for food, as well as cultivating kitchen gardens and potato fields, and raising domestic livestock such as chickens, cattle, sheep, and hogs. Children took on the work of adults Thomas Fleming, for example, states simply in *Told by the Pioneers*: "Like other boys of the community, I assumed work of a man while still of boyish age. I assisted the neighbors and worked out at various kinds of employment."[2] So, it must be kept in mind, while discussing the various enumerated "occupations," that this does not present a complete picture of the islands' economy.

Indigenous Seasons

> Some foods could be gathered at any time, others only in season; some could be gathered at many places and others only a few, but for the Straits peoples nearly everything had its proper time and place. Times and places were more or less fixed by the whole year's schedule of activities, and women's gathering and men's fishing and hunting were made to meet each other's requirements.
>
> —Wayne Suttles, Economic Life of the Coast Salish of Haro and Rosario Straits (1951)

Local Coast Salish groups had seasonal cycles of gathering, fishing, and hunting, based on the lunar year, which has 13 moons, with the lunar cycles of 28 days each. This cyclical system has been explained by Saanich Dave Elliott, Sr., in his *Saltwater People*, and by Swinomish tribal members Jamie Donatuto and Larry Campbell (with others). It is well articulated on the *Samish 13 Moons* story map of the Samish Tribe.[3]

The Samish articulate the year *Xws7ámesh Schel7óneng* according to the conventional four seasons, emphasizing the lunar months:

- *Chents'ólheng* (Winter): *Sch'elkwásen* Moon of putting paddles away (November), *S7elálexw* Moon of the Elders (December), *Ngíngene7* Moon of Children/Beginnings (mid-December to mid-January), *Wéxes* Moon of the frog (mid-February to mid-March).
- *Chenqw'íles* (Spring): *Pexsíseng*, Moon of Blossoming (March), *Sxwán7elh*, Moon of Little Bullheads (April), *Penáxweng*, Moon of Gathering Seaweed and Camas (May).
- *Chenséqi7* (Summer): *Chenelíle7* Moon of the Salmonberry (June), *Chenséqi7* Moon of the Sockeye (July), *Chent'áqe7* Moon of the Salal (August).
- *Píxwel* Season (Fall): *Chenq'échqs* Moon of the Coho (September), *Chenkw'ól7exw* Moon of the Chums (October), *Xwis7elánexw* Moon of the Howling Winds and Shaking Leaves (November).

Saanich elder Dave Elliott, Sr., begins *Saltwater People* with WEXES, the first moon of Spring, when the frogs come out of hibernation. It is the time when the herring arrive, and things begin to grow. SXANEL, or April, is named after the bullhead, a time for clam and plant gatherings. PEXSISEN, at the end of May, marked the time when the Saanich would venture out from their winter villages to their traditional gathering places in the San Juans, harvesting camas and gathering eggs, as well as fishing for codfish and halibut. With PENAWEN (June), the days were getting warmer, and the men prepared for fishing. CENŦEKI marked the time when the salmon runs began with the sockeye (ŦEKI); bullrushes and cedar bark would be collected for house, mat, and rope making. Elliott called the whole summer season CENQALES, with the middle part CENHENEN, when the pinks or humpbacks (HENEN) arrived; at this time marine mammals such as seals were also harvested. CENTAWEN, around September, was when the coho salmon, or ŦAWEN, arrived. By the time the dog or chum salmon (QOLEW) came, it was getting into PEKELANEW. With WESELANEW, "the shaker of leaves," Fall was coming on; the Saanich would catch ducks on their flights through the islands. When SJELCASEN arrived, the winter storms were beginning to blow, and the people settled down in their winter villages. During the long winter moon, *SISET*, which means "old ones," elders would relate stories, and winter dances were held in the longhouses. The last moon of this calendar was *NINENE*, "offspring" or "young ones," indoor activities continued, with some venturing forth to duck hunt.[4]

Gathering

The Coast Salish harvested a variety of marine invertebrates throughout the Salish Sea including mollusks, crustaceans, and echinoderms. Shell middens, ethnographic data, and tradition all indicate that Indigenous peoples have been harvesting shellfish in the Salish Sea for thousands of years. While occupying a harvesting or dwelling site, people deposited shells and other trash onto piles near their village or encampment, often by gathering them in baskets in the longhouses which were emptied behind the houses. These refuse piles are called middens. The shell midden at *Pe'pi'ow'elh* (English Camp), on the shores of Garrison Bay on San Juan Island, dating from around 1,000 years ago, is eight feet deep in some places, indicating an extensive period of use.

While it is a common assumption, based on modern-day recreational harvesting, that gathering along the shorelines and in the tidal zone is simple and straightforward, in fact it often requires an intimate knowledge of complex microenvironments. The occurrence of tides and the potential danger of currents and rogue waves, the specific location of shell beds and other resource areas, and in some cases the actual manipulation of the environment to foster certain organisms were all important factors. Shellfish could be gathered at any time, but the Coast Salish preferred summer. Harvesters—usually women—favored going to one location and processing large quantities of shellfish there, rather than moving around. Families often claimed ("owned") specific harvesting locations and handed down their use traditions through kinship lines. They could also grant access or rights to these places; along with use, however, came the obligation of stewardship.

Gathering was done either while walking along the shoreline at low tide or paddling in a canoe in shallow water. Shellfish harvested included barnacles, cockles, mussels, oysters, and scallops, as well as other marine organisms such as chitons, sea cucumbers, sea urchins, snails, and whelks. Clam types included bent-nose, butter, horse, little-neck (steamer), sand, and soft-shell. Cockles, edible mussels, native oysters, and sea cucumbers were picked up directly from the exposed shore or while wading in the shallow water. Barnacles, chitons, sea urchins, and snails were picked or pried from rocks. Clams were dug from sandy or gravelly flats, usually with a strong piece of wood called by the Lummi *skalax*. All of these were washed and placed in open-weave baskets to allow for drainage while transporting to the place for cooking (see Appendix: *Edible Marine Invertebrates*).[5]

> *They took the largest rocks that were in the clam bed and moved them out to extreme low water marks, setting them in rows like a fence along the edge of the water. This makes clam digging very easy compared to what it had previously been because there are only small pebbles and sand to dig in.*
>
> —Bernhard J. Stern, The Lummi Indians of Northwest Washington (1934)

There is a growing body of evidence of the practice of shellfish (specifically clam) "gardening" in the northern portions of the Salish Sea, such as near Quadra Island, as well as further north, to the Kwakwaka'wakw Islands west of the mouths of Knight and Kingcome Inlets in British Columbia. The Coast Salish modified existing clam beds, creating an extended tidal beach by forming a line of large rocks that held back the sand and gravel of the clam bed. It has also been suggested that harvesters transplanted favorite species of shellfish into the new beds for cultivation. The only known local example of this practice is mention of a family at West Sound on *Elelung* (Orcas) that cultivated a butter-clam bed. After Euro-Americans arrived in the islands, there is an instance of the American Camp sutler, Edward Warbass, helping Indigenous oyster gatherers by reseeding the oyster reefs in Griffin Bay.

OYSTER CULTURE
Its Beginning in the County

Prior to 1860—he [Captain Warbass] has no idea for how long a period—there were a great many native oysters in a small lagoon near the site of the American military camp on San Juan Island and also a great many in a small bay on the north end of Lopez island, long since filled up. The winter of 1860–61 was so cold that these shallow lagoons froze to the bottom and the oysters were all killed. During the summer of '61 Capt. Warbass sent some Indians to the Samish flats to get a supply of seed oysters and they brought over two or more sacks which were planted in the large lagoon in Griffin bay, about four miles from Argyle. The experiment was successful and for many years native oysters have been plentiful there and large quantities of them have been taken away by the Indians and sold.

The San Juan Islander, June 5, 1902

The Coast Salish used a variety of methods for cooking shellfish. Sea urchins, as well as some varieties of clams, were eaten raw. Other varieties of clams were steamed on a bed of hot rocks in a pit. Some varieties were first steamed open, and then strung on a stick that was then placed next to a fire for roasting. They were then strung on cedar bark line and placed in a sheltered place to dry. Strings of dried clams could be used for food later in the year or for trade for other items.

Gathering native plants for food was a significant part of the Coast Salish economy (see Appendix: *Edible Plants*). Several types of fruits and berries were gathered by Indigenous women, as well as Euro-Americans. They were both eaten fresh and dried for later consumption. To dry them, berries were placed in clumps on a 2½-foot long stick framework covered with dried maple leaves, and the resulting cakes were stored in "little crates" made from alder bark, as well as storage baskets, such as those found at the archaeological site of Ozette, which contained an average of 15.4 liters.[6] Jane Williams testified in *Duwamish et al. vs. United States* that there were "…huckleberries and savage berries, we call it, caps [Blackcap?], thimble berries, salmon berries, and the easter flowers, they have berries, blue berries [blue elderberry?], and they eat that. Then there is an elder-tree berry they eat." Upon further questioning, she mentioned blackberries, wild strawberries, and salal berries, as well as "the berries that Indians make ice cream from" [soapberry].[7] In the same court case, Cecilia Knowlsen mentioned cranberries: "It was big lakes all over, you know, and cranberries."[8] The native cranberry grew on several of the San Juan Islands in bogs. In his reminiscences James Tulloch mentions them on the slopes of Mount Constitution on Orcas Island and the Township and Range surveyors noted cranberries in the Sportsman's Lake vicinity on their 1874 map of San Juan Island.[9] In *Told by the Pioneers* Hannah Sandwith Jensen, daughter of Euro-American settlers, recollected that the Indians came to Garrison Bay for salal berries.[10] Wayne Suttles in his ethnographic work also recorded the use of serviceberry, black hawthorn, crabapple, Indian plum, small rose, gooseberry, Oregon grape, red elderberry, and kinnikinic (bearberry).[11] At English Camp on San Juan Island, Julie Stein wrote that archaeological investigations found charred seeds of serviceberry, kinnikinnick, Oregon grape, salal/huckleberry, rose, thimbleberry, and elderberry in almost every deposit in the shell midden.[12]

In other parts of the region, salal berries formed an essential part of the winter diet. Salal berries were harvested by taking whole branchlets—thus pruning them for enhanced cultivation and the next year's harvest—with about 10 berries per branchlet. Ethnobotanist Nancy Turner has calculated that there are 2,000 dried salal berries per liter; with 35.34 liters per bushel, this would equal 70,680 dried berries per bushel. Based on accounts from the Nuxalt, at the picking rate of about 1 liter per 32 minutes, a group of ten women could harvest about 12 bushels in 2-3 days. Given an estimated nutritional value of four calories and one gram of carbohydrates per berry, a bushel could provide up to 3,388,040 calories and 845,760 grams of carbohydrates. At an average requirement of 1,600 calories and 200 grams of carbohydrates per day, each family could be sustained with 4-5 baskets through the three months of winter during which they did not have access to fresh roots, stems, and bulbs.[13]

During the Spring, women gathered sprouts and stems from horsetail, thimbleberry, salmonberry, cow parsnip, and dock. Labrador (or Hudson's Bay) tea (*Rhododendron groenlandicum*), "a spicy shrub locally known as continental tea" according to James Tulloch, was used by Indigenous peoples and Euro-American settlers alike for a hot beverage.[14] Indigenous women also dug for wild roots, including onions (both nodding and Hooker's), "carrot," brake fern, tiger lily, and rice-root. Wapato (arrowroot), although mentioned as a local food source by several informants, was most likely collected on the mainland, not in the islands.

The most important root crop for the Coast Salish, as well as other Indigenous groups in the Pacific Northwest, was camas, a member of the lily family. Both great camas and small or purple camas grow in the San Juans, particularly in south-facing, well-drained soils. When harvesting, care had to be taken to distinguish the bulbs of these edible varieties, which have bluish or purplish blossoms, from poison camas (*Toxicoscordion venenosum*), which has white blossoms, so gathering most often occurred during the months of May, June, and July after the plants had blossomed. Women, who were the principal gatherers, would divide the beds—preferably in rocky areas with shallow soils—into rough sections and turn over the turf to reveal the bulbs. They used sticks pointed at one end and having a cross-handle on the other, which would facilitate the tool being used as a lever. They would return to favorite plots, which were sometimes marked with lines of stones, year after year; on May 15, 1854, Charles Griffin recorded in his *Post Journal* that "Klallams have arrived from 'Kamass' picking." When William J. Warren and Dr. C. B. R.

Salish Woman Digging Bulbs
(Washington State University, Washington Digital Archives)

Kennerly of the North West Boundary Commission were exploring the northern portion of San Juan Island they noted that "on the hills we saw in different places cobble stones placed in lines about 100 feet long" and later, on Stuart Island, they found more lines of stones, where "the slope of the mountain we were upon, facing towards the south, had been dug up a great deal by Indians gathering kamass roots."[15] The use of these delineated beds was traditionally handed down through maternal kinship lines. After harvest, the area was often burnt over to ensure the open prairie that makes for optimum camas habitat.

Camas was prized for its nutritional value and sweetness. The sweetness resulted from the conversion of carbohydrates in the form of inulin to fructose during cooking. The camas bulbs were roasted in pits and then stored in cattail bags (or, later, potato sacks) for use in the winter. Evidence of both digging sticks (a bone handle) and roasting sites (a large depression) were uncovered during Dr. Julie Stein's 1983-1991 excavations at English Camp, San Juan Island.

> You dig a hole about two feet deep and about four feet across. In this you lay fine dry wood, then heavy sticks parallel across it, then rocks across the heavy sticks. Now light the fire. When the rocks get red hot this means get ready. When the rocks drop down, take the ashes out and level the ground with a good hard stick. Then lay on kelp blades, salal branches, sword ferns, madrona bark, and the camas. With the camas, put all sorts of sweet bushes to infect it. The madrona bark and alder bark make it red. You must fix it so that no dirt gets in and yet leave it all full of holes. Leave a hole at the top and when it is all covered pour in more than a bucket of fresh water. When the water seeps through to the rocks, it steams up. Put grass on the top, then about four inches of dirt, then build a fire on top of that. Leave it all night until the next afternoon. After steaming the bulbs have to be dried a little before storing so they won't spoil.
>
> —*Saanich Woman in Wayne Suttles,* Economic Life of the Coast Salish of Haro and Rosario Straits *(1951)*[16]

The transition to agriculture, as it is defined in modern terms, was gradual, for, as described, the Coast Salish already managed the cultivation and harvesting of some of their resources, such as the case of the prepared clam beds on Orcas and the camas plots just described. The transition to a cultivated root crop—the potato—was not as abrupt as some have imagined. The potato was first introduced into the Northwest at Fort Astoria (1811) and later cultivation spread through Hudson's Bay Company forts. Fort Langley, established on the Fraser River in 1827, was probably the source for potatoes in this region. Groups of the Coast Salish who occupied the San Juan Islands readily adopted the potato, and were growing it as early as 1842.

Because of their cultural tradition of growing camas, women were the primary cultivators of potatoes within the Coast Salish groups. They used traditional methods such as digging with sticks, gathering in baskets, and roasting in pits, to cultivate and process the tubers. They even established and defined plots using low walls formed by roots, weeds, and other refuse from cultivating the plot. Because Coast Salish women married outside their kinship group, and resided at their husband's place, potatoes were spread throughout the region through women's relocation through marriage. Similar distribution probably occurred through the frequent cohabitation and marriage of Coast Salish women with the predominantly single Euro-American men who were newcomers to the area.

The Coast Salish also raised woolly dogs, which were a breed separate from village hunting dogs, for their pelage. Women would shear the hair of the dogs with shell razors (later metal knives) and combine it with fireweed tufts, mountain-goat hair (from the mainland), and other materials for weaving blankets. The dogs were sometimes sequestered on smaller islands, away from the village dogs, to keep their breed pure, and the women were responsible for paddling out with food—usually salmon—for their 'flock'. Coast Salish looms and weaving techniques were culturally distinctive. When the Hudson's Bay Company came into the area, workers introduced woolen blankets as trade for salmon and other native goods. After the introduction of Euro-American woolens and sheep, Coast Salish women gradually

Paul Kane, "Clal-lum Women Weaving a Blanket" Showing Woolly Dog (Washington State University, Washington Digital Archives)

abandoned woolly-dog culture and adapted to both spinning and weaving sheep wool or using manufactured woolen fabric and clothing.

> They have a peculiar breed of small dogs with long hair of a brownish black and a clear white. These dogs are bred for clothing purposes. The hair is cut off with a knife and mixed with goosedown and a little white earth, with a view to curing the feathers.
> —Paul Kane, Wanderings of an Artist among the Indians of North America (1859)

When the Hudson's Bay Company first established Belle Vue Sheep Farm on San Juan Island in 1853, employees lived and farmed on the open area ("Home Prairie") on the south end of the island where American Camp is today. From there, they established a series of sheep grazing sites on other open areas. The introduction of sheep, cattle, and particularly hogs destroyed the camas-growing beds in these areas, which had been kept clear through seasonal burning by the Coast Salish. Early accounts indicate that settlers on the mainland deliberately fed their hogs on camas; no doubt the Belle Vue Sheep Farm swineherds did likewise.

Logically, when Americans first began to settle (or squat, as the English would soon claim) in the islands in the mid- to late 1850s, they also chose lands that were treeless and therefore more easily cultivatable. One of them, Lyman Cutlar, settled on part of the Company's "most valuable sheep run" and, together with his Coast Salish wife, planted potatoes. Thus, it was that a Hudson's Bay Company pig was shot while rooting in an American's—and most probably Coast Salish's—potato patch, precipitating the "Pig War."

Hunting and Trapping

The Coast Salish hunted and gathered on their seasonal visits to the islands. Originally, hunting of both birds such as ducks and mammals such as deer was done with both nets and bow-and-arrow. Later, guns were introduced by Euro-Americans. According to Philip Drucker, in his *Indians of the Northwest Coast*, "spears and arrows were almost wholly out of use by the Tlingits by 1805," and "everyone" at Nootka, on the west side of Vancouver Island, had firearms by 1812.[17] Certainly, most of the Indigenous groups mentioned in the historic literature of this period had rifles.

Squamish Woman Spinning Wool
(Washington State University, Washington Digital Archives)

> *Game of several sorts is plentiful. Deer can be had whenever wanted. Some of the post go out and shoot them, or Indians bring them. Wild fowl is abundant. There were hanging up in the larder of the kitchen, geese, ducks, the common wild duck & the canvas backed, teal & wild muscovy. A fine wild goose can be had for half a dollar if you buy, later they will be much cheaper.*
>
> —Anglican Bishop George Hills, Diary (1860)[18]

Ducks were often netted in their customary flyways. Thirty-foot high nets, constructed of willow bark, nettle, or imported grass twine, and ranging in length up to a hundred feet, were strung off the ground or water between two poles. When the ducks flew into the mesh during the twilight hours of dawn or dusk, the hunters stationed at the poles at either end lowered the nets and the birds were clubbed by a third person either on the ground or, in the case of a net strung above water, in a canoe.[19] Several local place names reflect the sites of these activities: Pole Island in Mosquito Pass, where nets were strung across the narrow waterway to Henry Island, and Pole Pass between Crane Island and the point on Orcas Island between Deer Harbor and West Sound. Ducks were also either speared or shot with arrows at night from canoes lighted by fires; later, after the introduction of firearms, they were shot with guns.[20]

> *Having passed San Juan, and steering through a narrow passage near to Orcas Island, we observed a long pole with a crosspiece to it at the top. It is the native arrangement for catching wild-fowl. A net is spread on the cross-poles, fires are lighted at night, the wild—fowl seeking at this time their food, and not seeing the net, fly against it with such force that they drop down, and are seized by the Indians before they have time to recover themselves.*
>
> —Edward Coleman, Mountaineering in the Pacific (1869)[21]

"Four Remarkable, Supported Poles, in Port Townsend"
Captain George Vancouver, A Voyage of Discovery to the North Pacific Ocean and Around the World (1984)

Although there were elk in the islands in early prehistory, apparently there were few left upon Euro-American arrival, and the primary large game animal was deer. Bucks were hunted in the Spring and early Summer and does in the Fall when each was at its fattest. Deer were taken by nets and snares (and in some cases, staked pits) located in their customary pathways. In earlier times they were shot with bow-and-arrow; later, with guns. A common technique was to drive the deer into either ponds or the ocean, where they could be easily approached and shot.[22] When white settlers first came to the Olga area on Orcas in the 1860s, they named it Stockade Bay after the remnants of a stockade or barrier at the mouth of the bay; some have suggested that this was used to corral deer on the tidal flats for easy slaughter.[23]

Hunting continued after Euro-American contact and settlement of the islands. Edward Coleman, travelling through the islands in 1869, stated that "So plentiful is game that an hour's hunting suffices to catch a deer weighing from 75 to 150 pounds."[24] Several men made their living as hunters. Dr. C. B. R. Kennerly, along with the American survey crew of the North West Boundary Commission, ran across a group of Coast Salish off Decatur Island:

> *On a neighboring point we saw some Indians & saw a small canoe pull out from shore, & we arrived along side of it just as the Natives had captured a deer that, frightened by the dogs, had attempted escape by swimming to one of the small islands in the Macedonian Crescent."*[25]

They turned out to be Swinomish who had already bagged two deer earlier that morning:

> *Upon rounding Decatur Id. we saw a party of Swimamish[sic] Indians who were out on a deer hunt: Two hunters were in a small canoe, and had four deer in it, which they had shot, and as we rowed past them they were hauling in the fifth deer which they had killed while it was swimming over from one little island to another.*[26]

In Kennerly's formal report, he said that: "The island [Decatur] being well stocked with deer is constantly resorted to by the Indians for the purpose of hunting. Like other islands in the vicinity it is claimed by several tribes, the Lummis, Swinamish[sic], and Clalms [sic] all of whom hunt upon it in mutual peace." Kennerly's report also noted the presence of four men "living temporarily" on the eastern shore of Lopez Island, "engaged in hunting." French Canadians or Métis hunted deer in the islands, both for the military at Fort Victoria and the railroad survey crews on the mainland. The Hudson's Bay Company stationed four men at what would come to be known as Deer Harbor on Orcas to supply venison to the Fort. These men included James Bradshaw and Louis Cayou. William Moore, another Hudson's Bay Company deer hunter, later settled on Orcas at Olga, as did Charles Shattuck, at Eastsound. French Canadian Julien Lawrence first came to Shaw Island to hunt deer for the railroad crews working on the mainland.[27] Bishop Hills noted that the "French Canadian half breed" deer hunters Louis and Antoine he encountered in San Juan Valley took their venison to Victoria, where they sold it for four pence half-penny a pound.[28]

Rachel Hyland Ross, who taught school on Lopez Island during this period, noted:

> *Frequently as we walked to or from school we saw deer among the brakes or ferns. There were many on the island at that time. I lived with a young half-breed woman, a splendid cook and scrupulously clean. She had several admirers among the young men of the district and it was their custom to hang a haunch of venison on our door knob on their return from hunting.*[29]

Edward Coleman observed that deer "skins are sufficient to keep the settlers in tobacco and flour until they have cleared the ground for potatoes and grain."[30] "Addie" Chadwick recollected that when her father used to walk from his homestead at Watmough Head on the south end of Lopez Island to Hutchinson's near present Lopez Village, he would hunt deer, to trade as venison at the store.[31]

One method of shooting deer favored by farmers and orchardists was hunting at night. W. R. Griffin, in *Told by the Pioneers*, related:

> *When they first began hunting on Orcas Island with a lantern, it proved quite an improvement over the old way of shining with a pitch jack. The pitch jack was a home made affair, a heavy basket made of wire or thin iron bands. This was fastened with a crooked pole about six feet long and filled with pitch, lighted and the pole carried on the shoulder. This was not a successful method, being extremely dangerous in dry weather. The falling pitch would set fire to the orchards and woods. Balls of rags saturated with kerosene were also used in the early days of fire hunting.*[32]

In hunting with lanterns, as 1869 visitor Edward Coleman explained, the deer "come down to the shore to lick the salt off the stones, and are so thoroughly spell-bound by the lights that they easily fall victims to the hunters."[33] The purpose of this type of hunting was not only to provide meat for the table, but also to rid the orchards and crops of deer as a pest.

One of the prime reasons that the Hudson's Bay Company came to the Northwest Coast in the first place was fur trading. Company parties trapped and traded furs throughout the region, and there is evidence that this also occurred in the San Juans. The presence of beaver at the time is evident from Charles Griffin's mention of the "Riviere Castor" [Beaver Stream] (probably the watercourse located to the north of "Port L'Enfer" [modern-day Portland Fair]) and has survived in the place name of Beaverton Valley. In *Told by the Pioneers* Archibald Fleming recalled that there were many elk and beaver when the Company was still on the island.[34] Bishop Hills, while visiting the island in 1860, noted that the aforementioned "French Canadian half breed" hunters Louis and Antoine caught beaver in addition to deer, and inspected both a beaver dam and the skin of one of the animals shot by Louis.[35]

Archibald Fleming claimed that quail—specifically California mountain—had been introduced to San Juan Island by E. D. Warbass and Gus Hoffmeister from Victoria, at $5.00 a dozen.[36] Lila Hannah Firth recalled that her brothers trapped quail "by the dozens" and shipped them via sloop to Victoria, where apparently, the boys made enough money to carry around twenty-dollar gold pieces.[37] Mary L. Iotte wrote that the children of Freeman and Louisa Iotte earned spending money by trapping quail on Orcas Island; they used figure four traps and received three dollars per dozen.[38] (A figure four trap is basically a deadfall apparatus in which a simple configuration of sticks—one baited—upon being triggered by the prey eating the bait, leads to the fall of a weight that captures or kills the animal.)

Fishing

Indigenous peoples have been fishing in the Salish Sea for millennia (see Appendix: *Fishes and other Marine Seafood*). Fishing salmon, in particular, has been said to be the defining cultural trait of the Indigenous peoples of the Salish Sea, "The People of the Salmon," although it was also central to the culture and economy of other groups in the Pacific Northwest. As mentioned in the introductory discussion of the Thirteen Moons calendar, the Coast Salish designated different times of the year according to the salmon available during that time; for example, the Saanich named the months of July, August, and September for the types of salmon harvested then: *hananɛ'n*, "humpbacked salmon"; *sowantan*, "coho salmon"; and *skeyɛ'n*, "sockeye salmon," according to Diamond Jenness (*The WSÁNEĆ and Their Neighbors*), and *Chenséqi7* "Moon of the Sockeye" (July), *Chenqěchqs* "Moon of the Coho" (September), and *Chenkwől7exw* "Moon of the Chums" (October), according to Dave Elliott, Sr.[39]

> *O Shwanaylets, our children this day eat the first of the fish that you have sent us. We thank you. We shall treat the fish carefully as we have always done.*
>
> —Diamond Jenness, The WSÁNEĆ and Their Neighbors *(1935)*

The Coast Salish, along with many Pacific Coast groups that depended on salmon, believed that the salmon were like people who came to feed them with their flesh. To honor their arrival, the Coast Salish performed a First Salmon Ceremony, which, although it differed from group to group, had some essential features.

> *When the first sockeye is caught the little children sprinkle their hair with down, paint their faces and put on white blankets. They go out to the canoe and carry the fish on their arms as though they were carrying an infant. A woman cuts it with a mussel shell knife, after which the fish is boiled and given only to the children to eat. The sockeye is just like a person, they say; that is why they must be careful.*
>
> —Erna Gunther, Klallam Ethnology *(1927)*

When reef netting, the first salmon caught would be brought by the crew to the beach, where the children were assembled. With white down in their hair and their faces colored with red ochre, they met the canoes, each child taking a single fish in their arms like a baby, steadying it by taking the dorsal fin in their mouths. Walking with a limp, they carried them to where the women waited by racks over long fire trenches. The women would then cut the fish, usually starting from the head facing away from them to the tail on one side, and then in the opposite direction on the other. The head, bones, guts, and tail would be separated from the flesh as a single unit. The flesh would be roasted on the rack over the fire and consumed by the children. Then they would ritually dispose of the offal, often by either placing it on rocks running into the sea or directly into the water. This would ensure that the fish would tell their relatives that it was safe to return to be caught by the reef netters.

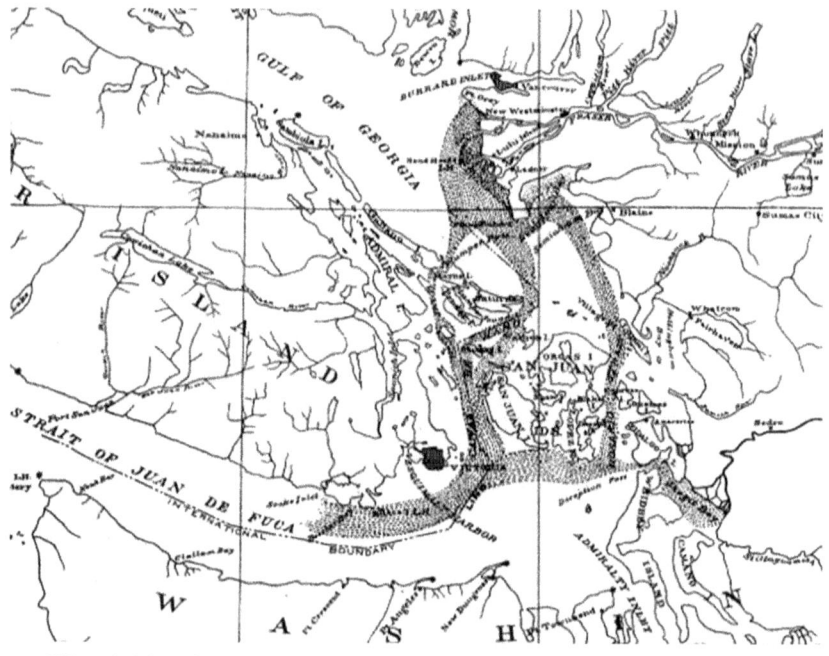

"Sketch Map Showing the Approximate Route of the Sockeye Salmon in Approaching the Fraser River and Skagit River from the Strait of Juan de Fuca" Richard Rathbun, A Review of the Fisheries in the Contiguous Waters of the State of Washington and British Columbia (1900)

In addition to salmon, the Coast Salish peoples fished for a wide variety of other species in local waters. These included dog fish, halibut, sturgeon, ling cod and rock fish, herring, smelt, and flounder. They also fished for other sea creatures, such as octopus, and mammals such as seals and porpoises. Salmon, however, was the principal fish available to the Coast Salish peoples of the San Juan Islands. There are five types of Pacific salmon: Chinook, which is also called "king," "spring," and "tyee;" coho, also known as "silver;" sockeye, or "red;" pink, "humpback," or "humpie;" and chum or "dog salmon." In addition to differing in size and quality of flesh, these salmon have different life histories and migration patterns, and therefore different fishing methods were used to catch them. Chinook are present in the region throughout most of the year, and coho are here from spring through the fall. Both are caught by trolling, and the latter could have been caught through netting or harpooning in the few smaller streams in the islands. Sockeye migrate via standard routes—principally Haro and Rosario Straits through the islands to the Fraser River—in midsummer. Together with pinks, which also migrate through the area in the summer—but only every other year, sockeye were largely taken by reef netting. Chum come later in the fall.

Salmon were dried for later consumption and trade. Women gutted and then filleted the fish by removing the head, tail, and spine, leaving two halves of flesh that could be kept splayed open with wooden splints. In some instances, the head and tail, still connected by the spine, were dried or smoked and stored to be used later as flavoring in stews and other meals. Long trenches were dug in the ground and a structure of upright posts with horizontal racks was erected. In some locations, such as near South Beach on San Juan Island, the prevailing winds were sufficient for drying the salmon fillets; often this was supplemented by smoky fires in the trenches, which helped dry out the flesh and kept insects from laying eggs on them. Julie Stein and others have conjectured that if located in a windy situation, the poles and racks were kept upright with clay footings and guy cords secured to anchor stones.[40]

> *They catch lingcod and split them in half. Take each half right off the backbone. You take that backbone right out and throw it away. And you take a pole and hang one half of one on one side and other half you hang on the other side so the backs aren't touching together. That's the way you hang them up to dry. They hang them up single too. They bust that up and make soup, the belly part. They take salmon and split it like you were going to hang it up to smoke, and you smoke it about a day and half or two days and you take it down and cut it right in half down the middle, split it again. Then you hang it up where it'll really be as dry as a board.*
>
> —Herman Olsen, quoted in Ann Nugent, Lummi Elders Speak (1982)

Anthropologist Gordon Hewes has estimated that the per capita annual intake of salmon in the precontact period averaged 365 pounds (i.e., a pound a day). This was based on a requirement of 2,000 calories per day and the assumption that half of this was met by salmon, which has an average caloric value of 1,000 per pound.[41] Russel Barsh, referring to Richard Rathbun's 1895 interview with Coast Salish reef-netters Joseph Cagey and Dick Edwards, noted that they "were operating eight gears off Iceberg Point on Lopez Island from July to September, landing sockeye salmon and some pinks for several weeks, followed by smaller numbers of coho salmon. While the sockeye were running, Cagey and Edwards estimated that they landed 3,000 to 4,000 fish on each outgoing tide..."[42] Although this occurred during a later period (1890s) and involved multiple gears, the numbers are substantial, indicating that traditional reef netting during the period in question yielded more fish than was necessary for subsistence. The Indigenous peoples of the Salish Sea often traded the bounty of their harvest with other groups, such as peoples of the mainland plateau region. Preserving the salmon by drying and storing them in woven cattail bags not only allowed for winter storage but also trade among other groups in the region and beyond.

Reef netting is probably the most distinctive cultural practice of the local Coast Salish peoples, and after a hiatus of several decades (1890-1935), when it was eclipsed by fish trapping, continues as an important Indigenous activity to this day. The method consists of forming an artificial reef such that the salmon, following the current, will then be funneled into a net and caught. Reef net sites were chosen where salmon naturally followed a course over relatively shallow reefs with kelp, often near a promontory that caused the backward sweep of a current.

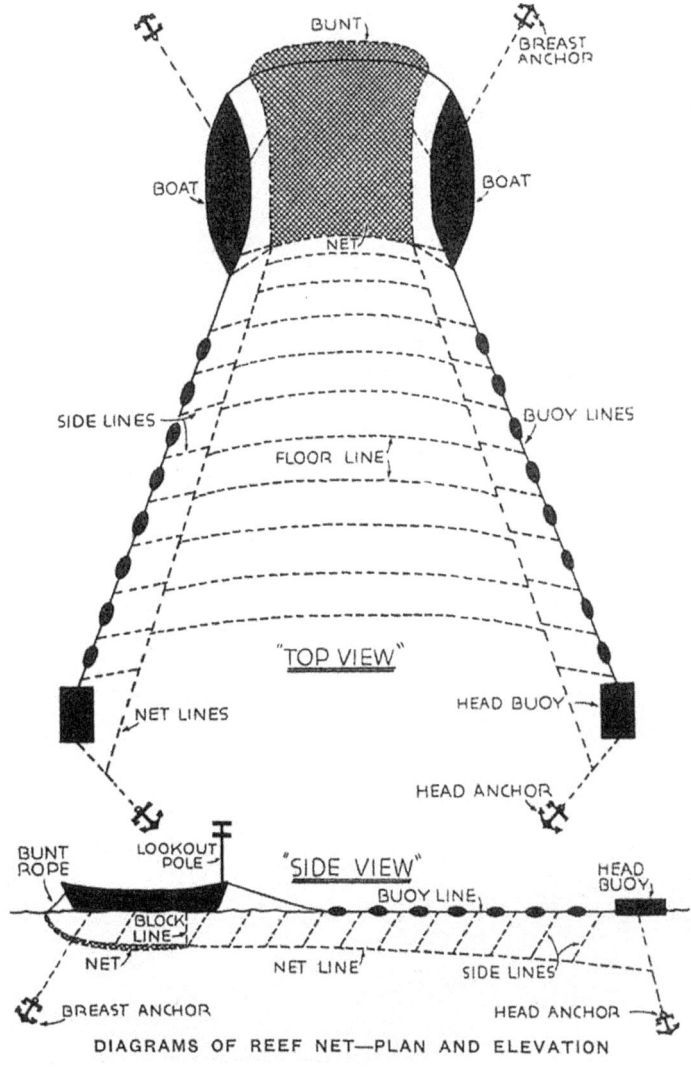

Diagram of a Reef-net
Pacific Fisherman, (June 1939)

Two canoes, specially designed for reef netting, were anchored approximately 15-25 feet apart, with their sterns facing the current (and therefore the incoming salmon). A net, made of dyed willow bark twine and approximately 20-30 feet wide and 30-40 feet long, was suspended in the water between the two canoes. If there was kelp, a channel was cut in the bed; if not, an artificial channel was created by laying out a funnel from each canoe towards the current. This funnel, consisting of "side" and "floor" lines attached to a top, buoyed lead line and a bottom, anchored net line, sometimes had beach rye grass tied to it to serve the illusion of eel grass at the bottom of a channel through which the salmon had to pass. Captains of the reef net crew, or their designees, stood at the stern of each boat and watched for the salmon entering the net, at which point ropes holding the boats apart would be slackened and the two canoes would swing together, capturing the fish in the net, which was then emptied into the shoreward canoe and paddled to the fishing camp.[43]

Several other methods of fishing were used by the Coast Salish such as fishing with hook and line. Bull kelp stipes were dried and then soaked in freshwater, stretched, and twisted for greater strength. They were then tied end to end with what is today called a "fisherman's knot": two overhand knots, each tied around the standing part of the other. Because of the length of the stipes—up to 80 feet—these lines could be used for deepwater fishing. Nettle fiber was also used for lines, as was the inner bark of the cedar tree. The latter, stripped from split lengths and twisted into a three-strand rope, was particularly useful for halibut fishing. Sinkers were made from stones that were either wrapped with cherry bark straps, grooved for lashing with lines, or perforated for a rope to pass through.[44]

The form of the hook depended on the catch. One of the most intricate was a halibut hook. The halibut, a right-eyed groundfish, swims horizontally and its jaws hinge sideways. A halibut hook was commonly made of yew wood (although balsam, fir, hemlock, and spruce knot wood were also used), steamed and then bent to form a U-shape, with a sharp barb, lashed to the shank, pointing inward from one of the ends of the bent hook, and the line on the other part of the shank. The halibut takes in the full hook and then, unable to swallow it, tries to eject it, resulting in the angled barb penetrating the mouth. Baited with either strips of octopus or a small fish impaled on the barb, two of these hooks were rigged to a spreader that hung several feet above where the line was anchored with sinkers to the sea bottom; the line was held up with a small, submerged bladder float and indicated with a larger bladder buoy riding on the surface.[45]

The Coast Salish trolled for salmon in canoes with the line attached to their hand or the paddle so that it jerked forward with each stroke (imitating a bait fish); a small sinker stone attached partway back from the hook kept the line at a certain depth. Hooks were made of wood, with a bone or shell barb lashed to face backward and baited with herring. Baited throat gorges were also used to catch bottom-feeding fish. The gorge, a slender bone sharpened at both ends, was firmly lashed in the middle to leaders attached to lines. The fish would swallow the bait and the gorge would toggle or turn sideways, causing it to lodge in the throat.

A distinctive method of using bait fish for cod was practiced by some Coast Salish. A small greenling or "tommycod" was attracted by crushed sea urchins and speared. The fisher would then put a rock in its stomach, cut away a portion of the fish from one side to make it uneven, and tie a line around it. This bait was lowered to the bottom and then rapidly pulled to the surface, making it spin or wobble. A lingcod, rising for the bait, could either be speared or, if it swallowed the greenling, pulled to the surface and then speared.

During March and April, when the herring congregated to spawn in shallow waters where eel grass grew, the Coast Salish would let down various materials such as kelp fronds and hemlock or cedar boughs, weighted with a stone and kept upright with a float, to catch the roe, which stuck to the surfaces. After several days the boughs would be removed and the roe dried, shaken off, and stored.

The principal means of catching herring and other small fish was by raking. A paddler in a canoe would sweep a rake—a 12-foot-long fir pole with hemlock, white fir, or bone (and later iron nail) teeth fastened at one-inch intervals into the three- to five-foot end cut flat—into a ball or school of herring and then deposit the impaled catch into the canoe.[46] Small fish like smelt were also shoveled into a canoe with a paddle or stick from the shallows when they congregated near the shore.

The importance of herring in the Northwest people's diet in the time before Euro-American contact is evident from a 2013 analysis of archaeological sites along the Northwest Coast that date from 10,700 B.P. to the contact era (A.D. 1740–1860). Of the 171 sites studied, 95 included bones, mostly found in middens, of herring, the single most numerous fish, and, in an additional 41 sites, it was the second most. All told, herring ranked among the three most abundant fish in 88% of the sites. This indicates that herring were not only an important food source but were consistently abundant enough during this long period to be the primary type of fish consumed. This is particularly true of archaeological sites in the Salish Sea, in comparison with sites in southeast Alaska, the northern British Columbia coast, and Haida Gwaii.[47]

The Coast Salish used gill nets to catch Chinook, coho, and pink salmon in the spring and summer whenever the fish were observed swimming close to shore. Gill nets were used on the Fraser River from the early historic period—the 1860s—by Indigenous peoples who sold their catch to Euro-Americans. Gill nets are webbing with meshes that allow the fish's head to enter and get caught by its gills; the size of mesh varied according to the species of fish. (This is in contrast to a seine, which impounds, not entangles, the fish.) The top of the net was kept at the water's surface with wooden floats, which were often upright three-foot cedar sticks, with half their length sticking out of the water, spaced three feet apart "like a picket fence," according to Wayne Suttles' Semiahmoo interviewee.[48] The bottom was weighted with stones, wrapped in cattails, secured to the lower edge. There are two types of gill nets: stationary, which are anchored in place; and drift, which are allowed to float loose. Because they work best when the fish cannot see, and therefore avoid, the net, either muddy water conditions or night fishing is optimal.

One of the principal methods of capturing salmon in the rivers of the region was by means of a weir, a framework of poles that supported a walkway with barriers and pots for catching the fish. Because there are few perennial streams—and no rivers—in the San Juans, this type of weir was not used, but a modification may have been utilized. There is a reference to an old weir at the entrance to a stream on Orcas Island—the locals called it "Fish Trap"—but it was not known when it had been used.[49]

The Coast Salish hunted seals and porpoises, but probably—according to Wayne Suttles and other anthropologists—did little whaling, except for taking advantage of a dead whale washed up on the shore. Harbor seals were speared with a harpoon with two fore-shafts, each of which had a three-piece female head. The harpoon shafts were made of fir; the fore-shafts of ironwood. The head was made of two spurs of elk bone fitted on either side of a blade made of antler, bone, or mussel shell, with a single barb, lashed together with nettle fiber and sealed with pitch. Porpoises were harpooned in the same manner as seals.[50]

Seals were also caught by net, made of willow bark twine and formed into a 10-inch mesh. Anchored by large stones at the ends and held up with cedar floats at the top, the net was set at night around a rock where the seals were known to sleep. The Songish and Samish would drive the seals into the net and then club them. The Saanich would lay the net around the rock at high tide, allowing the seals to swim in over it; in the morning, at low tide, the seals would get caught in the net when they tried to swim out. Seals were also clubbed, on the nose, as they slept on the beach. Hunters would steam the meat of porpoises and seals in a pit, often near where they were captured. Sometimes the meat was preserved by drying. Oil from both types of animals was saved in seal bladders and served in shells with meat or dried fish. Seal intestines were used as buoys.

It was the presence of the Straits Salish peoples fishing the seasonal runs of salmon that first attracted the Hudson's Bay Company to establish an outpost on San Juan Island. The initial Company operations on San Juan Island were seasonal fishing stations, encampments where items such as blankets were traded for salmon, which were then packed in salt brine in large wood barrels. In a letter dated June 25, 1851 to Company Secretary Archibald Barclay, Governor James Douglas wrote that a Company boat was "now taking in salt and barrels for a fishery which we propose establishing in the Island of San Juan."[51] (The Governor and Committee not only approved of the fishery, they said "it always affords us great satisfaction to learn that exertions are made to explore and turn to account the resources of the Colony".) William John MacDonald, who was sent at that time, stated:

> *In the month of June [1851] I was sent to San Juan Island to establish a salmon fishery, starting in a canoe, with an Indian crew, Joseph W. McKay as pilot and locator of a site, and four French Canadian workmen. We selected a small sheltered bay, erected a rough shed for salting, packing and curing of salmon, not known at that time, afterwards to become such an extensive and remunerative industry.*

That season the crew put up only 60 barrels of salted salmon.[52] Although it has not been determined exactly where this initial fishing camp was located, undoubtably it was on the west shore of San Juan Island. (Griffin refers to the "old Fishery" on November 7, 1859, in the *Post Journals*.) Later, the Company established a "fishing station" near their dock on Griffin Bay, close to Fish Creek (hence the name).[53]

Salmon had become an important export for the Company, surpassing fur at Fort Langley by the late 1840s. It was shipped primarily to San Francisco and the Sandwich Islands (Hawaii), although markets as far away as Australia and London were also attempted. The salmon, which was obtained by trading with the Indians (at a rate of 60 fish for a blanket worth $4), were placed in wooden barrels and packed in brine made with salt shipped as ballast from the Sandwich Islands. A writer in 1910 described the method as follows:

> *In dressing salmon for pickling the heads are removed, the fish split along the belly, the cut ending with a downward curve at the tail. The viscera and two thirds of the backbone are removed, and*

> *the blood gurry, and black stomach membrane scraped away. The fish are then scrubbed and washed in cold water. They are next placed in pickling butts with about 15 pounds of salt for every 100 pounds of fish. The fish remain here for about one week, when they are removed, rubbed clean with a scrub brush and repacked in market barrels, one sack of salt being used for every three barrels of 200 pounds each.*[54]

Each of these Company barrels, which contained 40 to 50 salmon and weighed 180 pounds, could fetch from 8 to 14 dollars. In addition to Belle Vue, fisheries were established at Fort Hope, Nanaimo, and Fort Victoria.[55]

One of the reasons for the establishment of the San Juan fishery was the failure of the Fraser River run in 1851.[56] What the precise yields were subsequent to the first season are not known, although Douglas wrote in early September of 1852 that about 290 barrels had already been put up and the catch was still in process.[57] Macdonald reminisced, perhaps exaggeratingly, that the annual output was between two and three thousand barrels.[58] According to another observer, by the mid-1850s Belle Vue fishery was producing around 300 barrels annually.[59] Catching or trading, salting down, and packing the salmon were certainly still a going concern in 1856, when Douglas wrote to Griffin:

> *...A cooper is now sent with Napoleon, to put up casks in order, and if the fish yield at all well, you may keep him at San Juan to put up as many fish as you can possibly cure, an additional number of casks and a quantity of salt will be sent over if required. Fish are very scarce in this quarter, and we shall be delighted if you succeed in curing 2 or 300 barrels.*[60]

In the *Post Journals* Griffin mentions fishing in late August/early September of 1858, but apparently the fish were not biting: "Let out net this morning at 9 am:- & left it until 8 pm:- in the water without the smallest success —although salmon were jumping all round it & even over it!"[61] A year later, George Gibbs mentions that in former times the operation had put up 1500 to 3000 barrels a year—a tenth of which is probably more likely—although he confirms that there was no catch in 1858. Griffin's journals in subsequent years mention the cleaning and repair of salmon barrels and cauldrons, but no catch.[62]

> *When we went out there and put in those reef nets, we caught fish right off starting the first day and the white fishermen never had one to eat. They didn't know how to catch them. They didn't know how to use a reef net. Every night when we'd go home, you could go down and sit on the beach and see them out there measuring our reef net and copying it. They'd wait until it was nighttime before they'd go and copy our reef net. Measure all the lines then they'd go back and try to fix theirs the same way.*
>
> —Herman Olsen, quoted in Ann Nugent, Lummi Elders Speak (1982)

Although there was clearly small-scale fishing by Euro-Americans during the subsequent years, there do not seem to have been wide-spread commercial operations in the island prior to the introduction of fish traps in the 1890s. On Waldron Island, Edouard Graignic, a Frenchman who had moved there in the late 1870s, fished for herring with his family by lighting a fire on the beach at night and rowing a net around the fish that were attracted by the light. Later, Ellery and Ashton Thomas established a herring smoker on Fishery Point in the 1890s.[63]

*Graignic Family in the City of Paris
(courtesy of San Juan Historical Museum)*

Farming

The introduction of Euro-American methods of farming began on December 15th, 1853, when Hudson's Bay Company Chief Factor James Douglas and a company of men consisting of a multiethnic mix of Europeans, Hawaiians, Métis, and Indigenous peoples landed on the southern end of San Juan bringing 1,369 sheep as well as 1 horse, 1 stallion, 1 mare, 2 cows and calves, 1 heifer, 1 boar, and 1 sow with young from Nisqually to establish Belle Vue Sheep Farm. Two years later, Douglas stated that the farm had 40 acres under cultivation, 2,200 sheep, 6 horses, 6 milch cows, 9 working oxen, 6 "other" cattle, 10 swine, and 40 poultry.[64]

Farming methods in the San Juans were similar to those at the Company's forts and posts throughout the Northwest. Livestock were grazed on naturally occurring (or Coast Salish-enhanced) open spaces (prairies), although at some places such as Fort Vancouver there was an effort to improve pasture by cultivating and then planting timothy and clover. During times of shortage, hay was cut from swamp areas, and during the winter the livestock were fed both peas and oats. Cultivated fields were kept fertile through manuring and rotation; in 1838, Douglas said of Fort Vancouver: "The method hitherto most successfully pursued in the management of the Farm, is a rotation of grain with occasional hoe crops, keeping the soil in good heart, by fallowing and manures, the latter operation being most commonly performed by folding the cattle upon the impoverished land."[65] At the Fort, animals such as cattle and sheep were folded in fields by means of moveable fences; at Belle Vue Sheep Farm, although there is some evidence of these fences (as opposed to the standard "park" or fixed fenced enclosure), it is not certain whether folding of this sort was practiced. Fertilizing was accomplished by hauling the manure from the barns and parks to the fields.

According to Douglas, the crops suited for the land at the Fort were, from best to worst: corn; barley or wheat; then a rotation of peas or oats. Not far from Fort Vancouver were outlying farms specializing in livestock (principally sheep) raising at Fort Nisqually (established 1833) and grain (principally wheat) production at Cowlitz Farm (established 1838). Upon the completion of the trade agreement with the Russian American Company and the establishment of the Puget Sound Agricultural Company in 1839, these farms grew in importance. It was from Nisqually that the original shipment of stock—mostly sheep—came to Belle Vue. The main crops on San Juan were sheep, cattle, and pigs for livestock and potatoes, oats, peas, and turnips for field crops, with an early, short-lived experiment with wheat. Corn was apparently never attempted, and there is no record of barley as a crop.

The number of sheep grew rapidly from the initial imported 1,369. By January 1857, Douglas could report to his directors that there were 4,250 sheep; two years later both George Gibbs and the tax assessors for Whatcom County numbered Griffin's sheep at 4,000.[66] This seems to be the maximum number achieved, and with dwindling pasturage due to "squatting" on Company-claimed land, as well as interference by American and English troops, the numbers probably had begun by fall by the early 1860s. Like the other Company farms at Cowlitz, Nisqually, and Vancouver, the principal breeds included Cheviot, Leicester, and Southdown, although Griffin also records some Merino, used to improve the quality of the wool.

Sheep operations varied little from year to year. Rams were introduced to the ewes for breeding, at a ratio of about one to thirty-five, in late October or early November. Lambing would then begin around the end of March and continue through April. In April and May those male lambs that were not kept as rams would be castrated (and thus become wethers, or, as Griffin writes, "wedders"). In May and June, the shepherds would then wash and shear the sheep flock by flock: first the wethers, then the young ewes, the old ewes, and the rams. After shearing, the sheep would then be dipped in a solution of tobacco boiled in water to prevent parasites (George B. Roberts, stationed at Fort Vancouver, wrote that the formula for this preparation was "32 tobacco in decoction 2-1/2 oz. corrosive sublimate per salmon Barrel of water"[67]). In July and August, the lambs would be separated from their mothers (weaned), and then the cycle would begin again in the winter.

> *I am glad to observe that you are making arrangements to part the ewes into flocks of 600 each; that is even too large a number to remain together, careful breeders generally making 500 the limit of their ewe flocks. In the lambing season, care must be taken to part the young lambs that have come during the night every morning from the flock, and to keep them apart until they are strong enough to range for themselves; shear each flock of ewes, within the lambing season, before then subdivided into two flocks each, so that you will require an additional number of hands to look after them, but the extra expense will be largely repaid by the increased number of lambs reared. The rams require much care and attention. The disease you describe as prevalent among those at San Juan is purely the effect of hardship and privation; if well fed and kept dry, the scab will soon disappear from among them; they should now receive a feed of oats daily, until they have perfectly recovered, and be well rubbed with a decoction of tobacco juice. I have spoken to McLeod about these matters; as a good shepherd ought to be well acquainted with them.*
>
> —James Douglas to Charles Griffin, July 5, 1856[68]

That the sheep raising was of primary interest to the Company is evident from frequent letters from Douglas to Griffin, which indicate the concern he felt for the proper management of the flocks. There were several products from the sheep operation. The North West Boundary Survey's *Geographical Memoir* noted that the average net weight of a San Juan fleece was 3½ pounds and that, "when full grown and fat", the sheep itself weighed fifty pounds."[69] After shearing, the wool was packed and shipped off, presumably to the Company headquarters at Fort Victoria; for instance, on February 9, 1860, 50 bales of wool were shipped. Sheep were periodically sold off as both breeding stock—on July 11, 1859, for example, Griffin sold 25 Black Face South Downs to some Americans—and meat: there are numerous entries concerning shipments to the other Company farms, Victoria, and the Royal Marines at English Camp.

The farm also had other livestock: horses and oxen, cattle, and pigs. The horses and oxen, although bred for reproduction, were principally used for transportation, hauling, and plowing. The cattle stock from Nisqually were probably descendants of California animals that were herded or shipped to Fort Vancouver. What methods, if any, were used in the husbandry of these animals is not known, although there are some references to cattle and horses being periodically rounded up from various locales on the island, and both a "calf park" and stables for horses are mentioned in the *Post Journals*.[70] McLoughlin, at Fort Vancouver, mentioned that the cattle were as wild as deer, and "could not be approached so that when we wanted to kill any for Beef we had to hunt them as Deer," and in *Told by the Pioneers* Archibald Fleming recalled of the cattle on the island "how wild they were, and the settlers ran to get out of the way of them."[71] That they were pastured at Home Prairie is evident from a letter of August 5, 1859, from Chief Factor Dallas to Governor Douglas about the damage sustained at Belle Vue upon the arrival of the American troops and establishment of their nearby camp: "Our sheep, cattle and horses are disturbed in their pasturage, and driven from the drinking springs, in the vicinity of which the troops are encamped. (Much of the pasture is also destroyed)."[72] There is also an obscure reference in the *Post Journals* to foals, again presumably loose on Home Prairie, being killed by U.S. Army mules.[73] The cattle were bred and raised for both meat and milk. Beef was a common ingredient of the men's weekly rations. In 1858, a "new" dairy was constructed, and the following spring Griffin noted with pride that there were 12 milch cows under the care of Alexander ("Aleck:") McDonald. There are also some *Post Journal* entries suggesting sale of butter to Victoria.[74]

It is likely that the Company first introduced native pigs from the Sandwich Islands (Hawaii) to Fort George in the1820s; later, Berkshire boars were imported from England to improve the stock. At Fort Vancouver, Kanakas were usually used as swineherds. Although there is no direct mention in the *Post Journals*, this was probably the case at Belle Vue, because of the large number of Kanaka shepherds. There is mention of at least one pig sty, although where it was is not known.[75] The pigs were slaughtered, and the pork served, either fresh or salted, as rations for the men, and possibly for export. There is no record of the manner in which pigs were kept or if there were any problems with poisonous weeds (such as death camas, which had occurred earlier at Fort Vancouver), although as the incident of 'The Pig' clearly indicates, they were let free to roam wild (or, as the frontier saying goes, 'root hog or die'). As for human predators, aside from the incident in which Lyman Cutlar shot a boar, there are further notations in the *Post Journals* of sows found killed around the island.[76]

FIG. 246.—BERKSHIRE BOAR.

Period Illustration of a Berkshire Boar

Several plant crops were grown on the farm. The largest field near the Establishment—40 to 80 acres, depending on the year and the observer—was sown in oats, principally for fodder for the livestock. The smaller field was sown in turnips and peas as well as other grain crops such as barley and wheat. Oats and peas were also planted out at Port L'Enfer and Little Mountain. Douglas wrote to Griffin on February 15, 1859:

> *Your plough is being repaired by the blacksmith and a new iron plough besides is sent which it is hoped will enable you to get on with your farming operations. It would be very advisable to get as much crop in the ground as you possibly can both grain and green crops so that you may have abundance offered for your stock ensuing winter, if you cannot procure natural grass in your swamps for hay, you might obtain this very necessary article by sowing a quantity of oats and having it cut when green, and cured, it would make good hay and not very expensive should the soil be such that the oats would grow pretty rank.*[77]

The *Post Journals* record the feeding of pea straw to sheep and cutting up turnips to feed to the oxen. In addition, on several occasions the men cut hay in swamps near Port L'Enfer to feed to the calves.[78]

While it is known that the oats, peas, and turnips were used for livestock, it is not clear to what extent flours or other products were made from the grain crops. Douglas had written to Griffin on July 5, 1856, "I hope the wheat crops will turn out as productive as you at present anticipate."[79] The following year, wheat was sent to Fort Victoria, where it was ground and then sent back to Belle Vue for consumption. There is a record of wheat being threshed March 15, 1858, but it is not mentioned again. Douglas estimated that the average yield per acre of good land at Fort Vancouver was 20 bushels of wheat, 30 of peas, 50 of oats, and 40 of barley; on poor soils, he reckoned half these amounts[80]. Unfortunately, the Belle Vue Sheep Farm *Post Journals* do not yield enough data to compare with these figures.

Some potatoes that had been sent to Victoria in 1857 for a trial in the mess "excited general admiration", according to Douglas.[81] A large field of potatoes—the seed stock having been obtained from the Cowichans—was planted every year thereafter.[82] The crop was substantial: in 1858, 1,497 bushels were harvested; 800 in 1859 (as well as 700 turnips); and 1,157 in 1860. Although it can be assumed that a generous portion of these were sent to Victoria and other Company outposts, the only known record is from the *Post Journal* of April 1859, when 300 bags for potatoes were sent from Fort Langley, and at least 197 returned full.

Griffin's kitchen garden included beets, cabbage, celery, lettuce, onions, and parsnips, in addition to small amounts of some of the other crops mentioned. A Fort Vancouver seed list dating from 1831 mentions several other vegetables—broccoli, cucumber, kale, leek, mustard, parsley, and radish—but it is not known whether these were also grown at Belle Vue.[83] Griffin mentions both fencing and pruning fruit trees, but species and varieties are not indicated. Apparently, he would often proudly show off his flowerbeds to visitors.

Because of the weather and crop characteristics, the cyclical farm year did not vary much. Plowing could commence as early as November but began in earnest after the first of the year and continued through March. Depending on the wetness of the soil, horses were first used, and then oxen. In March and April peas and oats were sown, while cabbage and lettuce seeds were planted, presumably in cold frames of some sort. Drills were plowed for potatoes in April, and seed potatoes cut up and sown, as were beets, carrots, and parsnips. Cabbages and celery were transplanted in May, and although no mention is made in the *Post Journal*, lettuce probably followed soon thereafter. Weeding, either through cross-plowing or hoeing, continued throughout the spring and summer. In August, cradles (scythes with teethlike attachments for laying grain in bunches at its was cut) were prepared and the oats and peas were cut and harvested into the barn or granary. Seeds were also collected at this time. In September, potatoes, then turnips, were dug and hauled to root houses. In September and October carrots were dug and onions gathered. Presumably other root crops, such as beets, as well as other kitchen garden vegetables, were harvested throughout the late summer and early fall, although Griffin does record digging parsnips as late as December one year. During the winter months of October through February, the grain crops were threshed and the potatoes and turnips were cleaned under the shelter of the barns, granaries, and root houses.

Also, during the winter months, farm operations and repairs that had been put off during the growing season were dispatched. Barnyards were cleaned and the manure hauled off to the fields. Drains were installed around the establishment, particularly in vicinity of the underground root houses ("pits"). (During the first winter—1854—it rained so much that the pits were flooded, and Griffin and his men were forced to move the potatoes to underneath one of the men's houses in order to keep them dry and free from frost.) The various structures such as the barns, granaries, and root houses, were repaired, replaced, or expanded, and fences repaired and heightened, particularly after strong windstorms.

Overall taking of inventory occurred in October or November. This involved rounding up all of the animals that ranged freely on the island and counting them. The October 17th, 1859 *Post Journal* mentioned that "Aleck:- Angus & "Little Man" out collecting cattle, horses &c. to be seen & counted & put in inventory"—as well as the more carefully herded animals, such as the sheep.[84] Accounts were then drawn up of all of the property—both real and livestock—and these were then sent by canoe to Victoria.

After the departure of the Hudson's Bay Company, large stock production (particularly sheep) was taken up by men such as the Keddy brothers—John on "Cady" Mountain and William at the head of Fisherman Bay on Lopez—who were British citizens originally from Victoria. Not only did they run their own sheep, but also let contracts to other shepherds for their stock. For instance, in a contract dated November 1, 1873, Sampson Chadwick agreed to take care of 200 of John Keddy's sheep and pay half the wool and increase in lambs (less loss), while clipping and sacking the wool for market.[85] (John left the islands for Victoria in 1877 worth some $20,000.[86])

Two other early stockmen were Augustus Hoffmeister, who was post sutler at English Camp, and Samuel Trueworthy, a native of Maine. Hoffmeister ran 60 head of cattle and hundreds of sheep, including some 500 Southdowns (probably of Hudson's Bay Company origin) that he had on his home ranch near the Camp as well as on Spieden Island. When Hoffmeister died in 1874 (his was the first probate file in the newly-formed San Juan County), his estate was divided between Isaac Sandwith, who leased his property on San Juan, and John Tod, Jr., who purchased the sheep, farm, livestock and improvements on Spieden and Henry Islands. Trueworthy ran his sheep—numbering 800—on his ranch near West Sound on Orcas Island, although according to his probate he also had some cattle and 300-350 goats on the mainland.[87]

In her reminiscences, Lila Hannah Firth relates that her father, James Hannah, raised free-range goats on Mount Dallas in the late 1860s, after the Hudson's Bay Company had withdrawn their sheep. However, this area was later used by sheepmen, who brought in their flocks from the north end of the island and, in an apparent 'range war', shot most of Hannah's goats.[88]

Homesteaders also raised stock on their farms, although on a much smaller scale than the larger stockmen. Lizzie Lawson summed up the subsistence requirements of a homesteader:

> *A horse and cow were the first tame animals a man needed on the island. A horse for riding through the trail as there were no roads. A horse helped clear the land. The cow had milk for the family to drink, and for cream and butter. People raised pigs. Pork was winter food. It was put in wooden barrels or earthen crocks and salted to keep. The fat from the pig, lard, was used for cooking and baking.*[89]

Few of the 'proving up' records on homestead applications mention livestock, but those that do indicate that most had at least one cow and calf ("milch" cows), several had cattle, sheep, and hogs, and most had chickens (see Appendix: *Homestead Livestock*). In addition, many of these farmers planted timothy and clover for hay. Grain crops included barley, oats, and wheat. Among the tools listed as part of the applications for homestead lands were seed drills and cultivators, hay scythes and grain cradles, and hay drags and pitch forks. In addition, they often planted orchards of fruit trees.

Orchards in Eastsound, Orcas Island ca. 1900 (courtesy of Orcas Island Historical Museum)

Farmers planted orchards on their homesteads as early as the 1860s and 70s, but the fruit industry in San Juan County did not really take off until the 1890s. This was due to the growing market for fruit on the West Coast and nationwide. Production began in mid-1800s in Oregon with stock developed and supplied by Dr. John McLoughlin at the Hudson's Bay Company farm at Fort Vancouver (established 1824). Orchards had become well established in western Oregon by the 1860s, but large-scale production west of the Cascades did not really begin until the 1880s; according to census figures, in the next decade "the annual value of fruit production nearly doubled…from $580,000 to $1,100,000."[90] In San Juan County, the Italian prune-plums, which had become very popular through the efforts of the Portland horticulturalist J. R. Cardwell, were first planted on Orcas in the mid-1870s. These were followed by apples and pears, as well as apricots, cherries, peaches, and plums. Berry fruits such as blackberries, raspberries, and strawberries were also grown in the islands. According to the recollections of E. L. Kimple, E. L. Von Gohren, who established and maintained the orchards of the Rev. S. R. S. Gray on Orcas Island, urged local growers to concentrate on a half-dozen varieties of apples, to make sorting and packing easier. He recommended Gravenstein, King, Wagner, R. I. Greening, and Spitzenberg, with Blue Pearmain in some locations.[91]

Details of the fruit industry can be gleaned from first-hand accounts offered in letters, journals, and memoirs, including the Diaries of Orcas orchardist James Tulloch. In 1877, he planted 300 apple trees, the first of what would become one of the largest orchards (1700 trees) in the islands. In addition to farming his own fruit trees, he also hired out to prune for others. Getting root stock at the time was pricey: when Waldron Island homesteader Sinclair A. McDonald bought his fruit seedlings from Victoria nurserymen Mitchell & Johnson in November of 1870, he paid a little over 50 cents each for apples, 75 cents each for pears and plums, and $1 each for cherries. Later, the proliferation of nurseries in the Northwest drove costs down.

Marketing island-grown fruit was always difficult. When the principal means of transportation in the region was shipping, the islands had a relative advantage over the mainland; later, when the railroads arrived in the Pacific Northwest, islanders faced greater competition. Tulloch's chief market was Seattle, although he also shipped to Bellingham, Port Townsend, Tacoma, and Victoria. Always wary of the commission agents—"These fellows pay a month's rent in advance and hang out their signs and are ready to fleece the unwary farmer and fruit growers out of thousands of dollars"—he made a habit of accompanying his shipments, and relates several amusing stories of getting the better of those who were trying to take advantage of him. Tulloch estimated that he shipped a total of 75,000 boxes of apples, or as many as 3-4,000 annually over his thirty-five-year career. Overall annual shipments from Eastsound on Orcas Island are estimated at 25-30,000 boxes per year each of apples and pears, with additional thousands going out from Olga, Orcas Village, and West Sound.

Limemaking

> It is to be found on the southern end, in the vicinity of the Hudson's Bay Company's station. On the western shore, near the base of Mount San Juan, immense masses raised up into perpendicular walls are seen at several localities, covering an area of many acres. The northeastern corner of the island is composed of an extensive ledge of the same material... Testing by acid and burning, it proved to be of a superior quality. It exists in sufficient quantities not only for lime, but might be profitably quarried for building stone. The value of these discoveries can better be appreciated from the fact that up to the time of the discovery of limestone on this island it was not known to exist at any point on Puget Sound, within United States territory, and for building purposes it was necessary to procure all the lime used, from California or Vancouver's Island.
>
> —Geographical Memoir of the Islands between the Continent and Vancouver's Island in the Vicinity of the Forty Ninth Parallel of North Latitude (1860)[92]

The North West Boundary Survey noted several mineral resources in the islands including coal, limestone, and sandstone. Of these, the deposits that generated the most excitement were limestone, which was discovered and tested on the west and north side of San Juan Island. The quarrying and processing of lime on San Juan Island began with Royal Marines stationed at English Camp. The British used the lime for paint, whitewash, and mortar in the construction of their buildings there. Sometime in 1860, Lyman Cutlar, E. C. Gillette, and Frank Newsome began producing lime at Lime Kiln on the west side of San Juan. The Victoria *Colonist* reported on September 25, 1860:

> We were yesterday shown some specimens of lime from San Juan Island. It is as white as chalk, and slacks much quicker than any lime we have yet seen on the Pacific Coast. It was burned in a rude kiln and without the usual precautions of lime-burners. The supply of the stone is almost inexhaustible.[93]

Clearly the partners were experimenting with production and testing the market, because the Olympia *Pioneer & Democrat* also reported on San Juan lime—"white as chalk"—just three days later.[94]

Gillette sold his interest to Augustin Hibbard after the first winter of operation, and Hibbard, Cutlar, and Newsome formed a new business—the San Juan Lime Company—on January 13, 1861. At the end of 1864, Hibbard bought out Cutlar and Newsome, and continued operations until the following year, when George R. Shotter and Company bought in. In 1868 Hibbard borrowed $1,500 for operations from Catherine McCurdy of Port Townsend, secured through a mortgage on the land, and bought out Shotter. A year later, on March 9th he formed a partnership, still known as the San Juan Lime Company, with Nicholas C. Bailey, Charles Huntington, and Charles Watts. Unfortunately, on June 17th of that same year Watts murdered Hibbard in an argument over work and stolen goods. Hibbard died intestate, and, after an ensuing legal battle between his heirs and creditors, the property was eventually sold in 1873 to Port Townsend entrepreneur Catherine McCurdy, who turned it over to her son, James McCurdy, to operate along with former company partner N. C. Bailey (see Appendix: *Appraisal of Property, Augustin Hibbard Probate*).[95]

San Juan Lime Company [Lime Kiln]
(courtesy of San Juan Historical Museum)

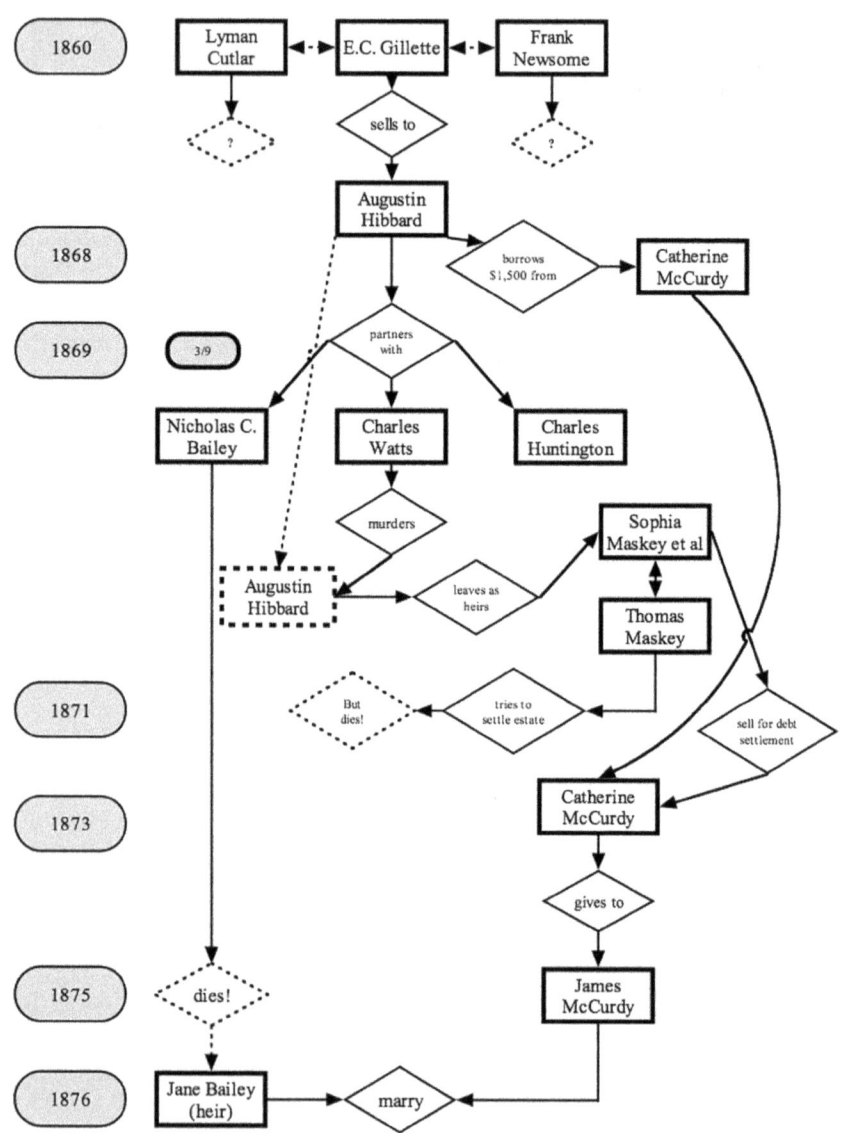

San Juan Lime Company Chart of Ownership
1860 - 1876

According to the *Products of Industry* portion of the 1870 census, "Thomas MacKey" at Lime Kiln produced $26,000 worth of lime—13,000 barrels at $2 a barrel—and employed 18 men for 6 months per year for a total payroll of $1,000. These 18 employees included 1 lime maker, 2 coopers, 2 carpenters, 4 quarrymen, 1 chopper, 3 laborers, and 2 cooks. Among the various ethnic groups working there, most of whom were American or Canadian, two groups stand out: the quarrymen were all from Cornwall (typical of western mining operations), and both cooks were Chinese.

On June 20, 1861, the Victoria *Colonist*, noting that "there are now two companies engaged in getting out lime on San Juan," reported:

> By the arrival of the Schooner General Harney yesterday, 345 barrels of San Juan Island lime, from the kiln of the Eureka Company were brought to this city... The kiln is situated about midway between the American and English Camps, and a wharf has lately been erected in a snug little cove for the accommodation of vessels. Some six men are constantly employed at the kiln...making bands, etc.[96]

Eureka, located on the east shore of San Juan, was later owned and operated by Daniel and William McLachlan and their cousin by marriage, Thomas Lee.[97]

Port Langdon, on the east shore of Orcas Island's East Sound, was first quarried in 1862 by George R. Shotter, who, as we saw, was also involved at Lime Kiln for several years. Listed as "Shotwell & Company" in the 1870 *Products of Industry*, the company had $7,000 in capital, 25 employees ($2,000 in wages), and produced 8000 barrels in 6 months, for a value of $16,000 at the going rate of $2/barrel. Associated with the kilns was a cooper shop, which produced the barrels for the lime (The Port Langdon dock, which was primarily used for loading and shipping barrels of lime, was also used for fruit and other agricultural shipments.) Port Langdon was later sold to Daniel McLaughlin and Robert Caines in 1874.

Because lime making required skill and knowledge, the men who worked in the industry often appear in the records of several locations in the islands. For instance, George R. Shotter, who first established the lime operations at Port Langdon on Orcas Island, later invested in Lime Kiln on San Juan Island with Augustin Hibbard in 1864. Colin Ross worked in 1875 at McCurdy's and later joined in partnership with the Scurr Brothers and his cousins Alexander and Donald Ross in 1879 to make lime at Roche Harbor. Daniel McLaughlin first worked with his cousin by marriage, Thomas Lee, at Eureka on San Juan Island, before moving to Port Langdon on Orcas Island.

Lime Kiln and Quarry Crew, Cowell's, San Juan Island (courtesy of San Juan Historical Museum)

Limestone was quarried either in pits or shelves. Pit quarries, where miners dug down into the ground in successive layers, were established at Roche Harbor and Mitchell Bay, whereas at San Juan Lime Company, Eureka, and Langdon miners removed the rock from the faces of ledges exposed on the hillsides. The resulting landscape was therefore either what appear to be sunken holes or terraced scoops out of hillsides.

Quarrying was heavy, loud, and dusty work that required a great deal of strength and endurance. Sections of rock were blasted from the vertical faces of the deposits and the resulting boulders were broken into smaller pieces for loading in the kilns. "Big holes," for blasting the rock off the face, were drilled six to eight feet back from and parallel to the cliff's edge. Drilling was done by hand by a team of three men called a "doublejack": two men with sledgehammers alternated hitting a drill bit, which was held and turned by the third man. They regularly added water, which would mix with the drilling dust to make "mud," sticking to the side of the drill; the third man would clear the hole by withdrawing the drill and knocking the mud loose. A series of progressively longer drill bits was used until the holes were about 20 feet deep, and then a small amount of black powder was poured down the hole and ignited to form a larger chamber, a "springing hole." This chamber was filled with a large amount of black powder and then set off with sticks of dynamite, resulting in the face of the cliff being blown off onto the quarry floor. A "single jacker," using a kit with different size bits and a double headed hammer, would then drill holes in the boulders, into which sticks of dynamite or black powder with fuse would be inserted for blowing the boulders up into smaller pieces. There was usually a specific person who actually ignited the explosion, although jackers would sometimes do so. A 9- or 12-pound rock hammer with a narrow bit was used to break medium sized rocks into useable chunks (usually 8-12 inches in diameter), care being taken to waste as little rock as possible in small chips. This size of rock allowed the hot gases to pass around the rocks piled in the kilns in order to heat them thoroughly.

These smaller rocks were then loaded by hand into rail or trestle cars and moved by either manpower or draft horse to the main processing area. Temporary, 36"-gauge tracks were laid from the more permanent lines and trestles to the quarry currently being worked on. In some cases, a form of tram system, operating by gravity, was used to convey the loads down the steep slopes to the sorting areas. The quarried limestone could then be either shipped unprocessed or burned in the kilns to produce lime.

Limestone (calcium carbonate—$CaCO_3$) must be subjected to a great heat to drive off carbon dioxide (CO_2), leaving pure lime (calcium oxide—CaO). This process—calcination or "burning"—yields about 60% lime and 40% gas. In order for this chemical reaction to occur, the limestone must be heated to temperatures ranging from 1650 to 2000 degrees Fahrenheit (900-1100 degrees Centigrade), and optimally around 1800 degrees Fahrenheit. This heating is done in kilns, the design of which varied through the nineteenth century. The two basic types were pot (or field) and shaft (or vertical) kilns.

Pot kilns consisted of a covered, one-time burning of the limestone. Some of them consisted of just a rock-lined pit in the ground, with the raw limestone mixed together with fuel (usually firewood) that was then burned (the so-called "heap kiln"). This fits a description of a contemporary kiln in Pierce County; according to Lucille McDonald:

> *The custom was to put in a layer of wood topped with a layer of rock and repeat the layers until the kiln was full. The wood was lighted and left. When the fire went out, the lime was ready.*[98]

A significant drawback of pot kilns was that the temperature of the burning could not be closely regulated. David Eselius noted, "Since no chemical determinations were run in those days, the men judged whether or not the rock was done by its appearance. At night the rock was transparent; in the day it had a yellow-golden color when cooked."[99]

North Kiln and Boarding House, Lime Kiln, San Juan Island (courtesy of San Juan Historical Museum)

Shaft kilns consisted of vertical structures that were often constructed against the side of a hill near the quarry to facilitate the loading of the ore at the top of the shaft. An early version was filled with alternating layers of stone and fuel, which would then be ignited and left to burn for about 3 days, and then cooled for a day or so before workers removed the lime from the kiln (hence the term "periodic" kiln). A later modification of this was an early version of the "continuous," "perpetual," or "draw" kiln, where the burnt stone—lime—was withdrawn from the bottom of the shaft and new limestone was added to the top for continuous burning. Heat was applied through fireboxes at the sides of the kiln; the wood fuel never came in contact with the limestone. The technical advantage of this was that the heat generated by the initial burning was not lost through the process of cooling down the kiln to empty out the full load.

> *[The kiln]…resembl[ing] a short, wide stack, of either square, round, or elliptical cross section. It consists of a casing of steel or stone which is lined with refractory material. The long, vertical chamber formed by this lining may be divided into three compartments by imaginary horizontal planes. The top compartment, called the hopper, is used for storing and preheating the middle compartment, the shaft. This shaft is the place where the lime is burned. It may be of either square, round, or elliptical cross section, independently of the outside of the kiln. …At the bottom of the shaft, the third component (the cooler) is used for storing the lime after it is burned [Processed lime is removed from the cooler section.] …The fuel used in burning the lime is consumed in the fire boxes usually arranged on two sides of the kiln. They are very similar to the common fire boxes in use under boilers.*
>
> —Warren E. Emley, "Manufacture of Lime" (1927) [100]

At Lime Kiln, on San Juan Island, the kilns were constructed of an inner lining of two courses of firebrick around a flattened oval that measured approximately 6 by 8 feet contained in squared outer walls of rough limestone with rubble fill in be-

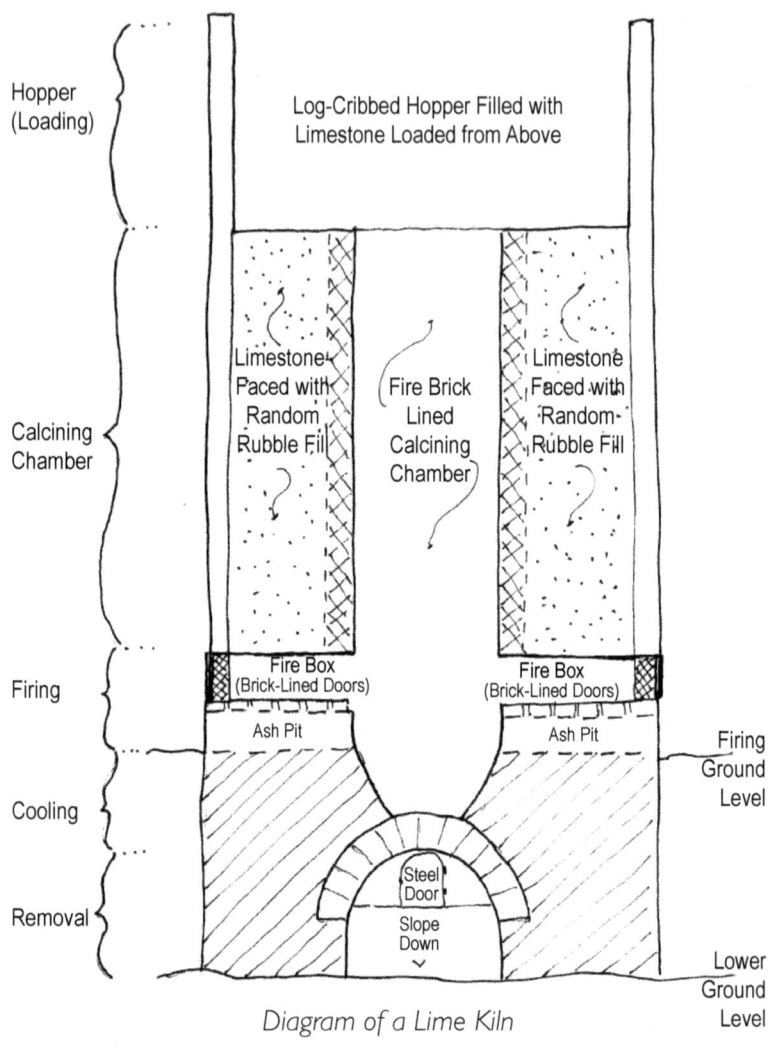

Diagram of a Lime Kiln

tween. Large horizontal and vertical timber frame beams and metal tie rods were used to encase the structure and keep it together. The stone shaft was extended upward another 10' or so by a wooden superstructure, which was used as the hopper for the unburnt limestone. Approximate dimensions of the masonry shafts were 18 feet high on the upslope side and 30 feet on the down slope, 18 feet wide (on the lime-removal side) and 20 deep (on the firebox sides). Sandstone was used in key places such as the arches over the bottom removal area as well as quoins of the shaft. The fireboxes, pairs of which were located midlevel on the north and south sides of the kilns, consisted of hinged steel doors covering arched openings lined with firebrick. Open-brickwork grates on the bottom let the ashes fall into cinder boxes below, for easy removal.

The firebrick had to be periodically replaced because the lime would chemically fuse with the surface of the bricks. The kilns would be shut down, and workmen would go inside the shafts to remove the big chunks of fused and melted firebrick and replace them with new brick. Large piles of discarded brick on the site bear witness to this process. Firebrick used for lining mainly came from England and Scotland during the 19th century; later brick came from both British Columbia and Washington State.

> *If…the limestone was properly heated and calcined into lime by the time it reached the hottest section at the firebox level, the whole charge would expand and stick to the kiln walls, creating a large cavity when the lime was removed from the cooler below. It was at this point that the experience of each fireman came into play, both physically and knowingly. The task now was to strategically poke the key pieces of red-hot lime in order to break the hung-arch, and thus bring down the whole kiln charge in a rattling thump to fill the gap. In order to accomplish this maneuver every three or four hours, strategic openings were located in the kiln shell and brickwork. 10' to 20' foot steel rods were then pushed through these poke-holes to dislodge and to drop the lime and overlying twenty feet of preheating limestone, often a five-foot drop. Slow removal of the rod when the charge crashed down could knock the firemen over or bend the rod in a stuck position.*
>
> —Wolfgang Bauer, "Roche Harbor During the Roaring" (2003)[101]

The quarrymen loaded the stone—about 15 tons—into the top of the shaft kiln, while the firemen, working twelve-hour shifts, fired the kiln and maintained the proper temperature, keeping it hot but not too hot. Guiding the mass of limestone through the shaft was often a tricky process. From the time it passed the firebox to its drawing from the bottom was about 24 hours. The firemen who kept the kilns burning also drew the rock from the kiln, sorted out any unburned rock—"core" —and then packed the burned lime in barrels. They drew about every 3-4 hours, with the average draw being 12-15 barrels.

Although some lime operations purchased staves elsewhere—specifically the Puyallup Stave Factory and stave operations on Orcas Island—the barrels were assembled at a cooperage on the site. The 1870 advertisement for the sale of Lime Kiln on San Juan noted "a large Cooper Shop with benches for 4 coopers to work," and the appraisal performed by court order the next year noted a cooper shop with 4 shave horses with benches, a set of cooper's tools, a grindstone, and 11 "Rack Wheels," as well as a stock of 1180 barrels on hand. In the industry portion of the 1870 census, several 'factories' for the production of barrel staves are mentioned, and, in addition to the mention of a cooper shop at Shotwell & Company's limekiln on Orcas Island, two cooperages are attributed to a Joseph Gibson and Charles Swift. Early on, rather than iron hoops the staves were bound together with

> *Logs are taken to the mill in rafts or on barges, cut to twice the length of a stave, and are known as "stave bolts"... The bolts are hauled up an incline, at the head of which they encounter a saw that quickly saws them into lengths for staves. After being steamed, another cuts them to the proper thickness, and a third machine shapes them so that when put together they will have the required bildge[sic] in the center. They are then tied up in bundles, loaded on cars and passed through the dry kiln, where they are thoroughly seasoned, and are then stored away for use. Heads are made from bolts of a different length. The slabs, after being sawed out of the bolt and being thoroughly kiln dried, are laid at proper widths on another machine and sawed into round and perfect heads, three pieces usually going into one head...*

*Coopers Displaying the Tools of Their Trade,
Roche Harbor, San Juan Island
(courtesy of San Juan Historical Museum)*

"liners," which were made of some flexible sapling material such as fir, hazel or vine maple, which was split down the center and then soaked to gain flexibility and bundled together in bunches of one hundred.[103]

> *...The coopers work in sets of four, grouped about a stove, upon which the barrels are heated after being "set up" and before "hooping". From a pile of staves the cooper selects enough to make a barrel and places them in position by confining the upper ends in a heavy hoop and letting the lower ends rest upon the ground. Another hoop is then driven down toward the center of the barrel. The barrel is then reversed and the upper ends of the staves, which are narrower than the center and are about two inches apart, are drawn together by a rope loop placed over the ends and tightened by power from a treadle or windlass sufficiently to permit another strong hoop to be slipped over the top. The barrel is then set over a drying cylinder on the stove, and when sufficiently dry the regular hoops are adjusted, the heads set in, the edges of the staves planed, champered and crozed, and the completed barrel is then rolled along an incline to a warehouse, where it is stored for seasoning...*
>
> —"One Thousand Barrels a Day," The West Shore, August 1889[102]

The rock, which was still in large chunks (6-8 inches in diameter), was raked out of the bottom part of the kilns by means of long (10-20') rods and channeled into a chute. From there it would be packed in barrels and the heads sealed in order to keep the lime from hydrating once again. Fireman Fred Wagner said:

> *The lime was so hot…just cool enough so it wouldn't burn the barrel—that's when they started drawing it, and them poor fellows—I know some of them would just bleed at the nose.*[104]

The barrels, weighing between 200 and 250 pounds each, were then transported to warehouses where they could be stored until shipped to market.

Lime in its pure state, called "quicklime," may also be further converted to hydrated or slaked lime. This process could be done in several ways: water could be sprinkled onto the quicklime and the lumps would crack open and form a dry powder; or the lime could be placed in a basket and immersed in water and then drawn up to complete the slaking process in the air. In either case, caution was necessary to control the chemical reaction that resulted, because it could be quite violent, even causing the water to boil. If left exposed to the air for a length of time, quick lime will naturally take on moisture or slake, but in the process it absorbs carbon dioxide and other impurities, which make it less useful. Quick lime could also be placed in a pit or vat and more water than necessary for slaking added, to form a paste, which could be kept for several months.[105]

One of the advantages of lime making in San Juan County was proximity to water, which allowed easy shipment of barreled lime to Seattle, Tacoma, Victoria, and other Puget Sound cities as well as to ports as far away as San Francisco and Hawaii. All the early local quarry operations had a wharf with attached warehouses, where the barreled lime could be stored and loaded for shipment. Ships laden with barrels of lime, some stacked on open decks, were carrying a very dangerous cargo since quicklime that becomes wet is highly combustible. Many ships from Puget Sound—the so-called "Mosquito Fleet"—that plied significant West Coast trade routes (the three-to-five-day run from Puget Sound to San Francisco and the Vancouver or Victoria to Portland run, for example) suffered severe damage or sank as the result of fires ignited by their lime cargo.

Logging

The Coast Salish used various trees for fuel, house construction, canoe making, and boxes built for storage of food and other goods. Principal among these trees was cedar (*Thuja plicata*), which could be easily split and contains a toxic oil (*thujaplicin*) that naturally preserves the wood against rot and insect attack.[106] Indigenous peoples used two basic means of obtaining cedar wood: by felling the tree so that the full log could be utilized and by splitting off planks from a tree that was left standing. Felling a tree occurred after summer and before the sap rose in spring. The fellers chiseled a cavity with stone adzes near the base of a tree and then placed hot stones in the cavity to burn away the wood, hewing away the charred matter before replacing the hot stones and repeating the process until the trunk was cut through. (This same method was used to remove the top portion from the felled tree.) The log could then be used whole—carved into the body of a canoe—or split into planks with wooden or elk antler wedges driven with stone mauls. Planks or boards could also be split from standing trees: first, cavities were chiseled with stone adzes at the top and bottom; then the separation of a plank of the desired thickness was begun by inserting wedges at the top; and finally the plank itself was split off either by pulling with ropes wrapped around the top or by inserting a round crosspiece into the initial split, which would gradually pressure the plank away from the trunk.

Sections of the planks could then be broken off by chiseling a narrow groove on each face of the plank and then bending until the section broke off. This method was used for the construction of cedar boxes. The carver chiseled kerfs—ranging from "V" to square and stepped, with several curved variations—creating the four sides of the box, which were then bent to form a cubicle and the two edges drilled and either sewn or pegged with cedar withes; a base was fitted and attached with diagonal pegs. A removable lid was then fitted to cover the box.

Indigenous peoples also used the bark of Douglas fir trees for hot, smokeless fires that didn't spark—an advantage in the summer when there was danger of fires spreading through the forest as well as smoke revealing one's location. Some local and regional archaeological sites revealed the use of Douglas fir bark. Excavations at English Camp indicated its ubiquity as well as the preference for its use in processing shellfish by steaming.[107] Gatherers would use bone, stone, or wooden wedges driven horizontally or tangentially under the outer bark, the fissures of which usually run vertically, and a section of bark pried away from the trunk.

Although Coast Salish groups that came to the islands probably used the timber resources available to them, evidence of cedar "heritage" trees that have been stripped of boards such as one finds in the forests of the surrounding lands such as Vancouver Island is rare in the San Juans. The principal examples are from the less-developed islands such as Patos and Sucia, places where the forests have survived extensive Euro-American logging. Culturally modified Douglas firs that have had portions of their bark stripped from them for use as firewood may also be present in the islands, but archaeologists have only recently recognized evidence for this.[108]

When the Euro-Americans came, they used the extensive forests on the islands for a variety of uses. One of the earliest settlers in the islands was William Pattie, a Hudson's Bay employee who was granted license to cut timber on the south side of Lopez Island in 1852. Although Pattie soon left to explore the coal mining opportunities in the Bellingham area, he was replaced by an American—Richard W. Cussans or Cousins—who continued with the timber operations, producing some 30,000 felled and squared feet. Governor James Douglas became alarmed about American settlement of the islands although Cussans claimed that he was British-born and would become member of the Colony. When his license expired in 1853, Douglas claimed the improvements.[109] As James Alden, Lieut. Com. U.S. Navy, who served as Assistant to the U.S. Coast Survey, wrote to his superintendent, Prof. A. D. Bache, on October 31, 1853:

He came to me with a long complaint, and the facts as near as I could get at them are as follows: His name is R. W. Cussans. He located a tract of land on Lopez or Rodger's Island and made improvements to the cost of about $1500, but owing to the action of the Governor of Vancouver's Island was obliged to abandon everything. He was compelled to take a License to cut timber (a copy of which I herewith enclose) and after he had cut and squared some 30000 feet was informed that it would be necessary for the vessel when she took it away to go to Victoria and clear at the Custom House.[110]

Belle Vue Sheep Farm manager Charles Griffin mentions the use of trees for buildings, farm implements, ship construction (spars and knees), and cordwood for steamships. Certain locations on San Juan Island were used for the harvest of specific trees: cedar (for shingles and fences) was usually cut near the "fork in Cowitchin Road"; oak (used for ship's knees, wagon trees, and harrow teeth) was first harvested from Oak Prairie (San Juan Valley) and later "Prairie du Chine" as well as from the north end of the island; and spruce was taken from nearby Mt. Finlayson. Griffin also mentions the use of a sawpit near the Establishment.[111] Another lumber production site, called a sawmill but probably just a covered sawpit, was listed next to the carpenter's shop at English Camp.[112] A saw pit was a large hole or pit dug into the ground (usually on a hillside) so that one man (the "box man") could stand beneath a piece of lumber while another stood on the beam above (the "tiller man"), both on either end of a long "pit saw."[113] Producing boards by means of pit sawing was a rather laborious process and averaged only about 200 board feet per day.

The North West Boundary Survey, in exploring the islands with an eye towards economic potential, noted the presence of a few creeks or streams that had enough of a fall to be able to establish mills, including the drainage from Beaverton Valley into

Friday Harbor on San Juan Island and Cascade Creek on Orcas Island. There is mention of some early sawmills in the islands. John Bowman, who settled in Olga on Orcas Island in the 1870s, established a creek-powered mill on Stockade Bay. He later sold the mill to Edward and Andrew Newhall, who then moved operations to Cascade Bay (currently Rosario).[114] Otherwise, most of the lumber in the islands came from the sawmills located in nearby Bellingham and Victoria.

In addition to producing shakes for their dwellings and outbuildings, several early settlers in the islands established "factories" for shakes and barrel staves. Both shakes and staves were split off a section of a log called a bolt with a mallet and froe. The froe, which was an L-shaped tool with an upright wooden handle and a metal blade with a sharp edge that faced away from the holder, was placed on the open grain of the bolt and struck with the mallet; the handle was then levered away from the plane of the blade to help split off a shake. Smaller strips could then be riven from this and shaved with a draw knife to form staves for barrels.[115]

*Hauling Cordwood, San Juan Island
(courtesy of San Juan Historical Museum)*

The North West Boundary Survey party encountered several groups on some of the smaller islands in the archipelago such as Decatur in the business of producing shakes for local mainland markets. Hiram E. Hutchinson, who established a store at Fisherman Bay on Lopez Island, cleared his land of the large trees and sold cordwood for steamers and barrel staves for the lime operations such as Port Langdon on Orcas. In the *Products of Industry* portion of the 1870 census, John L. Reed was mentioned as having a shingle factory that produced some 350,000 shingles, valued at $875. A couple of stave factories were also enumerated: Charles Swift (barrel staves, $600) and Hiram E. Hutchinson ($1480). The Port Townsend *Weekly Argus* of July 18, 1874, noted that "The Schooner Orcas arrived last Friday from Lopez Island, with 100,000 shingles for E. S. Fowler & Co."—an indication of the volume of manufacture at that time.[116] A thousand shingles—the product of a single day's work—were worth about $1.50 at the time.[117]

A common use for wood cut in the islands was for cord wood: logs bucked into four-foot lengths and then split. A stacked wood cord is 4 feet high by 8 feet long by 4 feet deep and there were about 120 sticks per cord. An 1883 "Map of Density" of forests in Washington State was scaled to cords per acre; San Juan County is rated among the lowest in the state.[118] Wood—principally old growth Douglas fir (*Pseudotsuga menziesii*), although some pieces of red alder (*Alnus rubra*), western red cedar (*Thuja plicata*), or madrona (*Arbutus menziesii*) could be present—was the fuel used to burn limestone throughout the San Juan Islands. Cutting local timber for cordwood for the lime kilns soon became a major source of income for residents. It took about 4 cords to fire a kiln continuously through a 24-hour period. Wood was supplied by woodcutters and farmers clearing their land on Lopez, Orcas, and San Juan, as well as many of the smaller islands located in the San Juan archipelago and hauled by wagon or shipped by scow to the kiln sites. James Tulloch remembered that one of his first jobs when he came to homestead on Orcas was cutting wood at $1.50 a cord for the lime works. It was a hard job—"the badly twisted timber of these windswept islands is the very hardest wood to cut or split that I have ever seen"—although he was finally able

*Woodcutters with Springboards and a Misery Whip
(courtesy of San Juan Historical Museum)*

to work up to 1½ cords a day.[119] Cord wood also supplied fuel for the many steamers that began to ply the waters of the Salish Sea, beginning with the British steamers such as the *Beaver*, *Julia*, and *Otter*, and continuing with early American vessels *Eliza*

Anderson, Wilson G. Hunt, and *Olympia.* Historic photographs of docks in the islands recorded large piles of cordwood stacked up and ready to be loaded onto steamers.

The method for cutting trees at that time was with an axe and two-man saw. The largest, straightest (usually first growth) trees were selected, and notches were cut at shoulder (i.e., swinging) height with a double- or single-bit axe. Springboards, or wide milled boards, were inserted into the notches, and the men, standing on these, would begin a cut with an ax, again at shoulder height, and then continue with a cross-cut saw (called a "misery whip"). Cutting at this height avoided the rich sap and gnarlier grain at the base of the tree. After felling, the top was cut off, and the trunk bucked into four-foot-long rounds that were then split into cordwood. Evidence of this type of logging can still be seen in areas of former old growth forest where there are 8-10-foot-high stumps with notches 4-5 feet above the ground. Sometimes, some 50 to 100 feet away, there will be a line of smaller trees that have seeded from the remains of the overstory.

Trades

Several trades were essential to the local economy of these times. Blacksmiths—and eventually liverymen, when concentrations of people developed in towns—played an essential role in an economy based on metal agricultural and hand tools and horsepower. James Douglas told Charles Griffin that his plow was being repaired by a blacksmith, no doubt at Fort Victoria. The blacksmith shop at American Camp was built in 1867; the coal that fueled the forge came from both California and nearby Nanaimo, BC. At English Camp, there are the remains of a stone structure with what appears to be a forge, which would have been an essential component of the operations of the Royal Marines. An 1877 receipt from the Langdon Lime Kiln operator Shotter & Co. records the sale of "all our blacksmith's tools" to William Moore on Orcas Island. Concomitant with blacksmithing was the use of grindstones, which were essential to sharpening the many metal tools used at this time. It is no accident that Grindstone Bay on Orcas Island was named that, reputedly because it was the only location on the island that had one. It was also called

Brown Bay, after Lars Brown, a Norwegian who practiced blacksmithing there.

There is also the mysterious case of the San Juan Manufacturing Company, located on the southeast coast of Friday Harbor in the early 1880s. Records begin with the lease of an acre of E. D. Warbass's land, near a stream, to Maria dos Reis Harbersham on January 24, 1884. (Maria, sometimes referred to as Mariquinha Dos Reis, was the wife of Robert Habersham, who purchased Brown Island in Friday Harbor.) Two years later the "San Juan Manufacturing Company" conveyed to James Steele of Portland Oregon "all its buildings, fixtures, machinery and appurtenances…upon a certain tract of two acres of land heretofore leased … by E. D. Warbass." A year later, the company was clearly in trouble, with three court claims, including a mortgage foreclosure by James Steele. All this begs the question: What was the company manufacturing, with its buildings, fixtures, machinery and appurtenances near what may have been a stream providing water power?

Recreational trades abounded with the establishment of San Juan Town, the first village on the island, catering to the needs of the soldiers at American Camp and other islanders. Saloon keepers flourished; at one time there were several operating in the small settlement. The *Victoria Gazette* reported that "some three or four persons had started little groggeries near the landing from the harbor and several parties had been in a state of drunkenness the night before."[120] Mike Vouri, writing about "Scofflaws and Moonshine," stated:

> *Alcohol abuse was considered a serious enough matter that the Washington Territorial Legislature passed a law in 1855 forbidding the manufacture and sale or gift of "Ardent Spirits." Only a public agent was permitted to sell liquor "for certain purposes as long as he conforms to regulations and is paid." Selling to Indians and Hawaiians was prohibited in all cases, and by 1863 violators were subject to imprisonment.*[121]

When Friday Harbor was established as the seat of San Juan County—which E. D. Warbass saw as a way of distancing the County from the reputation of San Juan Town—one of the early tasks of the newly formed county government was the regulation of liquor sales through the sale of licenses.

Other, associated recreation came with drinking. As noted at the beginning of this chapter, one of the occupations listed in the 1860 census was "gambler," and certainly not all those gambling relied upon it for a living. Prostitution was also a major occupation in San Juan Town. Grim as it is to recognize this fact, most prostitutes were Indigenous women who were either slaves used by their masters or girls set adrift from their traditional societies by the disruption wrought by introduced diseases and a market economy.

Laboring

In addition to those practicing specific crafts, trades, or occupations, there were "common laborers"—those who hired out their services for a wage or fixed fee. This group was quite broad and indefinite and included members of the various Indigenous groups that worked for the Hudson's Bay Company as well as employees ("servants") of the Company, soldiers at American and English Camps, and English and American citizens who hired out to the various enterprises in the islands. Examples of wage labor ranged from common tasks such as digging and grubbing, herding, plowing, and harvesting to more specialized skills such as butchering, construction, milk and butter production, and shearing. To examine wage labor in general, it is best to start with the Hudson's Bay Company, which not only established paid jobs in the islands, but set the precedent for going rates.

Belle Vue Sheep Farm operated within the corporate culture of the Hudson's Bay Company, and their employment practices had been codified well before the establishment of the farm. Hudson's Bay was a joint-stock company (i.e., owned by shareholders), which held a general meeting every year to elect a Governor and committee to oversee its business. Those who worked for (or were "engaged by") the Company were called "Servants," who were divided into "Gentlemen" ("Bourgeois" was the term that the North West Company had used) and "Labourers." The rank-and-file was organized in a quasi-military structure: a Chief Factor and his officers (Chief Traders) commanded each trading post, while Clerks (the equivalent of non-commissioned officers) and Labourers, Shepherds, and Voyageurs (enlisted soldiers) conducted the day-to-day work. To climb the ranks, a Gentleman must first have apprenticed for five years in order to become a Clerk. A Clerks' engagement was generally for five years, with the wage rising each year: starting at £20 per annum, £25 the second year, £30 the third, £40 the fourth, and £50 the fifth. They would then be re-engaged at £100, a salary that could then rise to as high as £150. After 13-20 years as a Clerk, one could then be appointed a Chief Trader (or half shareholder), and then hopefully attain the highest rank, Chief Factor (full shareholder). From 1821 to 1872, the average wage of a Chief Factor was £720, while a Chief Trader got half that, or £360. In 1858, George Gibbs estimated that the Chief Factor (James Douglas) received $7,000, while the Chief Trader (Charles Griffin) received $3,500 annually.[122]

The Company had a standard corporate procedure for hiring "Labourers" — an employee was "engaged" (*engagé*) through a contract ("paper") for a specific period of time (one month, one year), under specific conditions of work and pay. Employees could then be "discharged" or "re-engaged;" leaving during the unexpired term of one's engagement, however, was considered "desertion." Probably due to his French-Canadian origin and the influence of the North West Company on Hudson's Bay, Belle Vue Sheep Farm Manager Griffin also uses the French term *congé* when referring to the firing of an employee; this probably refers to the phrase *donner congé* (to give notice).[123] It is not clear if there was prejudicial hiring with regard to ethnicity, although the textual and comparative evidence seems to indicate that Europeans were assigned positions of supervision over Indians, and the latter had shorter periods of employment.

The Company-wide average annual servant's wage was £18, or about $550 (in 1976), which was calculated to cover purchase of clothing, some luxuries, and private tools and utensils, plus rations. At Belle Vue, however, the term of employment and wages varied according to position and duties. The Head Shepherd, who was engaged for a period from one to two years, received £35 per annum, while Shepherds and Labourers generally received £25 or less. Shepherds also received extra for shearing. In 1856, for instance, the two McCleods received one pound sterling per 100 fleeces. Temporary workers were also hired by the month. Younger employees, such as the sons of the Kanakas, who worked tending the flocks, were generally hired at a lower scale; Friday's son (Joe) was hired in 1858 for £5 per annum and a half ration. Wages were credited to "servants accounts," and items such as clothing, blankets, and extra provisions that were obtained from Company stores (in this case, at Fort Victoria) were deducted from these accounts. In the case of damages due to negligence or malfeasance on the part of an employee, such as the incident on June 5, 1854, when the Old Man's [Page's] dog killed a sheep, a penalty was assessed on their account.[124]

> *I have duly weighted your remarks in regards to providing Servants with food for their families, and admit their force, but there are reasons equally cogent against the practice. At an inland Post supported on the resources of the country the expense is trifling, but at this place where we have to import Provisions at a very serious expense, the business would not repay the cost. A man like Ferron might easily salt 3 or 4 barrels of salmon at San Juan in the proper season, and cultivate a patch of potatoes, for the support of his family, and every facility and assistance should be given him in breaking up the land, and you might also furnish him with barrels for the salmon he may cure. By that means he might keep his family in comfort. I will talk the matter over with him quietly & endeavor to prevail upon him to return to you.*
>
> —Chief Trader James Douglas to Post Trader Charles Griffin, March 31, 1856

All employees—but not their families—were provided on Saturdays with weekly rations of either salt or fresh meat (beef, mutton, or pork) and flour, sugar, and tea. The *Post Journals* often record the average ration of meat: 12-15 pounds of fresh beef, mutton, or pork, or 9 pounds of salted pork. For other items, we must look to places like Fort Vancouver for comparison. In 1838, for instance, the weekly ration there consisted of 4 qts. peas, ½ lb. tallow, 9 lb. salmon, and 3 lb. bread or potatoes, while yearly the men received two bags of flour, 60 lbs. sugar, 12 lbs. tea, and a small quantity of wine and brandy. By 1842-1845, the weekly ration was 21 pounds of salmon and either 1 bushel of potatoes or 12 lbs. of flour per week. (Chief Factors, in keeping with their higher salaries, received: 300 lbs. flour, 336 lbs. sugar, 18 lbs. black tea, 9 lbs. green tea, 42 lbs. raisins, 60 lbs. butter, 30 lbs. candles, 3 lbs. mustard, 16 gallons port, sherry and brandy; Chief Traders, in turn, received half this, while Clerks got half of the Chief Traders' amounts.[125] For the Christmas and New Year's holidays, the men were issued a "Regale" or, as Griffin calls it, "Regal": a portion and a half of their usual rations, and sometimes a pint of rum.

Talk of laboring would not be complete without mention of the men who worked at the two military camps on San Juan. The "special correspondent" who described the situation on San Juan Island in 1859 for the *San Francisco Daily Alta California* described the soldier's life:

> *Camp life begins at 5½ o'clock—and the fifes, drums and trumpets keep up a general hubbub for nigh an hour. At breakfast, which is often just coffee and toast, there are drills, various labors, including guard duty, artillery experiments, cooks, carpenters, brick-layers and tailors, while others cut firewood.... Dinner is at 1½ o'clock, there are various activities, at 4 o'clock, everyone parades and the tattoo beats at 8 o'clock. Those with passes seek amusement in town...and sleep to those not on duty soon leaves the camp to the solitude of the guard..."*

In the U.S. Army, enlisted infantrymen who had signed up for a 5-year hitch started at $7/month, which could rise to $13/month if they became sergeants. (Officers, on the other hand, received $25/month for a 2nd lieutenant to $75/month for a colonel, and received extra pay for quarters, remote service, and food.)

Daily rations consisted of fresh or salt beef or pork, fresh bread or hardtack, coffee, and beans, peas, or rice. Although payroll was supposed to be every 8 weeks, soldiers often went without pay for 6 months or more, and so became dependent on credit from the post sutler.[126]

At English Camp, in addition to their normal pay, the Royal Marines also received "colony pay"—recompense for work 'above and beyond usual duties' establishing forts or camps in a previously unsettled area—much to their delight and the consternation of the American commanding officers. According to Mike Vouri, during spring and summer of 1859 the marines received 14 shillings per day for Captains, Subalterns 9, Sergeants 4, and Privates 3, with a grant of land after a specified number of years.[127] Charles Whitlock wrote home that he received "very good pay, altogether about seventy pounds a year."[128] Daily fare for the British soldiers included 1 lb. biscuit, ¼ c. spirits, 1 lb. fresh meat, ½ lb. vegetables, 1¾ oz. sugar, 1 oz. chocolate, and ¼ oz. tea. Then, once a week, they received ¼ pt. oatmeal, ½ oz. mustard, ¼ oz. pepper and ¼ pt. vinegar. For beverages, they also got ½ pt. wine, 1 qt. strong beer and ½ gal small beer, as well as coffee, cocoa, chocolate, and tea.[129] It can be assumed that their daily work schedule was very similar to their American counterparts, consisting of an early start with breakfast, engagement in various drills and camp jobs, dinner midday, and then more work, parade, supper, and dismissal.

Many Euro-Americans and Indigenous peoples hired out their labor to neighbors for farm jobs. In 1879, several islanders were paid $5 per day for mowing and $6 per day for reaping. An example of wages paid for labor at various jobs can be gleaned from a Territorial court case in which Charles E. Powell sought unpaid wages incurred in 1859 and 1860 from San Juan resident John Henry. His ordinary rate for labor—including such tasks as building a house—was $2.50 a day. He charged a base fee of $6.00 for hauling, although if it was a heavy load requiring two yoke of oxen, the charge was doubled ($12.00). He also charged a base rate of $12.00/acre for plowing.[130] Another unpaid invoice, from Solomon Meyerbeck to Moses Eckstein, includes the costs of "Indian" labor in the Company garden: on one day Meyerbeck, who may have been brokering for the laborer, notes down a mere 25 cents, but later the charge is $5.00—unfortunately with no rate. He also lists hauling rails at $3.00.[131]

Several Chinese worked as servants in local households. Lila Hannah Firth reminisced that her mother brought a Chinese teenager ("Che Che") back from a shopping trip in Victoria; her only payment was to teach the boy English.[132] Chinese were brought from Canada through the San Juans to the United States by smugglers who allegedly could get $100 a person, and there are many tales of their being abandoned when the smugglers felt threatened by approaching revenue cutters; China Rock in San Juan Channel is one instance of a place named after such an incident. In speaking of household servants, Mary Julia Allen, wife of Major Harvey A. Allen, commander at American Camp, wrote to her sister Carrie on March 5, 1868, that "Our neighbors have Chinamen and pay them thirty dollars [a month]." She went on to say that they made "excellent servants, good cooks and excellent washermen and ironers. They are great imitators, and if you once tell them what to do, they go on doing it the same way till you tell them to stop."[133] As noted above, several of the lime kilns in the islands employed Chinese as cooks.

Slavery

A description of work during this period would not be complete without mention of labor without compensation, through human bondage, or slavery. The Coast Salish did have slaves, who were usually captives obtained in war or their offspring. Although slaves were assigned work that other members of the group did not want to do, such as gathering fuel and water and packing and hauling goods, they are said to have been treated well. William J. Warren, secretary to the North West Boundary Survey, on a tour of the San Juan Islands, noted that "I notice that nearly all the labor of packing up their baggage and loading the canoe was performed by the slave, who seemed to be perfectly satisfied and contented in the performance of his task."[134] Upon inquiry, the old man who was his "owner" said that he had paid $100 for the boy, which Warren estimated was about twice the ordinary price. After the coming of so many single Euro-American men to the islands, some Coast Salish prostituted their female slaves.

During the time prior to the U.S. Civil War, Washington Territory was considered "Free Soil," where slavery was forbidden. However, there are several cases on the mainland where those who came over the Oregon Trial as well as other immigrants brought slaves with them. One was James Tilton, the surveyor who worked on the 1870s Township and Range Survey in the islands, who brought the enslaved Charles Mitchell with him to Washington Territory in 1853. Mitchell escaped to Canada to seek his freedom, which generated a political firestorm pro and con his forced return; he eventually was returned to Tilton until the end of the Civil War.[135] Lyman Cutlar's plainly spoken prejudice against Blacks—he referred to the Hudson's Bay Company servant Jacob as a "collard [colored] man," "negro," and "nigger"—certainly is representative of his contemporary culture and the number of former U.S. officers who joined the Southern cause is testament to contemporary attitudes towards slavery. Whether there were other cases of enslavement in the islands during this period is not known.

> *When my father left Cowlitz County he brought an Indian woman slave with us. He took her away because the Indians were using her to earn money for them. After a short time father turned her loose. She was then taken by a white man with an Indian wife and again put into slavery.*
>
> *When father heard this, he told the man he must let her go—or he would kill him. He let her go.*
>
> —Interview with Victoria Taylor, Washington Pioneers Project

Work

During this period, the nature of work underwent a change from the substinence and trade economy of the Indigenous peoples to the introduction of wage labor and specific occupations by Euro-Americans. This change was already inherent in the various ways that people worked in the islands. The Coast Salish fished, gathered, and hunted to sustain their households, but they also did this work to produce a surplus for trade to groups in the Salish Sea region and beyond. Both camas cultivation and reef netting—the latter entailing stewardship of specific sites and equipment and the ability to manage large numbers of workers (the crews and processors)—both produced surpluses that were processed for long term storage and trade. With the introduction of Euro-American economies, Indigenous peoples supplemented their trade systems, adding market goods such as venison. As the economy of the islands gradually transitioned from one of relative self-sufficiency to that of being dependent upon the wider regional and even world-wide economy, both Indigenous and Euro-American islanders worked in several ways to 'make a living.' And, being islanders, they have always had to interact with those outside the islands through trade. Examination of the variety of occupations—gathering, hunting and trapping, fishing, farming, trades such as blacksmithing and saloon keeping, and even 'ordinary' laboring—indicates the many different ways islanders worked and how those occupations changed through time.

INTERCOURSE

When Lyman Cutler settled on San Juan Island, it was as one of a larger group of Americans who had begun arriving there after returning from the Fraser Gold Rush, joining other Euro-Americans working for the Hudson's Bay Company and Indigenous peoples who had been living in the islands for millennia. Cutlar probably arrived with his Indigenous wife in a Coast Salish canoe. While on the island, he used the "Cowichin Road"—which passed right in front of his place, and from which Jacob had espied the infamous boar digging in the potato garden—that had been established by the Hudson's Bay Company to connect the various pastures of the Belle Vue Sheep Farm. Later, renamed the Military Road, it would connect American Camp with English Camp during the joint military occupation. As part of the commercial network on the island and within the region, Cutlar would have bought and traded goods at local stores as well as mainland ones such as Waterman and Katz in Port Townsend. This chapter examines intercourse among the islanders and their wider economic milieu, through transportation, communication, merchandizing, and financing.

Boats and Shipping

Because the San Juan Islands, by definition, are not connected to the surrounding mainland and Vancouver Island, the only transportation throughout the Salish Sea was by means of boats and ships. When Chief Trader Charles Griffin gazed out from his "Establishment" at Belle Vue Sheep Farm on the south end of San Juan Island, he looked out over Haro Strait and the Strait of Juan de Fuca beyond to observe and record in his *Post Journals* a great variety of sea-going vessels, ranging from one-man canoes and row boats, to many-crewed Nootkan and Northern or Haida canoes, Euro-American sloops and schooners, and British and American war ships and steamers.[1] Just as it is important to understand the common ways in which inhabitants of the islands used and lived on the land, it is equally important to examine the many ways in which peoples navigated the waters surrounding the archipelago and throughout the greater region.

During the latter half of the nineteenth century, the Coast Salish in the San Juans used several types of canoes depending on function, the styles of which varied through time. All early canoes were carved from trunks of trees native to the region, most commonly cedar (*Thuja plicata*), which has a grain that can easily be split and carved and also contains a toxic oil (*thujaplicin*) that naturally preserves the wood against rot and insect attack.[2] Within a common building tradition of cedar dugouts, what distinguished the styles of regional canoes were features such as the lines of bow, stern, and gunwale and the section of the hull, all of which were influenced by the nature of the waters in which the canoes were used. The standard measures of the hull of a vessel are the length, beam (width at the widest point—usually the middle), and draw (depth). Canoe styles developed over time from Coast Salish (short and narrow, low prow)—for use in the calmer, inner waters—to Nootkan (larger, curved, pointed prow, and vertical stern)—for more stability, especially for reef netting. Finally, other tribes used the Northern style (largest, with vertical cutwater leading to angled prow and sloped stern with knob)—for long-distance freightage. Part of the reason for this change in style and size must have been increased reliance upon the larger

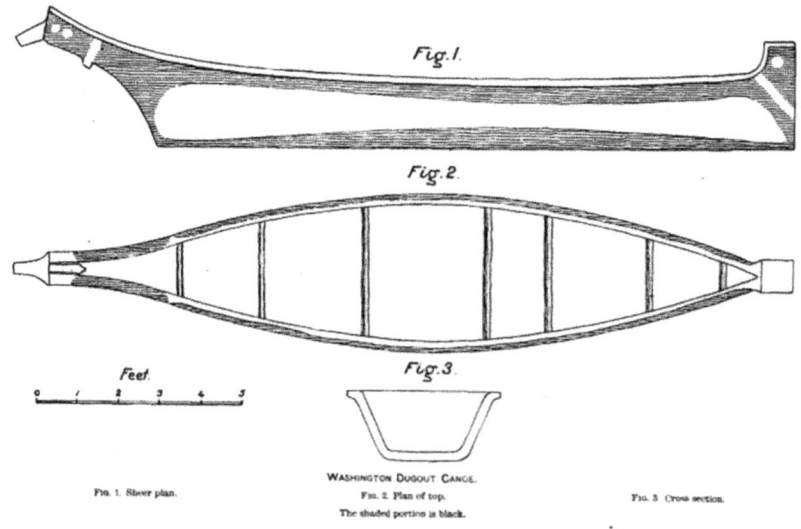

Washington Dugout Canoe
"Fishing Vessels of the Pacific Coast," Bulletin of the U.S. Fish Commission (1890)

cedar trees that were available on the west coast of Vancouver Island and Haida Gwaii (Queen Charlotte Islands).[3]

Both the Nootkan- and Northern-style canoes added material to the upper portions of the prow and stern, so that carvers were able to use only half of a large log for the main body of the canoe, and not have to be too picky about selecting core wood that was solid and not fungal and spongy.

> *[The canoe maker]...first softened the wood by filling... with water which he made to boil by putting red hot stones in it. The canoe was then partially spread and allowed to remain for a day....The next morning after heating the water again with hot stones he built a slow fire of rotten wood and bark on the ground along the sides of the canoe to render the wood perfectly soft, or as he said, "to cook it", and then stretched the sides apart as far as was safe and kept them in position by means of stretchers or thwarts. I measured this canoe before he commenced to widen it and found that amidship, the opening was two feet eight inches wide, after he had finished the canoe I again measured it at the same place and found it was four feet nine inches...*
>
> —James Swan at Neah Bay, quoted in Ivan Doig, Winter Brothers (1980)[4]

The lines of the canoe were carved with the eventual widening of the hull in mind. This widening was done by heating stones in a fire and then placing them in water in the hull, which was sometimes covered, to steam and soften the wooden hull fibers. Thwarts were then placed to both widen the hull and raise the gunwale and stem line.

The earliest type was the Salish canoe, which is long (averaging 20-30 feet, although it could reach up to 40 feet), narrow, and distinguished by an almost vertical cutwater with a long-angled prow and a steadily sloped stern that narrows to meet the rising gunwale. An important feature of the Salish canoe is the flare that is carved below the full length of the gunwales and is particularly pronounced at the bow and the stern. In the situation of either an approaching wave or a following sea, this feature effectively turns the force away, and prevents the water from going over the gunwale to swamp the hull. With its rounded bottom, this early

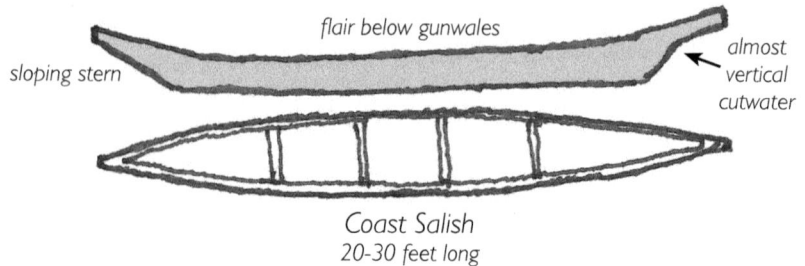

Coast Salish
20-30 feet long

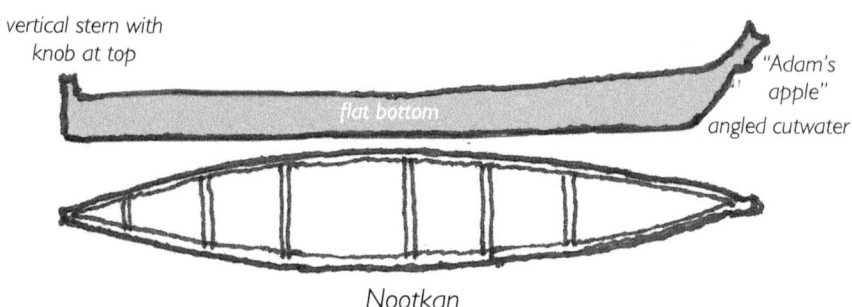

Nootkan
20-40 feet long; 5-7 feet wide

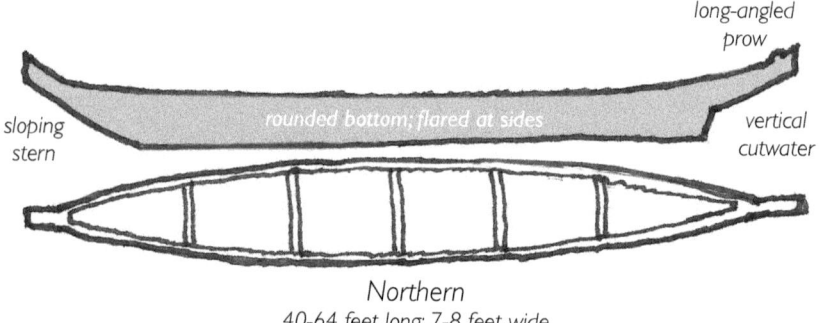

Northern
40-64 feet long; 7-8 feet wide

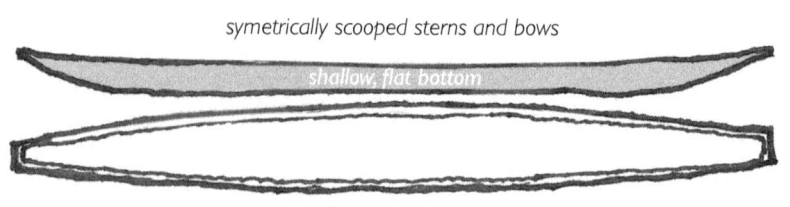

Shovel-nosed
10-40 feet long; 2-3 feet wide

Northwest Dugout Canoe Types
(adapted from: Leslie Lincoln, Coast Salish Canoes 1991)

Salish canoe was particularly seaworthy in the inner waters of Puget Sound, the Islands, and the Gulf of Georgia, which can feature strong winds and currents and choppy waters, but not the large swells and breaking waves of the outer Vancouver Island and Olympic Peninsula coast and ocean. While the lower prow cutwater slices through the waves, the upper portion flairs to resist boarding waves. Like most Indigenous canoes, these craft were beached with the bow facing water-ward, both to deflect beach waves and for quick launching.[5]

The West Coast, or Nootka, style of canoe originated among the Nootkan (*Nuu-chah-nulth*) peoples of the West Coast of Vancouver Island but was adopted by tribes as far south as the Columbia River and as far north as Haida Gwaii. This style of canoe was designed for the rougher waves of the Pacific Ocean. Unlike the Salish style, it features an angled cutwater that leads in one continuous, graceful curve to an animal head-like projection; below this, on the outside, is a knob that has been called, after Euro-American arrival, an "Adam's apple." The stern is almost vertical, with a knob at the top. The gunwale, which is close to horizontal, curves up to meet the prow, but essentially dies into the stern knob. The bottom is close to flat, lending stability when fishing or whaling. While whaling canoes, which carried a crew of eight (a helmsman, a harpooner, and six paddlers), ranged in length from 30 to 35 feet with a beam of 5 feet, those that were used in inland waters ranged from 20 to 40 feet in length, although there were historically recorded instances of canoes that were 55 feet long and over 7 feet wide.[6]

The third major type of canoe is called the Northern or Haida style, named for the principal Indigenous group that produced it, although others, such as the *Heiltsuk* (formerly Bella Bella), *Xa'islak'ala* (formerly Haisla), *Kwakwaka'wakw* (formerly Kwakiutl), Tlingit, and Tsimshian not only used them but probably built them as well. The Haida peoples were particularly known for their canoe-making abilities, so that extensive trade in Haida canoes occurred throughout the region, leading to confusion among Euro-American observers as to the identity of the groups who were using Haida-style craft for transport. Northern canoes traded for goods ranging from 10 to 15 blankets to one slave. The Haida traveled easily in these canoes from their territory in Haida Gwaii 500 miles south to Puget Sound.

Like the smaller Coast Salish canoes, which may have been the original inspiration for the style, the Northern canoe has both a vertical cutwater with a long, angled prow and a sloping stern. However, these vessels were on average larger and used several distinct pieces in their construction: one large log for the hull, with pieces added to the upper portions of the bow and stern. The hull section was rounded at the bottom and flared at the sides, leading to greater buoyancy and speed, and wash strakes—bands of wood—were sometimes added to the gunwales to provide the extra height needed to prevent waves striking against the sides from washing into the canoe. Although the average size has been estimated at around 40 feet in length, 7 feet at the beam, and 3 feet deep, they could be as large as 64 feet in length, 8 feet at the beam, and 7'3" at the bow. These canoes were valued for their carrying capacity: some of the larger examples could hold up to 50 men and from six to eight tons of cargo.[7] (This makes it seem more believable, in the Beigin family's story about Lucy Morris, that she could stow away in a canoe going south to elope, fleeing from her father who was a Northern tribal chief.)

> When these northern Indians start out upon their trading and marauding expeditions with a fleet of canoes, varying in number according to the object and extent of their excursions, they present a truly formidable array. Their canoes, made from the single trunk of the giant cedar of their country, are of the most beautiful model and workmanship; they are from seventy-five to one hundred feet in length, and will carry from fifty to sixty persons, and a plentiful supply of arms, ammunition, and stores. They have been known to capture large vessels. An idea may be formed of the seaworthiness of these craft, and of the Indians' skills in navigating them, from the fact that they make voyages along the coast of over five hundred miles in extent, and go far out to sea in pursuit of the whale. These canoes, propelled by fifty or sixty paddles, are driven through the water with great speed.
>
> —Geographical Memoir of the Islands between the Continent and Vancouver's Island in the Vicinity of the Forty Ninth Parallel of North Latitude (1860)[8]

Reef Netters off Stuart Island
(courtesy of San Juan Historical Museum)

A fourth type of regional canoe—what has been called in English the spoon or shovel-nosed style—was well adapted to river use, and thus probably not used much, if at all, in the San Juan Islands. Both the bow and the stern were symmetrically scooped, with flat ends and relatively shallow, flat bottoms. Ranging from 10 to 40 feet in length, a typical example from the Stillaguamish River measures 27' long but only 32" in the beam. These were designed to be poled through the rapid currents of the swift streams and rivers of the Nootsack, Upper Skagit, Sauk-Suiattle, Snohomish, Stillaguamish, Puyallup, Nisqually, Chehalis, Muckleshoot, and freshwater Duwamish.[9]

Wayne Suttles conjectured that a modified form of the shovel nose canoe was used by Coast Salish groups for reef netting. Suttle's interviewees, who had not actually seen one, referred to the reef net canoe's wide bow and flat stern, which accords with Boas' 1890 description of the "large fishing-boat" of the Songish:

> *The square stern is peculiar to the LkungEn fishing-boat. It seems that it was not made of one piece with the boat, but consisted of a board inserted into a groove, the joints being made water-tight by means of pitch.*[10]

Reef net canoes were anchored with their sterns at the forward end of the net; the watchman was able to observe better from the sheared-off stern, while the rest of the crew lay in the bottom towards the bow, for stability. Because the shovel-nose style of canoe was more appropriate to the calm waters of rivers and streams, and not the rougher waters of the Salish Sea, it was usually deployed for reef netting when the waters were calm.[11] By the mid-nineteenth century, reef netters had converted almost exclusively to the Nootkan canoe, because it offered greater stability. Eventually, modern plank ("clinker-built") boats replaced these. When examined from a stylistic point of view, although the fundamental construction materials changed, the form and details did not. Modern reef net boats still feature an almost vertical cutwater, a long projecting prow, flat bottoms with curved sides, and an upright stern.

Paddles varied among various Indigenous groups within the region. Like paddles of other canoe-using groups, such as South Pacific islanders, Coast Salish paddles can be classified according to the various shapes used to describe leaves: cordate, deltoid, and elliptic; lanceolate; and oblong, obovate, oval, and ovate.[12] Salish paddles were mostly oblanceolate, although some were elliptic with a narrowing point. They were usually constructed of broad-leaf maple, with crutch-like handles carved out of the same piece of wood. (Ruth Kirk mentions that the paddles found at Ozette were shaped so that they entered the water quietly and when removed would not drip, so as to not attract the attention of marine mammals.)[13] Men's paddles differed from women's: they were longer and narrower, while the latter's were shorter and carved with a slightly fuller blade; the handle was sometimes broadened out at the end to include two thumb holes. It is interesting to note that in a photo of Kanaka Bay Camp, there are at least two men holding paddles, clearly in the Coast Salish style. (While it is tempting to conjecture that there may have been a Hawaiian [Kanaka] influence on local paddle design; outrigger paddles from the Hawaiian Islands at the time were rounded.)

> *Now that is the sail of the ancient people before any white people came; to wit, short boards sewed together. The canoe-mast is short, for it just shows above the top edge of the board sail when it is standing up in the bow. The wind just blows against it and presses the board sail against the mast when the canoe is running before the wind.*
>
> —Franz Boas, "*Ethology of the Kwakiutl,*" Thirty-fifth Annual Report of the Bureau of American Ethnography, 1913-1914 *(1921)*

The Coast Salish sometimes used sails, which were made of rectangular mats woven of cedar bark, cattail, or rush. An older form of sail consisted of cedar boards thinly split and lashed together. Sails were rigged on a mast with two horizontal spars (top and bottom) and four lines. This could only be used to sail directly before the wind. After Euro-American contact, sprit-rigged cloth sails were adopted.[14] Within the canoe itself, there was a cedar-withe mat on the bottom and a sewed cattail mat on top of it, upon which the paddler knelt. Edward T. Coleman, in his 1869 travelogue through the San Juans, described a quite cushy arrangement, albeit as a privileged passenger:

> *The bottom of the canoe is spread with small branches and twigs, and then covered with matting of native manufacture. One's blankets are placed against the thwarts and form a soft cushion, against which he can recline and be as comfortable as in a first-class railway carriage.*[15]

Boating gear included a bailer made of folded cedar bark with a wooden handle and an anchor consisting of a rock about one foot in diameter with a hole through it and a cedar-withe ring, to which the anchor line was attached.[16]

The order of the paddlers in the canoe reflected that of the household, with the matriarch steering in the stern and paddlers arrayed according to family rank ahead of her. (This was also the order of living arrangement in the longhouse, and, in the case of reef net crews, the order of place in fish camps.) When the people moved from winter to summer villages, they would load the cedar boards that formed the siding of the longhouses and place them across two canoes, forming a catamaran platform that they could then load their belongings onto and paddle to their seasonal dwelling place.

The general outline of adaptation and change over time emerges—from Coast Salish canoes (short and narrow, low prow) for use in the calmer, inner waters; to Nootkan (larger, curved, pointed prow and vertical stern) for more stability and use in reef netting; and eventually to use by other tribes of Northern style (largest, with vertical cutwater leading to angled prow and sloped stern with knob) for long distance freightage. What is not always clear is who was using what type where and when. For instance, when Charles Griffin writes about his canoe in his *Post Journals*, what type was it? Or when, according to family tradition, Patrick Beigin traded for an Indian canoe to transport goods between San Juan and Victoria, what type was that? One of the few historic photographs from this period—taken of the Kanaka Bay settlement from the water—indicates a mixture of several canoe types, including both the Coast Salish and Nootkan, as well as Euro-American Columbia River Salmon boats.

In contrast to traditional Indigenous boats, which were carved out of tree trunks, European and Euro-American boats were primarily constructed of wooden planks that were fastened

*Canoes and Columbia River Salmon Boats at Kanaka Bay
(courtesy of San Juan Historical Museum)*

together to form a hull. Called "clinker-built" or "lapstrake" construction, these were comprised of long boards that were attached to a framework such that each course overlapped the one below. Although Indigenous use of dugout canoes persisted through the 1920s—and American and English settlers used them throughout the late nineteenth century—the Coast Salish gradually adopted clinker-built boats, primarily small 14- to 16-feet-long, oar-powered skiffs that were easily built or cheaply purchased.

Indigenous Fishers Bringing Their Catch to Sell (courtesy of San Juan Historical Museum)

Clinker-built boats ranged in size from small craft—dinghies, dories, long or whale boats, and gigs—to larger sailing craft such as sloops, schooners, brigs, and barks. Boats and ships can be classified by their motive power: oars or paddles, sails, or steam—and later gasoline—engines. Sailing craft were most often classified by how they were rigged, with spars or poles forming a mast, yard, boom, or gaffs, as well as the ropes (or lines) that secured the spars and sails. These classifications included the number of masts as well as the number, position, and type of the sails.

One of the easiest of the plank-formed boats, and most er-ergonomic considering the material used, was the dory, which is defined as a flat-bottomed boat with the boards that form the bottom running the length of the hull. Dories are constructed of wide (6-10"), thin (around 1") planks, which, when conformed to the outline of the flat bottom, form widely flared sides and a graceful prow and stern.[17] New World versions of the dory—particularly the French *bateau*, which was used to navigate the strong currents and rapids of the St. Lawrence and other Canadian and American rivers—were probably derived from Old World traditions, which ranged from Portuguese *flats* to French *bachots* and *bateaux* and English *flatners* and *wherries*.

The dory was introduced by the Hudson's Bay Company to the Northwest Coast in the eighteenth century, replacing the birchbark canoes used by the North West Company with the York Boat, named after the principal "factory" at the mouth of the Hayes River on Hudson's Bay that transshipped furs from the wide Company network of traders to London. The York Boat, which was allegedly based on Orkney designs and built by Orkney men employed by the Company, was long (32-36 feet) with a narrow bottom that flared to 6-8 feet and pointed bow and stern that were angled at about 45 degrees. They were clinker-built, with the ¼-1"-thick planks of the side hull overlapping each other. The crew consisted of six to eight oarsmen, who rowed with 18-foot-long oars from seats on the opposite side of the boat from the oarlock. York boats were sometimes poled or sailed with a square rig on an 8-foot-tall mast. Twice a year, the Company sent off the "York Express" to carry important papers and trade goods from Fort Vancouver to York Factory; this usually consisted of two York Boats carrying 40 men.[18] Locally, the Company may have used York Boats for the Nisqually Express, a similarly rapid journey between Fort Vancouver and Nisqually Farm—although other outposts, such as Fort Victoria and Belle Vue Sheep Farm, were often included.

Long boats and whale boats were developed by the English and used on the East Coast of North America as early as the eighteenth century, either on their own or in conjunction with a larger ship. During the mid-nineteenth century, these designs were modified to develop a boat that was faster both in terms of sailing and rowing.[19] Clinker-built, they were usually 20-28 feet long, with a straight keel. They could be either rowed (illustrations commonly show at least five oarlocks) or sailed, often with a centerboard and sprit or gaff mainsail. When Americans under the direction of Whatcom County Sheriff Barnes came from Bellingham Bay and auctioned off Belle Vue Sheep Farm sheep in lieu of purported taxes, the party, which consisted of eight men and two Indians in either two or three boats, must have been rowing substantial longboats or whaling craft (as well as a stolen canoe), because they were able to make away with 34 breeding rams as cargo. The American members of the North West Boundary Survey used whaleboats; they could either be rowed or sailed, and were convenient with for their ease of beaching for overnight camping while surveying. Islanders use them too; Thomas Fleming noted in his *Journal* on May 16, 1878: "Went to Victoria in Whale Boat."[20]

The sloop—defined as single-masted, fore-and-aft rigged with a jib or gaff mainsail, the latter sometimes with a gaff topsail, and one or more headsails—were well suited to island waters, particularly because they were small enough to handle with

Sloops
(courtesy of San Juan Historical Museum)

one or two sailors and could be hauled up on a beach if need be. Lila Hannah Firth recalled that:

> There was a man by the name of Harry Dwyer that ran a sloop from Kanaka Bay to Victoria for years. He freighted produce for the farmers on San Juan to Victoria. It was freighting on a small scale I imagine, but it seemed to be enough to about satisfy the demands, in those days.[21]

In a Superior Court case held in Jefferson County in 1877, Peter (Pierre) Lami, a "Boatman and Fisherman," testified that he had resided at Mitchell Bay for some nine years and that he was often employed in ferrying people (including the defendant) across the "Straits of Canal de Harrow" to Telegraph Bay, about 5 miles from Victoria.[22] In another case, Frederick Sparling sued Smith Burr in 1874 to recover his new sloop, which was 20 feet long and 10 feet broad, "said sloop not being of sufficient size and tonnage to be subject to customs regulations." Clearly sloops were not only common but were the primary means of transporting goods and people among the islands and to Vancouver Island and the mainland.[23]

One of the more common fishing boats to be seen in island waters, particularly in the last quarter of the nineteenth century, was the Columbia River Salmon Boat. Howard Chapelle, in his classic *American Small Sailing Craft*, attributes its origin to J. J. Griffin, who built a craft of this design in San Francisco in 1868 for a fisherman on the Sacramento River.[24] This was followed the next year by a similar boat built for Columbia River gill netting, and the type subsequently proliferated, mass-produced as a stock model. As a result, prices were relatively inexpensive: $220 in 1872. The Columbia River Salmon Boat has distinct double ends. Although early boats were 22-23 feet long, 8 feet wide, 4 feet deep, and open, by the late 1870s they had been lengthened to 28 feet, with washboards and end-decks added. They were built with steam-bent frames and planking of Douglas fir. The boats were rigged with a single mast with spritsail and sometimes a jib. The crew of two or three fishermen who sailed and rowed them often had to stay out for several nights, so they used the boom and the sail to form a cockpit tent and cooked on an oil stove. Designed for heavy use by the gillnetters who rented them from canneries, they were solidly enough designed and built to last 10-15 years. Historic photographs of Kanaka Bay and Victoria Harbor reveal myriads of Columbia River boats, probably sailed by Songhees and other Coast Salish gillnetters.

There were other, larger sailing ships plying the waters around the islands, but they were usually associated with either the American or English troops. These included schooners—having a foremast and a mainmast, with fore-and-aft sails on all lower masts; brigs—two-masted, square-rigged on both masts; and barks—three or more masts, square rigged on all but the aftermost mast, which is fore-and-aft rigged. In *Told by the Pioneers*, Archibald Fleming recollected that his brother James was skipper of an eighteen-ton schooner, the *Ontario*, which carried freight and passengers among the islands as well as to Port Townsend and Victoria.[25] (The *Ontario* was later used by the San Juan Lime Company for shipping lime throughout the region but sank off Lime Kiln during a storm on March 25, 1875.) One of the more famous transports was the *General Harney*, a 100-ton schooner that first sailed in the Salish Sea in 1859. Towed by a steamer, the *Harney* was used to transport troops, artillery, and later supplies to the American encampment on San Juan Island in the early days of the Pig War. Later that year, she was beached in Griffin Bay during a gale. From 1860 to 1876, when she was again beached after the load of lime that she was carrying caught fire, she hauled bricks, lime, and lumber, and stone as well as livestock throughout the region.[26]

Scows, defined as having a flat-bottomed rectangular hull with sloping ends, were used in the islands for transporting large loads. In the various court records, scows are mentioned as the means for freighting sheep and other livestock between Vancouver Island and the San Juans. In 1859, during the troubles with American 'squatters,' Griffin mentioned that he had "…heard them say they were going to hire a vessel, a scow I suppose, to bring over lumber, Provisions etc…"[27] The *General Harney*, although technically a schooner, was referred to as a scow because it was towed by a steamer to haul freight to the islands. An historic photograph by Asahel Curtis of "Purse Seiners in harbor, San Juan Island" (probably Kanaka Bay) shows "standard" open boats with wide sterns paired with scows, most probably for the catch, moored by tow lines behind them. Members of the North West Boundary Survey noted that some American settlers had even *rafted* over chickens, pigs, and a yoke of oxen to Orcas Island from Vancouver Island.[28]

The largest ships that serviced the transportation and trade within the Salish Sea region and throughout the islands were steamers. They not only brought passengers and mail from up Sound (Olympia and Seattle) to Victoria and back, but also hauled freight among the various Puget Sound and island ports.

The Hudson's Bay Company steamship *Beaver* was not only the first steamer in Puget Sound, but also the most venerable. Built in England in 1835, she was 101 feet long, 20 feet in the beam, and had an 11-foot-deep hold. After sailing around the Horn and arriving at the Fort Vancouver via the Sandwich Islands, the

Hudson's Bay Company "Beaver"
(courtesy of San Juan Island National Historical Park)

Beaver, which was originally meant for travel on the Columbia River, was assigned to routes from Fort Nisqually in Puget Sound and further north to other Company trading posts. The *Beaver* had a crew of thirty, ten of whom were wood choppers because she burned some 40 cords a day which was about all the fuel she could carry. In 1860, she took up the Victoria-New Westminster run as a passenger boat. She was sold as a tugboat by the Company in 1874, and after several more reincarnations and owners, she was abandoned after hitting the rocks near Vancouver Harbor in 1888.[29]

The *Beaver* was joined in 1853 by the Hudson's Bay Company ship *Julia*, a bark-rigged propeller steamer, 122 feet in length and 20 feet in beam.[30] The *Major Tompkins*, which was built in Philadelphia in 1847, also served as a freight and passenger steamer in the Salish Sea. In 1854, she was brought from San Francisco to Puget Sound, and commenced a run among Olympia, Seattle, Victoria, and other ports. Unfortunately, her service was short lived, for she hit rocks and foundered the next year.[31]

Advertisment for *Eliza Anderson* Washington Standard, May 11, 1867

Probably the most steadfast, although also the slowest, steamer to serve in these waters was the *Eliza Anderson*, a 140-foot-long and 24-foot-beam, 279-ton vessel. Launched in 1858 at Portland for the Columbia River trade, she was soon consigned to the inland seas, where she made a run from Olympia (departing at 7:00 a.m. on Mondays) to Victoria (departing 3:00 a.m. on Thursdays). Purser Rich C. R. Stark wrote of the route in a letter of August 19, 1859:

> *Leaving Olympia, we come down Sound to Port Townsend, touching at Steillacoom, Seattle, Port Madison, Tekalet and Port Ludlow; from thence to Victoria, touching at Dungeness, Whidbey's Island and San Juan; from thence across the Gulf of Georgia to Semiahmoo and Bellingham Bay, landing in the Bay at Whatcom and Sehome, there to lay six hours, in order to change the mails and coal the ship, and then return to Olympia by the same route...*[32]

The fares were $20, with freight ranging from $5 to $10 per ton, and cattle at $15 a head. Several other steamers competed with the *Eliza Anderson*, including the *Wilson G. Hunt*, a 185-foot-long side-wheeler with a 25-foot beam, and the *Olympia*, a 180-foot-long side-wheeler with a 30-foot beam.[33]

Trails and Roads

Although the Coast Salish certainly traveled throughout the San Juan Islands, there does not seem to be much evidence, either traditional or physical, of extensive Indigenous trails, because the main means of transportation was by canoe. Hannah Sandwith Jensen recalled in *Told by the Pioneers* that the Indians, coming to Garrison Bay on San Juan Island for salal berries, would walk overland to "Grassy Swamp" (probably Sportsman's Lake) many miles away.[34] However, we can assume that they often followed deer trails through the denser forested areas while hunting. Although there is little documentary evidence from the San Juan Islands, Charley Nelson of Fidalgo Island, reminiscing in *Told by the Pioneers*, noted that "There was absolutely no road through the island. A tiny path followed the shore line over logs and between rocks. Later this path was cleared out so one ox and a stone boat could travel it."

One of the first things that the Hudson's Bay Company did upon establishment of Belle Vue Sheep Farm was to construct a road to link the various "prairies," or sheep pastures on San Juan Island. James Douglas, in a December 13, 1855, letter to Sir William Molesworth, British Secretary of State for the Colonies, said that he "mustered a force of Indian labourers, and cut a passage through the forest to a fresh range of the west side of the island about 16 miles from the establishment to which the sheep were originally driven," and, within a year, roads had been completed "nearly from end to end of the island."[35] Because the work crew consisted of Indigenous peoples from nearby Vancouver Island, it was subsequently referred to as the "Cowichin Road."

In his *Post Journals*, Charles Griffin noted the construction of a series of roads on San Juan Island over the next few years, including a road from "the shore of Grande [Griffin] Bay to Winter Station [near Friday Harbor]," from "New Station to Oak Prairie [San Juan Valley]," from "Grande Prairie [American Camp] to another prairie more inland," from "Prairie to Old Fishery House

Sheep Station on North End of San Juan Island
(courtesy of San Juan Island National Historical Park)

(to drive sheep)," "through Oak Prairie Lamb Station through Oak Prairie [San Juan Valley] to Leroux's Prairie then to Park Hill [off North Bay, to the west of Bald Hill] other side of Harbor," "Two Roads from Park Hill to spring and through to Prairie," "Norwegian Road," and "Road from Leroux's Prairie ["off Prairie du Chien"] to Channel Prairie [Friday Harbor Laboratories]." Most of these were probably tracks cleared through the woods and fields, although specific structures, such as several bridges and at least one section of corduroy roadbed, are mentioned. The corduroy road consisted of logs laid in the ground parallel to each other in order to traverse swampy areas. When they were used to skid logs, fat or grease was applied to the surface of the logs. An early road down to the landing at Dolphin Bay on Orcas Island, called "Iotte's Landing Road," was a corduroy or "skid road."[36]

At the time the North West Boundary Survey arrived in the islands, deer trails were one of the few means of exploring the land that had not been accessed by the Hudson's Bay Company shepherds. While exploring San Juan Island in January 1860, William Warren noted that:

> *While the men were pitching tents, Dr. Kennerly and I started out in a southerly direction. We had gone only a few hundred yards when we came across the worst swamp we have yet seen. We didn't attempt to push our way throughout, but looking around we found a deer trail, which we followed till it brought us out at the western end of the swamp. Our condition was little improved as we were now in a country where the fires and winds had leveled the immense fir trees that had formerly stood there, as the young firs and pines had sprung up thick as ferns.*[37]

On a trip on horseback to inspect Oak Prairie on San Juan Island on January 26, 1860, Warren commented that "The roads were very muddy making the riding disagreeable."[38]

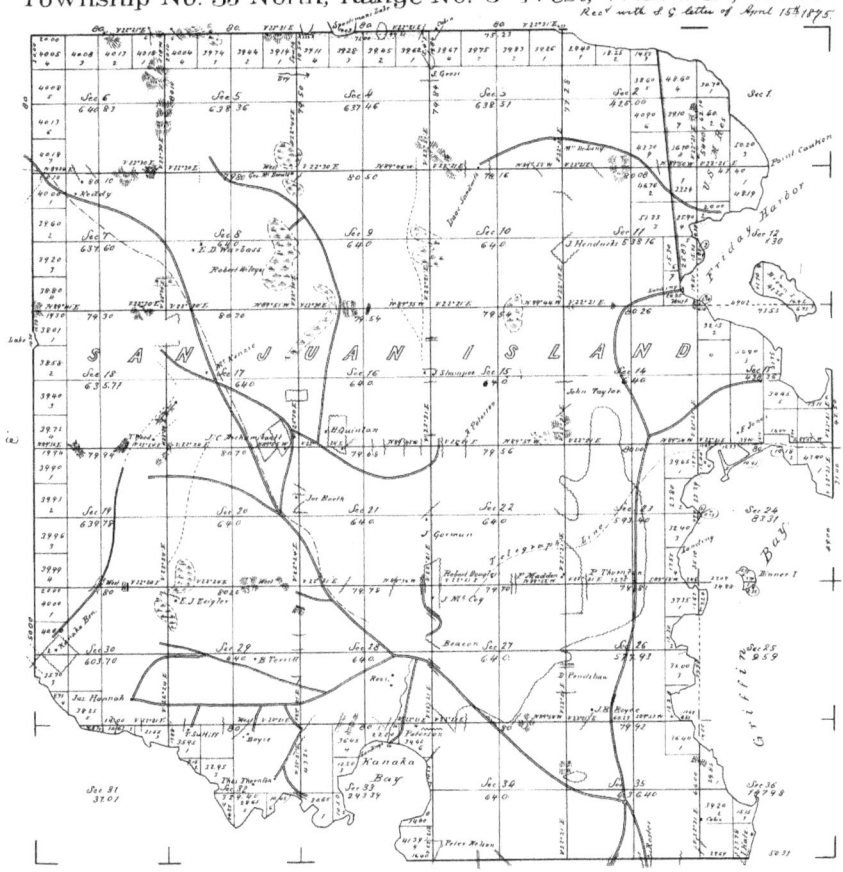

Township and Range Survey Map of San Juan Valley, San Juan Island (General Land Office, Bureau of Land Management)

In the wake of the decision to jointly occupy the island and the establishment of American and English camps, "Cowichin Road" was improved and widened and then renamed the "Military Road," functioning as a relatively rapid and essential means of communication between the two encampments. In addition, the importance of this route linking the north and south ends of San Juan Island to the growing number of settlers on the island is exemplified by a March 30th, 1861, petition by a score of island residents to the Whatcom County Board of Commissioners to appoint Peter Lawson and John Whitty to view and locate "a county road commencing at the Town of San Juan thence on the

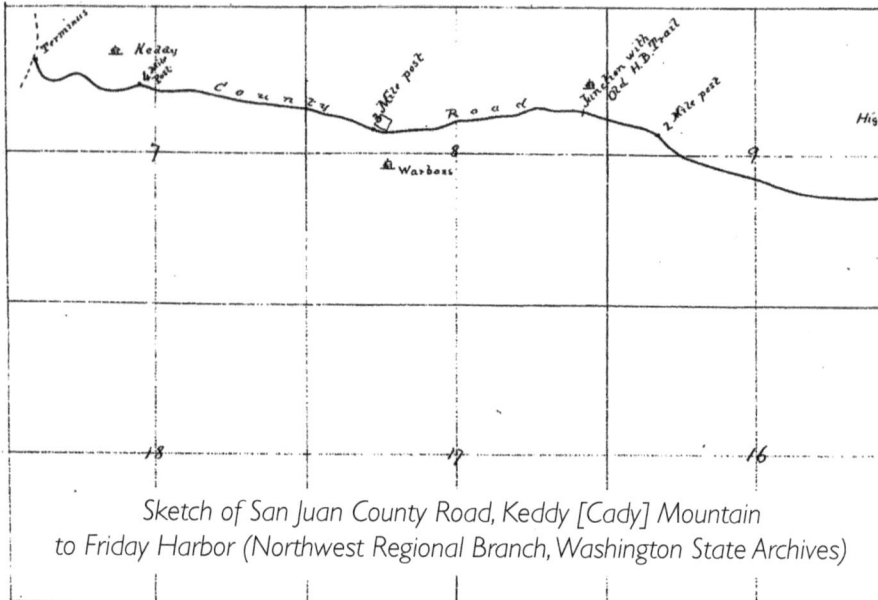

Sketch of San Juan County Road, Keddy [Cady] Mountain to Friday Harbor (Northwest Regional Branch, Washington State Archives)

most direct and practicable route to the North end of the island at or near the English Camp."[39] The Commissioners appointed John Whitty, Chas. Powell, and H. Wharton to meet on the May 18, at S. V. Boyce's house, and to view and locate the road within five days thereafter. There is no record of the outcome, but later maps indicate the intricate web of roads that stem from this central axis provided by the Cowichin/Military Road.

Euro-American settlers had to make do with the existing road system originally established by the Hudson's Bay Company. Lila Hannah reminisced:

> *We had 8 miles to go & do our trading [from their farm to the commissary at American Camp and back]… All this traveling back & forth to the store had to be done in farm wagons in good weather at that! for the roads became very bad in winter time, washouts here & there. Sometimes a Bridge would go out! Then we were hopelessly stranded until the settlers could get together & fix it.*[40]

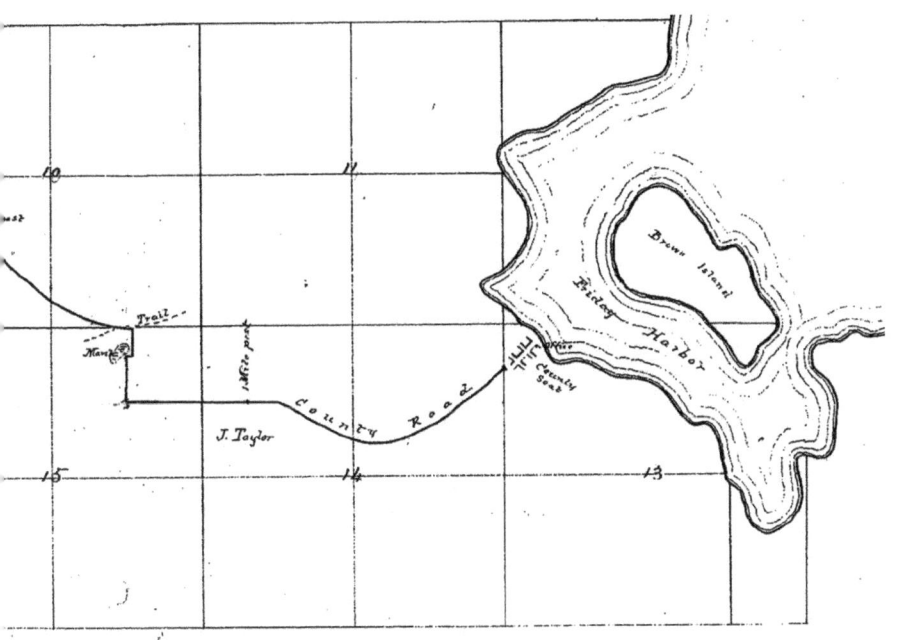

Thomas Fleming, who kept a journal during this period, made numerous entries about working on roads, such as "making bridges and roads this week."[41]

With the settlement of the boundary dispute and the establishment of San Juan County, the county commission was enabled to levy taxes (at the rate of 2 mills) for the purpose of constructing and maintaining county roads, and to appoint road supervisors. As early as August 1874, Peter Jewell, county road supervisor of the San Juan Island Road District, submitted a bill; the same year E. C. Gillette surveyed for a county road on Lopez. The *Journals* [minutes] of the county commission are full of petitions for various roads on several of the islands. For instance, Samuel Gross and A. F. McCuen petitioned for a road in 1877; I. Katz, P. Gorman, and P. McGraw petitioned in 1878, as did P. Gorman and E. F. Bailer ("Road to Kanaka Bay"), P. Madden and Francis Dean, E. D. Warbass, and A. Ross and Patrick Beigin. In the same year, both the "Ostergaard Road" and the "Road to Kanaka Bay" were ordered opened. Settlers were not always eager

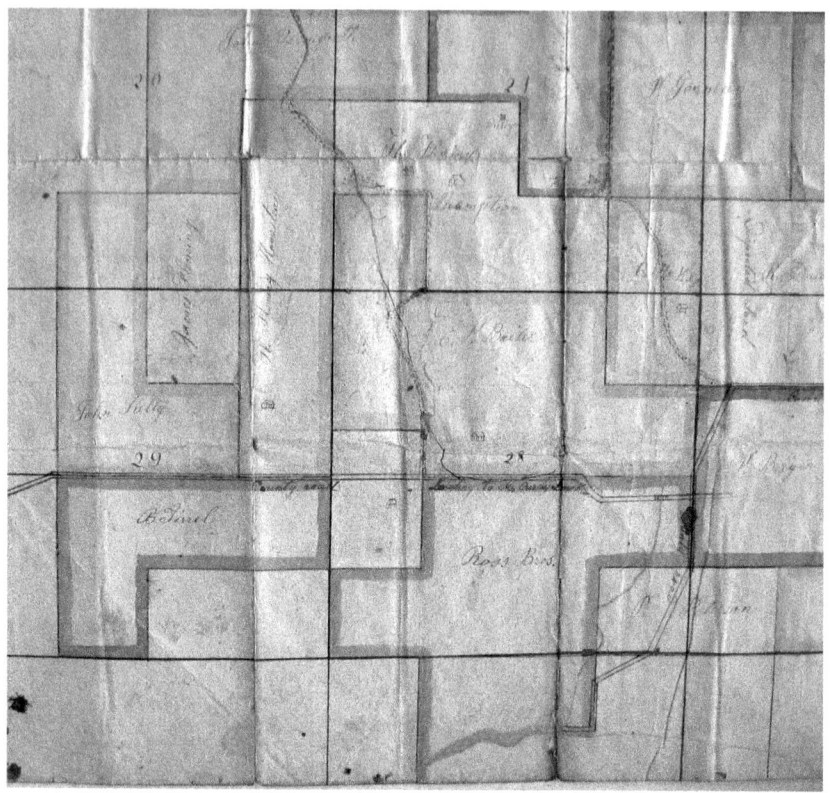

Map of 1887 Road Dispute in San Juan Valley, Including Parcels and Routes (Northwest Regional Branch, Washington State Archives)

to do their duty by way of road improvement, and several of the early court cases concern either non-payment of road levies or labor spent or disputes over right of way. In 1875, for instance, road supervisor Peter Jewell sold one of John Keddy's cows as reimbursement for the work that Keddy's hired hands were supposed to do on the road.[42]

Controversies over roads and their impact on private property were an ongoing issue, and a bundle of civil cases before the Superior Court in the 1882 was concerned with property damage associated with their location and construction. Typical of these was the 1887 dispute of E. P. and Gregory Bailer with San Juan County over a road that ran through their property in San Juan Valley. At issue was the imposition of a barrier between two of the Bailers' sheep pastures. A detailed colored map of the land holdings and roads within the Valley was drawn and submitted as evidence. Ultimately, a solution was arrived at with the construction of an underpass so that the sheep could move unimpeded from one side of the road to the other.[43]

A closer look at a controversy that played out in the pages of *The Islander* newspaper near the end of the nineteenth century reveals the manner in which roads were established, challenged, and changed in the islands. The opening salvo on January 27, 1898, was by H. A. Armstrong, who accused his neighbor D. W. Oakes of solely benefitting from the petition for the opening of a county road "beginning at county road near School House No. 1 and running through school lot of District No. 1 and through lands owned by Messrs. Goodridge, Armstrong, Oaks [sic], Boyce, Beigin and Ross." Oakes returned fire on February 3rd:

> *The road referred to is an old one, established years ago, of which there is a plat and record that any taxpayer can see if he so desires. When that road was viewed it commenced at the school house in District No. 1 and followed an old road that was made by the Hudson Bay Co. and used to get from the main station to the branch stock stations on the island, and was also used by us early settlers. The first school house was built on that road, and the only store and postoffice were at the old Hudson Bay landing, afterwards named San Juan Town; wherefore it became necessary to perpetuate that road while it could be done by mutual agreement all along the route. A few years since a new district was formed of the west half of district No. 1, which necessitated the building of a new school house in the center of the district. After San Juan Town was abandoned and Friday Harbor and Argyle sprung into prominence it was necessary to make changes in the roads for public convenience, and as a consequence portions of roads have fell into disuse and have been closed, being of no public utility, and are now pastures and field with growing crops. The potion of the road of which I am writing...has not been used for years and should be legally vacated.*[44]

The epistolatory battle went on for several issues of the paper.

The main means of transportation was either by horse or wagon; as Lila Hannah reminisced:

> *It was a very common scene to be riding through the country at any time, to see a young chap racing along with his 2 horses going after his girl, as we all rode horseback well! It was about our only mode of traveling, outside the farmwagon. No buggies there in those days.*[45]

San Juan homesteader Peter Lawson's daughter, Lizzie, recounted that a horse was essential to the settler "for riding through the trails as there were no roads."[46] Later, four-wheeled wagons were introduced for hauling crops and materials on the farm and supplies from stores. Personal property assessments from the 1890s indicate that almost every farmer had at least one wagon, if not two.[47]

Mail, Newspapers, and Telegraph

Mail was a vital means of intercourse between settlers in the islands and to the outside world. Early on, mail was delivered to the islands either through the military establishments or by means of steamers that travelled among Olympia, Seattle, Port Townsend, Victoria, and Bellingham. The earliest local United States post offices were established in stores, with the proprietors being the postmasters. The first of these was San Juan (established March 2, 1861), located in the saloon of Isaac E. Higgins in San Juan Town, near the Hudson's Bay Company wharf on Griffin Bay. It received the mail from a star route (a postal delivery route served by a private contractor) between Olympia and Victoria, which also served Steilacoom City, Seattle, Port Madison, Tekalet, Port Ludlow, Port Townsend, Coveland, New Dungeness, and Port Angeles to the south, and Unionville and Whatcom to the north. The steamers would leave Olympia on Monday and arrive in Victoria Tuesday afternoon, and then make a return trip at the same places Wednesday and Thursday.

However, troubles with the military commanders at American Camp exacerbated the mail delivery. On September 30, 1865, an American citizen wrote to the *Washington Standard*:

I have endeavored to have your paper circulated on the Island, but in vain. On requesting subscribers, the people cry with one voice—"We like the paper, but have no mail and cannot get it." Too truly, Mr. Editor, is this the case. We have no mail and can get no paper. A few days since I complained to Capt. J. E. Higgins, the Postmaster here, about the delinquency. He informed me that Major Bissell [current American Camp commander] had forbidden the Government mail carrier from carrying any mail for the citizens on his boat, and thus are we to be deprived of another privilege and excluded from the news of the continent.

Hiram Hutchinson established the Lopez Island post office at his store on Fisherman Bay on April 2, 1873; the name was later changed to simply Lopez. On the same date, the Orcas Island post office was established by Joseph Gibbons near present-day Orcas Landing; its name was also later shortened to Orcas. A succession of postmasters (and storekeepers) occurred annually for the next three years: James O. Turner in 1874, Robert M. Caines in 1875, and then Joseph Sweeney in 1876.

With the founding of Friday Harbor in 1874, San Juan Town was eventually abandoned, but another village—Argyle—sprang up on the North Bay portion of Griffin Bay. There, a new "San Juan" post office was established in 1873 by G. Herman Moore, who was succeeded a year later by the storekeeper Israel Katz. To the north, the post office at Friday Harbor proper was not established until January 12, 1876 (by John Taylor, with William H. Higgins succeeding him in March of that year). Joseph Sweeney, of Orcas Island fame, became the postmaster in late 1879, when he moved his store to Friday Harbor. This office, as well as Lopez Island and Orcas Island, received its mail from a once-a-week steamer on a star route between Port Townsend and Whatcom.

The expansion to other locations in the islands occurred slowly at first, and then accelerated during the boom times of the 1890s. Orcas Island developed post offices at East Sound [later changed to Eastsound] (1877), Doe Bay (1881), Olga (1890), Ocean (1890), Newhall [later Rosario] (1890), West Sound (1892), and Deer Harbor (1893); San Juan Island at Lime Kiln (1879) and Werner (1890); and Lopez Island at McKay (1880), Richardson (1887), and Edwards (1894). Shaw Island had Griswold (1891) and Shaw Island (1906); Decatur (1891); Thatcher (1892) on Blakely; and Prevost (1898) on Stuart. Today, it is interesting to note that Lopez, San Juan, and Shaw all have a single post offices (with an extension of Friday Harbor at Roche Harbor), while Orcas has four (Deer Harbor, East Sound, Olga, and West Sound).[48]

One of the items that residents of the island could receive through the mail was a newspaper, with news of both the local region and the two nations. Although a local newspaper was not published until 1890 (the *San Juan Graphic*), locals could subscribe to either American or British newspapers. The first newspaper in the northern part of then-Oregon Territory was the Olympia *Columbian* (renamed the *Olympia Pioneer and Democrat*) established on September 11, 1852, in part to agitate for the new territory that was to become Washington in 1853. One of its agents was Edward D. Warbass, then at Cowlitz Farms, who later had such an influence in the San Juans. Steilacoom followed with the *Puget Sound Courier* (1855) and then the *Puget Sound Herald* in 1858. Closer to the islands was the *Port Townsend Register*, established at the end of 1859, followed by *The North-West* (1860-1862). The paper that probably covered the islands the most during this period was the Port Townsend *Weekly Argus* (1870-1875, changing to the *Port Townsend Weekly Argus* in 1876). In Victoria, the *British Colonist* was first published in 1858 by Amor de Cosmos, who became the second premier of British Columbia. (Pickett, in a letter to his superior, mentions regaling de Cosmos, who was part of the English delegation to the island, after the establishment of his camp.)

The purpose of newspapers at the time was not only to convey news, but also to advertise for local merchants and, often,

THE BRITISH COLONIST.

VOL. 1.   VICTORIA, V. I., SATURDAY, DEC. 11, 1858.   NO. 1.

The British Colonist *Masthead*

to boost the economy of the town or city and region. The layout of the papers varied, but generally consisted of four pages with a banner at the top of the front page; pages were divided into 5-6 columns, which could be combined for larger advertisements. Placement varied, but usually the national and international news, available through other newspapers, was located on the front pages, with local news—often in the form of one or two liners—on subsequent pages. The papers also reported business information such as the shipping news (what ships had arrived with specific cargo or passengers), business openings, and store sales. Local government affairs, such as county commission meetings and court sessions, were also closely followed. Mention of the islands, therefore, took the form of reports from "correspondents," stringers, or visitors, or actual scouting expeditions by the editor or a reporter. Such an occasion was reported on May 12, 1877, by the editor of the *Puget Sound Weekly Argus*, Allen Weir, when he visited the San Juan Lime Company, as well as other places on the island:

> *This morning…we started off at about 7:30 for the purpose of making a tour of the island and chasing unfortunate prospective subscribes into fence-corners in order to make them surrender. By galloping around at a lively rate, climbing fences and "footing it" across fields all day, we managed to meet and form the acquaintance of a great many honest tillers of the soil; also, by way of diversion, to secure some 14 subscribers to the ARGUS.*[49]

Weir was able to obtain the national news through the telegraph, which was introduced into the region in the 1860s.

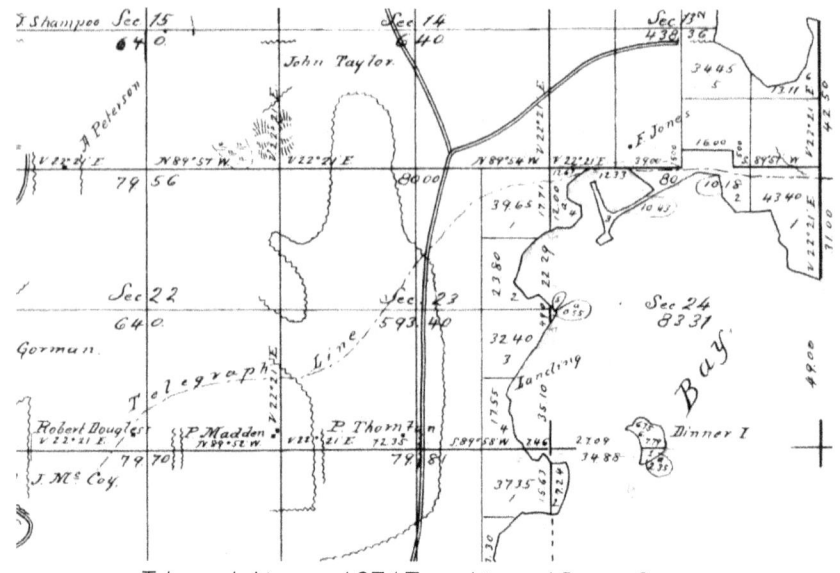

*Telegraph Line on 1874 Township and Range Survey
(General Land Office, Bureau of Land Management)*

On the township and range map that was prepared from the public land surveys of 1874 and 1875, a dotted line indicates the route of a telegraph line that runs from Pear Point across Jackson's Lagoon to San Juan Valley, and then proceeding northwest along the Military Road to the vicinity of English Camp, where it went to Hanbury Point. In 1866, the California State Telegraph Company established a section of line between Fidalgo and Lopez islands, coming to shore at Telegraph Bay. Because the line was meant to ultimately connect with Victoria, the British became concerned about American connections to Canadian wires. Reorganized under the Canadian firm Collins Overland Telegraph Company, a section between Lopez and San Juan was completed and the connection with Victoria secured. The *Puget Sound Weekly* reported on April 30, 1866:

> Victoria, April 24. The last stretch of the telegraph's cable, which connects this island with the main continent, was safely landed at Ladd Bay, San Juan Island, at one o'clock this afternoon.

The line was eventually disconnected in 1875 due to the increasing frequency of breaks and rising cost of maintenance.[50]

In 1866, twenty-four-year-old Georgius Kitchené, who had only been on the island for three months, was listed as a telegraph operator. At American Camp, the telegraph office, measuring 15 by 15 by 7 feet tall, was located southwest of the Adjutant's Office. Although it was listed as being in poor condition five years later, it is not known whether it was repaired or left as is. The location of the telegraph office at English Camp is not known, although in an apocryphal story about the American occupation of the camp after the British departure in 1872, the contingent, finding that the flagstaff had been removed, affixed an American flag to "a convenient telegraph pole near the wharf."[51]

Commerce

Commerce evolved in the islands from self-sufficient and trading economies, such as used by Indigenous peoples, to barter and trade (the introduction by the Hudson's Bay Company of the blanket as a means of exchange), to commerce (and mercantile financial systems—exchange based on credit—as well differing monetary systems—English and American). Prior to the arrival of Euro-Americans, the Coast Salish were known for their trading surplus production throughout the Salish Sea region and beyond—even as far away as the western Rocky Mountains. Analysis of reef net sites and their catch and processing indicate that the salmon caught during the season exceeded that needed for subsistence, and there is strong ethnographic evidence of processing clams specifically for the purpose of trade.

With the economies introduced by Euro-Americans, Indigenous peoples adapted their trade systems to the newcomers. For instance, the Coast Salish who reef netted along the west coast of San Juan Island traded their catch to the Hudson's Bay Company in exchange for blankets and other goods. Cross cultural marriage strengthened these networks. Traditionally, Straits Salish villages were linked through intermarriage, and families stove to establish ties to other family and village groups through strategic marriages. The wedding itself included exchanges of food and wealth, and it was expected that the ties so established would help bolster trade networks among the groups. With the arrival of the Hudson's Bay Company, servants were encouraged to marry Indigenous women in order to strengthen the Company's ties with local groups. This pattern was repeated with others who came later, such as the American and English soldiers who mustered out of their respective camps and the settlers and later homesteaders who stayed to farm the land. These marriages were initially conducted *à la façon du pays* (in the custom of the country), solidifying the kinship ties between the newcomers and their Indigenous wives and their families.

In addition to the trade economy among various Coast Salish groups—exporting goods such as salmon, clams, and camas—there was also a grimmer trade: that of slaves for trade or bondage through marriage or prostitution. Local Coast Salish groups had slaves—most likely war captives and their descendants—who were treated as a lower class and made to work menial tasks.[52] Slavery among Northern tribes, often resulting from their raids among Salish Sea groups, was harsher. There is historical documentation of human trafficking in the islands; specific instances include forcing slaves from the North into prostitution in San Juan Town, and offering young girls as brides to local Euro-American men (see *Work* above).

Since time immemorial, there has always been commerce among and between the San Juan Islands, Vancouver Island, and the mainland. This was facilitated by new forms of transportation and communications, which strengthened intercourse within the island communities and with the larger region and the world. Victoria, just 14 miles across Haro Strait from the west coast of San Juan Island, was the main port of trade for the islands, particularly during the period of a more porous boundary. In 1908, the December 12 *San Juan Islander* reported that J. L. Davis, "the well-known pioneer farmer of Lopez Island," had shipped apples to Victoria via his boat *Hermosa*.

> It is over forty-one years [i.e., 1867] since Mr. Davis took his first shipment of produce from Lopez Island to Victoria. That was five years before the settlement of the boundary controversy. There were no customs officers on the islands then and settlers going to Victoria with produce reported to Capt. Delacombe, in command of the garrison at English camp, and secured a permit from him.

In 1860, 79 vessels arrived in Victoria Harbor from San Juan Island; by 1870, of the 652 vessels that entered the Harbor, 417 were local, 152 from Puget Sound, 58 from West Coast ports, and 25 foreign. Interestingly, 124 of the vessels classified as "local" were from San Juan Island (it is not clear what the other "local" ports were). Sloops such as the *Alarm, Lady Franklin, Ringleader,* and *Ocean Queen* regularly plied Haro Strait to bring goods from the islands to Victoria and vice versa.[53] The column "Shipping Intelligence" in the Victoria *Daily British Colonist* lists visits from ships from Port Townsend and later San Juan Island. One captain who sailed regularly is Thomas Thornton with the schooner *Amelia* in 1859, joined by the *Elizabeth* in 1860, and then the sloop *J. K. Thorndyke*. Captain Love sailed the sloop *Random* in 1864 and Captain Mercer sailed to Victoria in the sloop *W. B. Naylor* in 1865.

Lime was a common export from the islands. On June 20, 1861, the *Victoria Colonist* reported: "By the arrival of the Schooner General Harney yesterday, 345 barrels of San Juan Island lime, from the kiln of the Eureka Company were brought to this city..."[54] According to an 1878 newspaper article, of the 8,000 barrels produced in the San Juans by August of that year, two-thirds had been shipped to Tacoma and thence to Portland via railroad, while another 1,000 had been sent to British Columbia and other parts of the Salish Sea. Ships laden with barrels of lime, some stacked on open decks, were carrying a very dangerous cargo since quicklime that becomes wet is highly combustible. The list of ships that suffered severe damage or sank as the result of fires ignited by their lime cargo is a long one. The fire and subsequent beaching of the *General Harney* was mentioned earlier.[55] In 1873 N. C. Bailey and James McCurdy at Lime Kiln furnished 1,000 barrels of lime for the construction of the Territorial Prison on McNeil Island; they transported it there with their schooner *Ontario*, which unfortunately came loose and was driven ashore by an April 1875 storm. Other lime-bearing ships included the schooner *Shoo Fly*, the sloop *Magnolia*, and the 95-foot-long *Dispatch*, a sternwheel steamer, launched by Captain Hornbeck at Port Madison in 1876 and sold to Captain J. C. Brittain for part of his fleet.[56]

Euro-American trade was first introduced by early explorers in the region but became established with the presence of the Hudson's Bay Company. Iron, which replaced traditional stone tools—such as the ax taking the place of the stone chisel for canoe building—became prevalent early on, such that the Tlingit began forging their own as early as 1786, and the Haida beginning in 1798. The Company traded utilitarian goods such as firearms, ammunition, fishhooks, hatchets, pots, and pans; woven goods such as blankets, cloth, and clothing; and consumables (food stuffs) such as molasses and rice. (In his 1984 M. A. Thesis, *Colonial Lands, Indian Labor, and Company Capital: The Economy of Vancouver Island, 1849-1858*, Richard Somerset Mackie gives a table of selected rates of exchange throughout the region from 1824-1847, including 'currency' such as awls, fish hooks, butcher knives, powder and shot, twists of tobacco, handkerchiefs, shirts, and, above all, blankets.[57]) The standard trade item for the Company was an English-made blanket, which was rated on a point system based on its size and value in beaver. Post Trader Griffin, for instance, records exchanging a 2½-point blanket for 3 barrels of potatoes.[58] As James Gilchrist Swan, who lived with the Makah Indians at Neah Bay on the Olympic Peninsula, said ca. 1859:

> *Blankets are the principal item of wealth, and the value of anything is fixed by the number of blankets it is worth. In the early days of the Hudson's Bay Company, and until within the past ten years, a blanket was considered equal in trade to five dollars; but since so many different traders have settled on the Sound, with such a variety of qualities and prices, the Indian in naming the number of blankets he expects to receive...will state what kind he demands. Thus, if the price is to be twenty blankets, he will say, 'how many large blue ones,' which are the most costly, 'how many red, and how many white ones?'*[59]

Trade among the various Indigenous groups and Euro-American settlers continued during the 1860s and 1870s. Many journals or reminiscences recall "Indians" coming to homesteader's cabins in order to barter fish or venison for goods. (In fact, the casualness with which Coast Salish visitors 'showed up' at their doorsteps led several Euro-Americans to establish spatial boundaries such as fences; Lila Hannah Firth's account, mentioned earlier, of her father constructing a fence and getting a dog in order to deter unexpected visits, is a good example.[60])

Euro-Americans also introduced the framework for an exchange economy, as can be seen in the records kept by the Hudson's Bay Company with regard to credits and debits at their Company store in Victoria. The introduction of double entry accounting in the early eighteenth century allowed for both credits and debits to be accounted for each customer. As Warren Hofstra has pointed out regarding the Shenandoah Valley in the eighteenth century, in "sprawling but rapidly developing cultural frontiers," barter economies break down, frustrating capital accumulation because the face-to-face transaction cannot be extended over space and time.[61] Exchange economies based on credit and debit, which, although valued in relation to currency, do not necessarily involve the actual exchange of money, facilitate the flow of goods and services. This can be seen through an examination of markets, prices, and credit during this period.

One of the earliest markets for farmers' produce was the various trading posts and military establishments in the region. For the operations at Belle Vue Sheep Farm, for instance, it was the supply network that the Hudson's Bay Company established throughout the region, including Fort Victoria and the officer's mess at Esquimalt (est. 1855), that offered a market for their potatoes and wheat; beef, mutton, and pork; and milk and butter. Both American and English camps also needed supplies, and the sutlers for the camps became major livestock raisers. Augustus Hoffmeister at English Camp, for instance, had some 60 head of cattle and over 500 head of sheep. Less is known about American Camp sutler Edward Warbass and his successors, but it is not unlikely that they also ran livestock to supply the camp with meat.

Fort Steilacoom, the U.S. Army garrison on upper Puget Sound near Hudson's Bay Company's Nisqually Farm, was a major customer for agricultural products. Prices there ranged from 8 to 19 cents per pound for beef during the early 1850s. They rose from 16 cents in 1854-55, to 17 in 1856-57, and 18 in 1858-1859. During the 1860s, the price again fluctuated between 8 and 14 cents. The price of mutton averaged 17 cents per pound during those years. Per head livestock prices for the Hudson's Bay Company during this period were $33 for a horse; milch cows cost about $45-50 from 1850 to 1858 and $30 from 1858 to 1865. Work oxen, which were more valuable, ranged from $150 to $200 a yoke during the same period.[62]

During the "San Juan Sheep War" of 1855, American custom officials and the sheriff of Whatcom County seized and then auctioned Hudson's Bay Company livestock in lieu of back taxes; they sold the breeding rams for 50¢-$1.00 a head. The British, however, in their claim for damages, requested £650 for the 34 breeding rams and £650:13/ for the 267 ewes and 142 lambs they allegedly lost, the equivalent of $24 per ram and $1.97 for each ewe and lamb.[63] (General Harney, in speaking of the San Juan situation, claimed that the Company exported sheep from Belle Vue at $8.00 per head.) This adds to the confusion over the question: Was the Hudson's Bay Company pig that Cutlar shot really worth the $100 allegedly demanded by Griffin and his superiors, or the $10 or less that he offered to reimburse?

Merchandizing

The earliest commercial establishments in the islands were those of the various sutlers to American and English camp. (A sutler was a civilian merchant who sold provisions to an army.) Although U.S. Army payroll was supposed to be every 8 weeks, soldiers often went without pay for 6 months or more, and so became dependent on credit from the post sutler, who supplied goods as varied as canned foods, beverages, writing paper, and other necessities and sundries. According to the August 1st, 1859, edition of the *British Colonist*, one of the first structures in "San Juan Town" that sprang up around the Hudson's Bay Company wharf on Griffin Bay, where Pickett and his company had encamped upon landing, was the log building of the camp sutler and butcher, Edward D. Warbass.[64] Warbass, born an Easterner, had migrated West for the California Gold Rush, and then moved into the Northwest. While he would later run into a dispute regarding the formation of San Juan Town, Warbass would become instrumental, while in the Territorial legislature, in the formation of San Juan County in 1873 as well as the homesteading of the original 160 acres that formed the townsite of the county seat, Friday Harbor.[65]

Warbass had originally obtained his appointment at Fort Bellingham for a term of three years and was succeeded by at least two others in the position of sutler to the American garrison: George L. Mercer and William S. Taylor. On January 19, 1869, Mercer petitioned the camp commander for six months to allow him to sell out his stock and settle up his business. Taylor, his successor, responded with the articles of agreement, stating that the transition should have occurred on December 16, 1868.[66] After the settlement of the international boundary, Taylor was obliged to give up his business, which was sold by the new San Juan County Sheriff, Stephen V. Boyce.[67] (Appendix: *List of Property of William F. Tayor Sold at Sheriff's Sale, January 28, 1874*, lists the property that he owned in San Juan Town.)

Augustus (Guss) Hoffmeister was the German-born sutler at English Camp. (Guss Island, in Garrison Bay, was named after him.) In addition to supplying the garrison with beef and lamb, Hoffmeister obtained large property holdings, including a quarter section southwest of the camp, an orchard of 100 bearing trees, 100 head of cattle, and some 300 sheep on Henry Island and 500 sheep on Spieden Island. By the time he died in 1874—the first probate in newly-formed San Juan County—his estate was allegedly worth $10,000. The estate was liquidated, and part of his land on San Juan, which was found to fall on a section designated for school land, was leased by Isaac Sandwith; his holdings and stock on Henry and Spieden were sold to John Tod, Jr.

Both sutlers—George Mercer at American Camp and Hoffmeister at English Camp—petitioned the Governor of British Columbia, Frederick Seymour, to obtain goods from Victoria duty-free, in the same manner as those from Port Townsend and other ports. Apparently, a paramount issue was the transshipment of goods from San Francisco to Victoria and then on to San Juan Island, and the sutlers did not want to be taxed.

For early settlers, trade still occurred with off-island settlements. Until the establishment of local stores, the most common centers of commerce for island residents were the two closest port towns: Victoria, across from the west coast of San Juan Island, and Port Townsend, the first port encountered on Puget Sound in Washington Territory. William Moore, in an October 6, 1859, statement sworn before officers at American Camp where he had been taken prisoner for selling liquor, stated that "I have been trading with my canoe between Victoria and Bellevue [San Juan] Island for nearly two months, dealing in onions, potatoes, bread, milk, and sometimes liquor...." From the invoices entered as evidence in lawsuits as well as accounts of the brisk trade by sloop between the San Juans and Vancouver Island and the mainland, the most frequented mercantile establishments were Bowker and Tod and Henry Saunders in Victoria and Rothschild & Co and Waterman & Katz in Port Townsend.

John Sylvester Bowker, a native of Massachusetts, had first established a store in San Juan Town. (He was listed as a "bookkeeper" in the 1860 U.S. Census). However, after run-ins with the U.S. military authorities over supplying liquor, he was forced to close his store in 1865 when the U.S. commander decreed that only two stores could exist on the island. On May 24, 1864, he married Mary Tod, the daughter of Hudson's Bay Company Trader John Tod and his wife Sophia, in Victoria. Bowker went into business with Tod's son, John Jr.—who had bought Hoffmeister's sheep, land, and improvements on Henry and Spieden Islands. The two are named in several civil actions seeking collection of debt from islanders. In some cases, Bowker and Tod are listed as the principals, with D. C. H. Rothschild and Sigmund Waterman as sureties.

Henry Saunders was born in Stratford, England, and emigrated to New York City in 1862 at the age of 25. He probably moved to Victoria, BC, around 1874, for there is the record of a son born there to him and his wife, Elizabeth Jane Foster, in July of 1875. Both the 1881 and 1891 Canadian censuses enumerate him as a grocer. A historic photograph of his store on 561-563 Johnson Street, as well several civil cases from that period confirm that his grocery store was an important source of goods for islanders. Saunders joined Edward D. Warbass in offering a reward leading to the arrest and conviction of the murderers of James "Harry" and Selina Dwyer, and it was he who brought their bodies back to Victoria.[68]

D. C. H. Rothschild was one of several German immigrants who provided general merchandise to Port Townsend and the region, including the San Juans. David Charles Henry Rothschild was born in Sultzback, Bavaria, in 1824, and after receiving an education there, moved to the United States in 1843. After working in Kentucky and California, he located in Port Townsend in 1858, where he ran a general merchandise shop under the name Kentucky Store, an allusion to the state where he had formerly worked but also perhaps an effort to evoke an American—not foreign—establishment. Later, together with his sons Henry and Louis, he went into the "Shipping and Commission" business as Rothschild & Co., supplying ship's chandlery throughout Puget Sound. He committed suicide in 1886. James F. Tulloch, in his usual crusty manner, did not think much of the "Baron," as his friends called him, acknowledging that though he had "the principal ship chandlery in Port Townsend" and "one of the chief supply houses for the extensive lumber and logging interests of the Sound," he regularly cheated and swindled his customers. According to Tulloch, when Rothschild began to dun him for accounts overdue, he replied with a letter:

> *Mr. D.C.H. Rothschild, Will you please go to hell.*
> *Very truly yours, James F. Tulloch.*

He did pay up as soon as he could, however.[69]

The other large mercantile firm in Port Townsend was Waterman and Katz. It was begun in 1861 by Sigmund Waterman and Solomon Katz, both German Jewish immigrants. Katz later employed his two nephews, Israel and William. Israel had emigrated in 1866 and two years later moved to Port Townsend. In

*Israel Katz Invoice for Samuel H. Gross
(Northwest Regional Branch, Washington State Archives)*

an effort to expand the business of the firm, he established a store in San Juan Town, and was involved in several real estate transactions. Solomon Katz died in 1879, and his interest in the Port Townsend store passed to Israel and his brother William. When William died by drowning in 1888, Israel moved back to Port Townsend and bought Waterman's entire interest. Waterman died later that year, but the firm continued under the old name. Israel Katz later served as mayor of Port Townsend but disappeared on January 14, 1917—a mystery that has not been solved to this day.

Local stores soon became centers of trade for each of the islands or regions on each island. At San Juan Town, where a conglomeration of saloons and hotels developed near the old Hudson's Bay Company wharf on Griffin Bay, there were several stores in addition to U.S. Army sutler Warbass' original structure. According to the November 23rd, 1859, edition of the *Daily Alta California*, these consisted of "…a bakery, a butchery, three or four bar-rooms, one aristocratic 'two-bit' house, a fruitery, grocery, etc., etc." Among these were the "establishments" of Isaac Higgins, a "ware-house of Baker [probably Bowker] & Roberts," and other stores. In November of 1865, military officials at American Camp forced J. K. Bowker to close his mercantile establishment that had been in business since at least 1860. The resulting inventory of goods indicates what would have been available to islanders at that time (see Appendix: *Inventory of Goods, J. K. Bowker Store, San Juan Town, November 1865*). In a letter of January 20, 1871, Brigadier General E. R. S. Canby reported that:

> ...to keep the trading on the islands under control of the American and British Commanders, it has been found necessary to limit trading establishments to one at each of the Military posts...thus preventing smuggling etc. ... There has certainly been less trouble in the Island since it was adopted, and it is to be apprehended that if other establishments were authorized some of them at least would degenerate into whiskey drops, and depots of smuggling.[70]

Stores were soon established on the other islands. Hiram Hutchinson, familiarly known as 'Hutch,' established a store on Fisherman Bay in the 1850s, where he eventually claimed a homestead on the site of what is now Lopez Village. At first, he traded with local Indigenous peoples, but his commerce soon expanded to include Euro-Americans who had settled on Lopez and other neighboring islands. Over time, his goods changed from necessities such as powder and lead, flour and salt, and blankets and tobacco to more domestic items such as shoes, gingham cloth, and remedies. As with many of the local stores, his establishment became the locus of the first post office on the island.

Another early store was established by Paul K. Hubbs on Orcas Island at what came to be known as Grindstone Bay—allegedly because Hubbs had the only grindstone in the area. The Robinson brothers—John and Allan—homesteaded in Crow Valley after making a stake in California (and allegedly not being able to return to their native Virginia because of the Civil War); at their store they traded goods from Port Townsend and Victoria to the Fraser River area and supplied stock to island residents, including Paul Hubbs for his store. Their account books record sales of crushed sugar at 28 cents per pound, kerosene oil for $2 per gallon, and dried apples for 28 cents per pound.[71]

Charles Shattuck opened a store at Eastsound on Orcas Island in the late 1850s. He first lived in a tent at the head of East Sound, and later built a house of lumber that he had shipped in.

After Hubbs moved away, Stephen Sweeney received a homestead in 1882 and established a store west of Grindstone Bay. He traded with a schooner, and later a steamboat (which was lost in Deception Pass, with Sweeney succumbing to injuries he received then). Stephen was the brother of John and Joseph, who would eventually move to San Juan Island to establish a ranch in San Juan Valley (John) and a store in Friday Harbor (Joseph); Joseph became a major real estate broker on the island.

After the commencement of the operations at Lime Kiln in 1860, a store was established nearby. Records of trades for lime barrel "liners" in exchange for goods at the store by Samuel Gross in the 1870s indicate that he obtained staples such as sugar, lard, and soap, as well as caps, powder, and shot; tobacco; hair oil; and writing paper.[72] In the records of Gross's insolvency, one of his creditors was the then-operator of the lime company, James McCurdy. In 1879, McCurdy petitioned for the establishment of a post office named Lime Kiln.[73]

Until the establishment of stores in Friday Harbor such as Joseph Sweeney's (1876) and William Douglas' (1882), Israel Katz dominated the trade on San Juan Island. Katz established a store in San Juan Town and a ranch nearby; it is also claimed that he later had a store in Argyle on San Juan. Eventually he bought a lot in the new town of Friday Harbor and built a store, The Produce Exchange, there.

Homesteaders such as Peter Lawson purchased goods in bulk from Victoria or San Juan Town. These included 100-pound barrels of brown sugar; 25-pound sacks of table salt; 100-pound sacks of rock salt (for meat and hides); flour in 50-pound sacks or 100-pound barrels; unroasted coffee beans in 100-pound sacks; green tea in 5-pound boxes; soda crackers in 24" high by 18" wide tins; and matches in small batches.[74] Extant invoices and credit accounts from local stores indicate purchase of staples similar to these as well as credit for farm goods. James Tulloch notes that he sold potatoes to Hutchinson at his store on Lopez for $2.75 per ton—less than one-seventh of a cent. Much of the information that is available on goods and prices during this period comes from credit accounts and invoices at Israel Katz's store in San Juan Town, which provide prices on several commodities and crops during the mid-to-late 1870s. Christopher Rosler's 1876 account at Katz' store lists: credits for barley (at 1 cent per pound); peas (1½ cents/pound); eggs (25 cents/dozen); wool (23 cents/pound); rams, ewes, and lambs; and sheepskins (25 cents each). Cows were valued at $20 each, as were hogs; sheep were $2 each. Chickens were 50¢, turkeys $1.50. Beehives sold for $10.00. Wool ranged from 19 to 23¢ per pound; sheep skins were 25¢ each. Beef was 8¢ per pound; cow hides (green or dry), $1.50 each. Katz bought 4 dozen eggs for $1.00, or 25¢ a dozen. Barley sold for 1¢ per pound, peas for 1½¢.[75] Potatoes ranged from $4/5$ to ½ of a cent.[76]

This data can be compared with prices given for livestock sold at auction to satisfy creditors for default on loans and mortgages in various court cases from the 1870s through the 1880s. For instance, in 1879 when Samuel H. Gross petitioned for insolvency, his possessions were sold at auction. Sheep went for $1.25 a head; hogs for $2.50; and chickens for about 25 cents each. Three steers were sold for $17.00, and a cow for $7.00. His yoke of oxen was sold for only $80.00, which seems very low. Three hundred and sixty-eight pounds of wool were sold for 18 cents per pound.[77] All these prices seem low, perhaps because of the situation—an insolvency auction. Gross was certainly not alone in needing to obtain credit for the expenditures of settlement in the San Juans.

Financing

Many of the early American settlers in the San Juan Islands had made their fortunes elsewhere, principally in the gold fields of the Fraser River during 1858-9, but also through other occupations such as freighting by boat in the Salish Sea region. Even with these initial investments, however, additional funds were often needed for goods and services for farms and businesses in the islands. The most common financing in the San Juan Islands during this period was in the form of credit, either for goods—in the form of running accounts at local stores—or loans, from local or regional merchants. Principal among the regional financiers were J. K. Bowker and John Tod in Victoria and Rothschild & Company and Waterman & Katz in Port Townsend, and later Israel Katz at his store in San Juan Town.

The most common form of loan, at least from the evidence of defaults, was in the form of a promissory note, to be paid after a certain period ranging from several months to a year, at an interest rate of 1-2 percent per month or, in the case of longer terms, ten percent per annum, and usually specified as "payable in United States gold coins." Notes and loans were secured either through chattel mortgages on livestock such as cattle, hogs, and sheep, or on crops and land (see Appendix: *Mortgages and Loans*).

Samuel H. Gross is exemplary of someone who came to San Juan Island to farm and proceeded to run up enough debts that he was eventually forced to file for insolvency. Gross was born in Ellsworth, Maine, and moved to California to prospect when he was 22 years old. After heading north to Port Gamble (possibly because of the affiliation with the lumber firm of Pope and Talbot with Maine) in 1862, he struck out for the Fraser River gold fields two years later. In 1868, with some $2,500 to his name, he moved to San Juan Island, married a member of the Mitchell Bay Band, Jane Jennie Quinalt Satart (also spelled Jane Z-tat or Satartz, as he wrote it in his *Account Book*), and began farming. A series of unfortunate investments in land and downright bad luck eventually led to his petitioning the 3rd District Court in Port Townsend for insolvency in 1879, with accumulated debts equal to his original stake (see Appendix: *Petition of Samule H. Gross for Insolvency*).[78] Among his creditors was none other than Israel Katz and included in the evidence submitted for the case were both an invoice for items attained at Katz's store (see Appendix: *Samuel H. Gross, Exhibit One, Account of Sales*) and records of property and chattel mortgages from Katz and others (see Appendix: *Creditors of Samuel H. Gross*). Gross was allowed to retain some possessions "as necessary to his support and that of his family," viz.:

To himself a bed and bedding and two beds and bedding for his children, one cow, and calf 3 swine ten chickens...one colt coming two years old in lieu of a team and all necessary household furniture not exceeding in value one hundred dollars and all firearms, family pictures and all books constituting petitioners library. Also ~~all~~ necessary ~~seed~~ grain and potatoes not exceeding $30.00 in value" [crossed out in original].

Eventually, Gross found other employment, and even succeeded in fish trapping for salmon later in life.

> *Now therefore you the said Sheriff are hereby commanded and required to notice for sale, and to sell the said chattel property and mentioned in said bill of complaint, to wit—1 pair oxen, nine years old marked white and red 1 pair steers three years old, red color, three cows, one white 9 years old, and two white and black 4 years old, and two yearlings dark red, also about two dozen chickens, fifty hogs together with all the increase of said cattle hogs and chickens, also a plow, harrow, wagon, and all the farming implements upon the farm of said Peterson together with one half of all crops grown on said farm of Peterson for the year of 1873 consisting of oats, peas, barley, and sell the same according to law for gold coins, and to apply the proceeds of such sale in gold coin to the satisfaction of said judgment, with the interest thereon and costs together with your fees and to make and file you return of such sale to the Clerk of said District Court within sixty days from the date hereof.*
>
> *Waterman & Katz v. Peter Peterson Case #761 (1873)*[79]

Gross's possessions were sold at auction, mostly to his creditors. In the case of chattel mortgages, problems of assigning or attaching livestock such as cattle and sheep that were often scattered on several ranges or even islands were substantial. Court records reveal many cases of attachment that bear witness to debtors who were not able to make good on their accounts or loans. In 1877, for instance, Israel Katz accused British Columbia resident James Peers of having run up a bill at Katz's store in San Juan Town and then leaving for Victoria, taking his 300 sheep with him.[80] In a later case involving the same parties and Peers' partner John Anderson, $700 worth of sheep were attached, but a report filed by the sheriff expressed great frustration over trying to watch over several hundred sheep scattered over Flat Top, Spieden, Johns, Waldron, and Orcas Islands.[81]

> Frend Bowker
>
> Dear Sir
>
> I ham Sore that I hav bee the cas of wonding you feelings. But I will not be so ... a gan I hav ben a long tim tring to send sheep hover but no bot an wen I got a bot I was on the way to the Post hofes with leter the anser to Mr John tods leter so it was not poste. The Sheep that I brot over wold not Sut you for thay was lams as I had no tim. The Bot was loded with Shingls and I sold to Stafort for 3 dollers and Payd to Rup and Company 100 dollers and frat 25 dollers Duty. So you will See that I tend to pay my Dets. Now my old frend Bowker you will not hav to find any mor falt as I ham old Bill Smith agan. So I hop that haur frenship will last. It was my intencen to com with mor Sheep. But the bot went to the Squinish ... and hav loaded and cold not tak no Sheep but promist to bee back in Six days. To day I hav Sent aman to hutchinson for a bot if no bot to go to San Jun this tusty the 13 no word of bot or man and Snowing fast. I ham Sorey to hear that mrs Bowker is Sick and hop She will sun get beter. Giv my best wishes to all of the family and a hapy new year. So I must clos as I hav to go Six mils to the Pos hofes and the Sno faling fast
>
> > Your truly
> > —William Smith, Orcas Island,
> > to J. S. Bowker of the firm Bowker and Tod,
> > Victoria, January 10, 1874

In the case of Orcas resident William Smith, proof had to be given that Smith was indeed earnest in his efforts to pay his creditors, and not taking sheep to Victoria to remove them from attachment. Smith had run up a debt at the firm of Bowker and Tod in Victoria, eventually signing two promissory notes at 2% per month: one for $100 on the first of August 1872, and the second for $259.88 on the day following. Smith wrote several letters to the firm, answering their requests for payment. In 1874, Bowker and Todd, principles, with D. C. H. Rothschild and Sigmund Waterman as sureties, sued to attach Smith's sheep, accusing him of selling them to others to avoid debt. The case included testimony from his neighbors such as H. E. Hutchinson, proprietor of the store on Lopez:

> ...W. Smith is a neighbor and he [Hutchinson] well knows his condition financially, that he has a few hundred sheep and they are his only source of income, that Victoria V.I. is his market for fat sheep, that sometime in September and October last he took a quantity of sheep to Victoria and after his return paid me one hundred and fifty dollars which he owed me for supplies from my store. That affiant knows said sale of sheep was not for the purpose of defrauding his creditors but for the purpose of paying his obligations."[82]

The case was dismissed.

Customs and Smuggling

The Puget Sound Customs Collection District, established in 1853, was moved from Olympia to Port Townsend a year later (and only three years after that city was founded), under the direction of Col. Isaac Neff Ebey, Customs Collector. Every vessel entering Puget Sound from foreign ports—and that meant Victoria and other Canadian ports—had to clear customs at Port Townsend first. Prior to the settlement of the international boundary, customs officials were assigned to San Juan, but only in the capacity of directing ships to Port Townsend, not collecting customs. Several of these men became famous for their involvement in the settlement of the San Juans. Henry Webber was the first, brought to the island by Ebey himself, and it was his claim to the land where Belle Vue Sheep Farm and later American Camp were sited that became the only filing under the Donation Act. Webber left after a year, to be replaced by Oscar Olney, but he, too, soon left. Paul K. Hubbs, Jr, received his commission on April 29, 1857, and soon resided in Webber's and Olney's cabin near Belle Vue Sheep Farm. Hubbs was not only involved in the actual events of the Pig War and its settlement but homesteaded the south end of the island, originally called Hubb's Point. He subsequently settled on Blakely Island, Grindstone Harbor on Orcas Island, and John's Island. After the boundary decision, Customs was reorganized, with John M. Izett, who lived on Whidbey Island, in charge of the San Juans.

Because the main exports from San Juan Island during this period were lime and agricultural goods, which probably did not account for that much trade, it has been suggested that most of the traffic consisted of other, illegal goods—liquor and wool—that could be brought into the United States over the disputed boundary at the time. After the establishment of a fixed international boundary, clearer cases of using the relative porosity of this border to move goods are evident in another lucrative avenue of commerce: smuggling. In 1873 Izett noted several seizures, including "The British sloop ATALANTA, Todd master, over 5 tons, for loading sheep at San Juan for Victoria without entering at Port Townsend." The next year he caught several vessels bringing goods to the islands without paying duty, including materials for an (illegal) distillery at English Camp. A growing sense of the frustration in trying to apprehend smugglers in the seas around the islands can be gathered from Izett's 1875 entry on the seizure of the British Columbian sloop *Invincible*, bringing 400 pounds of wool to a store on San Juan:

> *Found here whereabouts from Paul K. Hubbs, but it was blowing too hard for me to go to her with my small boat until the tide turned. The cutter WALCOTT'S large boat came along and Lieut.*

> Burkes assisted me in getting to her. I made the seizure. Boatman Newton and myself took her to Port Townsend. Sloop and goods sold at public action, Paul K. Hubbs getting the informer's share.[83]

By 1882, Izett was stationed in Friday Harbor, although there was quite a controversy over the requirements that small boats stop there; a year later, port of entry was moved to Roche Harbor, nearer to the Victoria.[84]

One of the most popular items for smuggling was wool. This was exacerbated in part by the 1860 Morrill Tariff, a Republican protectionist tax bill introduced by U.S. Senator Justin Morrill, which raised the dutiable tax on imports from the just under 20 percent of the former 1857 Act, to over 36 percent in 1862, with dutiable rates scheduled to go to 47 percent within three years. As it played out, the Tariff increased the rate by 67 percent to over 26 percent by 1862 and to 36 percent—more than double—by 1865. This had the specific effect of making it very expensive to legally import wool from Canada, so that it became economically advantageous to smuggle it across the border. Here's how James Tulloch put it:

> *The price of wool on the Canadian side being about half that paid on our side made raising wool on a foggy night extremely profitable and J. L. Sherer, our county auditor who made a careful canvas, found that the yearly yield of San Juan County was 27 lbs. while the actual clip was 2-½ lbs.*[85]

In 1883 Customs Collector Izett, apprised that large shipments of wool were being planned, took a pre-emptive five-day boat trip among the islands counting the potential wool clip, in order to be on guard. Opium was also a popular item; although it was not illegal in the United States at the time, it was subject to a substantial, $12 per pound duty.

> *One stormy morning Father and Uncle Eber were at the barn above the bay when they heard a commotion below and saw a boat that...was about to sink. Two men were yelling for help. Father and Uncle Eber threw a rope over the side of the bank and the men were brought to safety. Then they noticed strange sounds coming from the hold of the ship. [The] men who had been rescued said, "It's nothing. Forget it. We may as well get going. Let the boat sink." But Father and Uncle Eber wouldn't go along with that. Pretty soon the passengers broke out of the hold which had been locked and...it was apparent they were chinamen being smuggled into this country...*
> —Ethel Bruns-Shull, quoted in Amy Frost, "The San Juans in the Bigger Picture: Chinese Exclusion," The Islands' Weekly August 30, 2005

The customs official also served as immigration officer, and after the Chinese Exclusion Act was passed in 1882, served to detain smugglers of Chinese immigrants. Chinese would pay smugglers $300-500 for clandestine passage from Canada, through the islands, to the mainland; they were often stowed in a ship's hold, sometimes sewn in potato sacks. The geography of the islands abetted this: smugglers would land their 'cargo' at North Beach on Orcas Island and have them run to Eastsound, where they would be picked up by another boat, thus eluding customs agents. Among the more horrific tales of the islands is the abandonment, when approached by customs agents, of Chinese on rocks such as Goose Island in San Juan Channel, leaving them to the vagaries of storms and tides. Amelia Davis recorded in her diary that her husband James rescued a boat load of Chinese who had been abandoned on a barren rock in the straits, presumably when a revenue cutter had come too close to their smuggler.

Intercourse

From the historical precedent of Indigenous trade, based largely on transportation by canoe, among the various Coast Salish groups in the San Juan Islands with their regional neighbors, intercourse evolved through the introduction of Euro-American boats and ships coincident with the development of road systems on the land. These networks were abetted by the emergent mercantile system of post sutlers and stores, which as the foci of monetary and trade transactions became the de facto lending institutions of period. With the imposition of an international border separating the islands from their major British trade ports—principally Victoria on nearby Vancouver Island, the difference in laws and tariffs led to smuggling across what had previously been a porous boundary.

Alfred and Annie Burke and Family, Shaw Island
(Courtest San Juan Historical Museum)

SOCIETY & GOVERNANCE

When Lyman Cutlar came to San Juan Island, he was with an Indigenous wife and child; presumably they had been married *á la façon du pays* ("according to the custom of the country"), i.e., through her tribe's traditional practices. Although it is not specifically mentioned in the historical records, he also must have participated in important personal events that had a societal aspect, such as their child's birth and education. Nearby, he witnessed the formation of San Juan Town, and he was instrumental in founding the community that developed around the works at Lime Kiln. Beyond the everyday social interactions among islanders engendered by work and trade, the social element was a vital force during this period. Important life events included marriage, death and burial, festivities and celebrations, religious observation, education, communication, and the formation of concentrated populations such as towns and villages. The principal reason that Lyman Cutlar settled on San Juan Island was that he thought it was American territory, upon which he and other Americans could stake a claim on land which they could eventually own—not the Colony of Vancouver claimed by Great Britain. This was the reason that they were called "The Disputed Islands." However, after the shooting of the pig, and disputing what he considered to be the exorbitant value of the Hudson's Bay Company boar, Cutlar offered Belle Vue Sheep Farm Chief Trader Charles Griffin to gather three neighbors to determine an appropriate cost. While this may have been the American way of settling disputes, it was not that of the hierarchical Hudson's Bay Company and the English judicial system. In the following years of the Joint Occupation, there would be many differences concerning governmental and judicial decision making.

Marriages

The Coast Salish had specific practices for courting and marriage. Most commonly, young men asked for marriage to a young woman. Wayne Suttles outlined three steps to this process:

negotiations by the supplicant's family; a vigil, including fasting, at the girl's house; and an exchange of property between the two families, at the girl's house.[1] The principal form of exchange was wealth represented by blankets and sometimes food. Later, this took the form of food shared at a banquet, and even the exchange of money. As a rule, the bride would leave with the groom by canoe for his house, even if he lived nearby. Later exchanges of wealth occurred between the families, cementing their relationship through the marriage itself as well as economic ties. (This custom, perhaps not too different than some modern-day cultures, may have given rise to the Euro-American perception that Indigenous wives were available for a price; for instance, men like Paul K. Hubbs boasted that the going rate for a young and beautiful girl was four sacks of flour, a pair of Hudson's Bay blankets, a musket and some powder and shot.)[2]

Despite the greater proportion of Euro-American unmarried men to women in the San Juan Islands, some of these men sought Euro-American women as partners. If they did not come to the islands already married, some were able to obtain wives through "bride ships." In 1862, a British Columbia clergyman wrote to the Lord Mayor of London, requesting eligible women. In response, the ship *Tynemouth* left Newcastle-on-Tyne, England, on June 9, 1862, with 60 women aboard; after a difficult sailing, it arrived on September 17 in the same year. More than half of the passengers were married within a few weeks; others took jobs as governesses or servants but eventually married in the area. One instance of a ship bride in the San Juans is Fanny Dearden, who married Peter Lawson. They met at the house of Peter's neighbors, Stephen and Lucinda Boyce, and were married on June 9, 1865, at Christ Church in Victoria.[3]

With the introduction of so many single Euro-American men into the social network of the San Juan Islands, the majority of marriages occurred between them and Indigenous women. These men encountered several different Indigenous groups: local families, associated with the Mitchell Bay Band; tribes from Vancouver Island and various parts of the mainland, who were fishing, hunting, and gathering, often with their relatives, in their traditional islands resource areas; and Northern Tribes who were visiting the San Juans. William Moore, for instance, met his future bride Sara Seymour at an encampment at Stockade Bay on Orcas Island and asked permission of the chief to marry her. Christopher Rosler, a soldier at American Camp, met his wife-to-be, Anna Pike, when she and her Tsimshian family were encamped at a rancherie on the south end of San Juan Island. Several Kanakas, servants of the Hudson's Bay Company, met their partners, most of whom were related to Mitchell Bay Band members, while doing their work on San Juan Island. All these men undoubtedly married *à la façon du pays* (in the custom of the country), i.e., through Indigenous marriage ceremonies.

> *These islands were settled by former employees of the Hudson's Bay Co. and it was settled policy of that thrifty company that their employees should all take Indian women for mates. Both that it gave them control of the fur trade of those tribes and it also prevented the tribes from raising against them.*
>
> *These Indian women were obtained by purchase price ranging from $20 to $50 according to looks and social position in the tribe. Having a Chief's daughter gave a squaw man a fancied superiority over his fellows. Quite a proportion of these women [men?] were French Canadian, but there were also a number of Americans both from the North and the South.*
>
> —The Diary of James Francis Tulloch (1970)[4]

White attitudes towards "mixed" marriages varied. The Hudson's Bay Company encouraged their servants to marry local Indian women, to promote stability and establish and strengthen commercial ties. The Church of England, however, disapproved of cross-cultural marriages, which reinforced the custom of most such marriages being sanctioned through the Roman Catholic Church.[5]

Civil laws were no less ambivalent. Washington Territory, for instance, had passed laws against "fornication;" due to societal pressure in 1878 and 1879 many settlers who had married by Indian custom were required to obtain a "legal" marriage or face prosecution. Reactions varied. Tulloch told it this way:

> *Judge Lewis of the Superior Court had just rendered a decision that all squaw men must marry their squaws or give them one third of their property and send them back to their tribes in a certain time or be punished severely. The feeling ran high among them and they burned the Judge in effigy, and would have murdered him if they had dared. They professed great indignation that they should have to marry squaws though they seemed to think it was all right for them to have families by them.*[6]

Some couples were 'remarried' before civil judges, while others chose to ignore the law. A typical example is Samuel H. Gross, who had moved to San Juan Island and married Jane "Z-tat" (which he wrote as "Satartz") of the Malahat (Saanich) Tribe around 1869 or 1870, the year of birth of their first child, Alice. (Family tradition says that they married by 'Indian custom' as early as 1862, but this seems unlikely, given that Gross was in Port Gamble then, and did not come to San Juan Island until 1868, after spending time in Caribou, BC.) In 1877 he recorded this event before a civil judge as their legal marriage in his account book.

This situation changed in 1879, when Roger S. Greene, as Judge of the Third District Court (in Port Townsend), who was also Chief Justice of the Supreme Court of the Territory of Washington, ruled in support of Charles W. Beale's marriage to Julia Ke-Shugush (a Lummi also known as Neshagusho) through an Indigenous ceremony. Beale, along with eight other Whatcom County men with cross-cultural families, were charged with "open and notorious fornication" because they had not made their marriages official through Euro-American civil or religious ceremonies. All, including Beale, but excepting Henry Barkhousen, married their Indigenous spouses in an approved Euro-American ceremony prior to going to trial; Barkhousen refused to dishonor his tribal marriage to Julia Sea-hom Fitzhugh, daughter of Samish Chief Sehome and Clallam Tsis-Wah-use.

> *Like many others of the early settlers of the Northwest, Mr. Barkhousen took a wife from the native tribes, marrying her according to Indian ceremony at Whatcom in 1860, but unlike many other white men in similar relation he declined to hold that [the] marriage was not binding in the eyes of the law. He held that relation sacred and argued that an admission of its lack of force would brand his children as illegitimate. As a result he would not be remarried according to civilized usages and was indited by a grand jury for the offense against the stature...*
>
> —"Henry C. Barkhousen," Illustrated History of Skagit and Snohomish Counties (1906)

Although Beale did marry in the approved fashion, he hired a lawyer to challenge the meaning of "marriage." In particular, he asked:

> *1st. The defendant and the woman that he claims to be his wife commenced to cohabit together as man and wife...on or about A. D. 1857...*
> *2nd No license was taken out. None of the persons authorized by the statue to perform the marriage ceremony were present; that is, there was no Justice of the Peace, Priest, Minister or Judge or clergyman of any denomination present at the time said parties agreed in presence of witnesses to take each other as man and wife. The Question is, do the above facts constitute a valid marriage in this Territory?*

This stems from a complicated history of cross-cultural marriages in Washington Territory. After the initial Marriage Act of 1854, the Color Act of 1855 forbad interracial marriages. Although this was modified in 1858, exceptions to the interracial law were prohibited in 1866. This, in turn, was reversed when the entire Color Act was repealed in 1868. Some of the impetus for this repeal was the concern about the offspring of cross-cultural marriages, particularly in regard to inheritance; in fact, the title of the 1868 act was "Declaring Legitimate the Issue of Marriages of White Men with Indian Women." When Judge Samuel Greene heard the case, he considered the following:

> *1st Whether, in this Territory, at any time since the passage of the Marriage Act of 1854, a good and valid marriage contract could have been entered into, per verba de presenti [by verbal presentation], with out any statutory form or solemnization?*
>
> *And 2nd Whether, assuming such a marriage valid, it could, subsequent to the 29th of January, 1855, and prior to the 18th of January, 1868, have been lawfully entered into by a white person with a person of one-half or more Indian blood?*

Judge Greene ruled that tribal custom marriages were as valid as those imposed by whites, and, in doing so, wrote an encomium to the nature of the marriage contract.[7]

> *The marriage contract stands, among all contracts, chief. It exists not by the law of a particular nation, but by the law of all nations. It is before all nations, and it is the legitimate source of them all...where the relationship of parties apparently living together as husband and wife, is in question, the presumptions of the law are always that they are married.*

> *The great weight of legislative, judicial and speculative authority is that marriage among English-speaking peoples, and particularly throughout the United States, is a civil contract, and needs for its validity nothing more that the mutual assent of two persons legally capable of making and fulfilling such a contract. Such is our English common law. And a statute, therefore, providing for a license, publication, witnesses, an officiating civil or religious officer, or ceremonies of any kind, is not held to make these formalities necessary to constitute a marriage...for it is not the act of the State, but the act of the couple, that makes the wedding.*[8]

Past histories have often either denigrated or made light of cross-cultural marriages, but examples indicate the lasting nature of these attachments. The marriage of Patrick Beigin and Lucy Morris endured for more than 30 years. According to their grandchildren, Lucy's father died the first year she lived on the island with Patrick Beigin. Some tribal members were sent to kidnap her and take her back to the tribe, because they didn't want her married to a white man. As Babe Jewett, Beigin's granddaughter, told the story:

> *So it was sometime after 1860 that these six Indians came down to kidnap her. Well grandpa had built, planted a big orchard. And he built a fence around it and the log cabin was inside of the orchard. And he put this big fence around so the animals couldn't get to it. And while he was traveling back and forth he got grandma a great big white dog. She heard a noise outside, she had two children by then, and she went downstairs. The log cabin was a two-story cabin. She went downstairs and the dog went running out after these Indians.*

> *The Indians are quite superstitious you know. They saw this big white thing come out of this house running at them and they thought it was her father's ghost and they ran and never came back.*

Not all such marriages worked out, however. Peter Teeters, for instance, in suing for divorce from his wife Nancy on grounds of abandonment and adultery in 1875, stated that:

> ...she has been living in adultery with an other man. That is she has been living, sleeping and cohabiting with an other man, or in other words, has been guilty of sexual intercourse with him. And affiant says he has never forgiving her for it, or received her back, or cohabited with her since said adultery were committed by her.

Furthermore, he complained "that when defendant deserted Plaintiff as aforesaid and abandoned his house, bed and board, she took all of her own property with her and nearly all of Plaintiff's clothing, besides all of Plaintiff's chickens, half his hogs, all the provisions he laid by for winter, dishes lamps &c &c, and in company with an other man departed from the Territory of Washington." Specifically, he noted

> ...that she is an Indian woman and has no particular place of abode, but wanders about with her tribe from place to place, and the last time [he] heard of her whereabouts she was somewhere on the west coast of Vancouver Island about 150 miles from Plaintiff's said home [San Juan Island].[9]

In the 1867 Superior Court Civil Case #527, Hannah Meyers, who lived in San Juan Town, sued for divorce from Henry Meyers, saying that

> *She has conducted herself towards the defendant as a good and chaste wife, and that the defendant has beaten and cursed the plaintiff and accused her falsely of having been unfaithful to him and bearing a child to another from criminal intercourse while his wife, and the defendant prefers to live with a squaw and proposes to get one.*[10]

This case illustrates two significant aspects of some island marriages: the disadvantageous position of wives in the marriage relationship, and the perception of a relationship with an Indigenous woman as being without the duties and responsibilities of a 'normal' marriage.

Another example reflects how one couple handled this societal situation: when Samuel Trueworthy's estate was probated in 1876, he bequeathed his sons the revenue from his 800 sheep and 300-350 goats for their education, while he willed his Indigenous wife, Jennie, "50 sheep, two cows, a pair of goats, his poultry, household furniture and $6 a month for one year." Although it does not seem that Jennie Trueworthy got most of the estate, she was clearly left with enough to get by on, while the boys' future was secured.[11]

Burials and Cemeteries

When a person died in Coast Salish societies, there was a concern about disposing of the body so that surviving family members and relatives would not be physically and spiritually contaminated, while at the same time honoring the dead person. If the person died in a house, the body was carried out feet-first through an opening other than the door. It was wrapped in blankets or mats and carried to a sacred spot used as a graveyard. There the body was left in a coffin-like box or canoe that was supported by upright posts or trees.[12] Local Indigenous peoples had special places in the islands for burial grounds. Most were associated with sites significant to the origin or prehistory of the groups, such as ancient settlement areas, peninsulas, or smaller islands. In his deposition to the United States Court of Claims Case *Duwamish et al* concerning local Indian claims of lands in the San Juans, F. D. Sexton said:

> *[The Coast Salish] lived on that side of the island, most of them and had their burying ground over there at our place. It is there yet; a little island there adjoining this island. When the tide was out you could go across. They buried their dead in canoes and laid them on that island, and then there are several graves on the banks now that you can see.*"[13]

There are known and protected Indigenous burial grounds on Guss Island in Garrison Bay, at the She-Kla-Malt/Pearl Little place on San Juan Island, and Madrona Point near East Sound.

Soon after death, female relatives mourned the deceased by wailing over the body. This seems to be the case of the Haida man who was murdered in the main street of San Juan Town; the family of the victim formed a circle around the body and wailed for days. Victoria LaPlante Taylor, who as a little girl landed with her family at Cattle Point on the San Juan Island, only to find themselves in the midst of an Indigenous mourning ceremony, recalled: "On the day we arrived an Indian woman had been killed. The Indians had gathered there and all night long they kept up a wailing moans and beat tom toms." Captain Pickett, fearing reprisals, eventually paid the widow provisions.[14]

For those Euro-Americans who died in the islands, cemeteries were first established at English and American Camps so that the deceased could be buried in the ground. The one at English Camp is a small plot of ground on the slopes of Young Hill, above and behind the camp. It is surrounded by a picket fence, and contains seven gravesites, five of which are marked by wooden headstones; two are unmarked. Four of those that are marked are for Royal Marines, the earliest of which dates to June 1, 1865. The other gravesite is of a civilian. The cemetery at American Camp was located about 500 yards south of the post. It was also enclosed by a picket fence but was larger—about 34 feet by 34 feet, according to the lieutenant who measured it in 1873—and included a gate with a wooden arch above. Divided into three sections—A, B, and C—the plot contained at least 14 graves therein, including several unmarked that were considered to be those of civilians. The grave sites ranged from unmarked to wooden headboards to sandstone and marble monuments. Upon abandonment of the camp, the bodies were disinterred and moved to Fort Townsend—and later reburied at The Presidio when the Fort was abandoned.[15]

At the May 29, 1869, meeting of the subscribers of the schoolhouse at Portland Fair, the minutes of the building committee were closed, and it was moved that "a committee of three be appointed to wait upon the commanding officers of both camps to obtain permission to select a suitable piece of ground for a burying place."[16] Joseph Sandwith, P. Lawson, and Thomas Fleming were selected. Both the Catholic and Protestant cemeteries overlooking San Juan Valley probably evolved around the same time. The earliest recorded burial in St. Francis Cemetery is that of Edward McGeary, who died on May 28, 1872, but there are probably earlier, unmarked graves at this site, because Catholic Mass was held near this location as early as 1860. When the construction of the Presbyterian Church was begun across the road in 1878, the grave of James M. Hannah, an early pioneer who died in 1880, had to be moved, suggesting that there were possibly other, earlier graves from the 1860s and 1870s.[17]

On Orcas, James Tulloch, along with several others, formed the Orcas Island Cemetery Association to formally own and regulate Madrona Point, where there had been Indigenous, as well as later Euro-American and cross-cultural, burials for a long time.[18] However, they were persuaded to sell the Point and purchase land further inland. On Lopez, in 1882, John Carr donated land near the center of the island for what eventually became the Lopez Union Cemetery.

Festivities, Political Meetings, and Celebrations

In addition to inviting neighbors over for dances and other festivities, holidays were a ready reason for company. Island residents often gathered for political meetings as well as celebrations of important events. There are several records of Indigenous celebrations upon arrival on the island for the fishing season or camas gathering. Unfortunately, during the 'Disputed' years, so-

> *I remember also that it was the usual thing to celebrate on Christmas Eve. Many neighbors came to the home and from the large front room the furniture would be moved out of doors in rain or snow. The folks would dance and make merry until the morning hours.*
>
> *We always made room for company. Mother would get out a feather bed. It was placed on the floor. There was always room and company was always welcome*
>
> —Orpha Higgins Sutton, IN Told by the Pioneers (1938)[19]

cial intercourse among the soldiers stationed at American Camp and settlers and Indigenous peoples was often fraught with trouble, particularly when alcohol was introduced into the situation. Captain Pickett, in a letter of June 19th, 1860, noted:

> *The islands become a depot for whiskey. Not only do the northern Indians flock here, but our own tribes make it their market. It has been and is now being sold wholesale. The consequences are too obvious—robbery, raping, even murder are enumerated by a determined combination of civil, Indian, and military authorities.*[20]

The commanding officer's repeated attempts to delimit the military reservation was principally in order to prohibit bootleggers from selling their goods to the soldiers, and repeated raids were made on surrounding residences in search of alcohol. James Hannah, an early settler, established a short-lived local chapter (Lodge) of the Independent Order of Good Templars, a national fraternal organization loosely based on freemasonry, which was founded in 1851 and dedicated to temperance; the Order met at the first schoolhouse on San Juan.[21]

In addition to the attractions offered in San Juan Town to the soldiers at American Camp, entertainment came to the garrison. According to a November 23, 1859, report from a special correspondent to the *Daily Alta California*, "A short distance from camp, in this direction [down slope towards the north], is located the "Temple of the Muses," presided over by the Chapman Family. It is a round tent, not over large, and nightly entertainments (!) are here given to the soldiers."[22] There may well have been other travelling shows encamped nearby during this period.

The American newcomers lost little time in asserting their perceived right to the land through political meetings including caucuses and celebrations such as the Fourth of July. For instance, after the pig incident, fourteen Americans gathered at Paul Hubbs's cabin near Belle Vue Sheep Farm and celebrated the Fourth, raising a flag on a fifty-five-foot-high pole.[23] Later, when American Camp was established, the soldiers would set up a bandstand and a large platform with a tent over it, as well as picnic tables also covered by a tent, where the Fourth could be celebrated. A San Juan Island correspondent for a Port Townsend paper, the *Register*, reported on July 17, 1861:

> *The Fourth was celebrated by reading the Declaration of Independence, horse racing, etc. Early in the day the U.S. flag was raised at the Post office and San Juan Exchange at 10 o'clock, a.m. The Declaration of Independence was read by Paul L. Hubbs, Jr., after which, extemporaneous speeches were made by several gentlemen.*[24]

All of this patriotic Americanism did not deter British military and citizens from participating in the horse races; among the winners were Captain Bazalgette and Charles J. Griffin.

Lila Hannah Firth recalled that

> *In those days, there were no fences on the old Prairie down at the south end of the Island near the American Garrison, it was all an open country free for all &, grant it was too, there, this 4th of July, out on the Prairie they had erected a Bandstand, & a very large platform with a tent over it for a dance hall. Another long tent was arranged with tables under it for Picnickers to bring their baskets & dine.*

She goes on to relate how the garrison soldiers approached all the settler families for girls around 10 years old to take part in a parade from the landing, where they would meet an excursion boat, to the prairie, each "queen" in a white dress with a red sashed lettered with the state of the Union she represented. The parade featured Lila's brother Henry as George Washington and sutler John Taylor's daughter Lucy as "Goddess of Liberty."

> *When we made the circle & all got back to the Picnic ground…our Mothers had the tables all set, tea, coffee steaming hot, & the baskets all ready for the big spread. After a big feast for all hands & the cooks, they started the sports, Boys foot-race, girls foot rain. Mens race, & womans race, high jumping, womans horse race, mans horse race.* [25]

Other excursions from Victoria to American Camp occurred without the excuse of holiday (see Appendix: *The Excursion to San Juan*). Fourth of July celebrations were also held at the San Juan Lime Company.

The English, in turn, often celebrated Queen Victoria's birthday (May 24th) at their camp. In 1866, Lieutenant Sparshott, in Captain Bazalgette's absence, entertained the Royal Marines, officers and soldiers, and about 180 excursionists from Victoria who came to celebrate the holiday:

> *The wheel-barrow race blindfolded evoked intense amusement, the men rushed about in all directions and several of them disappeared, barrow and all, over the embankment… As the steamer was about to get under weigh the last game which consisted of walking a greasy pole extending 15 feet from the end of the wharf at the extremity of which was a stick three feet high with a bunch of evergreens, worth $3 to the person who could reach came off… From the deck of the vessel the excursionists witnessed several men who attempted the perilous journey take an involuntary header into the briny deep….*

To conclude the celebration, the celebrants, sang "God Save the Queen" and gave speeches.[26]

During the joint occupation, the commanders of the two camps often exchanged invitations to social events at their respective quarters. The Americans, for instance, invited the British to come for horseracing on the prairie near the camp, while the British invited the Americans up for Christmas celebrations at their barracks.[27] Newspapers offer accounts of excursionists, including several of the Masonic Lodges in Victoria, visiting English Camp, and being entertained by dances in the barracks and dinners at the commanding officer's quarters, as well as picnics at American Camp followed by dancing.[28]

Religious Observances and Churches

The Coast Salish practiced various rites and rituals, but without specific shrines or religious places. First salmon ceremonies, for instance, were held on the shore, usually at a fishing camp where the first catch of the season was landed. Longhouses provided the setting for observation of rituals, particularly during the winter months when there was little outdoor activity. In the Saanich culture, during the long winter moon, *SISET*, which means "old ones," elders would relate stories, and winter dances were held in the longhouses; in Samish it is similarly called *S7elálexw*, Moon of the Elders (December). This was followed by *NINENE*, "offspring" or "young ones," when indoor activities continued (for the Samish, *Ngíngene7* Moon of Children/Beginnings, mid-December to mid-January). Elders trained youth in their traditional culture, which would include not only proper observation of ceremonies and rituals but also how to conduct oneself as a member of the family and society.

The first Euro-American settlers in the islands—Hudson's Bay Company employees—were mostly English, Scottish, French Canadian, or Métis; the latter two groups were predominantly Catholic, and farm manager Charles Griffin notes several cases where servants went to Victoria for Catholic religious rites such as burials and marriages. A large contingent of American settlers was Irish Catholic, and they mostly settled in San Juan Valley, with a nucleus around Madden's Corner. The first church—a log cabin—was built there around 1860. This served for Mass and

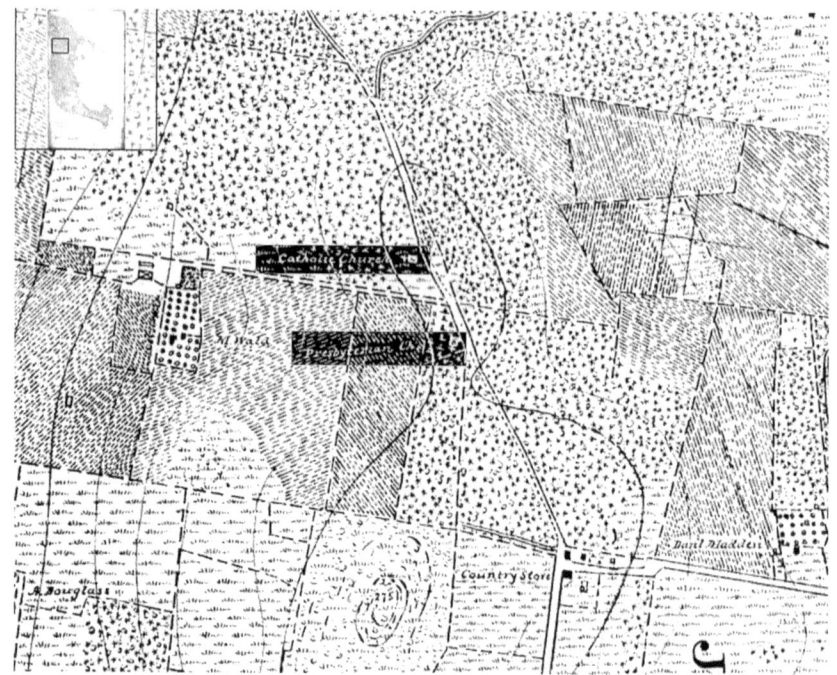

Catholic and Presbyterian Churches [highlighted], San Juan Valley, 1897 (U.S. Coast Guard & Geodetic Survey)

other sacraments whenever a priest was able to visit. In 1874, the log structure burned, and a new church, completed ca. 1884, was constructed of frame lumber, with the substructure consisting of three large timbers hauled by Patrick Beigin with his team of draft horses. Early Catholic families included Daniel and Patrick Madden, Patrick Gorman, John Doyle, Cornelius Coghlan, Edward McGeary, John Sweeney, John Delaney, and Patrick Beigin and their wives and children.

Protestant itinerant preachers occasionally came to the islands. Mary Jane Fraser recalled that "the first minister to come to the island was a negro…from Victoria."[29] Upon his return, he reported the need for a minister on the island to a Mr. Summerville, a Presbyterian. Anglican Bishop George Hills visited San Juan Island in 1860 and held a service for the soldiers and their families in the supply depot at English Camp. The Reverend Thomas J. Weeks came to the island in January of 1870. In 1872, he married Margaret Ann Naylor, the teacher at School House No. 1, where he held Sunday services. He eventually lived in the commanding officer's quarters at American Camp and went on to found two churches in the Islands: Valley Presbyterian Church (now Valley Church) on San Juan and Calvary Presbyterian Church (now Center Church) on Lopez. Although money was raised by him and Mrs. Michler, wife of visiting General Nathaniel Michler, in 1874, the cornerstone of the San Juan Church (on land donated by Norwegian settler Matthias Lundbland) was not laid until August 1878 and the Gothic Revival structure was not finished until 1882. The Lopez Church was begun in 1877 and dedicated on August 14, 1889.[30] The first Methodist church in East Sound was not built until 1887.[31]

Education and Schools

The Coast Salish considered the education of their children an integral part of their family life. According to Wayne Suttles, children were taught through early morning lectures, evening storytelling, and occasional private conferences.[32] Children were taught to be quiet and develop their bodies through hardship and dietary restrictions, both for endurance to hardships and to make them receptive to "power." Both boys and girls were rousted early in the morning to bathe, often in icy weather. Certain foods with adverse properties were denied them, and they were urged to restrict their meals to one or two a day. As part of their coming of age, both boys and girls were sent out to look for power. Boy's puberty was recognized through a change in voice and was celebrated through rituals either in the outdoors—going to the woods, bathing, and scrubbing themselves with cedar boughs—or a four-day fast in the house, followed by bathing. A girl's puberty was recognized through first menstruation, when she was isolated in a partitioned-off corner of the house. She would then be subject to ritual purification by elder women, including bathing and performing ritual acts. Richer families would then celebrate her passage to womanhood with a public feast.

The Euro-American and cross-cultural settlers on San Juan Island placed great value on formal education and established private schools very early on (see Appendix: *School House No. 1 Minutes*). Hattie Rosler Merrifield relates in *Told by the Pioneers*:

> For a while some of the children near American Camp attended a private school. The neighbors hired a teacher and this school was held in one of the smaller Hudson's Bay buildings.[33]

Lila Hannah Firth said that: "My mother taught one of the earliest private schools that I can remember of, in an old log house, on a hill, about 2 miles from our home, where Henry Baylors [Bailer's] house now stands."[34] In 1865 a group of settlers got together to establish a public school for their children. The list of subscribers to the new school is testimony to the ethnic diversity of the population (Appendix: *Subscribers to Portland Fair Schoolhouse*). Hattie Rosler Merrifield described it in *Told by the Pioneers* as "built of logs with a shake roof ...[and] larger than the usual log house of two rooms and furnished with long home make tables and benches."[35] Lila Hannah Firth described the same building as

> ...built of large hewn logs with plaster between them. Plenty of windows. It was built on a hillside, the back of the building set on the ground, but, in front we had to walk up about 5 or 6 steps to the door. These steps were also made of hewd logs, & reached clear across the front of the building. Plenty of room to gang up on them, which we often did.[36]

Archibald Fleming recalled in *Told by the Pioneers* that it "had gun holes all around," which caused the English commander, who thought it intended as a blockhouse, to order it torn down.[37] However, he was countermanded, and an Englishman from Victoria, William Bell, was hired as the first teacher.[38] Students from the year 1870 included children of the Archambault, Beigin, Boyce, Brown, Comoy [Komoi], Douglas, Fleming, Friday, Hannah, McCoy, Rosler, and Whity families.

The Portland Fair School House not only functioned as a schoolhouse. It was used by residents for a variety of meetings, such as religious services, fraternal lodges, and civil government; Lila Hannah Firth related: "That school building was used for

*No. 1 Schoolhouse, Portland Fair, San Juan Island
(courtesy of San Juan Historical Museum)*

every public meeting on our side of the Island, Church & Sunday school for many years, Good Templars Lodge, Elections. At Christmas time, we had a large public Xmas tree there on Christmas Eve."[39] Another specific use of the building is represented by the 1874 case of *John Keddy v. Peter Jewell* over road taxes, the parties of which were summoned to the Portland Fair School House for a hearing by Justice of the Peace D. W. Oakes.

Due to the geography of the islands, the schools scattered throughout the county were situated near the approximate center of settlement in each region of each island. Lila Hannah Firth said:

> *Our first district school, called No. 1 District, was placed as near the center of the Island, from Cattle Point to Mount Dallas, along the west coast of the Island, this distance was about 8 miles, giving we children 4 miles to walk to school, and the Jakles children 4 miles. The Firth children 3 miles & so on. The children came from all directions in walking distance.*[40]

After District Number 2 was established, Lila Hannah went to school there; although it seemed just as far away as the Number 1 School, she did not have to climb Portland Fair Hill to get there. The school session was only 3 months during the summer, because of the poor quality of the roads during the winter. Later, with the improvement in roads, the summer session was extended to six months. There was a relatively high degree of absenteeism due to the difficulty of getting to school.

William Bell was county superintendent of schools from 1879-1885; he was succeeded by E. C. Gillette. The reports of the latter are quite detailed, and although they come from a period later than that of this study (1887), they are revealing of early schooling in the islands.[41] At that time, the county had nine school districts located on the three major islands (Lopez, Orcas, and San Juan), with a school just having been built the year before (1886) on Shaw. San Juan Island had four districts: 1, 2, 8, and 9. The first two were at Portland Fair, "built of squared logs, and whitewashed inside and out" and San Juan Valley, which was also a hewn log structure, but more run down. Number 8 was located near English Camp at Mitchell Bay, although the "frame building whitewashed" was struggling to accommodate the growing numbers of children of the worker's families at Roche Harbor. The latest district, Number 9, was just completing a building in Friday Harbor.

On Orcas Island, the first school (Number 5) was of hewn log—but not whitewashed—at the head of "Buck Bay" [East Sound] at the village of Eastsound. Number 6 was located "on the road between the mouth of Buck Bay and Doe Bay" and served a less dense population. The latest district at that time, No. 7, which was located "in the western portion of the island at Low Valley... situated on the road connecting west and east sounds," had just (1886) been enlarged.

Lopez Island had two districts, one each for the north and south halves of the island. The south district (Number 3) had two schoolhouses, and terms of three months each were alternated between the two locations. Rachel Hyland Ross, who taught there during this period, recalled:

> *I had a term of nine months at a salary of forty dollars per month. I felt that I was well paid. My school was held in two different places, in a log building each time, and the time was divided evenly. There were no desks in these buildings. Benches with book rests faced the center of the building. I had from twelve to fourteen children in each school. At the last school the children were mostly from homes where the fathers were American or British sailors and the mothers native women.*[42]

District 4, on the north end of the island, had "an old building of rough logs, ill lighted but thoroughly ventilated by numerous cracks and crevices in the chinking so that both pupils and teacher were almost constantly taking colds."[43] A new, painted frame structure had just been built to replace it the year before (1885).

Fraternities

Although there is evidence of a chapter of the Knights of Pythias, possibly among the soldiers of American Camp, it wasn't until the turn of the century that charitable institutions such as fraternities began constructing meeting halls in the islands. The Odd Fellows built their two-story Hall—Mount Dallas Lodge #95 of the International Order of the Odd Fellows—in Friday Harbor in 1892. Union Grove Hall, centrally located on San Juan Island at the corner of Cattle Point Road and Madden's Lane, seems to have been constructed around 1897; a branch of the Modern Woodmen of America, San Juan Camp No. 5899, was organized there in 1898. Both served as important meeting centers as well as places for dancing and other social activities.

Towns

Groupings of two or more Coast Salish longhouses formed villages, whose inhabitants were generally related through family ties among the various houses. They were sited with their long sides parallel to the shore, usually on the bench above the high-water line, with the lower wall of the shed roof facing the water and the higher wall facing inland. (The Coast Salish, like other Indigenous groups, hauled their canoes out with the bows facing toward the water, so that they could be launched rapidly.) The spaces between the buildings could include racks for drying fish and middens of discarded shells. Unlike northern tribes, who placed totem poles in front of, within, or flanking the villages, there is mention of house posts—carved timbers that framed doorways or accentuated the interior of the longhouses—created by the Coast Salish.[44]

The dispersed pattern of settlement of the early Euro-American inhabitants of the islands did not lend itself to concentrated clusters such as hamlets, villages, and towns. Such groupings usually resulted from the establishment of a trading center, such

James Madison Alden, View of Griffin Bay and San Juan Town [on right] (courtesy of San Juan Island National Historical Park)

as a mercantile store, that then served as the nucleus of a more concentrated settlement. Most of the villages—Town of San Juan (aka San Juan Town and San Juan Village), Lopez Village, Richardson, and East Sound, began that way.

The Town of San Juan started as a cluster of tents located along the road near the wharf that Hudson's Bay Company servants had constructed on Griffin Bay (at various times called "Grande Bay," "San Juan Harbor," and "Ontario Roads"). This is where Captain George Pickett and his troops landed at the beginning of the Pig War, and, in fact, the first American encampment was near what has come to be called "Old Town Lagoon." According to the August 1, 1859, *British Colonist*, one of the first structures built was that of the post sutler:

> ...at the head of the wharf a log building was in course of erection, by the sutler and butcher of the company. Next it lay large quantity of provisions. Around were gathered a dozen or so American settlers, who all claimed the island as American territory.[45]

The town grew rapidly around this nucleus. As in many western frontier settlements of the period, most of the early structures were tents, which served as bars; the *Gazette* reported on August 11, 1859, that "Some three or four persons had started little tent groggeries near the land from the harbor...."[46] Liquor, as well as prostitution, was a major problem for the military authorities, and San Juan Town continued to be a source of trouble throughout the joint occupation.

Several frame structures were built within a few months of the troop's arrival. These were located on narrow lots perpendicular to the street (one lot is described as 43 by 75 feet). Most structures were probably of box frame construction, wherein wide boards of milled lumber are nailed vertically to a hewn log sill at the bottom, supported on either cedar rounds or stones as a foundation, and a plate at the top. Most probably had gable roofs with shingles. Archaeological investigations uncovered evidence of this type of construction, as well as several basements or cellars that had brick-lined floors.[47] While the predominant use of the buildings seemed to be as bars or saloons, there were also several general merchandise stores, including a "ware house of Baker and Roberts" (where U.S. citizens met to petition the government) as well as Higgin's and Bowker's stores. As noted elsewhere, these stores were the only local source of provisions for the settlers.

In January 1860, when William I. Warren and Dr. C. B. R. Kennerly of the North West Boundary Survey visited the place, they described it thus:

> *There are about 20 houses: one of them is occupied by a store keeper who keeps an exceedingly limited supply of goods; five or six are 'rum mills', and the balance are vacant. The population of the place numbers about 30 or 40; the number being made up of …white men, Chinamen and Indians. Whiskey drinking seems to be the principal occupation.*[48]

Later that year Edward D. Warbass, the post sutler, described the town. He refers to the problem of ownership of land that was already in dispute, in this specific case, among the Hudson's Bay Company (who had constructed both the road and the wharf), Stephen Boyce, a farmer who claimed the land to there and the west for cultivation, and Isaac Higgins, who had set up shop in the budding town:

> *There are some twenty buildings in the town, built on lots by permission; some from Higgins, some from Boyce, some from both and others [from neither]… The land is claimed by the agent of the Hudson Bay Company, is claimed by Boyce as a farm, and Higgins as a town site. Higgins has plowed up recently the road used by the company to their wharf…and he is now engaged in carrying rails to fence it.*[49]

Higgins was later forcibly removed from the island after having several run-ins with the American military commanders.

After the boundary decision in 1872, San Juan County was established in 1873, with Friday Harbor as the county seat. Two documents help us envision the Town of San Juan at this time: Deputy Surveyor John Whitworth's notes on that section, ("It is composed of about a dozen houses, among which is a large store, also a hotel"[50]) and General Nathaniel Michler's Map, which indicates the road to the wharf lined by structures on either side, including a hotel, store, and two lots labeled "government." The town continued for several years after the departure of the troops, particularly because of the establishment of a branch of Waterman and Katz of Port Townsend, under the direction of Israel Katz, who also became postmaster. However, commerce and settlement eventually moved north to Argyle and Friday Harbor. The *Daily Colonist* reported on September 4, 1890, that the town, which had been abandoned, burned to the ground in a fire that spread from the nearby debris of an old stable.[51]

The problem remains as to how land or lots were allotted on property that had not been settled during the period of joint occupation. The reference to the actual measurements of several lots seems to indicate that some form of division had been applied to the site, but the legal contests mentioned earlier regarding ownership among the Hudson's Bay Company, a store owner (Higgins), and a farmer (Boyce) indicate that there was no clear solution to this problem. Furthermore, that several of the lots were later labeled "government" only highlights the issue: why could the "government," which is assumed to be the military, claim land even if it had seized it from a criminal through court proceedings?

This same problem applies to Lopez Village and East Sound on Orcas, both of which evolved as villages that grew up around stores established on land that had been privately homesteaded. On Lopez Island, Hiram Hutchinson came in the 1850s to establish a general mercantile store, but it wasn't really until the 1880s that other settlers began locating near him to form a village. In the case of East Sound, Charles Shattuck built a log cabin and opened a store there in the late 1850s. Shattuck applied for a homestead on land that would later become half of the village of Eastsound; the other half was homesteaded by Ephraim Langell, another Fraser River miner. (The name "Eastsound" devolved from the two-word name of nearby body of water: "East Sound.")

Orcas Island also saw the growth of several other small hamlets and villages: Deer Harbor, around the residences of Louis Cayou and James Bradshaw; West Sound with Joseph Bull and other trappers in the 1860s; Olga in 1860 with William Moore, another Hudson's Bay Company deer hunter; and Doe Bay, where German sailor John Viereck had settled with his Indigenous wife Jennie in 1872, later joined by Henry Langbadt and Peter Morris.

Friday Harbor

Friday Harbor is a case unto itself: a town that was homesteaded specifically as the county seat, although its relatively slow rate of growth certainly mirrored that of the other incipient hamlets on the islands.[52] The newly appointed Commissioners of San Juan County first met in November 1873, but it was not until August of the following year that the Commissioners selected a site for the county seat, officially naming it Friday Harbor:

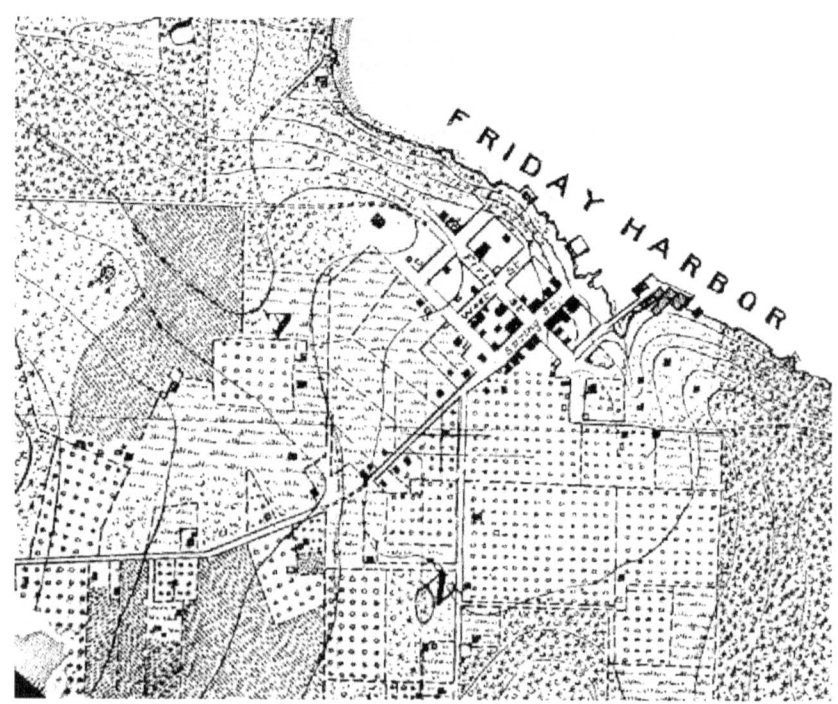

Map of Friday Harbor, 1895
(U.S. Coast and Geodetic Survey)

*Earliest Photo of Friday Harbor
(courtesy of San Juan Historical Museum)*

2 oclock PM Commissioners proceeded to examine the west shore of Fryday's[sic] Harbor with a view of selecting a desirable site for the county seat and Auditors office convenient to fresh water with a bold shore for the landing of boats and vessels and after careful examination selected a site about one quarter of a mile south east of Rees[?] warehouse and just in front of a large spring of fresh water named the place Friday Harbor...[53]

They then authorized the construction of a 16 by 24 foot "building suitable for the present purposes of the County," i.e., a courthouse.

The townsite of Friday Harbor was laid out to take advantage of its location. The main street—named for the spring that furnished an abundant quantity of fresh water for the town—led from the harbor to the farmlands up the slope to the southwest; it was intersected by Front, nearest the water, and First (what was to become Second was merely marked "Road") and paralleled by East and West. Interestingly, although the narrow side of the 50-foot by 100-foot lots fronted Spring, those along Front (including the corner lots) faced the water, the source of commerce. The streets were wide—80 feet—possibly for the convenience of turning a wagon team around.

In January 1876, Friday Harbor was established as a post office. That same year, Joseph Sweeney moved from Orcas to establish a store at the corner of Spring and Second Streets. However, very few people chose to buy lots and settle in town until the early 1880s, when Israel Katz established a second store—the "Produce Exchange"—at the corner of Front and Spring, which later served proprietor John "Jack" Douglas as a saloon (the "Saloon Best"). This apparently led to a building boom. Lots that originally sold for just $20 on Front Street and $10 inland soon went for hundreds of dollars. A new courthouse was built at the corner of Spring and First Streets, up the street from the old one, in 1883. However, it would not be until the 1890s that the town—and the island economy along with it—really grew with the founding of the San Juan County Bank, the Friday Harbor Packing Company (cannery), and other waterfront industries.

Government

The Disputed Islands were the result of the Treaty of 1846, which established the boundary between Great Britain and the United States of America. These two countries had been arguing over mutually claimed territory in the Pacific Northwest ever since 1818. The treaty establishing a boundary at the 49th parallel, a compromise decision because some in the United States had been advocating for a boundary farther north—54 degrees 40 minutes—to the rallying cry, "Fifty-Four Forty or Fight!"

The treaty recognized American control of all territory north of California to the 49th parallel of latitude, except for Vancouver Island; all territory north of the 49th parallel fell under the jurisdiction of Great Britain. While the boundary was clear on the mainland, it was ambiguous in regard to the water line between the mainland and Vancouver Island: the treaty simply said that the boundary

> *shall be continued westward along the said forty-ninth parallel of north latitude to the middle of the channel which separates the continent from Vancouver's Island; and thence southerly through the middle of the said channel, and of Fuca's Straits to the Pacific Ocean.*[54]

While this decidedly meant that the Gulf Islands were north of the border, what about the San Juans? Was this channel Haro Strait to the west or Rosario to the east, or even perhaps the "Middle Channel" that ran through the midst of the islands?

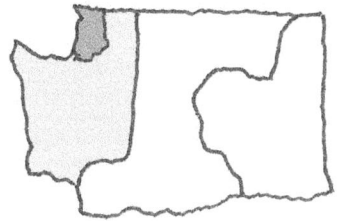
1850 - Lewis County

As a result of the Treaty, Oregon Territory, covering most of the territory gained, was established in 1848; it ranged from California on the south to the 49th parallel in the north, and from the Pacific Ocean east to the Continental Divide. In the next five years before the creation of Washington Territory, the Oregon Territorial Legislature created a total of eight counties north of the Columbia River: Clark, Lewis, Jefferson, King, Pacific, Pierce, Thurston, and Island—the latter in January 1853, less than two months before Washington Territory was established. Island County, carved out of Thurston County, encompassed what are the present-day Island, San Juan, Skagit, Snohomish, and Whatcom counties.[55]

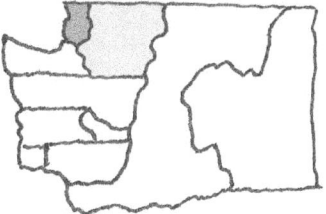
1853 - Island County

1854 - Whatcom County

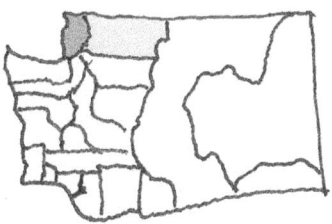
1860 - Whatcom County

Changes in Washington Territory Counties (in light gray)
That Include the San Juan Islands (in dark gray)
(Adapted from: Scott and De Lorme, Historical Atlas of Washington, *1988)*

Washington Territory was created on March 2, 1853. The first session of the Washington Territorial Legislature met at Olympia beginning on February 27, 1854. Before it adjourned, eight new counties had been established: Whatcom County, created on March 9, 1854, consisted of the northernmost portion of the existing Island County, up to the U.S.-Canadian border at the 49th parallel. On January 14, 1858, the Washington Territorial Legislature enlarged Whatcom County by adjusting its southern boundary, taking even more of Island County. Exactly three years later, on January 14, 1861, the legislature created Snohomish County from the remaining mainland portion of Island County, which was left with only two populated areas, Whidbey and Camano Islands.

The Organic Act that established Washington Territory in 1853 created a Legislative Assembly comprised of a Council (the equivalent of a senate) and a House of Representatives. This system remained intact until 1883. Whatcom County was represented on the 12-member Council by James Power, who also represented Island and Snohomish counties, and in the 24-member House of Representatives by Orin Kincaid, who also represented San Juan County. Both resided in the southern half of Whatcom County, and when the legislature met in the fall of 1883, both were given seats on the Standing Committee on County Matters.

The international boundary dispute (called, depending on the side, "the San Juan Imbroglio," "Pig War," and "The Disputed Islands") came to a crisis point with Lyman Cutlar's shooting of the Belle Vue Sheep Farm boar on June 15, 1859. American troops were requested by American settlers, with the excuse that they would defend them from Northern tribal raids—a real threat at the time, but not for this immediate situation. The landing of Pickett's force and subsequent sword rattling has been well covered elsewhere. After cooler minds prevailed, it was agreed by the "warring" factions to occupy (and govern) the islands jointly until the location of the boundary was settled.

With the agreement to jointly occupy San Juan Island, leading to the establishment of American and English Camps, jurisdiction of the island fell to the commanders of the two camps, and it was agreed that each would deal with their own countrymen. However, the nationality of suspected miscreants was not always clear, and they often played the nationality card when apprehended by military authorities on either side. Captain George Pickett described the situation in a June 1, 1860, letter to Captain Alfred Pleasonton:

> *Ever since knowledge of the joint occupancy, the desperadoes of all countries have fought [sic] hither. It has become a depot for murderers, robbers, whiskey sellers—in a word all refugees from justice. Openly and boldly they've come and there's no civil law over them. All the Indian tribes in the neighborhood—Lummi, Swinomish, the Skagit and even the Cowichan and the Victoria Indians flock here in quantities to supply themselves with poisonous whiskey. As a result, this is a perfect bedlam day and night.*[56]

As the letter indicates, an ongoing issue was the supplying of liquor to Indigenous peoples, a practice prohibited by both the Americans and the English. In September 1860 when Pickett and a squad of soldiers confronted John Taylor selling liquor to American soldiers as well as Indians, who had rafted their canoes to his boat near the beach, the Indians identified Taylor as "a Boston" (i.e., American) but he himself claimed to be a British subject. Pickett proceeded to send him to English Camp Commander Captain Bazalgette.[57]

It was a similar dispute over access to San Juan Island resources that ultimately forced Pickett and Bazalgette to delineate their zones of influence on the island. The Royal Marines apprehended two U.S. citizens, Paul K. Hubbs, Jr., and Solomon Meyerbach [Meyerback] while they were quarrying lime near the British works at Roche Harbor. Hubbs and Meyerbach protested that the deposits they were working were a far distance from English Camp, but Bazalgette subsequently claimed as a reserve the whole northern part of the island, including the Roche Harbor area, prompting Pickett to claim the southern end, including Cattle Point.

> *His mode of procedure appears to have been this: he would shoot the animal in the bush and skin and dress the carcass, and, under the cover of night, would send it across by his confederates to this side for sale. On searching his premises, the skins of eleven head of cattle were found buried, the brands on the skins establishing their identity with those of a corresponding number of cattle that had been missing of late…*
>
> —Seattle Weekly Gazette *September 9, 1865*

The situation of miscreants claiming either nationality depending on circumstance continued, however. As Captain Lyman Bissell, in charge of American Camp from 1862 to 1865, wrote in 1863, "When I assumed command of this camp in February 1862, I found the island infested with thieves and vagabonds of no particular nationality."[58] There are several other prominent instances of using the islands during their disputed status as a refuge. In the September 9, 1865, *Seattle Weekly Gazette*'s article "Important Arrest on San Juan Island," the paper reported that the American military authorities had seized a "well-known cattle thief named Parsons" who "ostensibly passed for a farmer" and was married "a few weeks ago to an English girl in Victoria."[59] Bissell also came to the aid of Royal Marine commander Captain George Bazalgette, who appealed for his help in evicting William Andrews, an American citizen accused of killing an Indigenous man near English Camp, as well as one near San Juan Town several years earlier. With witnesses from an Indian camp, Bissell and Royal Marine Lieutenant Henry Cooper discovered him in the company of Augustin Hibbard at Lime Kiln and proceeded to expel him from the island. This situation was exacerbated by the handling of several incidents by American commanding officers. Bissell intervened when the Whatcom County Justice of the Peace E. T. Hamblett tried to evict a British subject who had laid claim to some land coveted by an American, going so far as suspending Hamblett "as a functionary of Washington Territory." In this case, he was backed up by Department of the Pacific commander Major General George Wright, who cited as the basis of his support Winfield Scott's orders that territorial officials not intervene in cases involving British citizens.[60]

> *No civilized people on earth are subjected to the same degrading despotism as practiced upon the residents of San Juan. While the British residents resort to their civil tribunals for the settlement of their quarrels… The Americans are denied all law, and subjected by the force of the bayonet to obey the caprices a petty military officer, and their persons and property subjected to outrages nowhere else tolerated among civilized people. By what authority can a military officer require that no sale of property, nor lease, nor erection of a fence, nor building, shall take place on San Juan without his consent is first obtained.*
> —Isaac Higgins, Deposition, U.S. Third Judicial District Court, Sept. 6, 1866

Things came to a head when Bissell's successor, Captain Thomas Grey, who commanded American Camp from 1865 to 1867, confronted San Juan Town saloon owner (and mail contractor) Isaac Higgins over the latter's plowing up and putting up a fence across the military road between the town and the Hudson's Bay Company dock that was now used by all arrivals on the south end of the island. Grey sent his First Lieutenant William Graves to demolish the offending fencing. An altercation ensued, resulting in Higgins being first incarcerated in the camp blockhouse and then expelled from the island. Frustrated by what appeared to him as the excessive power of the military authorities, Higgins brought several cases before the District Court in Port Townsend, starting with a charge of "malicious trespass" on September 7, 1866, followed by obstruction of legal process when the U.S. Deputy Marshall was repulsed, not only once, but a second time armed with a posse. Eventually Judge B. F. Dennison, basing his decision on the fact that San Juan Island was under "military rule," refused to issue an "alias arrest"; this decision was upheld by Secretary of State William H. Seward. Higgins and others had to resort to a civil suit for damages, but after an initial award of $5,000 (of the $10,000 petitioned), the case was thrown out upon appeal. In 1868, subsequent commanders U.S. Captain Joseph Haskell and Royal Marine Captain William A. Delacombe ended the sale of liquor on the island by limiting sales to their respective post sutlers. Continuing challenges to the actions and decisions of commanders led representatives to making several attempts in the Territorial Legislature to assign the islands to Whatcom County for purposes of jurisdiction.

Negotiations over both the water boundary between the United States and Great Britain, and the claims of the Hudson's Bay Company on lands now held by Americans in the Pacific Northwest, had continued even to the brink of the Civil War; in April 1861, the British proffered arbitration over the claims as well as the boundary. The Civil War soon distracted the United States, so it was not until 1869, when Reverdy Johnson, envoy for President Ulysses S. Grant to the Court of St. James, concluded a deal to submit the question to a third-party arbitration. After a delay caused by rancor over Britain's role in the Civil War, the Treaty of Washington was signed on May 8, 1871, and ratified by the U.S. Congress a month later. Under the influence of George Bancroft, ambassador to Great Britain, Kaiser (Emperor) Wilhelm of German was chosen as arbiter. He appointed three men, all German—Professor Heinrich Kiepert, who taught geography at the University of Berlin, Councilor Levin Goldschmidt of the Imperial High Court of Commerce, and Dr. Ferdinand Grimm, Vice President of the High Court—to meet in Geneva to review the evidence. Despite disagreements—Goldschmidt, for instance, advocated for a "Middle Channel" (President's and San Juan Channels) solution, which would have placed the boundary between San Juan Island and Lopez, Orcas, and Shaw Islands—the commission finally voted for Haro Strait two to one, Goldschmidt being the minority, with a lengthy dissent. Endorsed by the Kaiser, the judgement was officially issued as a ruling on October 21, 1872. News of the decision was sent to both camps by telegraph. The English withdrew their troops by the end of November, and the Americans soldiers left in 1874.

During these disputes and negotiations, Indigenous peoples were largely ignored. With the initial settlement in the 1840s of Indigenously populated areas of what was to become British Columbia, the British government, represented by James Douglas, negotiated what have come to be called the "Douglas Treaties" with a half dozen Coast Salish groups on southern Vancouver Island. These treaties, in exchange for access to First Nations lands, guaranteed them the right to hunt, fish, and forage "as formerly," which clearly included traditional fishing methods, catches, and areas. In the Territory of Washington, Governor Isaac Stevens negotiated a series of thirteen treaties with Indigenous groups; among these was the Treaty of Point Elliott (1855), which was signed by what were taken to be representatives of Indigenous groups in the greater Puget Sound region. The Treaty did not acknowledge ownership or reservations for Indians in the San Juan Islands, which were attributed to the Lummi, despite the acknowledgement by the secretary to the treaty commission, George Gibbs, at least graphically on an 1856 map, that the northwest part of San Juan was used by the Saanich and the southeast by the Songhees. After the ratification of the Treaty in 1859, the Lummi were to remove to their reservation on Lummi Island and nearby mainland and the Samish to Guemes Island. The Clallam, under the Treaty of Point-No-Point, were supposed to go to the Skokomish Reservation on Hood Canal, but many remained in their traditional villages along the Strait of Juan de Fuca. The drawing of the International Boundary in 1872 exacerbated relations among Indigenous groups in the San Juan Islands, particularly the Mitchell Bay Band, because many families consisted of kin from groups in what was now the other side of the border: Sooke, Songhees, Saanich, and Cowichan.

With the boundary decision, the San Juan Islands fell under the jurisdiction of Whatcom County. This meant that they were to pay Whatcom County taxes, and be subject to the county administration, laws, and regulations as all other residents. Whatcom County soon imposed an eight-mil-per-dollar tax on personal property and collected road taxes, poll taxes, territorial taxes, and school taxes. In order to vote, islanders not only had to row to mainland Whatcom County but also pay a $2 poll tax to vote. It is little wonder that island residents, who were used to little or no governance in these areas, soon petitioned to establish their own county. On October 31, 1873, the Washington Territorial Legislature passed an act "to create and organize the County San Juan" out of Whatcom County.[61] Pursuant to the mandate of organizing the county on the third Monday of November, two of the appointed commissioners—Charles McCoy (later spelled McKay) and Joseph H. Morrill (the third, Samuel Trueworthy, was absent)—met on November 17, 1873, and proceeded to elect McKay as chairman and appoint county offices:

Auditor and Clerk Edward D. Warbass
Sheriff Steven H. Boyce
Treasurer Robert H. Frazer
Judge of Probate John H. Bowman
Superintendent of Schools William J. Deyerle
Coroner John L. Sherer
Wreckmaster James Fleming
County Surveyor E. C. Gillette
Justice of the Peace D. W. Oakes (in place of S. V. Boyce whose term had expired)
Justice of the Peace Thomas Fleming (in place of Edward D. Warbass).

The next day, they established four voting precincts in the islands. San Juan Island was divided into two districts, the northern District 1, which included Henry, Spieden, Stuart, and Waldron Islands, was delineated on San Juan Island by a boundary "south of Andrews Bay and north of John Keddy's," with polls at Augustin Hoffmeister's store. In the southern District 2, polls were to be held at either the school or the church. District #3 consisted of all of Lopez, Blakely, Decatur, Shaw and Charles Islands, with polls at Hutchinson's store on Lopez Island. Orcas Island made up District #4, with polling at the "school or church at the head of Buck Bay [East Sound]." Christopher Rosler was appointed the Constable for the "Precinct of the San Juan Island." William J. Deyerle was appointed Justice of the Peace (JP) for Lopez, with J. L. Sherer as Constable of the Lopez Precinct and Paul K. Hubbs became JP for Orcas, with Joseph Bridges as Constable. (Apparently Hubbs did not hang around for long, for in May 4, 1874, the County Commissioners *Journal* mentions Allan Robinson as JP as well as Charles W. Shattuck.

Within a few years the new citizens of San Juan County elected their officials, including G. W. Gray, Charles McKay, and

Gideon Brownfield as Commissioners. The Commission moved quickly to County business: establishing roads, providing for the indigent, and establishing taxes, as well as the first order of business—granting liquor licenses at $125 each to Israel Katz and Hiram Hutchinson.

Taxes

As territory claimed by the United States, the San Juan Islands were subject to local, territorial, and federal taxes. A customs collector in the federal Puget Sound Customs District, which had been moved from Seattle to Port Townsend in 1854, traveled to San Juan Island to assess the property of and collect taxes from the Hudson's Bay Company's prosperous Belle Vue Sheep Farm on livestock that he claimed had been smuggled into U.S. territory. His efforts were summarily rebuffed. The Whatcom County sheriff also made several attempts, beginning in 1854, to collect taxes on Belle Vue Sheep Farm (see Appendix: *Assessment of Property on San Juan Island, Henry R. Crosbie, Whatcom County Assessor, May 20th, 1859*). One trip resulted in what must have been a comical scene when Sheriff Ellis Barnes, having been refused payment, seized approximately 50 rams that he said were taken in compensation for tax claims; the sheep to be auctioned-off right on the beach to a group of bidders. After the auction and before the sheep could all be herded onto boats for a swift get-away, Belle Vue Sheep Farm personnel arrived, and the result of the ensuing melee involving men and sheep with differing agendas could be deemed, at best, only a partial success for either party, as only some 34 of the rams were eventually transported to the mainland. The British were incensed and determined to enforce their claim to jurisdiction. Farm manager Charles Griffin was appointed as a justice of the peace and magistrate that year specifically "to enable him to treat the U.S. collector of taxes on San Juan as a common offender, as Douglas reported to the British Colonial Office."[62]

When the newly appointed San Juan County Commissioners met on May 7, 1874, they determined the worth of taxable property at $128,000. They then established an 8-mil tax of "$2 on every male 25-50" (interestingly, the word "white" originally modified "male," but was struck out). A poll tax of 4 mils on the dollar was set for schools; 3 for the Territory, and 2 for road purposes.[63]

Judicial Courts

Established in 1854, the 3rd District Court, which was held in Port Townsend, covered most of the northwest region of Washington Territory, including the counties of Clallam, Island, Jefferson, San Juan, Skagit, and Whatcom. Skagit and Whatcom counties broke off around 1878, but San Juan remained in Port Townsend until after statehood (1889). Cases were categorized as civil, criminal, chancery, admiralty, and probate. It was also here that islanders had to go for naturalization—petitioning the United States government for citizenship. Washington District and Probate Court cases during the Territorial Period (1853-1889) have been compiled in a document called *"Frontier Justice."*[64] The Frontier Justice Records Project catalogued over 37,000 cases; approximately 70% were civil, 20% criminal, and 10% probate. Interestingly, civil cases rose in proportion to population growth during this period, while criminal and probate grew at a far lower rate.[65]

In order to get a sense of the context for San Juan Island and later San Juan County cases, there were a total number of 25,093 civil cases during the Territorial Period; along with population growth, this number jumped from 292 in the 1850s to 2,310 in the 1860s, 5,549 in the 1870s, and 16,873 in the 1880s, leading up to Statehood in 1889. The most common early civil cases had to do with collection of monies owed; later, property disputes and foreclosures became more common. Damage suits were a late (1880s) phenomenon; contract disputes, while being present from the start, grew slowly during this period.[66] Some 66 civil cases involved residents of the San Juan Islands. Similar to the trends Territory-wide, they begin with a small number in the 1860s—10—and then jump to 46 in the 1870s. Only 10 cases occur in the 1880s, but this is largely because local cases were being handled by the county court.

The total number of Territorial criminal cases was 6,834, rising from 262 in the 1850s to 713 in the 1860s, 1,212 in the

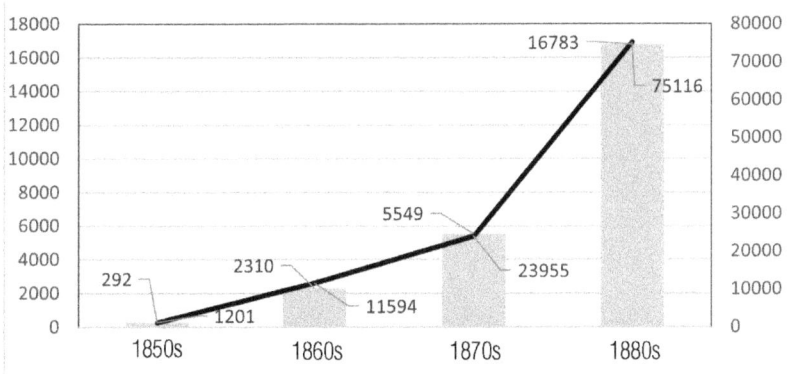

Washington Territory Civil Cases (left scale)
Compared to Population (right scale)
(adapted from "Frontier Justice" 1987)

1870s, and 4,604 in the 1880s. As the editors of *Frontier Justice* point out, despite popular images of the Territory being part of the "Wild West," less than half of these cases involved violent crimes such as assault, murder, and rape, and only 110 included the crime of "Exhibiting a Dangerous Weapon." A good portion of these involved substance abuse, most relevantly sale of liquor to Indigenous peoples. (Another major aspect of this situation, Chinese railroad laborers smoking opium, was absent in the San Juans.)[67] Approximately 29 of the total Territorial criminal cases involved residents of the San Juan Islands; these increased from just one in the 1850s—a robbery at Post Sutler Edward D. Warbass' newly-established store at American Camp—to twelve in the 1860s, eleven in the 1870s, and then fell to five in the 1880s, the latter probably because of the assumption of local cases by the county court.

In the San Juans, early (1860s) civil cases involved property damages or improper detention—largely related to the rather raucous goings-on at San Juan Town—or non-payment of wages. The majority of civil cases were for debt collection, principally from mercantile firms of Bowker and Tod and Henry Saunders in Victoria and Rothschild & Co and Waterman & Katz in Port Townsend. Israel Katz alone had a total of 47 San Juan cases before the Port Townsend court from 1876 to 1889. In the San Juans, civil cases for debt collection amounted to eight cases for Waterman & Katz or Israel Katz alone and two each for Bowker & Tod,

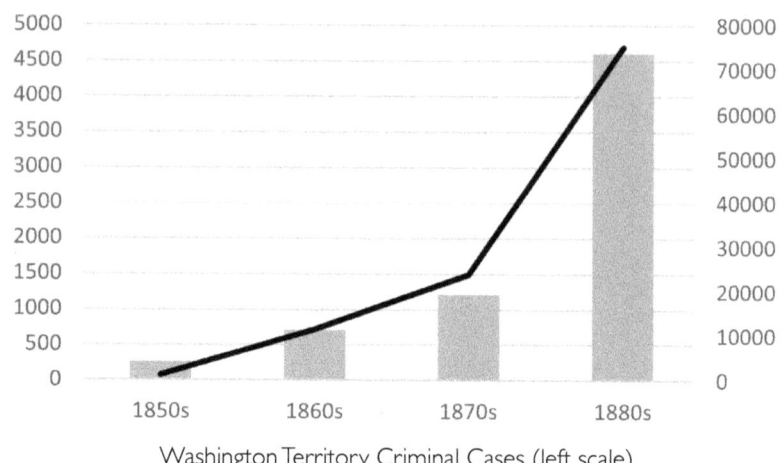

Washington Territory Criminal Cases (left scale)
Compared to Population (right scale)
(adapted from "Frontier Justice" 1987)

Rothchild & Company, and Saunders. After San Juan County was established and the county commissioners authorized roads, civil cases involving "property damage" as a result of siting of roads soared, clearly occurring in batches around the time of the actual road designation. One settler stands out as for some reason being more litigious than others: Edward D. Warbass, with four cases.

Among the civil caseload were divorces. In 1863 the Washington Territorial Legislature had passed a liberal divorce law, allowing for "any other cause" leading the court to the conclusion that "the parties can no longer live together." In addition to the 1867 Superior Court Civil Case #527 (see *Society*), in which Hannah Mayers, who lived in San Juan Town, sued for divorce from Henry Mayers, on the grounds that the defendant has beaten and cursed the plaintiff and accused her falsely of having been unfaithful to him and bearing a child to another from criminal intercourse while his wife, there was also the case of Flora Ross's divorce from her husband Paul K. Hubbs, Jr. Flora had married Paul on December 6, 1859 in Christ Church in Victoria after he wooed her while she was nursing the wife of Aleck McDonald, the Belle Vue Sheep Farm's dairyman. She separated from him on January 25, 1866, on the grounds of abuse as well as his cohabitation with an Indigenous woman. Hiring Port Townsend attorney B. F. Denison, she filed for a Petition for Divorce in September

(Superior Court Case #482); the decree, which came down on September 14, 1866, stipulated that Flora retained custody of their son, there was no alimony, and both parties assumed their own costs. Furthermore, they both retained their respective properties on either side of the (presumed) boundary: Flora kept her family farm at Ross Bay south of Victoria and Hubbs kept his homestead at Cattle Point on San Juan Island.[68]

Third District criminal cases in the islands during the period from 1854 to 1888 involved a wide variety of charges, from more egregious crimes of assault (4), murder (4), rape (1), and robbery (2) to destruction of property (2), sale of liquor to Indians (1), non-payment of liquor and tobacco taxes (4), and smuggling (1). As with the overall character of criminal cases in Washington Territory, and despite the more titillating descriptions of the early days of that "virtual Bedlam" that was San Juan Town, most citizens of the islands were relatively law abiding. Perhaps it is not altogether flip to attribute the violence that occurred at the works associated with the lime kilns to the predominantly male society there.

The exception seems to be the killing of Mr. Fuller, an Englishman who had claimed a farm next to the Hannah's, and the subsequent murders of James "Harry" and Selina Dwyer, by Kanaka Joe Nuana; these events particularly roiled a community that was looking to coexist peacefully. (Thomas Fleming noted in his *Diary*, "May 16 [1873]—James Dwyer and Wife found Murdered shot dead.") When confessing, Nuana said that he had planned to kill Benjamin Terrell and his wife Sarah, and then John and William Keddy, all because they supposedly had money. Lila Hannah Firth conjectured that soon after the Keddys heard this, they sold off their sheep and left the island. The events may have precipitated most of the Kanakas' removal north across the border to the Gulf Islands, notably Salt Spring. The overall sentiment among those who remained seemed to be that this act was an outlier, performed by a "monster." [69]

A signal case that illustrates the complexity of jurisprudence in disputed territory was the trying by the Territory of Washington of Charles Watts for the murder of Augustin Hibbard. On

June 17, 1869, Watts killed Hibbard, his partner in the San Juan Lime Company, at the company office. Watts and Hibbard had argued about the amount and quality of Watts' contribution to the lime kiln operation. When Hibbard accused Watts of the theft of several personal items, Watts interpreted Hibbard's actions as a threat of aggression and fired two shots: one directly into Hibbard's face and another into his chest. Hibbard barely managed to stagger down the steps of the boarding house, where the office was located, only to collapse and die several hours later. The subsequent legal action went through several lengthy jurisdictional challenges due to the uncertain status of the "Disputed Islands." A trial (*Territory of Washington v. Charles Watts*) was eventually held before the Superior Court in Port Townsend and ended up with a guilty verdict on September 14, 1871. Watts first appealed to the Supreme Court of the Territory of Washington over the question of federal jurisdiction of the islands; after this was put to rest and he was tried and found guilty again, Watts appealed again (*Watts v. Washington Territory*, 1 Wash. Terr. 409 [1872]) over further jurisdictional disputes and procedural errors. This appeal went to the U.S. Supreme Court; seven years after the event, when news arrived that this Court had declined the case—

> *This court can only review the final judgements of the Supreme Court of the Territory of Washington in criminal cases, when the Constitution or a statute or treaty of the United States is drawn into question (Watts v. Territory of Washington 91 U.S. 580 [1876])*

Watts managed to escape his prison keepers, and his hanging, and was never seen or heard from again.

Another signal case in the San Juan Islands was the 1880 trial of James Smith for the rape of Nora [sometimes spelled Norah] Jewell (*Territory of Washington v. James Smith*) which revealed the complex socioeconomic milieu of Indigenous and Euro-American residents in the islands.[70] Nora was the daughter of Peter Jewell, a Dane by birth who had settled in the islands in the 1860s, and his Indigenous wife Fanny Yackship. After homesteading in San Juan Valley, Peter died in 1874, and Israel Katz, to whom Peter was indebted, administered the estate, recognizing the twelve-year-old Nora as the sole heir; it is conjectured that Nora's mother Fanny may have left for Vancouver with her younger children, Roma and Eliza, to seek support from her family. (Katz would see Peter's homestead application through to certification, which occurred on November 25, 1879.) Nora was assigned T. W. Boggess as a guardian, but that was soon switched to James Smith and his wife, curiously bypassing the family of her aunt Ellen Yackship, who had married Frederick Jones and lived nearby. The Smith family raised Nora until 1880, when she entered a complaint of rape against Smith on February 9.[71] The trial included several witnesses to the character—both good and bad—of both Nora and James, some of which devolved from ethnic stereotyping of "Siwashes" and their morality versus the implied upright character of the islands "white" citizens. James Smith was acquitted at the end of February and a marriage of convenience was arranged for Nora, who was fourteen, with Orcas farmer Edward Hitchens, who was forty-one. The marriage did not last; Nora divorced Hitchens in 1883 and moved back to San Juan Island, where she and her cousin Jennie Jones worked in the Ole Wold household, probably as domestic servants (Wold was a Dane, possibly related to Peter Jewell). In 1886, Nora sold the homestead she had inherited from her father. Sometime later she moved to the mainland, where she is enumerated in the Tacoma 1910 federal census as a childless "white" widow, stating that her father was Danish, but her mother was from California. She eventually remarried.

The cost of transporting sheriffs, witnesses, and even jurors to Port Townsend was substantial, and many of the case files include reimbursement for transportation as well as other expenses. After the formation of San Juan County, the county clerk—first Edward D. Warbass and later John Bowman—would sign an affidavit for homestead applicants who could not file their claims with the land office in Olympia in person. Several San Juan Islands residents, including Charles Watts, were represented by Port Townsend attorneys. One of them was Charles M. Bradshaw, who had set up a law firm in 1867; he was later elected as mayor of Port Townsend in 1884, serving two terms.[72]

Witness Transportation Costs
Territory of Washington v James Smith, 1880
(Northwest Regional Branch, Washington State Archives)

The Probate Court handled cases regarding the settlement of people's estates. Most cases dealt with the appointment of administrators for the estates of deceased persons and the appointment of guardians for minor heirs. Typical cases included a sometimes-elaborate process: the issuance of a decree appointing administrator; presentation of last will of deceased; petition of probate of will; certificate of testimony in proof of will; order appointing and administering oath of appraisers; order setting time and place of hearing; final inventory; decree order of discharge; invoices; petition for final hearing and discharge; and final account. During the Territorial Period, Washington handled over 5,000 cases of probate. Records of probate cases in Whatcom County only date from 1872; those in San Juan from 1874 beginning with Augustus Hoffmeiser, the post sutler at English Camp (SJC-1). (There are a few Jefferson County cases, identifiable as being residents of the San Juan Islands, heard in the District Court prior to 1873.) Through the 1870s, there were only one or two cases heard each year; with the growth in population in the 1880s, this increased to four to five a year.

When the international boundary was settled, local island residents who could not claim American citizenship decided to apply for naturalization (citizenship) *en masse* in Port Townsend, and a group of 39 were recorded in the Superior Court's *Declaration of Intention, Book 3*, on January 13, 1873 (see Appendix: *List of Petitioneers for Naturalization, January 15, 1873*). The vast majority of these (32) were from Great Britain and Ireland; others included citizens from Austria, Denmark, Germany, Norway, and Sweden. Naturalizations continued steadily in the years following this initial mass application and increased to three to five per year in the 1880s; 1890 was a banner year, with nine declarations of intent for citizenship. Most of these were associated with the application for homesteads in the islands. During the mid-1890s this dwindled to none or sometimes only one per year, a trend that continued through the 1920s.

Local court cases were first heard at schoolhouses and later at the county courthouse when it was eventually built in 1883. The schoolhouse at Portland Fair, for instance, was used by Justice of the Peace Oakes in resolving a local dispute (*Keddy vs. Peter Jewell*) over payment of road taxes (or duty). In 1889 court was set up in Friday Harbor, with second Mondays in March and October as court days. The first meeting was held on March 10, 1890, with the Honorable M. B. Sachs as Judge, John Kelly as sheriff, R. H. Wansborough as Clerk, and J. J. Calvin as Prosecuting Attorney; S. V. Boyce and J. Edwards served as bailiffs and Charles McCoy [McKay] as crier.

Society & Governance

By the mid-1870s, the San Juan Islands had not only seen the settlement of the international boundary dispute between the United States and Great Britain, but also the beginnings of the domination of Euro-American civic society through formalized institutions and an organized county government. Civil society, as expressed through marriage, death, and religious practices as well as informal associations such as political meetings, festivities, and celebrations, grew more formal through the enactment of laws about marriage and the growth of institutions such as schools, churches, and cemeteries. Disputes arose from differing cultural expressions and interpretations of customs such as marriage and burial practices. The development of the hamlets, villages, and towns that replaced Indigenous settlements concentrated population to form the foundations of a societal identity for the San Juan Islands within the political framework of the Washington territorial government. This became formalized through the establishment of San Juan County itself, with Friday Harbor as its seat, together with a regional and local court system. The Disputed Islands had become the San Juan Islands, self-governing within the context of Washington Territory and the United States.

EPILOGUE

Definition of an island: an argument surrounded by water.
—*an anonymous Gulf Islander, ca. 1970s*

There's something about islands that lends themselves to dispute. Perhaps it's relative closeness; you must live with your neighbors whether you like them or not. In my relatively brief stay of some 60 years on San Juan Island, it seems like every winter some issue comes up that riles everybody; we get all worked up over it, with deep splits in the community—often to the point of old timers saying that it is the most divisive issue that the community has ever faced—and then, when tourist season begins, we all go back to our normal lives. But there's also the flip side; I have rarely experienced such charity and magnanimity of spirit as when 'one of ours' is in trouble: meal trains for the seriously ill; flights for those with major medical expense; fundraisers for seeking medical treatment off the island or those who lost their homes to fire. This is not only a modern phenomenon; one of the first acts of the newly-formed San Juan County Board of Commissioners was the allocation of financial support for a destitute islander.

Lyman Cutlar's shooting of a Hudson's Bay Company pig, which precipitated the Pig War and resulted in the Joint Occupation of The Disputed Islands, was not the only dispute in the islands. It had been preceded by many acts bearing on the possession of the San Juan Archipelago. But looking past the politics of international diplomacy of the period, ordinary, everyday disputes occurred among peoples with diverse ethnic and cultural backgrounds, some of whose ancestors had lived here for millennia and others who were coming to a relatively new world. For a brief period, a multi-ethnic and polyglot community existed in relative harmony, just trying to get along and make a living. The 'Wild West' frontier in the islands, although it had many of the basic economic and social conditions of frontier communities elsewhere, realized a community where a wide range of peoples strove to create a society in which most islanders recognized and respected each other as fellow islanders. And then, as the values and mores of mainland society assumed dominance in the late nineteenth century, the historical narrative changed into a story of the Euro-American 'pioneers' settling in a wilderness.

On October 15, 1924—almost a hundred years ago—descendants of San Juan Islands families dedicated a "Pioneer's Building" on the newly opened San Juan County Fairgrounds. Earlier that year, San Juan County citizens had issued stock for the purchase of land and construction of buildings near Friday Harbor for the fairgrounds. As part of this effort, the Fair Committee had decided to construct a "Pioneer's Building" to commemorate the role of early families in the settlement of the islands. On July 31st they issued an appeal for a "peeled log" from each pioneer family. By September, work had been progressing nicely under the supervision of William Buchanan, Sr., Andy Buchanan, and Stafford Merrifield "as boss"—to be completed in time for the Fair, October 9-11. On October 16th, the Friday Harbor Journal reported:

Jesse Douglas, Pioneer Cabin, San Juan County Fairgrounds (courtesy of San Juan Historical Museum)

> On Thursday afternoon the visitors on the grounds were invited to attend a dedication program under direction of Mr. L. B. Carter, of the Pioneer's Building and the presentation to the association by the local American Legion Post of an American flag. The presentation speech was made by County Attorney S. R. Buck in a few well chosen remarks. The acceptance speech in behalf of the fair association and the pioneers was made by John L. Murray. This was followed by Attorney Ivan L. Blair, who paid tribute to the pioneers, who likened the work of the citizens and fair association to the hospitality of the early pioneers in their unselfishness in community affairs. This feature of the program closed by George Mullis in reciting ... "The Old Settler."

Representatives of the island families had chosen to construct the "Pioneer's Building" of logs left round and connected with saddle notching, with the ends of the logs jutting several feet past the corners. This reflected more the contemporary image of a "log cabin" than the actual homes that the first Euro-American settlers built, with logs 'hewed outside and in' set in full dovetail notches flush at the corners.

One cannot have expected the builders to replicate their ancestor's structures—after all, most if not all were children when their parents first settled—but they also conveyed a sense of history that was tied up in the term "pioneer." The prevalent assumption was that Euro-Americans came to a largely-uninhabited land and "carved" their farms "out of the wilderness." In fact, the islands had been occupied and used by the Coast Salish for millennia. Many of these lands that Euro-American "pioneers" "settled" had already been kept free of tree and brush growth and cultivated; furthermore, the Hudson's Bay Company, through its Belle Vue Sheep Farm, had taken advantage of these very tracts to graze their sheep. These pastures, in turn, attracted American "settlers."

And then there's the multi-ethnic origin of these island families. While many were American (and proud of it!), many were English of many ethnicities—English, Irish, Scots, French Canadians, Métis, and Kanakas. The majority formed families through cross-cultural marriages with local and regional Coast Salish women (Cowichan, Saanich, Songish, Sooke, Lummi, Samish, and S'Klallam) as well as those from the North (Bella Coola, Haida, Tsimshian). Not only were these men indebted to their wives and Indigenous relatives for their livelihood in the islands but also for trade relations throughout the region. Early in the recorded history of the islands, this was acknowledged and valued; it was only later that the history of these earlier times was reworked to reflect the values of comtemporary times. Nor am I different in that I have tried to understand the past by examining it through the prevalent criteria of my own era.

2024, the year that this book was published, marks the 152nd anniversary of the settlement of the boundary dispute, bringing to an end the status of "The Disputed Islands." But not all was settled with the Kaiser's decision. Clearly, islanders still feel the ramifications of that decision: the separation of related Indigenous groups by an international boundary; the dominant historical narrative of pioneering—discovery, possession, and settlement; and the legacy of a one-sided story. Challenges to that come in many forms; mine has been a re-examination of the history itself.

> *I pay tribute to the past as a resource that can serve as a foundation for us to revision and renew our commitment to the present, to making a world where all people can live fully and well; where everyone can belong.*
>
> —bell hooks, Belonging: A Culture of Place (2008)

THE OLD SETTLER

I've travelled all over this country,
    Prospectin' and diggin' for gold.
I've tunneled, hydrauliced and cradled
    And I've quite often been sold.
For one who gets riches by minin'
    Perceivin' that hundreds grow poor,
I made up my mind to try farmin'—
    The only pursuit that is sure.
So rollin' my grub in my blankets
    And leavin' my tools on the ground,
I started one mornin' to shank it
    For a place they called Puget Sound.
Arriving dead broke in mid-winter,
    I found it enveloped in fog
And covered all over in timber,
    Thick as hair on the back of a dog.
As I gazed on the prospect so lonely,
    The tears trickled down my face;
For I thought that my journey had brought me
    To the edge of the jumping off place.
But I took up a claim in the forest
    And settled myself to hard toil—
For two years, I chopped and I niggered,*
    But I never got down to the soil.
I tried to get out of the country,
    But poverty forced me to stay
Till I became an old settler—
    Then you couldn't drive me away.
And now I'm used to the climate,
    I think that if man ever found
A place to live easy and happy,
    That Eden is on Puget Sound.
No longer a slave to ambition,
    I laugh at the world and its shams,
As I think of my splendid condition
    Surrounded by acres of clams.

            —George Mullis, October 15, 1924

[*"Niggered" referred to clearing stones from fields.)

End Notes

Introduction
1. Ivan Doig, *Winter Brothers: A Season at the Edge of America* (New York and London: Harcourt Brace Jovanovich, 1980) p. 4.
2. Edward Gibbon, *Miscellaneous Works* (1815) III:126

What About the Pig?
1. Margaret Visser, *Much Depends on Dinner* (New York: Collier Books, 1986), p. 12.
2. Mike Vouri, *The Pig War: Standoff at Griffin Bay* (Pullman, WA: Basalt Books, 2022).
3. Sources differ as to the spelling of Lyman Cutlar's [Cutler's] name; this book opts for Cutlar because of the preponderance of mentions.
4. Belle Vue Sheep Farm *Post Journals* June 15, 1859; emphasis in original.
5. Charles Griffin to James Douglas, June 15, 1859, *HBC Archives*.
6. Lyman Cutlar to Paul K. Hubbs, Jr., June 23, 1859, Hunter Miller, *San Juan Archipelago: Study of the Joint Occupation of San Juan Island* (Bellows Falls, VT: Wyndham Press, 1943) p. 54-55.
7. Cutlar Affidavit September 7, 1859, Miller 1943:53-54.
8. Alexander Grant Dallas to General Harney, May 10, 1860, Miller 1943:55-56.

Identity
1. Wayne Suttles, "Post-Contact Culture Change among the Lummi Indians," *British Columbia Historical Quarterly*, Vol. XVIII, Nos. 1 & 2 (1954), p. 51.
2. Suttles 1954:52.
3. Boyd, Robert T. "Demographic History, 1774-1874" IN *Handbook of North American Indians*, Volume 7, The Northwest Coast (Washington DC: Smithsonian Institution Press, 1990) pp. 137-142; Grant Keddie, *Songhees Pictorial: A History of the Songhees People as Seen by Outsiders, 1790-1912* (Victoria, BC: The Royal British Columbia Museum, 2004), pp. 77-81.
4. Boyd 1990:147.
5. The, "Challams-Cowaitchims, 24 tribes, speaking the Challam and Cowaitzchim languages" and located "from lat 500 along the Coast South to Whidby Island in lat. 480; part of Vancouver's Island and the Mouth of the Franc's River," numbered another 9,427 (R. M. Martin, "Census of the Indian Tribes in the Oregon Territory from latitude 42° to latitude 54°, derived from the trading lists of the Hudson's Bay

Company, and from the best possible information," IN *The Hudson's Bay Territories and Vancouver's Island, with an Exposition of the Chartered Rights, Conduct, and Policy of the Honble Hudson's Bay Company* 1849).
6. Boyd 1990:136, Table 1.
7. Wayne Suttles, "Prehistoric and Early History Fisheries in the San Juan Archipelago," ms. prepared for the National Park Service, May 1998, on file, San Juan Island National Historical Park, p. 7, f.n.4.
8. Suttles 1998:7
9. Vouri 2022.
10. Daniel L Boxberger, *San Juan Island Cultural Affiliation Study. Prepared for National Park Service, Pacific Northwest Region* (1994), on file, San Juan Island National Historical Park, pp. 5-6, 14-18; Suttles Wayne Suttles, *Economic Life of the Coast Salish of Haro and Rosario Straits*, Unpublished PhD dissertation, University of Washington, 1951.
11. *Post Journals* April 4, 1854.
12. Anita Melanie Garrett, "The Indian Women" *San Juan Journal* June 23, 1982, B1.
13. Vouri 2022:218.
14. Geographical Memoir, "*Appendix C, Report of George Gibbs, Geologist, of an Examination of San Juan Island and of the Cowitchin Archipelago and Channel,*" *N. W. Boundary Survey*, March 18, 1859.
15. R. M. Ballantyne, *Hudson's Bay: or, Life in the Wilds of North America* (1848).
16. Quoted in Patricia C. Erigero, *Cultural Landscape Report: Fort Vancouver National Historic Site* Volume II (Seattle: National Park Service, 1992), p. 65.
17. Erigero 1992:65; see also Sylvia Van Kirk, *Many Tender Ties: Women in Fur Trade Society*, 1670-1870 (Norman, OK: University of Oklahoma Press, 1980).
18. Boxberger 1994:37; the Hudson's Bay Company used the term "Servant" for their regular employees, who were "enlisted" into the organization in a manner similar to the Army.
19. Mary Kawena Pukui and Samuel H. Elbert, *Hawaiian Dictionary* (Honolulu: University of Hawaii Press, 1957); Jean Barman and Bruce McIntyre Watson, *Leaving Paradise: Indigenous Hawaiians in the Pacific Northwest*, 1787-1898 (Honolulu: University of Hawaii Press, 2006), p. x.
20. James Robert Anderson, "Notes and Comments on Early Days and Events, 1925, British Columbia Archives, Add. Ms. 1912, Box 9/18.
21. Candace Wellman, *Peace Weavers: Uniting the Salish Coast Through Cross-Cultural Marriages* (Pullman, WA: *Washington State University Press*, 2017), p. 139ff.
22. Barman and Watson 2006:364-5.

23. Barman and Watson 2006; E. Momilani Naughton, " *Hawaiians in the Fur Trade: Cultural Influence on the Northwest Coast, 1811-1875,"* MA thesis, Western Washington University, 1983; Tom Koppel, *Kanaka: The Untold Story of Hawaiian Pioneers in British Columbia and the Pacific Northwest* (North Vancouver, British Columbia, Canada: Whitecap Books Ltd, 1995).
24. Brenda C. Pratt, *"Thank God It's (Still) Friday"* San Juan Museum Newsletter, 2003.
25. Edwin T. Coman and Helen M. Gibbs, *Time, Tide, and Timber: A Century of Pope & Talbot* (Stanford, CA: Stanford University Press, 1949).
26. *Peace Weavers and Interwoven Lives: Indigenous Mothers of Salish Coast Communities* (Pullman, WA: Washington State University Press, 2019).
27. Lynn Weber-Roochvarg, "McKay, Charles (1828-1918), *HistoryLink* Essay 21033 posted 5/11/2020.
28. James Francis Tulloch's career is detailed in his eponymous "Diary" of 1875-1910, although the manuscript should more properly be called a memoir; Tulloch, the son of a Methodist minister, moved to Orcas Island in 1875 and married and settled on a farm near East Sound; Gordon. Keith (compiler and editor), *The Diary of James Francis Tulloch, 1875-1910* (Portland, OR: Binford & Mort, 1978), p. 15.
29. Lila Hannah Firth,*"Early Life on San Juan Island,"* (1943), ms. on file, University of Washington Manuscripts and University Archives, p. 27.
30. *San Juan Islander* April 21, 1898.
31. B. F. Shattuck, " First Store in Eastsound Owned by Chas. W. Shattuck,, *Orcas Island Sounder* December 14, 1944.
32. Jackilee Wray and Mike Vouri, Interview with Bill Mason and Babe Jewett, September 25, 2001, on file, San Juan Island National Historical Park.
33. *The Victoria Colonist,* August 15, 1859.
34. Pauline R. Hilaire, *Rights Remembered: A Salish Grandmother Speaks on American Indian History and the Future* (Omaha, University of Nebraska Press, 2016), p.155.
35. Boxberger 1994:21,35-36.

Place

1. Ned Brown, *Geology of the San Juan Islands* (Bellingham: Chuckanut Editions, 2014); Bates McKee, *Cascadia; the Geologic Evolution of the Pacific Northwest* (New York: McGraw-Hill, 1972); Robert Russell (editor), *Geology and Water Resources of the San Juan Islands, San Juan County Washington* (Washington Department of Ecology Office of Technical Services Water Supply Bulletin No. 46, 1975).

2. McKee 1972:128.
3. Wilbert R. Danner, *Limestone Resources of Western Washington* (Olympia: Department of Conservation, 1966), p. 11.
4. Russell 1975; Schlots et al, *Soil Survey of San Juan County, Washington* (United States Department of Agriculture, Soil Conservation Service, in cooperation with Washington Agricultural Experiment Station, 1962).
5. Audrey DeLella Benedict and Joseph K. Gaydos, *The Salish Sea: Jewel of the Pacific Northwest* (Seattle: Sasquatch Books, 2015); Kathryn L. Sobocinski, *The State of the Salish Sea* (Salish Sea Institute, Western Washington University 2021).
6. Russell 1975; Schlots et al 1962.
7. David Laskin, *Rains All the Time: A Connoisseur's History of Weather in the Pacific Northwest* (Seattle: Sasquatch Books, 1997), p. 141.
8. Michael Leon Olsen, *The Beginnings of Agriculture in Western Oregon and Western Washington*, unpublished PhD dissertation 1970, p. 61.
9. Charles Kahn, *Salt Spring: The Story of an Island* (Madeira Park, BC: Harbour Publishing, 1998), p. 52.
10. *Post Journals* June 12, 1858; Thomas Fleming *Journal* September 18-19, 1868.
11. F. I. Trotter and F. H. and J. R. Loutzenhiser, *Told by the Pioneers: Reminiscences of Pioneer Life in Washington, Volume III* (Washington Pioneer Project, 1938), p. 102.
12. Theodore Winthrop, *The Canoe and the Saddle* (Portland, OR: Binfords & Mort, 1955), p. 26
13. Suttles 1951:36.
14. *Saltwater People as told by Dave Elliot Sr.: A Resource Book for the Saanich Native Studies Program*, edited by Janet Poth (Native Education: School District 63 (Saanich) 1983.
15. Suttles 1951:37.
16. C. F. Newcombe, *Menzies Journal of Vancouver's Voyage: April to October, 1792* (Victoria, B.C.: William H. Cullin, 1923), p. 60.
17. Samish Indian Nation, "Coast Salish Place Names of the San Juan Islands" https://storymaps.arcgis.com/stories/9b0f86b51e054ba78b83ab-39c4d0b1a6; https://itservices.cas.unt.edu/~montler/saanich/wordlist/placenames.htm
18. Bernhard J. Stern, *The Lummi Indians of Northwest Washington* (New York: AMS Press, 1969).
19. Lucille S. McDonald, *Making History: The People Who Shaped the San Juan Islands* (Friday Harbor: Harbor Press,1990), p. 3.
20. Samish Indian Nation, "Coast Salish Place Names of the San Juan Islands" https://storymaps.arcgis.com/stories/9b0f86b51e054ba78b83ab-39c4d0b1a6
21. *U. S. Coast Survey*, 1854.
22. *Post Journal* September 25, 1854.

23. Township and Range Survey Field Notes.
24. *Duwamish et al v. United States.*
25. *San Juan Islander* April 19, 1900.
26. Boxberger 1994 Map; 1892 US C&GS Map.
27. "*Coast Salish Place Names of the San Juan Islands*" website.
28. Suttles 1951; *Lummi Island Rural Heritage, Reef Nets*, lists of reef net sites.
29. Laskin 1997:36.
30. Victor J. Farrar (editor), "Diary of Colonel and Mrs. I. N. Ebey," *Washington Historical Quarterly* v. 7 (March 1977).
31. McDonald 1990:5-8; David Richardson, *Pig War Islands: The San Juans of Northwest Washington* (Eastsound, WA: Orcas Publishing Company, 1971), pp. 20-22.
32. McDonald 1990:9-10; Richardson 1971:23-28
33. Newcombe 1923:18.
34. David M. Buerge, "The Wilkes Exploring Expedition in the Pacific Northwest 1987," *Columbia Magazine*, Spring 1987: Vol. 1, No. 1, p. 35; Nathaniel Philbrick, *Sea of Glory: America's Voyage of Discovery, The U.S. Exploring Expedition*, 1838-1842 (London: Penguin Books, 2003), pp. 275-276
36. James S. Lawson, *Autobiography of James S. Lawson* (NOAA website, Stories and Tales), pp. 25-27.
37. Vouri 2022:258-259; Mike Vouri, notes on file, San Juan Island National Historical Park.
38. George Davidson, *Appendix No. 26, Report of the Superintendent of the United States Coast Survey*, 1855, p. 177.
39. James Alden to Prof. A. D. Bache, October 31, 1853.
40. Bailey 1977.
41. Fred Beckey, *Range of Glaciers: The Exploration and Survey of the Northern Cascade Range.* (Portland, OR: Oregon Historical Society Press, 2003), p. 155; John Keast Lord, T*he Naturalist in Vancouver Island and British Columbia* (1866).
42. Beckey 2003:151; Archibald Campbell's *Geographical Memoir of the Islands between the Continent and Vancouver, Island in the Vicinity of the Forty Ninth Parallel of North Latitude Geographic Memoir* was published as part of the record of the 40th Congress (1860). The journals of the Survey by Dr. C. B. R. Kennerly, George Gibbs, Henry Custer, and W. J. Warren, which figured as appendices to the *Geographical Memoir*, were hand-copied by Greg Lange and provided to the San Juan Island National Historical Park.
43. North West Boundary Survey, *Appendix E: Report of Dr. C. B. R. Kennerly of a Reconnaissance of the Haro Archieplago.*
44. Miller 1943:12.

45. Miller 1943:19.
46. Richard Somerset Mackie, *The Hudson's Bay Company on the Pacific, 1821-1843*, PhD dissertation, University of British Columbia, 1993, p. 7.
47. Richard Somerset Mackie, *Colonial Land, Indian Labor, and Company Capital: The Economy of Vancouver Island, 1849-1858*, MA thesis, University of Victoria, 1984.
48. James Douglas to Sir E. Lytton Lytton February 19, 1859, quoted in Erwin N. Thompson, *Historic Resource Study San Juan Island, National Historic Park*, Washington (Denver: National Park Service, 1972), p.190.
49. Charles Griffin to James Douglas, February 20, 1859, British Columbia Provincial Archives.
50. North West Boundary Survey, *Appendix B: Report of George Gibbs, Geologist, of an Examination of San Juan Island and of the Cowitchin Archipelago and Channel* (1859).
51. Frederick John Splitstone, *Orcas: Gem of the San Juans* (Sedro-Woolley: The Courier-Times Press, 1946), pp. 29-30.
52. Mackie. 1984:82
53. James W. Scott and Roland L. De Lorme, *Historical Atlas of Washington* (Norman: University of Oklahoma Press, 1988), p. 31.
54. Homestead applications, on file, Shaw Island Historical Museum.
55. Jefferson County Clerk Third Territorial District Court, File #195, June 30, 1879.
56. *Portland West Shore* 1876.
57. Washington State Northwest Regional Archives, Case# 2-106.
58. *Sacramento Daily Union* November 25, 1859.
59. Homestead applications, on file, Shaw Island Historical Museum.
60. Washington State Northwest Regional Archives, San Juan County, Miscellaneous and Mortgages, 1882-1895, p. 51
61. Quoted in Kahn 1998:44.
62. Olsen 1970:87.
63. Homestead applications, on file, Shaw Island Historical Museum.
64. Olsen 1970:86.
65. Hugh Parks Probate, cited in Andrew Hilen, "Murder on Shaw Island," *The Pacific Northwest Quarterly* Vol. 69, No. 3 (July 1978), p. 104.
66. James K. Agee, *Historic Landscapes of San Juan Island National Historical Park* (1984), on file, San Juan Island National Historical Park, pp. 18-19; Romo 1987:183-184
67. Charles Pickering, "Introduced Animals and Plants of America" (Chapter XXI) p. 307, *Volume IX of the Reports of the US Ex Ex*.
68. Richard White, *Land Use, Environment, and Social Change: The Shaping of Island County*, Washington (Seattle: University of Washington Press, 1980), p. 47.
69. Scott Atkinson and Fred Sharpe, *Wild Plants of the San Juan Islands* (Seattle: Mountaineers Books, 1993).

70. Erigero 1992:29
71. *Post Journal*, August 7 and 24, 1854; Personal communication, Grant Keddie, Royal Museum of British Columbia.
72. Washington State Northwest Regional Archives, Gross Petition.
73. Wolves are mentioned in the *Post Journals* May 20, May 30, June 17, September 17, October 2 and 3 [setting traps and catching a she wolf), and December 1 and 8, 1854; November 15, 1858; and March 16 and December 27, 1859.
74. *Told By the Pioneers* Volume III 1938:51.
75. Roberta L. Beyshaw, N*o Better Land: The 1860 Diaries of the Anglican Colonial Bishop George Hills* (Victoria, B.C.: Sono Nis Press, 1966), p. 243.
76. Erigero 1992:80.
77. North West Boundary Survey, Kennerly 1960:59.
78. Tharald homestead application, on file, Shaw Island Historical Museum.
79. Charles Whitlock correspondence, on file, San Juan Island National Historical Park.
80. Charles H. Ludwig, *A Brief History of Waldron Island* (1959), ms. on file, San Juan Island Library, p. 23.
81. Charles Whitlock, February 14, 1869, letter to his sister.
82. Richardson 1971:209-211.
83. *Laws of Washington*, 1855.
84. Washington State Northwest Regional Archives, San Juan County, *Marks and Brands*.
85. Keith 1978:32.
86. Candace Wellman, "Skexe: Birch and other Wool Dogs of the Coast Salish," *The Journal of the Whatcom County Historical Society* Number Two (October 2001), p. 10.
87. John Brinkerhoff Jackson, *American Space: The Centennial Years, 1865-1876* (New York: W. W. Norton & Company, 197), pp. 64-67.
88. Keith 1978:52.
89. Washington State Northwest Regional Archives, *San Juan County Commissioners Journal*, p. 59.
90. *Laws of Washington*, 1855:22.
91. *General Laws of Washington* 1869:323-326.

Dwelling

1. Geographic Memoir, "*Appendix F, Journal of William J. Warren, Secretary, North West Boundary Commission of a Expedition in Company with Dr. C. B. R. Kennerly, Surgeon and Naturalist, to the Haro Archipelago*," 1860, pp. 115-116.
2. Julie K. Stein, *Exploring Coast Salish Prehistory: The Archaeology of San Juan Island* (Seattle: University of Washington Press, 2000).

3. Amanda K. Taylor and Julie K. Stein, *Is It a House? Archaeological Excavations at English Camp San Juan Island*, Washington, Burke Museum of Natural History and Culture Research Report No. 9 (Seattle: University of Washington Press, 2011); in addition to the "Housing" chapter of Suttles (1951), see also Chapter 6: "Shed Roof Houses in the Pacific Northwest" in Stephen R. Samuels (ed.), *Ozette Archaeological Project Research Reports Volume 1: House Structure and Floor Midden*, WSU Department of Archaeology, Report of Investigations 63, National Park Service, Pacific Northwest Regional Office 1991; Wayne Suttles "The Shed-Roof House" IN Robin K. Wright (ed.), *A Time of Gathering: Native Heritage in Washington State* (Seattle: University of Washington Press, 1961); R. G. Matson, "The Coast Salish House: Lessons from Shingle Point, Valdes Island, British Columbia," IN R. G. Matson et al, *Emerging from the Mist: Studies in Northwest Coast Culture History* (Vancouver: University of British Columbia, 2003); and A. Katherine Patton, "Elements of an Ancient Tsimshian Dwelling: An Archaeology of Architecture in Prince Rupert Harbour, British Columbia, *Canadian Journal of Archaeology* (2017) 41:269-307.
4. Suttles 1951:258-259.
5. Newcombe 1923:60.
6. Suttles 1991:214.
7. Suttles 1951:259-260.
8. Franz Boas, *Second General Report on the Indians of the Pacific Coast. I The Lku'ñgEn* (1890), p. 568.
9. Bernhard Stern, *The Lummi Indians of Northwest Washington* (New York: AMS Press, 1969) p. 43; Suttles 1951:163-166.
10. *Duwamish et al v. United States* 1927:439.
11. Newcombe 1923:58.
12. Newcombe 1923:59.
13. William John Macdonald, *"Notes by a Pioneer"* (n.d.), ms. on file, Provincial Archives of British Columbia.
14. Nugent 1982:46.
15. *Told By the Pioneers* III 1938: 187.
16. *Duwamish et al v. The United States* 1927.
17. Jo Bailey-Cummings and Al Cummings, *The Powder-Keg Island* (Friday Harbor, WA: Beachcombers, Inc., 1987), p. 169.
18. Suttles 1951:257.
19. Suttles 1954:61.
20. Suttles 1954:61-2; David G. Tremaine, *Indian & Pioneer Settlement of the Nooksack Lowland, Washington to 1890*, Occasional Paper #4 (Center for Pacific Northwest Studies, Western Washington State College, 1975) pp. 27-30.
21. Tremaine 1975:61.

22. Steven A. Anderson, *The Physical Structure of Fort Nisqually* (Tacoma: Metropolitan Park District of Tacoma, 1988); John A. Hussey, *The History of Fort Vancouver and Its Physical Structure* (Portland, OR: Abbott, Kerns & Bell Company, 1957); David H. Chance, *Fort Colvile the Structure of a Hudson's Bay Company Post, 1825 To 1871, and After* (Moscow, ID: University of Idaho Anthropological Research Manuscript Series 1, 1972); Bryn Thomas ad Charles Hibbs, Jr., *Report of the Investigations at Kanaka Village, Vancouver Barracks*, Washington 1980/81 Volumes I1 & 2 (prepared for the Washington State Department of Transportation by Archaeological and Historical Services, Easter Washington University, 1984); Roderick Sprague (editor), *San Juan Archaeology Volume I* (Moscow, WA: University of Idaho Laboratory of Anthropology, 1983) p. 343-345.
23. Extensive fires during the 1840s at both Forts Langley (1840) and Vancouver (1844) drove home this lesson; later conflagrations were contained by means of isolating the structure on fire.
24. Sprague 1983:344.
25. Chance 1972:41; Anderson 1988:24-30,36-40.
26. Sprague 1983:315-356.
27. Hudson's Bay Company Archives, James Douglas to Charles Griffin November 12, 1856.
28. John Hussey, "The Fort Vancouver Farm," ms. on file, Fort Vancouver, Washington, p. 150; Erigero 1982:187-188.
29. Philip Dole, "The Rural Landscape," IN Thomas Vaughan (editor), *Space, Style, and Structure: Building in Northwest America* (Portland, OR: Oregon Historical Society, 1974), p. 89.
30. In Alberta, Métis had log houses at permanent settlements but used tipis when travelling: Donald G. Wetherell and Irene R.A. Kmet, *Homes in Alberta: Building, Trends, and Design* (Edmonton: University of Alberta, 1991), p. 13.
31. Alexander Henry, *New Light on the Early History of the Greater Northwest: Volume 1*. The Red River of the North (New York: Francis P. Harper, 1897), p. 743.
32. Thompson 1972:29.
33. Marius Barbeau, "The House That Mac Built," *The Beaver* December 1945, pp. 10-13; Harold Kalman, *A History of Canadian Architecture, Volume 1* (Toronto: Oxford University Press, 1994), pp. 323-328; Peter N. Moogk, *Building a House in New France* (Toronto: McClelland and Stewart, 1977); Jill Wade, "Log Construction at Red River," *Canadian Antiques Collector* 6 (Nov/Dec 1971), pp. 36-38; William C. Wonders, "Log Dwellings in Canadian Folk Architecture," *Annals of the Association of American Geographers* 69 (2) (1979), pp. 196-197, 205.
34. *Post Journals* August 30, 1854; July 28, 1858.

35. Anderson 1988: 90-92.
36. De Courcy to Young, April 11, 1859, PABC SAJU 1859 Correspondence, quoted in Thompson 1972:171. Thompson correctly points out that because De Courcy didn't arrive until July of that year, the date cannot be correct; however, the Journal entry concerning the improvements to his room is dated November 11, 1859, when presumably the cold would have begun to be felt.
37. *Post Journal* October 23, 1854.
38. Quoted in Thompson 1972:132.
39. *Victoria Gazette* August 23, 1859.
40. Randolph B. Marcy, *The Prairie Traveler: A Handbook for Overland Expeditions* (Published by Authority of the War Department, 1859).
41. According to Thompson (1972:159) there were six guns removed, but only five emplacements.
42. Quoted in Thompson 1972:159-160.
43. CEHP Incorporated, *Comparative Analysis, American Camp Fortifications, San Juan Island*, National Historical Park. Prepared for the National Park Service (September 1966), on file, San Juan Island National Historical Park; Thompson 1972:132-133.
44. Henry Roder, *Bellingham Bay and the San Juan Difficulty*, Port Townsend, 1878, ms. on file, Hubert Howe Bancroft Collection, Bancroft Library, Berkeley, California, pp. 21-22.
45. Roder 1878.
46. Artifacts Consulting, Inc., *Miller-Brown House Historic Structures Report* (Tacoma: Artifacts Consulting, 2007); Harold A. LaFleur, Jr., *Historic Structure Report: Officers Quarters HS-11, Laundress, Quarters HS-6, and English Camp Hospital HS-18, Architectural Data, San Juan Island National Historical Park, Washington* (Denver: National Park Service, 1977).
47. Personal communication, Michael Sullivan, Artifacts Consulting, August 21, 2007.
48. Captain Haskell, quoted in Thompson 1972:141.
49. Quoted in Thompson 1972:138.
50. Quoted in Thompson 1972:138.
51. Thompson 1972:140-141.
52. Thompson 1972:142-143.
53. Quoted in Thompson 1972:199.
54. Thompson 1972:202-204.
55. Thompson 1972:204-206.
56. Quoted in Thompson 1972:206.
57. Thompson 1972:206-207.
58. Firth 1943:3.
59. Barman and Watson 2006:169,175.

60. Keith 1978:11.
61. Philip Dole, "The Picket Fence at Home," IN Gregory K. Dreicer, (editor), *Between Fences* (Washington and New York: The National Building Museum and Princeton Architectural Press, 1996).
62. Wetherell and Kmet 1991:4.
63. Richardson 1971:194
64. Hudson homestead application, on file, Shaw Island Historical Museum.
65. Charles Whitlock, February 14, 1869.
66. *Told by the Pioneers II* 1938:181.
67. Tremaine, 1975:91.
68. Allen G. Noble, *Wood, Brick, and Stone: The North American Settlement Landscape. Volume 1: Houses and Volume 2: Barns and Farm Structures* (Amherst: The University of Massachusetts Press, 1984), Volume I, pp. 121-2.
69. *Told by the Pioneers II* 1938:181; Tremaine 1975:99.
70. Wetherell and Kmet 1991:19.
71. *Told by the Pioneers III* 1938:177.
72. *Told by the Pioneers III* 1938:166.
73. *Told by the Pioneers III* 1938:156.
74. *Told by the Pioneers III* 1938:169.
75. Bailey-Cummings and Cummings 1987:75-76.
76. *Told by the Pioneers III* 1938:157.
77. Bailey-Cummings and Cummings 1987:75.
78. Tremaine 1975:90
79. *Told by the Pioneers III* 1938:169.
80. Bailey-Cummings and Cummings 71987:6.
81. Fred Bischof, "Analysis of Selected English Camp and American Camp Nails," IN Roderick Sprague (editor), *San Juan Archaeology Volume II* (Moscow, WA: University of Idaho Laboratory of Anthropology, 1983), pp. 759-765.
82. One of her witnesses said that it was "a frame house 18 x 24 ft 1 story floored, roofed and ceiled. 3 rooms 4 doors 4 windows an addition to the main building 12 x 16 feet with panty and porch."); the apparent discrepancy in the dimensions, number of rooms, etc., can be partially reconciled by the inclusion of the addition in the widow's account.
83. Rader homestead application, on file, Shaw Island Historical Museum.
84. Al Wilding, "History of a Shaw's Island farm on Blind Bay" (1995), ms. on file, Al Wilding, Shaw Island.
85. Firth 1943:25.
86. Boyd C. Pratt, *Beaverton Valley Cultural History Study*, prepared for the San Juan Preservation Trust (1979).
87. *General Laws of Washington* 1869:323-326.
88. Dole 1996.

89. George A. Martin, *Fences, Gates, and Bridges* (New York: O. Judd Co. 1909; reprint, Brattleboro, CT: Alan C. Hood & Co., 1992), p. 43.
90. *Laws of Washington* 1855:22.
91. *General Laws of Washington* 1869:323-326.
92. Gary Kulik, "The Worm Fence," IN Gregory K. Dreicer, (editor), *Between Fences* (Washington and New York: The National Building Museum and Princeton Architectural Press, 1996), pp. 22-23.
93. Thomas Fleming *Journal*, on file, San Juan Historical Museum.
94. Thompson 1972:197-8.
95. *General Laws of Washington* 1869:323.
96. Firth 1943:5.
97. *Post Journals* June 16, 1854 and April 26, 1858; David M. Tucker, *Kitchen Gardening in America* (Ames: Iowa State University Press, 1993), pp. 18-20.
98. Johnson n.d.:57-58.
99. Personal communication, William Patterson, 2008.

Work

1. Edward T. Coleman, "Mountaineering in the Pacific," *Harper's New Monthly Magazine* (November 1869), p. 795.
2. *Told by the Pioneers III* 1938:51.
3. Elliott 1983; Jamie Donatuto et al, "The Story of 13 Moons: Developing an Environmental Health and Sustainability Curriculum Founded on Indigenous First Foods and Technologies," *Sustainability* 2020 (12) 8913; https://storymaps.arcgis.com/stories/01a27caf1f414ca1aac2dfd73db1ede6
4. Elliott 1983:41-54.
5. Suttles 1951:65-69,505; Stein 2000:25-28.
6. Suttles 1951:63-64; Dale R. Croes, "Archaeological Wet Sites Indicate Salal Berries and Acorns were Staple Foods on the Central Northwest Coast," *Journal of Northwest Anthropology* 57(1) (Spring 2023); 131-137.
7. *Duwamish et al v. United States* 1927:434-435.
8. *Duwamish et al v. United States* 1927:456.
9. Keith 1978:119; Township and Range Survey Map.
10. *Told by the Pioneers III* 1938:187.
11. Suttles 1951:63-64.
12. Stein 2000:85.
13. Nancy Turner, *Ancient Pathways, Ancestral Knowledge, and Ecological Wisdom of Indigenous Peoples of Northwestern Washington* Volume 1 (Montreal and Kingston: McGill-Queen's University Press) 2014:169, 174; Dale R. Croes, "Northwest Coast Wet Site Artifacts: A Key to Understanding Ancient Resource Procurement, Storage, Management, and Exchange," In *Emerging from the Mist: Studies in Northwest Coast Culture History,* edited by R. G. Maston, Gary Coupland, and Quentin

Mackie (Vancouver, BCs: UBC Press, 2003), pp. 62-66; Dana Lepofsky, Nancy J. Turner, and Harriet V. Kuhnlein, "Determining the Availability of Tradition Wild Plant Foods, Bella Coola, B. C." *Ecology of Food and Nutrition* (1985) p. 16 Table 6; Croes 2023:136.

14. Keith 1978:119
15. Warren, *Journal*, February 8 and 9, 1860.
16. Suttles 1951:61-62.
17. Philip Drucker, *Indians of the Norwest Coast* (New York: McGraw-Hill Book Company, 1955).
18. Beyshaw 1996:243.
19. *Told by the Pioneers III* 1938:51.
20. Suttles 1951:70ff.
21. Coleman 1869:794-795.
22. Suttles 1951:87-90.
23. Jen Vollmer, "Stockade Bay-Buck Bay," *The Islands Weekly* September 16, 2003, p. 4.
24. Coleman 1869:795.
25. Kennerly 1860.
26. Warren, *Journal*, February 4, 1860.
27. Wilding 1995.
28. Beyshaw 1996:243.
29. Angie Burt Bowden, *Early Schools of Washington Territory* (Seattle: Lowman and Hanford Company, 1935), p. 414.
30. Coleman 1869:795.
31. Richardson 1971:209.
32. *Told by the Pioneers II* 1938:186.
33. Coleman 1869:795.
34. *Told by the Pioneers III* 1938:51.
35. Beyshaw 1996:243-244.
36. *Told by the Pioneers III* 1938:52.
37. Firth 1943:6.
38. Mary L. Iotte, "Freeman Iotte Walked to the West in 1849; Lived, Worked on Orcas Is," ms. on file, Orcas Illand Historical Museum 1966.
39. Elliott 1983.
40. Stein 2000:42.
41. Gordon W. Hewes, "Indian Fisheries Productivity in Pre-Contact Times in the Pacific Salmon Area." *Northwest Anthropology Research Notes* 7 (Fall 1973), 133-55.
42. Russel Barsh, "Coast Salish Reef-net Fishery, Part 2," HistoryLink Essay 21238 posted 5/23/2021.
43. Stein 2000:29ff; Suttles 1951.

44. Suttles 1951:135; Hilary Stewart, *Indian Fishing: Early Methods on the Northwest* Coast (Toronto: Douglas & McIntyre Ltd, 2003), pp. 26-29
45. Suttles 1951:114-117.
46. Suttles 1951:126-127.
47. Iain McKechnie et al, "Archaeological data provide alternative hypothesis on Pacific Herring (*Clupea pallasii*) distribution, abundance, and variability," *Pacific Northwest Archaeological Society*, published online February 18, 2014, E807-816.
48. Suttles 1951:137-138.
49. North West Boundary Survey, *Report of Dr. C. B. R. Kennerly of a Reconnaissance of the Haro Archipelago* (1860).
50. Suttles 1951:106-108.
51. Hartwell Bowsfield (editor), *Fort Victoria Letters 1846-1851* (Winnipeg: Hudson's Bay Record Society, 1979), p. 193.
52. Macdonald n.d.
53. Bryce Woods, *San Juan Island: Coastal Place Names and Cartographic Nomenclature* (Tacoma: Washington State Historical Society, 1980), p. 97.
54. John N. Cobb, "Salmon Fisheries of the Pacific Coast," *Bureau of Fisheries Document 751*, Report of the Commissioner of Fisheries for 1910 (Washington, DC: 1911), p. 62.
55. Mackie 1984:28-39.
56. Bowsfield 1979:xxxi.
57. James Douglas to Archibald Barclay, September 9, 1852, Hudson's Bay Company Archives, B.226/b/6.
58. Macdonald n.d.
59. W. Colquhoun Grant, "Description of Vancouver Island," *Journal of the Royal Geographical Society* XXVII (1857), p. 282.
60. James Douglas to Charles Griffin, August 8, 1856, Hudson's Bay Company Archives.
61. *Post Journal* September 1, 1858.
62. *Post Journal*, September 2, 1859, and July 12, 1860.
63. Ludwig 1959:16,22.
64. Belle Vue Sheep Farm *Account Book*, 1853-1858, Hudson's Bay Company Archives.
65. Quoted in John Hussey, "Fort Vancouver Farm," on file, Fort Vancouver National Historical Site, p. 160.
66. Gibbs 1859.
67. "The Round Hand of George B. Roberts," *Oregon Historical Quarterly* LXII (June-September 1962), p. 183.
68. James Douglas to Charles Griffin, July 5, 1856, Hudson's Bay Company Archives.
69. North West Boundary Survey 1860:133

70. *Post Journal* February 10, 1859; October 15, 1860.
71. *Told by the Pioneers III* 1938:52.
72. Miller 1943:68.
73. *Post Journal* May 8, 1861.
74. *Post Journal* April 11 and June 16, 1859.
75. *Post Journal* September 13, 1859.
76. Erigero 1992:29,87-88; *Post Journal* May 8, 1861.
77. James Douglas to Charles Griffin February 15, 1859, Provincial Archives of British Columbia.
78. *Post Journals* February 16, 1858; April 15 and June 22, 1858; February 5, 1860.
79. James Douglas to Charles Griffin June 15, 1857, Provincial Archives of British Columbia.
80. Erigero 1992:146.
81. James Douglas to Charles Griffin, September 24, 1857, Provincial Archives of British Columbia.
82. *Post Journal* April 9 and 13, 1858.
83. Erigero 1992:355.
84. *Post Journal* October 17, 1859.
85. McDonald 1990:115.
86. *Friday Harbor Journal*, January 15, 1907.
87. McDonald 1987.
88. Firth 1943:8.
89. Bailey and Cummings 1987:76.
90. Michael Leon Olsen, *The Beginnings of Agriculture in Western Oregon and Western Washington*, PhD dissertation (1970), p. 242.
91. Kimple files, Orcas Island Historical Museum, 1986.
92. *Geographical Memoir* 1860:137.
93. *The Victoria Colonist*, September 25, 1860.
94. *Olympia Pioneer & Democrat*.
95. Documents on Settlers, National Archives Record Group 393.
96. *The Victoria Colonist*, June 20, 1861.
97. DayVincent 2004.
98. Lucille McDonald, "Old Water Mill in Pierce County Ground Limestone," *The Seattle Times*, Sunday, November 17, 1957.
99. David G. Eselius, *Cowell Home Ranch Cultural Landscape Report* (2004), p. 16.
100. Warren E. Emley, "Manufacture of Lime," *Circular of the Bureau of Standards* No. 337, Department of Commerce (Washington, DC: U.S. Government Printing Office, 1927), pp. 22-23.
101. Wolf Bauer, "Roche Harbor During the Recovering Thirties," *The Journal of the San Juan Islands* January 8, 2003.
102. "One Thousand Barrels a day," *The West Shore* 1889, p. 414.
103. McDonald 1990:91.

104. Fred Wagner, Interview, 1966, on file, San Juan Historical Museum, Friday Harbor, WA.
105. Harley J. McKee, *Introduction to Early American Masonry: Stone, Brick, Mortar and Plaster* (Washington, DC: The Preservation Press, 1973), p. 53.
106. Hilary Stewart, *Cedar: Tree of Life to the Northwest Coast Indians* (Vancouver/Toronto: Douglas & McIntyre, 1984), p. 22.
107. Stein 2000:85-86.
108. Darcy Mathews and Pete Dady, "Douglas Fir Culturally Modified Trees: Some Initial Considerations," paper presented at the Northwest Anthropological Conference, April 24, 2008.
109. Richardson 1971:34.
110. James Alden to Prof. A. D. Bache, October 31, 1853.
111. *Post Journal* July 25, 1854.
112. Thompson 1972:221.
113. Eric Sloane, *A Museum of Early American Tools* (New York: Dodd, Mead and Company, 1964), pp. 70-71.
114. Vollmer 2004; Tom Welch, "Newhall," *Islands' Weekly*, February 1, 2005, p. 2.
115. Sloane 1964:39,41.
116. *Port Townsend Weekly Argus*, July 18, 1874, p. 3 col. 2.
117. Tremaine 1975:88.
118. "Density of Forests Washington State" (1883), "Report on the Forests of North America (exclusive of Mexico)," United States Congressional serial set, House Mis. Doc. 42, Part 9 [after p. 574].
119. Keith 1978:12-13.
120. *Victoria Gazette* August 11, 1859.
121. Mike Vouri "Scofflaws and Moonshine: San Juan's Stormy Occupation," posted on *sanjuanislander.com* December 8, 2022.
122. John Hussey Archives, Box 4 File 95 [Grades and Ranks], Fort Vancouver National Historical Site; Gibbs 1859.
123. *Post Journal* June 21, 1854.
124. John Hussey Archives, Box 4 File 97 [Wages], Fort Vancouver National Historical Site; Hudson's Bay Company Archives, Fort Victoria, Servant's Accounts [B226].
125. John Hussey Archives, Box 4 File 100 [Rations], Fort Vancouver National Historical Site.
126. Mike Vouri, personal correspondence.
127. Vouri 2004:38.
128. Whitlock correspondence, on file, San Juan Island National Historical Park.
129. Vouri 2004:54.

130. Washington State Northwest Regional Archives, Jefferson County Civil Court Case 291.
131. Washington State Northwest Regional Archives, Jefferson County Civil Case 339.
132. Bailey-Cummings and Cummings 1987:112.
133. Bailey-Cummings and Cummings 1987:88.
134. Warren, *Journal*, February 4, 1860.
135. A. J. Dent, "A Little-Known Story of Slavery in Washington Territory," *Humanities Washington* blog May 1, 2014.

Intercourse

1. Although currently referred to as Nuu-chah-nulth, the term Nootka and Nootkan are used here because of their historical usage.
2. Stewart 1984:22.
3. Stewart 1984:52-75.
4. Doig 1980:191.
5. George Durham, "Canoes from Cedar Logs: A Study of Early Types and Designs," *Pacific Northwest Quarterly* April 1955:34-35; Leslie Lincoln, *Coast Salish Canoes* (Seattle: Center for Wooden Boats, 1991), pp. 9-10; Ronald L. Olson, "Adze, Canoe, and House Types of the Northwest Coast," *University of Washington Publications in Anthropology* Vol. 2, No. 1 (November 1927), p. 21; Stewart 1984:51-52; Suttles 1951:248-249; T. T. Waterman and Geraldine Coffin, "Types of Canoes on Puget Sound," *Indian Notes and Monographs* (New York: Museum of the American Indian, 1920), pp. 17-18.
6. Durham 1955:33-34; Lincoln 1991:14; Olson 1927:20; Stewart 1984:52; Suttles 1951:251-252; Waterman and Coffin 1920:14-17.
7. Lincoln 1991:10-11; Olson 1927:21; Stewart 1984:50-52; Waterman and Coffin 1920:12-14.
8. *Geographical Memoir* 135.
9. Durham 1955:35-36; Lincoln 1991:12-13; Olson 1927:19-20; Stewart 1984:51-52; Waterman and Coffin 1920:19-20.
10. Boas 1890:566.
11. Suttles 1951:250-251.
12. Kenneth Brower, *A Song for Satawal* (London: Penguin Books, 1984), pp. 73-74.
13. Ruth Kirk, *Ozette: Excavating a Makah Whaling Village* (Seattle: University of Washington Press, 2015), p 64.
14. Lincoln 1991:33-34; Stewart 1984:59; Suttles 1951:254-255; Waterman and Coffin 1920:27.
15. Coleman 1869:794.
16. Suttles 1951:254.
17. John Gardner, *The Dory Book* (New York: Intl Marine Pub Co, 1978), pp. 10-11.

18. Richard Somerset Mackie, *Trading Beyond the Mountains: The British Fur Trade on the Pacific, 1793-1843* (Vancouver, BC: University of British Columbia Press, 1997), pp. 61-62.
19. Howard Chapelle, *American Small Sailing Craft* (New York: W. W. Norton & Company, 1951), pp. 22-23, 41-43.
20. Beckey 2003:150.
21. Firth 1943:6.
22. Washington State Northwest Regional Archives, Case File #2-106.
23. Washington State Northwest Regional Archives, Case File # 880.
24. Chapelle 1951:187-190.
25. *Told by the Pioneers III* 1938:51.
26. Ronald Garner and Carol Garner, "The *General Harney*," ms. on file, San Juan Island National Historical Park, 1986.
27. *Post Journal* February 20, 1859.
28. *Geographical Memoir* 110.
29. Gordon R. Newell, *Ships of the Inland Sea: The Story of the Puget Sound* (Portland OR: Binford & Mort Publishing, 1960), pp. 5-9.
30. Newell 1960:9.
31. Newell 1960:11-12.
32. James C. Orcott "'I Have Never Seen a Ship Make So Much Money Traveling So Slow' Richard C. R. Stark Correspondence Aboard the Puget Sound Steamer 'Eliza Anderson," *La Posta: A Journal of American Postal History* (November 1989), pp. 49-55.
33. Newell 1960:22-23,53-55.
34. *Told by the Pioneers III* 1938:187.
35. Baynes, March 16, 1860; HBC, Douglas to Sir William Molesworth, December 13, 1855, SAJU Correspondence, 1860, 3, BCPA.
36. Tom Welch, "Orcas Island Roads," *The Islands Weekly* January 4, 2006, p. 2.
37. Warren, *Journal*, January 1860.
38. Warren, *Journal*, January 26, 1860.
39. Washington State Northwest Regional Archives, Petition to the Whatcom County Board of Commissioners, Record Book 1.
40. Firth 1943:24.
41. Fleming *Journal* July 9, 1864; see also June 30, 1866, and October 13, 1867.
42. Washington State Northwest Regional Archives, San Juan County Commissioners, *Journal*, 77-121.
43. Washington State Northwest Regional Archives, *E. P. and Gregory Bailer v. San Juan County Commissioners*, Cases 985 and 986.
44. *The Islander* February 3, 1898, p. 3.
45. Firth 1943:30.
46. Bailey-Cummings and Cummings 1987:76.
47. Washington State Northwest Regional Archives, Assessment Roll of

Personal Property, San Juan County; for an analysis of the remains of later-period (early 1900s) wagons, see Linda L. Ferguson et al, "Three Late Wagons from Bellevue Farm" IN Sprague 1983:441-455.
48. Guy Reed Ramsey, *Postmarked Washington: San Juan County* (Wenatchee: Wenatchee World, 1976).
49. *Puget Sound Weekly Argus* May 12, 1877.
50. Julia McCallum, "Dots and Dashes in the 19th Century," *The Islands Weekly* October 18,.2005, p. 8.
51. Thompson 1972:157, 194, 208.
52. Suttles 1951:305.
53. James H. Hitchman, *The Waterborne Commerce of British Columbia & Washington 1850-1870* (Bellingham: Center for Pacific Northwest Studies, Western Washington State College, 1976), pp. 4-6.
54. *Victoria Colonist* June 20, 1861.
55. Lucile McDonald, "1860-1956 The San Juan Limestone Trade," *The Sea Chest*, March 1983.
56. McDonald 1983.
57. Mackie 1984:276.
58. *Post Journal* November 18, 1854.
59. Quoted in Doig 1980:31.
60. Firth 1943.
61. Warren R. Hofstra, *The Planting of New Virginia: Settlement and Landscape in the Shenandoah Valley* (Baltimore: Johns Hopkins University Press, 2004), pp. 224-225.
62. Olsen 1970:54.
63. Vouri 2022:43-44.
64. *British Colonist* August 1, 1859.
65. Lynn Weber/Roochvarg, "Warbass, Edward (1825-1906)" *Historylink.org* Essay 20162, posted 10/14/2016.
66. Thompson 1972:115.
67. *Frontier Justice*, Civil Case #760, List of property of William F. Taylor, January 28th, 1874.
68. *Victoria Daily Colonist* May 18, 1873.
69. Keith 1978.
70. National Archives Record Group 393, Dept. of the Columbia Letters Sent Letterbook 1871 v.1.
71. Splitstone 1946:37-38.
72. *Frontier Justice* Case #231, "Inventory."
73. Ramsey 1976.
74. Bailey-Cummings and Cummings 1987:76.
75. Keith 1978:29.
76. C. Rosler, Invoices, Israel Katz Accounts, on file, Sundstrom Family, San Juan Island, inspected October 31, 2007.
77. *Frontier Justice* Case #231, "Exhibit One, Account of Sales."
78. *Frontier Justice* Case #231.

79. *Frontier Justice* Case #823.
80. *Frontier Justice* Case #2-53, Israel Katz v. James Peers.
81. *Frontier Justice* Case #2-98, Israel Katz v. Anderson & Peers.
82. *Frontier Justice* Case #890, Bowker and Tod v. Smith.
83. Lucile McDonald, "San Juan Customs Inspector," *Puget Sound Historical Society The Sea Chest*, June 4, 1971, p. 152.
84. McDonald 1971:150-154.
85. Keith 1978:27.
86. John Goekler, "Smuggling: Big Part of Island Life," *The Islands' Sounder* Wednesday, August 18, 1993; John Goekler, "A Confluence of Contraband," *The Islands' Weekly*, December 5-December 12, 1995; Tom Welch, "Smugglers," *The Islands' Weekly* August 16, 2005; and Lucille S. McDonald, *Making History: The People Who Shaped the San Juan Islands* (Friday Harbor: Harbor Press, 1990), pp. 78-81.
87. John Goekler, "Midnight Importers," *The Islands' Weekly* June 8, 2004.

Society & Governance

1. Suttles 1951:456-471.
2. Splitstone, 1946:39.
3. Bailey-Cummings and Cummings 1987:73-75.
4. Keith 1978:15.
5. Brown 1980; Jackson 1995; Van Kirk 1999.
6. Keith 1978:11-12.
7. *Territory of Washington v Charles W. Beale* (1879), *Frontier Justice* Case #52 (SKG-51); Peyton Kane, "The Whatcom Nine: Legal and Political Ramifications of Métis Family Life in Washington Territory" *Columbia The Magazine of Northwest History* (Summer 2000) 14(2):39-44; for an instance of miscegenationist reaction to the decision, see "Question Suggested by Judge Green's Decision in the Indian Marriage Cases," *Puget Sound Mail* (La Conner, WA), September 25, 1880, p. 2, col. 3. I am indebted to Candace Wellman for her advice on this, particularly her coverage of the subject and quotation of Judge Roger S. Greene in *Peace Weavers*.
8. "Judicial Review by Chief Justice Roger S. Green, Territory of Washington v Charles Beale Territory of Washington, 3rd Judicial District. In the District Court of Whatcom County of the June Term," *Bellingham Bay Mail* June 14, 1879.
9. *Frontier Justice*, Civil Case #978 (1875).
10. *Frontier Justice*, Civil Case #527 (1867).
11. McDonald 1987.
12. Suttles 1951:472-484.
13. *Duwamish et al v. United States* 1927:429.
14. Vouri 2022:218.
15. Thompson 1972:223.

16. Bowden 1935:412.
17. Personal Communication, Beth Wilks, San Juan County Cemetery District #1, October 2023.
18. Keith 1978:70-73.
19. *Told by the Pioneers III* 1938:157.
20. Pickett to Pleasanton, June 19, 1860.
21. Firth 1943:15,27.
22. *Daily Alta California* November 23, 1859.
23. McKay 1908:290.
24. *Port Townsend Register* July 17, 1861.
25. Firth 1943:10-13.
26. *Daily Colonist* May 26, 1866, as quoted in Vouri 2022:237.
27. Bailey-Cummings and Cummings 1987:57-58.
28. Thompson 1972:207.
29. *Told by the Pioneers III* 1938:168.
30. McCoy 2001.
31. Richardson 1971:294.
32. Suttles 1951:444-455.
33. *Told by the Pioneers II* 1938:199.
34. Firth 1943:4.
35. *Told by the Pioneers II* 1938:199.
36. Firth 1943:26.
37. *Told by the Pioneers III* 1938:199.
38. *Told by the Pioneers III* 1938:202.
39. Firth 1943:27.
40. Firth 1943:26.
41. "1887 Report of E. C. Gillette, Superintendent of San Juan County Schools" IN Bowden 1935:415-419.
42. Bowden 1935:414.
43. Bowden 1935:417.
44. Samish elder reference.
45. *British Colonist* August 1, 1859.
46. *Gazette* August 11, 1859.
47. Tyler 1983:205-248.
48. Thompson 1972:184.
49. Thompson 1972:185.
50. Survey Notes, Township and Range Survey, on file, Bureau of Land Management, General Land Office Records.
51. *Daily Colonist* September 4, 1890.
52. *Land Act of 1820* (Revised Statutes of the United States, Title XXXII, Section 2286, "Pre-emption by Counties for Seats of Justice" [1873].
53. Washington State Northwest Regional Archives, San Juan County Board of County Commissioners *Journal* August 2, 1875.

54. Miller 1943:12.
55. Scott and De Lorme 1988:maps 39 and 40.
56. Pickett to Pleasonton, quoted in Vouri 2022:218.
57. Vouri 2022:226.
58. Quoted in Vouri 2022:226.
59. *Seattle Weekly Gazette* September 9, 1865 p 2 col 2
60. Mike Vouri, "Scofflaws and Moonshine: San Juan's Stormy Joint Occupation" (2023), ms. on file, Mike Vouri, Friday Harbor, WA, p. 4.
61. Lynn Weber/Rochvaarg, "Washington Territorial Legislature establishes San Juan County on October 31, 1873," HistoryLink Essay 20453 posted 10/17/2017.
62. James O. McCabe, *The San Juan Boundary Question* (Toronto: University of Toronto Press, 1965), p.11.
63. San Juan County Commissioners *Journal* May 7, 1874.
64. "Frontier Justice": Guide to the Court Records of Washington Territory, 1853-1889. State of Washington, Office of the Secretary of State, Division of Archives and Records Management. Olympia, WA, 1987.
65. *Frontier Justice* 1987:12-13.
66. *Frontier Justice* 1987:8-9.
67. *Frontier Justice* 1987:6-7.
68. D. J. Richardson, "Before the Colonies Had Divorce Laws: Escaping a Toxic Marriage in the Colonial West," posted on *djrichardson,.ca/blog* May 18, 2020.
69. *Frontier Justice*, Case # 811 (JEF 799), Territory of Washington v Joseph Newana/Nuana; *Fleming Diary*; Firth 1943:15-23.
70. For a contextual analysis of this case, see Katrina Jagodinsky, *Legal Codes and Talking Trees* (New Haven: Yale University Press, 2016), 58-92. Primary sources are the federal censuses, *Ancestry.com*, and *Territory of Washington v. James Smith*, Case #1088.
71. In the 1854 "Act Relative to Crimes and Punishments, and Proceedings in Criminal Cases" rape is defined as: "Every person who shall unlawfully have carnal knowledge of a woman against her will, or of a female child under twelve years of age, shall be deemed guilty of a rape…, and in prosecutions for such offence, proof of penetration shall be sufficient evidence of the commission thereof."
72. *Ancestry.com*, Charles Minor Bradshaw (1831-1897). In 1859 at Dungeness, he married a Clallam woman named Betsy; she died several days after childbirth but was survived by their daughter, Adelia Bradshaw (1859-1944). Adelia married Sampson George Chadwick (1847-1924) on Lopez Island in 1877 and they had six children. In 1870, Charles M. Bradshaw married Florence Holmes (1854-1916), who was born in Wisconsin.

Islanders
(Abbreviations: *HBC* Hudson's Bay Company)

Mike (Michael) L. Adams (1830–1913): born in Pennsylvania; hunted and trapped; married *Louisa* (1845-?), Indigenous, born in Oregon; arrived on Orcas Island in 1858; settled in 1865; homesteaded (1879); farmed and ran a nursery, Eastsound, Orcas Island.

John Anderson: partner with *James Peers* in open range sheep raising.

John Anderson (ca. 1837–1882): boot and shoemaker; formerly of Port Ludlow, Washington; farmed, Lopez Island; shot to death by his neighbor *John Kay* in an argument over a "breachy cow."

J. C. (Jacques Cyprien) Archambault (1826–1901): French Canadian; married *Mary Delaunais* (1850–1924), French Canadian/Cowlitz, in 1863; homesteaded (1883) and farmed, San Juan Valley, San Juan Island.

Gregory (1817-1882) and ***E. P. (Engelbert Phillip) Bailer*** (1826-1913): German; E. P. married *Dorothy A. Schwartz* (1839-1931) in 1871; homesteaded (1883 and 1884, respectively), San Juan Valley, San Juan Island.

N. C. (Nicholas Charles) Bailey (1829-1875): born in Cornwall, England, in 1829; married *Jane Parker* (1833-1935) in British Columbia in 1863; they had seven children; in 1869, formed a partnership at Lime Kiln on San Juan Island with *Augustin Hibbard*, *Charles Huntington*, and *Charles Watts*; three months later, Watts murdered Hibbard; Bailey was naturalized in 1873; the property was sold in 1873 to *Catherine McCurdy*, who turned it over to her son, James; Bailey died two years later, leaving his half of the company and property to his wife, Jane, and their two surviving children; Jane married *James McCurdy*, thus uniting their ownership.

Arthur "Billy" Barlow (1824-1899): Irish; came to Northwest in 1855; married *Lucinda "Lucy" Kenanski* (1843-1898?), from the Stikine River, Alaska, in 1860 when Lucy was 16 or 17, at Homes' Harbor, Whidbey Island; they had eight children.

Patrick Beigin (1837–1908): Irish; U.S. Army soldier stationed at American Camp; naturalized 1873; married *Lucy Morris* (1848–1923), Howcan (Sitka) Tribe, in 1860; homesteaded (1888) and farmed, San Juan Valley, San Juan Island.

William Bell (1825-1908?): born in England; San Juan County Superintendent of Schools 1879-1885; married *Ella Terry*; homesteaded (1883) on San Juan Island.

Mary Jane "Jennie" Berdillon (1861-1932): daughter of Mitchell Bay born *Ellen Thloynnock Yackship* (1840-1918) and *Berdillon* (1835-1912); married *Peter Archambault* (1866-1913); married *Charles Williams* (1865-1932).

John Sylvester Bowker (1821-1898): born in Phillipston, MA; established a store in San Juan Town, but after run-ins with the U.S. military authorities over supplying liquor, forced to close store in 1865; married *Mary Tod*, the daughter of HBC Trader John Tod and his wife Sophia, in Victoria in 1864; went into business with Tod's son, John Jr, in Victoria, BC.

John H. Bowman (1821-1906): born in Tennessee; come to Orcas Island in 1872; homesteaded (1879) and farmed; moved to San Juan Island; elected San Juan County Auditor in 1876; purchased a large portion of the Friday Harbor San Juan County seat homestead, which he proceeded to sell off as town lots.

Stephen Boyce (1827–1909): born in Greene County, NY; moved to California and married *Lucinda Elizabeth Stewart* (1836–1913) in 1856; moved to San Juan Island in 1860; ran a store, farmed, and was San Juan County sheriff, San Juan Island; Lucinda worked as a nurse and midwife.

James Bradshaw (1844-1873): married *Idel LaPlante* (1855-1928), daughter of *Peter LaPlante* and *Catherine Delaunais*; hunted deer; came to Deer Harbor with three other men in the 1860s.

John Wesley Briggs (1824-1912): shoe/bootmaker; worked for Paul K. Hubbs, Jr. at Grindstone Bay; married Mitchell Bay Band *Mary Jones Seamtnaut [Seamtenitt]* (1850-1901) at Whatcom in 1869; homesteaded (1883) and farmed in the Mitchell Bay area.

Charles Brown (1828-1908): Swedish; arrived in the United States in 1852; married *K-naugh "Conna" (Mary Jane)* (1835-1920), Tsimshian; they had ten children; came to Lopez Island in 1870; built and sailed a boat throughout the Salish Sea and later farmed on land bought from James Nelson.

John Collins Brown (1835?-1886): married *Jane "Cecilia" Chanique* and they had one child; homesteaded (1884, completed by heirs) and farmed, Waldron Island.

Lars Brown (1828-?): born in Norway; emigrated in 1850; blacksmithed and homesteaded (1888), Brown Bay (Grindstone Harbor), Orcas Island.

Catherine Bull (ca. 1852–1932): daughter of *John Bull*, Kanaka, and *Fu–hue–wut Mary Skqulap*, Clallam/Lummi; married *Joseph Emmerling* (?-1873); married *John Vermouth* (1851-?) in 1880; homesteaded (1883) and farmed, San Juan Valley, San Juan Island; sold homestead and bought property in Crow Valley, Orcas Island; sold Crow Valley property and moved to mainland.

Joseph Bull (1851-1913): son of *John Bull*, Kanaka, and *Fu–hue–wut Mary Skqulap*, Clallam/Lummi; married *Mary Jane Iotte* (1857-1908), daughter of *Fermin Iotte* and *Louise Louisa Kiloup Billum*, in 1874 and they had seven children; homesteaded (1883) and farmed, Crow Valley, Orcas Island.

Smith Burr (1824-1874): married *Mary Adelaide Delaunais* (1850-1909), daughter of Louis *Henry Delaunais* and *Marie (Wak Tah) Quatanna Qatama*; they had eight children; after Burr's death, Adelaide married *Peter W. Smith* (1850-1934) and they had six children.

Robert Marshall Caines (1850-1927): born in 1850 in New Orleans, LA, the son of Captain Joseph and Mary Caines; came round the Horn, while still an infant, to Port Townsend, where he resided until 1874 when he moved to Orcas Island; managed the Port Langdon quarry and kilns; married *Margaret Douglas* in 1876; bought a farm in San Juan Valley in 1883; in 1911, moved to Saanichton, BC, where he died in 1927; buried in the San Juan Valley Cemetery.

Sarah Dorse "Lucy" Campbell (1845-1912); born in Metlakatla, British Columbia to James "Tsimshian" Campbell and Nishquaddy; married *Wesley Henry Whitener* by custom of the country in 1864 in Seattle, in San Juan County in 1877, and they had eight children; married *Charles Williams* (1865-1932) and they had six children; lived on Blakely and Lopez Islands.

Louis Owen Cayou (1834-1900): born in Louisville, KY; came to Deer Harbor, Orcas Island in the 1860s; married *Mary Ann Sulwham* (1836-1934) of the Mitchell Bay Band in 1866; they had several children, including *Henry T. Cayou*; farmed at Deer Harbor. After Louis' death, Mary Ann married the chief fisherman of the San Juan (Mitchell Bay) Tribe, *Pe-el (Harry Seawalton Sturgeon)*.

Sampson Chadwick (1846-1924): born in Ontario, Canada; arrived in United States between 1864 and 1869; hired by John Keddy in 1873 to herd sheep Lopez Island; in 1877 married *Adelia Bradshaw* (1846-1944), daughter of Charles M. Bradshaw and a Clallam woman, and they had six children; homesteaded (1888) and farmed, Lopez Island.

Jane "Cecilia" Che'ha'nook [Chanique] (also known as **Higlolucolus** and **Sluequlite**) (?-1924): Semiahmoo; married *Dr. C. B. R. Kennerly* and they had one child, George Kinley, Semiahmoo; married *Samuel James Trueworthy*, Orcas Island; married *William "Billy" Clark*, Orcas Island, and they had two children; married *John Collins Brown*, Waldron Island, and they had one child, Mary Jane Brown; moved to Lummi and married *Qui-ach-tun Joseph (Yel-Chent) Toby* and they had three children.

Mary Min-a-cla-it Cha-owa-thoit (ca. 1840-after 1919): Clallam; daughter of *Cha-owa-thoit* (1810-1882) and *Qua-qushul-wit* (1810-1855); married *Dick Teawhalem* (?-1876) in 1865; they had three children; married *Louis Trudell* (1817-1876) in 1879.

Hans Lee Christensen (took his middle name, Lee, as his last name; known as both ***Hans Christensen*** and ***Hans Lee***) (1841–1926): Norwegian; emigrated in 1868; bought property on Shaw Island in 1879; married *Henrietta Kathrina (Catharina) Krafft Carr* (1851–1938) in 1902; farmed, Shaw Island.

John Crook (1831–1889): English; brother of William; veteran of the 9th U.S. Infantry and 2nd U.S. Artillery; came to San Juan Island in 1869; carpenter and farmer; obtained a "Soldier's and Sailor's Homestead" (1883) in San Juan Valley, San Juan Island.

William Crook (1837–1901): English; came to San Juan Island in the mid-1870s; brother of *John* and father of *James*; carpenter, shipwright, and farmer; homesteaded English Camp, San Juan Island.

Richard W. Cussans (Cousins?): got a license to cut timber on the south end of Lopez Island but was turned away by Governor Douglas.

Lyman A. Cutlar (1832-1874): born in either Kentucky or New York; involved in the gold rush in British Columbia in 1858; moved to San Juan Island in 1859 with an unnamed Coast Salish wife and their child; shot an HBC pig, which touched off the Pig War controversy; partnered with *E. C. Gillette* and *Frank Newsome* in 1860 to produce lime at what would become the San Juan Lime Company on the west side of San Juan Island; out of the business in a few years and disappeared from the island; reappeared in Skagit County in 1871 and died in the Bellingham area in 1874.

Mary Adelaide Delaunais (1850-1909): daughter of *Louis Henry Delaunais*, French Canadian, and *Mary Wak Tah Qatama*, Cowlitz; married *Smith Burr* (1824-1874); they had eight children; after Burr's death, she married *Peter W. Smith* (1850-1934); they had six children; farmed near Mitchell Bay, San Juan Island.

Catherine Delaunais (1832-1902): daughter of *Louis Henry Delaunais*, French Canadian, and *Elizabeth Hepi (Heepee) Kwothe*, Cowlitz; married *Pierre [Peter] Paschal dit LaPlante* (1805-1857); after he died, married *Lezim Verrier* (1822-

1877); Catherine and Lezim ("Catharine and Liginet Varrier") homesteaded on the north end of San Juan Island; after Lezim died, Catherine moved to Deer Harbor on Orcas Island.

Louis Henry Delaunais (1797-1852): married Cowlitz *Elizabeth Hepi [or Heepee] Kwoithe* (1807-1843); they had *Catherine Delaunais* (1832-1902); upon Hepi's death, married *Mary Wak Tah Qatama* (1821-1852), Cowlitz daughter of *Elias Qatama* and *Schookpie*; they had *Mary Agnes* (1849-1924) and *Mary Adelaide* (1850-1909).

Mary Agnes Delaunais (1849-1924): daughter of *Louis Henry Delaunais*, French Canadian, and *Mary Wak Tah Qatama*, Cowlitz; married *Jacques Cyprien Archambault* (1826-1901); they had fifteen children.

C. L. Denman: along with *E. C. Gillette* had apparently arrived on San Juan in 1859 to survey the island for the purposes of preemption by Americans; Griffin stated in a February 20, 1859, letter to Douglas that Denman was "formerly in Mr Pemberton's [the Surveyor of Vancouver Island] office."

Thomas Dixon (1835-1898): hunted and trapped on Orcas Island; married *Isabel "Belle" Ladebauche* in 1875, when she was 16 years old; they had four children; homesteaded and farmed in Crow Valley.

Robert Douglas (1827–1881): from Ontario; married *Matilda Kyle* (1833–1901) in 1851; homesteaded and farmed, San Juan Valley, San Juan Island.

James "Harry" Dwyer (1838-1873): born River John, Nova Scotia; sailed goods between San Juan Island and Victoria; had a child, *Nellie D. Dwyer* (1872-1901) with *Ellen Chatalin Chatallen*, Haida; married *Selina Jane Hayes* (1853-1873); farmed; murdered in 1873 by *"Kanaka Joe" Nuana*.

Moses Exstine (1841-): restaurant proprietor, San Juan Town, San Juan Island.

Robert Firth (1831–1901): Scot; born Pomona [Mainland], Orkney, Scotland; married *Jessie Grant* (1830–1889) in 1857; managed Belle Vue Sheep Farm until 1873; naturalized in 1878; homesteaded (1884) and farmed, San Juan Island.

Edmund C. Fitzhugh (1818-1883): born in Falmouth, VA; married *"Mary" Xwelas* (1830-1920); Whatcom County Judge and one of Sheriff Barnes' party that raided the HBC's sheep in 1855; manager of the Bellingham Bay Coal Company.

Thomas Fleming (1822–1907): Scot; married *Mary Jane Matier* (1821–1902) in 1847; homesteaded (1877) and farmed, San Juan Valley, San Juan Island.

William (1818–1878) and ***Robert Frazer*** (1825–1912): William born in Scotland, Robert in Louisiana; arrived on San Juan Island in 1859; Robert married *Mary Jane Fleming* in 1867; homesteaded (1883) and farmed; they owned the property where *Lyman Cutlar* shot the pig.

Peter Frechette (1826–1897): French Canadian/Cowlitz; married *Catherine LaPlante*, daughter of *Catherine Delaunais* and *Pierre [Peter] Paschal dit LaPlante*; homesteaded (1894) and farmed, Crow Valley, Orcas Island.

Joe Friday (1851-1895): son of *Peter Friday*, Kanaka, and an unknown Indigenous woman; moved to San Juan with his father in 1858, working as a shepherd, apparently leaving in 1860, but returned to settle ca. 1864; homesteaded on San Juan in the 1870s; presumably died while working as a cook on a sealing schooner in Alaska.

William M. Fuller (?-1872): English; farmed, San Juan Island; murdered by "*Kanaka Joe*."

"Captain George" (1830-1909): born on San Juan Island to a Clallam father and a Samish mother, possibly at Fish Creek; occupied a rancherie near Belle Vue Sheep Farm; died in Victoria, BC, in 1909.

E. (Edward) C. Gillette (1823-1905?): born in Massachusetts about 1823; may have been the surveyor mentioned by Belle Vue Sheep Farm Chief Trader *Charles Griffin* and the North West Boundary Survey team as platting parcels for preemption in San Juan Valley; along with *Lyman Cutlar* and *Frank Newsome*, one of the founders of the operations at Lime Kiln on San Juan Island in 1860; listed as a mining engineer and surveyor in the 1860s and 1870s in the mining districts of British Columbia; appointed San Juan County Surveyor in 1873; elected as Surveyor in the 1880s; served as Superintendent of Schools from 1887-1890; in the 1890s bought and sold land on Decatur Island; appears to have died around 1905.

Patrick Gorman (1827–1892): born in Ireland; married *Ellen* (1826–1899); moved to San Juan Island in 1869; they had three children: Joseph, Mary, and Peter; farmed, San Juan Valley, San Juan Island.

Edouard Graignic (1849-1900): born in France; jumped ship in Victoria, BC; homesteaded on Waldron Island; married *Lena Skickliss Thomas* (1855-1925), Swinomish; they had eight children; fished for herring and halibut as well as dog fish for oil.

Samuel H. (Harriman) Gross (1835-1907): born in Ellsworth, ME; moved to California in his 20s and then north to the Fraser River Gold Rush; married Mitchell Bay *Jane "Jennie" Quinalt Satart* in 1862; homesteaded (1868) and farmed, San Juan Island; declared bankruptcy (1879); around 1897 teamed up with *William Shultz* in the fish trap business and was very successful, making a considerable amount of money before his death.

Harriet Delila "Lila" Hannah (1865–1954): daughter of *James Hannah*; married *L. Robert Firth* (1857–1927), son of Robert Firth; farmed, San Juan Island.

James "Jim" Madison Hannah (1832–1880): from Missouri; married *Minerva Elizabeth Cahoon* (1845–1929); homesteaded (1882) and farmed, San Juan Island.

Augustin Hibbard (-1869): in 1861, *E. C. Gillette* sold his interest in the lime kiln that he had started with *Lyman Cutlar* and *Frank Newcombe* to Augustin Hibbard, and the three formed a new business—the San Juan Lime Company; bought out Cutlar and Newsome at the end of 1864, and continued operations until the following year, when *George R. Shotter* and Company bought in; in 1868 bought out Shotter; a year later, formed a partnership with *Nicholas C. Bailey, Charles Huntington*, and *Charles Watts*; murdered by Watts three months later.

Isaac E. Higgins (1825-?): from Massachusetts; appointed postmaster San Juan Town, July 17, 1861; saloon keeper.

Augustus Hoffmeister (1829–1874): German; post sutler, English Camp, San Juan Island; sheepman, San Juan and Spieden Islands; first probate in San Juan County.

Hon-Hontoo (1848-1890): born on Orcas, a "Mitchell Bay Indian"; in 1863 married at Port Townsend *Charles Crawford* (1844-1884), who was born in Pennsylvania and died in Los Angeles.

Paul K. (Krispin) Hubbs, Jr. (1832-1910): born near Nashville, TN, to his father of the same name and his mother *Eliza Hedelius*; came to San Juan Island in 1858 as Deputy Inspector of Customs; married *Flora Ross* (1842-1897), who was from Victoria, on December 3, 1859; one child, Paul K. (later changed to Charles Ross); separated January 25, 1866, eventually divorcing in the spring of that year; two subsequent marriages, *Mary Talah* (Skagit) at Port Townsend and *Sallie (What-Qut-Sah) Allen* (S'Klallam) at Dungeness, as well as a series of relations with other Indigenous women; lived on Blakely Island, Grindstone Bay (Orcas Island), Port Townsend, and Dungeness before returning to San Juan Island, where he died.

Hiram E. (Edson) Hutchinson Jr. (1831–1881): born in Vermont; married *Marion Bone* (1835–1895) ca. 1866; traded and kept store, homesteaded (1879), and farmed, Lopez Village, Lopez Island.

Rachel Morris "Daisy" Hyland (1870-1936): daughter of Rev. Peter E. Hyland; came to Territory of Washington in 1860; taught school on Lopez Island; married Alfred Morris Ross.

Fermin Lloyd Freeman Iotte (1818-1907): born near Ottawa, Canada; came to Pacific Northwest in 1850s; married *Louisa Agneis Ignac Kiloup Billum* (1840-1904), part Lummi, at Fort Langley, BC; they had eight children, six of whom survived infancy; in the 1860s moved from Sehome to Orcas Island; first staked claim at Crescent Beach; exchanged for place at Dolphin Bay.

John M. (May) Izett (1831-1909): born Dunfermline, Scotland; emigrated in 1852; married *Nancy Martha Findley* in 1858 in Oak Harbor; established shipyard and built many ships, including the schooner *Growler* (1859) for Capt. Ed Barrington; Assistant Collector of Customs.

Lucy Ontonna Jack (1858-1894?): born in 1858 at Qualicum Bay, Vancouver Island (Tswahout First Nation of Central Saanich); married *Robert Smith* (1835-1889) in 1876 and lived on Spieden Island; after Smith's death married *John "Jack" Henry Balam* (1845-1928), a Royal Marine who mustered out from English Camp, in 1893; they moved to Stuart Island with Lucy's mother *Nu-Wask-Lak*.

Yves Jaffrett (?-1882): victim of an 1882? shooting by *Lars Brown* at Brown Bay (Grindstone Harbor), Orcas Island.

Nora Jewell (1865-1939): daughter of *Peter Jewell* (1826–1876) and *Fanny Yakship* (1843-1897); subject in a rape trial on San Juan Island; arranged marriage to *Edwin Hitchens* (1839-?); moved to mainland; married *Henry Hunt Tripler* (1864-?); married *Charles M. Wirges* (1883-1949); died in Tacoma.

Peter Jewell (1826–1876): married *Fanny Yakship* (1843-1897); three children *Nora* (1865-1939), *Roma* (1868-?), and *Eliza* (1869-1952); homesteaded (1879) and farmed, San Juan Valley, San Juan Island.

Frederick Albert Jones (1835-1912): born in Holstein, Germany; came to San Juan Island in the 1860s; married *Ellen Thloynnock Yackship* (1840-1918), Mitchell Bay Tribe, in 1865; they had six children; homesteaded and farmed, San Juan Valley.

Mary Lucy Katona ("Ka-tone") (1850-1893): probably Haida; orphaned as a girl and raised by Mitchell Bay Indians; married *John W. Gray* (1828-1917), born in Kentucky; raised a large family on Orcas Island.

Israel Katz (1851-1917): born in Germany; emigrated in 1866 and two years later moved to Port Townsend; nephew of Solomon Katz, cofounder of mercantile firm Waterman and Katz; inherited Solomon's share when his uncle died; after brother William died by drowning in 1888, bought Waterman's interest; married *Adele Maas*; established stores in San Juan Town and Friday Harbor; served as mayor of Port Townsend; disappeared on January 14, 1917—a mystery that has not been solved to this day.

John Kay (?–1907): homesteaded (1882) and farmed, Lopez Island; in 1882 shot his neighbor *John Anderson* to death during an argument over a "breachy cow."

John (1833–1907) and ***William Keddy*** (1844–1919): British; *John* born in Exeter, Ontario; preempted (1877) and ran sheep, Cady Mountain, San Juan Island; *William* born in Port Hope, Ontario; ran sheep, Lopez Island; both left the island after the murder of *James "Harry"* and *Selina Dwyer*.

James F. (Franklin) King (1857–1932): born in Yamhill County, Oregon; son of *Francis* and *Sarah King*; arrived in the San Juan Islands in 1877; married *Adeline Verrier* (1864–1942) of West Sound, Orcas, in 1880 and they had six children; farmed and grew fruit, Friday Harbor, San Juan Island.

Georgius Kitchené (1841-?): telegraph operator.

John Taylor Kittles (1867-1907): born St. Clair Island, Washington Territory; married *Isabelle "Belle" Ladebauche* at Deer Harbor in 1900.

Isabel "Belle" Ladebauche (1859-1922): daughter of *Pierre (Peter) Ladebauche* and *Marie (Mary) Spence*r; married *Thomas Dixon*, a hunter and trapper on Orcas Island in 1875; homesteaded in Crow Valley and had four children; after Dixon's death, married *John Taylor Kittles* at Deer Harbor in 1900; upon his death in 1907, married *George Shattuck*, the son of *Charles Shattuck*, and settled in Bellingham.

Joseph Ladebauche (1854/6/9-1929): son of *Pierre (Peter) Ladebauche* and *Marie (Mary) Spencer* and brother of *Isabelle*; homesteaded (1884) and farmed in Crow Valley, Orcas Island.

Pierre (Peter) Lami (1815-1904): born in Bordeaux, France; emigrated in 1859; naturalized 1882; married *Rosalea* (1835-1890), Indigenous; they had *Susan* (1869-1923), who married *J. B. Archambault*, and *William* (1876-?); homesteaded (1883); skippered and fished, Mitchell Bay, San Juan Island.

Catherine LaPlante (1850-1923): daughter of *Catherine Delaunais* and *Pierre [Peter] Paschal dit LaPlante*; married *Peter Frechette* (1827-1897) and they had one child; homesteaded and farmed in Crow Valley, Orcas Island.

Pierre (Peter) LaPlante (1852-1925): son of *Catherine Delaunais* and *Pierre [Peter] Paschal dit LaPlante*; married *Idele Iotte* (1859-1884) and farmed in Deer Harbor, Orcas Island.

Victoria Frances LaPlante (1857-1943): daughter of *Catherine Delaunais* and *Pierre [Peter] Paschal dit LaPlante*; married *John Taylor* (1830-1884) and settled in San Juan Valley, San Juan Island.

Louis La Porte (1840-1890): French; traveled with *Edouard Graignic* and jumped ship at Victoria in the 1870s; married *Louisa (Louise) So-Be-Nat-Za Thomas* (1857-1907), Swinomish, and they had three children; homesteaded (1897, completed after his death), fished, and farmed, Waldron Island.

Julien (Julian) Laurence (Lawrence) (1837-1905): French Canadian; came from the Fraser River gold rush to Shaw Island to hunt game for railroad crews on the mainland; married *Terice (Teresa) Seymour* (1849-1950), Chemainus group of Cowichans, daughter of *Thomas Seymour* and *Sarah Tomsemu*, in 1878; naturalized in 1873; farmed, Shaw Island.

Peter Lawson (1827–1927): Danish; possibly HBC servant, worked on the *Beaver* and several other ships; married *Fanny Dearden* (1841–1900); father to *Lizzie Lawson*; skipper and farmer, San Juan Island.

George (John) "Sghi-agh-kin" (1847-1892) and **Mary "Sith Cay" Littleman** (1852-?); George son of *James ("Captain James")*, Clallam and *Youtchen (Youtch-ken)* (1813-?), mixed Clallam and Cowichan; lived on San Juan Island in the late 1800s; filed an "Indian Homestead" claim (1892), located near a traditional reef net site at False Bay.

Jacob Low(e) (1830-?): HBC servant; first mentioned April 1, 1854; hired for one year September 11, 1854; engaged for one year January 24, 1859; discharged for drunkenness June 28, 1859; may have been the same Jacob who laughed at the pig rooting in Lyman Cutlar's potato patch (Cutlar called him a "collard [colored] man"); in the 1870 census Jacob Low, Black, is enumerated as married to an Indian woman, *Amelia*, from British Columbia, with several children; at that time, he was farming on the north end of San Juan Island.

Charles A. McKay (McCoy) (1828-1918): born in Pictou, Nova Scotia; arrived on San Juan Island in 1859; married *Mary Josephine Innis* (1846-1927), probably a Mitchell Bay, in 1862; they had eleven children; homesteaded (1879) in San Juan Valley; moved to Friday Harbor; appointed Commissioner of the newly created San Juan County (1873); ran a blacksmith shop.

William (1842-1905), **Daniel** (1844-1916), and **Robert** (1848-1907) **McLachlan**: brothers born in Ontario, Canada; William in 1842, Daniel in 1844, and Robert in 1848; in 1863 Daniel came to Orcas Island, where he joined with *George R. Shotter* to begin the lime works at Port Langdon on the east shore of East Sound; in 1865 he and Shotter operated the works at

Lime Kiln on San Juan Island; Shotter & Company went back to Orcas and operated there at least until 1870; after Shotter's departure, Daniel ran Port Langdon with *Robert Caines*; Daniel and William McLachlan later owned and operated Eureka on the northeast coast of San Juan Island with their cousin by marriage, *Thomas Lee*; William, who moved to Seattle in the early 1880s, died there in 1905; Robert, who lived in Deer Harbor, Orcas Island, died there in 1907; Daniel died in 1916 at Victoria, British Columbia.

John S. (Stafford) McMillin (1855-1936): born in Indiana; moved to Tacoma in 1882; in 1886, incorporated the Tacoma and Roche Harbor Lime Company and bought the lime works at Roche Harbor from *Alexander, Colin, and Donald Ross* and *Richard and Robert Scurr*; built the operations into the largest lime works on the West Coast; married *Louella Hiett* (1857-1943) in 1877 and they had four children.

Daniel (1835–1914) and ***Patrick Madden*** (1842–1919): Irish; *Daniel* arrived on San Juan Island in 1862; married *Mary Ellen Gorman* (1857–1890) in 1882; homesteaded (1877) and farmed, San Juan Valley, San Juan Island; *Patrick* married *Agnes Catherine Flynn* (1864–1946) in 1881; homesteaded (1882) and farmed, San Juan Valley, San Juan Island.

Enoch May (1827-?): born in Massachusetts; came to Orcas Island in the 1860s; married *Elizabeth Cahom* (1842-?) in 1874; married *Frances "Fannie" Jane Clark* (1866-1900), daughter of *William "Billy" Clark* and *Cecilia Chanique*, with whom he had one daughter; moved to San Francisco in 1900.

George I. Mercer: sutler at American Camp, 1865-1868.

Stafford Merrifield (1843-1924): born in Eardley or Onslow, Ottawa, Canada; emigrated in 1870; naturalized 1873; married *Harriet M. Rosler* (1863-1944), daughter of *Christopher Rosler* and *Anna Pike*; homesteaded (1879) and farmed at what is now called Merrifield Cove, San Juan Island.

Solomon Meyerbeck (Meyerbach) (1817-1883): born in Hanover, Germany; married *Bridgit* and they had six children; baker, San Juan Town, San Juan Island.

Hanna and ***Henry Meyers [Mayers*** and ***Myers]***: divorced 1867; hotel keepers in San Juan Town, San Juan Island.

William Moore (1827-1897): originally from South Carolina; possibly came to the islands from the Fraser River Gold Rush; at Olga on Orcas Island around 1866; married *Sarah Seymour* (1843-1913), Chemainus group of Cowichans, and they had twelve children; homesteaded (1882) and farmed, Olga, Orcas Island.

Bernhardt Mordhorst (1843-1936): born in Schleswig-Holstein, Germany; emigrated to the United States sometime in the 1860s; applied for a homestead on Reid Harbor on Stuart Island in 1876 and received the patent in 1883; there, together with his fellow German *Frederick Hay* (or *Hayes*) (?-1887), ran a herring fish operation, including a saltery on his property and a smoking house on the cove outside the harbor; sold fresh herring to the halibut schooners that would stop by on their way to fish in Alaska; married *Katherine "Kate" Rosler* (1868-1950) and they had six children.

Thomas Mulno (1831–1902): from Eastport, ME; married *Amanda Clark* (1833–1913); adopted daughter *Annie Emily* (1853-1922) who married *Alexander F. Ackerly* (1843-1929) from Cutler, ME; homesteaded (1882) and farmed, Mulno Cove, San Juan Island.

George Na-ME-At-Cha (1835-?): Lummi; brother of *She-Kla-Malt*; granted Indian Homestead on the west side of East Sound; married *Mary Nani Dadh-rah* (1834-?), Cowichan, and they had four children.

Frank Newsome (Newsom) (1821-?); born in Virginia; worked with *Lyman* Cutlar and *E. C. Gillette* as a lime burner at the San Juan Lime Company at Lime Kiln on the west coast of San Juan Island; it is not known what happened to him after he left in 1861.

Daniel W. Oakes (1831-1905): born in Maine; married *Mariah (Maria, Marie) Quiah* (1850/1851-?), born in either Alaska or British Columbia, in 1863 and they had eight children; homesteaded (1883) and farmed, San Juan Island; San Juan County Justice of the Peace.

Ella Elizabeth B. O'Bryant (1864-1901): born in White River, King County, WA, to *Humphrey O'Bryant*, an Indian Agent at the Port Madison Indian Reservation, and *Julia Whatulach*, a full-blooded member of the Duwamish, Snohomish, and Snoqualmie Tribes; in 1878 she married *Charles E. Basford* (1860-1944), born in Iowa, and moved to Orcas Island; Charles received a patent for a homestead in Eastsound (1889); Ella and Charles had four children.

Mary Elizabeth "Lizzie" O'Clain (1827-1912): Tsimshian from Lax Kw'alaams (Fort [later Port] Simpson); married American naval officer *Richard Davis* of Nova Scotia in 1864 in Victoria B.C.; came to Lopez Island and settled at Shoal Bay; homesteaded (1886) Davis's claim after he died; married *Peter Sery* on January 19, 1881, in Friday Harbor.

Hugh Park (1839-1885): born in Canada; naturalized 1873; came to Shaw Island 1873; homesteaded (1882) and farmed; murdered in altercation with Sheriff and posse.

William Pattle (1819-?): Suffolk, England; married *Ann* in Harbor Grace, Newfoundland, in 1845; alleged HBC servant; granted the right to cut timber on the south side of Lopez Island in 1852; discovered coal in Bellingham in 1852; naturalized 1855; filed a donation land claim (1870), Whatcom County.

Pe-el (Harry Sewalton Sturgeon) (1843-1914): said by his stepson *Henry Cayou* to be "the chief fisherman of the San Juan (Mitchell Bay) Tribe"; in 1903 married *Mary Ann Sulwham* (1836-1934) the widow of *Louis Cayou*; her son Henry claimed later in life that he learned how to fish from his stepfather starting at age nine.

James Peers (1851?-1886?): Victoria?; ran sheep, partner with John Anderson; petitioner for use of San Juan County open range.

Mary Quimican (?-ca. 1850): born to the "San Juan Tribe of Indians"; married *Joseph Eneas Tebo Innis (Enis) Lebeau* and they had two daughters: *Cecelia* (1840/41-1928) and *Mary Josephine* (1845-1927).

Henry Quinlan (ca. 1832–1880): Irish; naturalized in 1877; homesteaded (1880, finalized by heirs) and farmed, San Juan Valley, San Juan Island.

John P. (Paul) Reed (1831-1895): born in Washington, PA; married *Mary Tacee "Little Bird" Weldon* (1846-1918), Tlingit, in 1872; they had eleven children; ran a lumber mill and shipyard on Decatur Island.

Matthias Paul Rethlefsen (1832-1895): married *Nellie George* (1846-1902), born at Snohomish to *Khemath* and *Qua-ils-ia*, and they had six children; homesteaded (1879) in Beaverton Valley, San Juan Island.

George Stillman Richardson (ca. 1847–1915): born Mount Desert Island, ME; married *Ellen Bishop* (1850–1909) in 1871; homesteaded (1879) and farmed, Richardson, Lopez Island.

Allen Y. (Young) (1820-?) and *John B. (Burrell)* (1831-1890) *Robinson*: born in Brunswick County, Virginia; *John* married *Louisa* (1845-?), Indigenous; sailed trading goods between Port Townsend and Victoria and the islands; both homesteaded (1882) and farmed on adjoining plats, Crow Valley, Orcas Island.

Christopher Rosler (1840–1906): German; U.S. Army soldier stationed at American Camp 1859–1861; married *Anna Pike* (1846–1909), Tsimshian, in 1861; they had ten children; homesteaded (1877) and farmed, south end of San Juan Island.

Alexander (1824-1903), *Colin* (1826-1910), and *Donald* (1841-1924) *Ross*: *Alexander* born in Nova Scotia, Canada, in 1824 and emigrated to the United States in 1851; *Donald* also born in Nova Scotia and emigrated in 1861; their cousin, *Colin*, born in Scotland in 1826 and naturalized at Port Townsend in 1877; in 1882 Alexander and Donald became partners with the *Scurr* brothers in the initial development of the lime works at Roche Harbor; Colin joined them in 1884; *John S. McMillin* bought them all out in 1886; ranched and farmed in San Juan Valley, San Juan Island.

Jennie Bee-osh Sacom-Dack (1859-1919): born at Mitchell Bay, her father was *Bee-osh (Cole?)*, a full-blooded Snohomish; her mother was *Ooks-al-ga* (?-1911), a full-blooded Mitchell Bay; married *George Dingman* (1829?-1887) on Waldron Island in 1884 and they had one child; married *John H. Lawson* (1855-1916) at Deer Harbor in 1890 and they had four children.

"Harry" (Ho-Hal-Tet Ite) Samish (xwuhl-xwhal-tun) *(also known as* ***"Old Harry"****)* (1834-1899): leader of a village on the eastern end of Samish Island; operated reef nets off Iceberg Point, Lopez Island.

Isaac Sandwith (1852–1923): English; arrived on San Juan Island in the 1860s; married *Sarah Harriet Potter* (1855–1933) in 1873 and they had three children; naturalized in 1873; farmed, San Juan Island.

Richard (1831-1909) and ***Robert*** (1834-1913) ***Scurr***: born in England; came to the United States in 1850, eventually moving to California; Robert came to San Juan Island in 1870 and worked as a foreman at the San Juan Lime Company/McCurdy's; in 1881 Robert and Richard established the lime works at Roche Harbor; in 1886 sold their operation to *John S. McMillin*, who formed the Tacoma and Roche Harbor Lime Company; bought farmland on White Point; Richard died in 1909; Robert married *Annetta (Nettie) Hill* (1866-1935); he died in 1913 and Nettie continued to farm on their place.

Thomas (Lopson or Stotmish) Robinson (Staut O Mish) Seymour: Chemainus group of Cowichans (Stz'uminus First Nation); married *Sarah (Neesemu) Tomsemu*; their daughter *Sarah Seymour* married *William Moore* and settled on Orcas Island and their daughter *Theresa (Teresa or Terice)* married *Julian Laurence* and settled on Shaw Island.

Charles W. (William) Shattuck (1828-1900): born in Massachusetts; came to Orcas Iland as a deer hunter; opened a store there in the 1860s; married *Mary Ann Mitchell* (1852-?) and they had four children; married *Jeannie* (1846-?); homesteaded (1879) on land that would later become the village of Eastsound.

George R. Shotter (1838-1915): born in Sussex, England; emigrated to the United States in the early 1860s; in Victoria, BC, met up with *Daniel McLachlan*; they quarried Port Langdon, on the east shore of Orcas' East Sound, in 1863; in 1865 he and McLachlan bought in to the operation at Lime Kiln on San Juan Island; *Augustin Hibbard* bought Shotter out in 1868; Shotter & Company went back to Orcas and operated there at least until 1870; in the late 1860s married *Lucy Cunningham* (1851-1893) and they had several children; after the boundary settlement Shotter and his family moved to Victoria, BC, and stayed in Canada until around 1893, when he moved to Alaska to superintend the Treadwell gold mine in Douglas.

Thomas Sit-Sa-Lum (Siscilam, Boston Tom, Indian Tom, and ***Chechitem)*** (1840-1912): resided on land at North Beach on Orcas Island; received as an Indian Homestead Trust; reef netted off Point Doughty; married *Whee-wel-so (Walwhets)* (1840-1887) and they had six children.

Chief Jim Skomiax (1815-1891); Songhees; married *Mary Skomiaxx* (1821-1892); their daughters *Mary Ann Skomiax* (?-1826?) and *Mary Saaptenar or Skomiax* (1835-26), married Kanaka Bay kanakas, *Kama (Charles) (Andrew) Kamai* and *Peter (Pierre) Friday*, respectively.

Fu-hue-wut Mary Skqulap (1830-1892): father was Lummi and mother was S'Klallam; married *John Bull* (1823–ca. 1860) and had eight children, including *Catherine* and *Joseph Bull*; upon his death around 1860 married *John Kahana* (also called *John Hallum Kahano, Kahanan,* or *Alum Kioni*; they had seven children.

John (1833–1914) and ***Joseph Sweeney*** (1841–1920): Irish; *John* married *Johannah (Hannah) Antonia? Jane Burkhart* (1845-) in 1865 and they had two children; farmed, San Juan Valley, San Juan Island; *Joseph* married *Alice Lucinda Boyce* (1860-1943) in 1880 and they had four children; kept a merchandise store, brokered real estate, and farmed, Orcas and San Juan Islands.

William F. Taylor (1823-?): born in Scotland; sutler, American Camp, San Juan Island, 1869-1872; married *Jane (Isabella?)* and they had three children; homesteaded (1879) and farmed, south end of San Juan Island.

Thomas (1854-1923) and ***Theodore Tharald*** (1857-1926): Norwegian; *Theodore* arrived on Shaw Island from Port Gamble in 1883; *Thomas* arrived in 1885; homesteaded (1883) and farmed, Shaw Island.

John "Johnny Tom" Thomas (1853-?): born at Mitchell Bay, San Juan Island; son of *She-Kla-Malt Thomas* and *Mary Yakship Sluckhachwa*; married *Rose* (1866-?); they had a daughter, *Tillie* (1874-?); in 1879 obtained a homestead at the entrance to Reid Harbor on Stuart Island, offshore of which was a prime location for reef netting.

She-Kla-Malt Thomas (1825-1900): married *Mary Yakship Sluckhachwa*; their children included *John "Johnny Tom"* (1854-?), *Margaret Maggie S. Playwhilloot SheKlaMalt* (1855-1943), and *Emma Marie Shuclamat* (1867-1929); obtained an "Indian Homestead" to ancestral land on the north end of San Juan Island.

Thomas Thornton (1828-?): from Ireland; skippered boats in the Salish Sea, including the schooners *Amelia* and *Elizabeth*, and the sloop *J. K. Thorndyke*; cash entry homestead (1877) near False Bay, San Juan Island.

John Tod Jr. (1845–1889): Scots/Thompson River Indian; son of *John Tod*, Chief Trader, HBC, and *Sophie Martha Lolo*; together with his brother *Alexander* (1847-1889) ran sheep on Spieden and Henry Islands; partnered with *John Sylvester Bowker*.

Louis Trudelle (1821-1895): HBC servant, worked in a variety of locations, including Forts Langley, Nisqually, Vancouver, and Victoria; in the 1850s bought a city lot in Victoria; after retiring in 1852, farmed on Vancouver Island; moved to Orcas Island; in 1879, married *Mary Min-a-cla-it Chairwaythoit*, who had two children by a previous marriage.

Samuel James Trueworthy (1835-1875): born Bangor, ME; married *Jeanine (Jane) Sluequitti Chanique* (1852-1924) in 1866 and they had two children; homestead (1879, finalized by heirs); ran sheep, Orcas Island.

James Francis Tulloch (1848–1936): came to Orcas Island in the 1870s; married *Nancy Anne "Annie" Brown* (1856–1941) in 1876 and they had nine children; worked at Port Langdon as a wood cutter and feeding the kilns; homesteaded (1907); farmed and hired out as an orchardist.

Adeline Verrier (1864-1942): daughter of *Catherine Delaunais* and *Lezim Verrier*; married *James F. King* (1857-1932), who homesteaded the west side of Friday Harbor.

Johann (John) Gottlieb Viereck (1831-1899): born in Stettin Stadt, Prussia; a sailor, settled first in Port Rupert; at Port Townsend purchased and lived with as a common law wife *Maria Ketonah Samish (Gilbert)* (1842-1871), Tsimshian from Metlakatla on Annette Island, in 1859; they had six children; purchased at Port Townsend and later married Maria's sister *Jenny Kahlan* in 1872; they had seven children; homesteaded (1891) and farmed at Doe Bay.

E. L. (Ernest Louis) Von Gohren (1851-1931): from Tennessee; arrived Orcas in 1879; married *Mary Emma Fry* (1861-1934) in 1878; civil engineer and San Juan County Surveyor; had an orchard and ran a nursery, Eastsound, Orcas Island.

Edward D. (Dunlop) Warbass (1825–1906): born in Sussex County, NJ; claimed homestead in San Juan Valley; with *Suxsollia* (1830-1910) had a daughter, *Jessie Fremont Warbass* (1862-1898); one of the founders of Friday Harbor; first San Juan County Auditor; appointed by Commissioners Probate Judge; appointed Deputy Collector of Customs; farmed, Idlewild, Friday Harbor, San Juan Island.

Charles Watts (1831-?): on June 17, 1869, murdered his San Juan Lime Company partner *Augustin Hibbard* at the company office; subsequent trial went through several lengthy jurisdictional venues ending up with an appeal to the U.S. Supreme Court; in 1876, after the Supreme Court upheld the guilty verdict, Watts managed to escape his prison keepers—and his hanging—and was never seen or heard from again.

Henry Webber (1826-1894): born in Maine; appointed by *Isaac N. Ebey*, U.S. Inspector of Customs on San Juan Island; filed the only Donation Land Claim in the islands, covering both American Camp and Belle Vue Sheep Farm; died in Port Townsend.

Reverend Thomas J. Weeks (1840-??): came to San Juan Island in 1870; in 1872, married *Margaret Ann Naylor*, the teacher at School House No. 1, where he held Sunday services; lived in the commanding officer's quarters at American Camp; founded two churches, Valley Presbyterian Church (now Valley Church) on San Juan Island and Calvary Presbyterian Church (now Center Church) on Lopez Island.

Tacee "Little Bird" Weldon (1846-1918) born in Stikine, AK (Tlingit); married *John P. Reed* (1831-1895), probably "in the manner of the country" in the 1860s and by Euro-American law in 1872; they had eleven children.

Wesley Henry Whitener (1839-1881): born in Lincoln County, NC; married *Sarah Dorse "Lucy" Campbell*, Tsimshian, by the custom of the country in Seattle in 1864, married in San Juan County in 1877, and they had eight children; Sheriff; lived on Blakely Island.

Charles Whitlock: English; Royal Marine stationed at English Camp; discharged December 5, 1865; farmed on San Juan Island.

John Frederick Witty (Whitty) (?-1873): Metchosin, BC; married *Charlotte Thibault* (1842-1900) and they had five children; farmed near south end of San Juan Island.

Spanish, English, and American Explorers

Lieutenant Commander James Alden (1810-1877): served as a lieutenant on board the *Vincennes* under the command of Capt. Wilkes; Assistant to the U.S. Coast Survey; commanded the *U.S. Surveying Steamer Active* during the years 1852-1860, started work in the fall of 1853 in the Gulf of Georgia and adjoining coast, linking up with the British survey of *Captain Prevost* of the Plumper and the land survey of *Assistant George Davidson*; his nephew, *James Madison Alden*, served as survey artist.

Captain Francisco de Eliza (1759-1825): in June of 1791 sent First Pilot *Juan Pantoja y Arriaga*, commanding the schooner *Santa Saturnina*, to explore Haro and Georgia Straits as well as the San Juan Islands.

Lieutenants Dionisio Alcalá Galiano (1760-1805) and **Cayetano Valdéz y Flores** (1767-1835): commanding the *Sutil* and *Mexicana*, respectively, explored Rosario Strait; met Vancouver and agreed to explore Georgia and Queen Charlotte Straits to the Pacific Ocean together.

Lt. Richard Charles Mayne (1835-1892): served under *Captain George H. Richards* on the *HMS Plumper*; Mayne Island in the Gulf Islands (Canadian San Juans) was named after him.

Archibald Menzies (1754-1842): botanist for George Vancouver; gathered specimens and described landscapes of the San Juan Islands.

Staff Commander (later Captain) Daniel Pender (1832-1892): served under *Captain George H. Richards* on the *HMS Plumper*; North and South Pender islands, in the Gulf Islands (Canadian San Juans), were named after him.

Ensign Manuel Quimper (1757-1844): in 1790, together with Pilot *Gonzalo Lopez de Haro*, explored in the sloop *Princesas Real* Nootka Sound and the Strait of Juan de Fuca.

Captain George Henry Richards (1819-1896): born in Antony, Cornwall, England; entered the Royal Navy in 1832; Captain of the *HMS Plumper* which, along with two boats (*Shark* and *Whale*), was assigned the task of surveying the coastal waters in the region (1857-1862).

Captain George Vancouver (1757-1798): entered Admiralty Inlet with his boats *Discovery* and *Chatham*; ordered his lieutenant, *William Broughton,* to reconnoiter the islands while he explored what he came to name Puget Sound.

Captain Charles Wilkes (1798-1877); Captain of the *U.S.S. Vincennes,* commander of the "Great United States Exploring Expedition"; explored San Juan Islands in 1841.

Hudson's Bay Company Officers

John Fitzroy de Courcy (1821-1890): Irish; born in Corfu, Greece; appointed Justice of the Peace and Stipendiary Magistrate for the District of San Juan by Governor Douglas on July 23, 1859, where he served for two years; volunteered to the U.S. Army for the Civil War; died in Florence, Italy.

Alexander Dallas (1816-1882): English; Governor of the Hudson's Bay Company west of the Rockies; James Douglas' son-in-law; arrived in Victoria in 1857; took over Douglas' duties when the latter became Governor of the Colony; in 1864 left the West Coast to become Governor of Rupert's Land in Fort Garry; eventually returned to England where he died.

James Douglas (1803–1877): English; born Demerara (later Guyana); Chief Trader and then Chief Factor (and head of farming operations), Hudson's Bay Company, Fort Vancouver; founder (1849) of Fort Victoria; Governor, Colony of Vancouver Island; Governor, British Columbia; established Belle Vue Sheep Farm (1853), San Juan Island.

Roderick Finlayson (1818-1892): Scot; born Ross-shire, Scotland; joined the Company in 1837, oversaw Fort Victoria from 1844 until Douglas' arrival in 1849; married *Sarah Work* (1829-1906); eventually became Chief Factor; left the service in 1872; in 1878 became Mayor of Victoria. Mt. Finlayson on San Juan Island was named after him.

Donald Fraser (ca.1810-1897): Scot; friend and confidant of James Douglas; appointed by him to the Council of Vancouver Island in 1858, a position he held for four years; later served on the Legislative Council from 1864-66.

Charles John Griffin (1827–1874): English; born in Lower Canada; HBC servant starting in 1846; Clerk, later Chief Trader, Belle Vue Sheep Farm; moved to Red River in 1862 and then Churchill (1864-1873); married; died at Ottawa.

James Sangster (?-1858): Scot; born Port Glasgow, Scotland; joined the HBC as a ship's boy in 1827 and worked his way up to become a ships' commander; when retired from the Company in 1851, became Her Majesty's Collector of Customs for Vancouver Island, as well as harbormaster and postmaster for Victoria.

Dr. William Fraser Tolmie (1812-1886): Scot; born Inverness, Scotland; HBC Chief Factor as well as one of the founders of the Puget Sound Agricultural Company, having managed that Company's farm at Nisqually (Watson 2010:932).

Belle Vue Sheep Farm Servants
("mention" refers to *Post Journals*; "Company" and "HBC" both refer to Hudson's Bay Company)

Antoine Banne: French Canadian; first mentioned April 1, 1854; left April 14, 1858?

Baptiste Bohn: French Canadian; born La Prairie, Lower Canada; first mentioned April 9, 1854; engaged August 29, 1854, for one year. This may have been Jean Baptiste Bolne [or Bone], a middleman who worked at Fort Simpson from 1844-1849; he married *Marie* in Nanaimo on May 25, 1855. (Watson 2010:226).

George Berishe: French Canadian; first mentioned January 13, 1858; contract expired June 7, 1859; turned away for drunkenness September 12, 1859.

Chapuis: mentioned in the *Post Journals*.

Joseph Charboneau (c.1820-1854?): Metis, Saulteaux (Plains Ojibwe); worked for HBC on the *Beaver* from 1841 to 1855; married to *Genevieve* (?-1868?), a Tongass; first mentioned April 13, 1858 (Watson 2010:279).

Napoleon Dease (c.1827-1861): mixed English and Salish (Flathead); born into the fur trade and began work as a servant at Fort Vancouver in 1841; worked as a carpenter at Forts Colville, Hope, and Langley, and continued that work on San Juan; arrived July 31, 1854, left for Ft. Hope June 17, 1859; after leaving Belle Vue Sheep Farm he moved to Fort Langley, where he died in 1861; married to *Marguerite Smok-we-ah (?-1883)*, a Saanich, who may have been Mitchell Bay Band; they had three children; daughter *Mary* married *Godfrey McKay* (1843-1927) (Watson 2010:336).

Thomas Holland (?-1854): British; HBC servant from 1837-1840; served on various Company ships; discharged in London in 1840; first mentioned January 3, 1854; drowned July 13, 1854 (Watson 2010:478).

Jean(?) Ignace: French Canadian?; engaged April 18, 1859 for one year; discharged for habitual drunkenness January 24, 1860.

Lamane: ethnicity unknown; HBC servant; first mentioned April 26, 1859; engaged for one year April 30, 1859, as shepherd; contract expired May 8, 1860.

Alexander McDonald (1827-?): Scot; born Barras, Isle of Lewis; signed up in Stornoway in 1850; worked in the interior for several years before joining Belle Vue Sheep Farm in 1857; first mentioned January 13, 1858; contract expired April 23, 1859; returned April 27, 1859; discharged for habitual drunkenness and general bad conduct October 21, 1860 (apparently, the death of his wife on October 12, 1859, led to his drinking problems); re-engaged January 22, 1861 (Watson 2010:637).

Angus McDonald (1828-?): Scot; born Markethill, Stornoway, Ross; married; engaged in Stornoway in 1849; worked in the interior for several years, before returning to Scotland; reenlisted and came to Belle Vue Sheep Farm as a shepherd on January 6, 1854, taking over from William Page as head shepherd March 31, 1859; contract expired April 23, 1859; returned April 27, 1859 (Watson 2010:639).

William John McDonald (1829-1861): Scot; born Bay, Isle of Skye; emigrated and joined Company in 1851; sent to San Juan Island in 1851 to establish a salmon fishery, which continued for several seasons; married *Catherine "Kate" Balfour Reid* in 1857 at Victoria and they had six children.

Murdoch (Murdo) McLeod [Sr.] (c.1811-1859): Scot; born Sandwick, Lochs, Ross; arrived August 17, 1854. A Murdoch McLeod, probably from Stornoway, was hired as a servant in 1841, and worked as a farm laborer and dairyman throughout the Columbia Department, mainly at Fort Vancouver; died at Fort Nisqually in 1859 (Watson 2010:689).

Murdoch McLeod, [Jr.]: Scot?; most likely the son of *Murdoch McLeod, Sr.*; arrived August 17, 1854.

Leroux Montigny: French Canadian?; first mentioned March 8, 1858; contract expired 5/3/1858.

William "Old Man" Page: called a "Skatchet" [Skagit] (June 13, 1854); first mentioned April 3, 1854, two-year contract expires March 18,1859.

Young Page; son of William ("Old Man") Page?; first mentioned April 11, 1858, engaged for one year May 5, 1858, discharged August 11, 1858.

Richard K. Powell: first mentioned October 28, 1858; engaged as assistant June 17, 1859.

Joseph Robillard (c.1832-?): French Canadian; born Ste. Elizabeth, Montreal, Lower Canada; HBC servant; joined the

Company at St. Felix de Valois in 1841 and worked at Fort Rupert (1848-1853); after leaving the company, worked as a laborer at Belle Vue Sheep Farm while also working on a farm on the island; first mentioned January 13, 1858; left July 19, 1859; was married twice: his first wife, *Rose*, Kwakiutl, bore him four children and his second, *Louise*, Tsutsalia, one (Watson 2010:825).

John Ross (c.1822-1863): Metis; born into the fur trade and worked as a middleman at Forts McLoughlin and Victoria; arrived on San Juan Island February 28, 1854(?); first mentioned April 3, 1854; bought farm near Victoria and left June 15, 1854; left for Cowlitz and farmed there; left San Juan Island to build a barn for his mother; died in Victoria in 1863 (Watson 2010:854).

Robert Scudder: British; engaged June 23, 1854, as servant. (A Thomas Scudder came to Fort Victoria in 1853 and worked for the company for a year; he then moved to Belle Vue Sheep Farm, where he worked as a shepherd.) (Watson 2010:878)

John Williams: English?; married; arrived December 15, 1853, first mentioned April 29, 1854, dismissed June 21, 1854. (There are several John Williams on the HBC records, but none seem to be this man.) (Watson 2010:999)

Richard Williams: English?; arrived December 15, 1853, first mentioned May 31, 1854; drowned July 13, 1854.

James Williamson: discharged November 19, 1859. (A James Williamson from Uist, Scotland, was engaged by the Company in 1851 and worked in the Columbia Department for a year.) (Watson 2010:1001)

Belle Vue Sheep Farm Kanaka Servants
("Company" and "HBC" both refer to the Hudson's Bay Company)

John Bull (1823–ca. 1860): Kanaka; married *Fu–hue–wut Mary Skqulap* (1830–1892), Clallam/Lummi; HBC shepherd, San Juan Island; upon his death around 1860 she married *John Kahana* (also called *John Hallum Kahano, Kahanan,* or *Alum Kioni*).

George Faito: Kanaka; joined the Company in Hawaii in 1830, and worked at several posts, including Forts Vancouver, Simpson, and Victoria; laborer at Belle Vue Sheep Farm in 1860 (Barman and Watson 2006:245).

*Freizie "King Freezy" also known as **Chea-clach, Chee-al-thluc, Jeeatthuck, Tsilathack, and Tshiaschac***: (?-1864); Clallum/Kanaka?; possibly the "Chea-clach," head chief of the "Clallums"; sketched by Paul Kane in 1847; later references say that he was chief of the Songhees from 1840s to 1864.

Pierre (Peter) Friday (1830–1894): Kanaka; HBC servant; shepherd, Belle Vue Sheep Farm, San Juan Island; father, with a Cowlitz woman, of *Joe* (1851–1895); married *Mary Saaptenar* (ca. 1834-1926), daughter of Chief Jim Skomiax of the Songhees, at St. Andrew's Cathedral, Victoria, in 1870, and, in becoming a Catholic, received the Christian name Pierre (Peter); they had three children—*Lassel* (1866), *John* (1872), and *Emma* (1875); lived on the farm that Joe homesteaded in San Juan Valley; died in 1894 in Victoria, BC.

Kahahopa: Kanaka; HBC servant; engaged April 30, 1859, for one year as shepherd (Barman and Watson 2006:265).

Kahaliopua: Kanaka; HBC servant; first mentioned July 26, 1859; contract expired May 8, 1860 (Barman and Watson 2006:265).

John Kahana (John Hallum Kahano, Kahanan, or Alum Kioni) (ca. 1835-1901): Kanaka; HBC servant (shepherd), San Juan Island; upon the death of *John Bull* around 1860 Kahana married his widow *Fu–hue–wut Mary Skqulap* (1830–1892), Clallam/Lummi.

Kama Kamai (ca.1830-1890): Kanaka; joined the HBC in Hawaii in 1844; worked as a laborer at Fort Vancouver, New Caledonia, and Fort Victoria before coming to Belle Vue Sheep Farm in 1854; in 1855 after accidently blowing off his left hand, returned to Hawaii but then moved back to San Juan to farm until the boundary resolution in 1872; moved north to Coal Island; had several children by several women; died on June 19, 1890; buried on Salt Spring Island (Barman and Watson 2006:284-5).

Kamaka: Kanaka; HBC servant; first engaged with the HBC in 1844; worked as a laborer at Cowlitz, and then Fort Vancouver; signed up on May 4, 1859, for a one-year contact at Belle Vue Sheep Farm; contract expired May 8, 1860 (Barman and Watson 2006:285).

Kaukana: Kanaka; HBC servant; engaged one year May 11, 1858. See *Kauna* (below).

Kauna: Kanaka; possibly the same as *Kaukana* (above); HBC servant, worked as a shepherd at Belle Vue Sheep Farm from May 1858 to July 1859 (Barman and Watson 2006:304).

William Keaini (ca.1849-?): Kanaka; living on San Juan Island in 1870 with his indigenous wife *Mary* (ca. 1853-?) (Barman and Watson 2006:306).

Konea: Kanaka; joined HBC in Hawaii in 1840; worked at several posts, including Forts Vancouver and Victoria and Cowlitz Farm; farm laborer at Belle Vue Sheep Farm from 1859-1860; he moved to Fort Vancouver and then returned to Hawaii (Barman and Watson 2006:325).

La Laima: Kanaka; possibly *Lahaina*, (born on Maui); HBC servant; first mentioned August 15, 1858; worked as a young boy at Belle Vue Sheep Farm; apparently deserted with some Americans, possibly for the Fraser River gold fields (Barman and Watson 2006:330).

Nahouree: Kanaka; HBC servant, laborer at Belle Vue Sheep Farm in 1860 (Barman and Watson 2006:357).

Nahua (also ***Nahona***, ***Nahowa***, ***Nahoua***, and ***Nahor***): Kanaka; joined the HBC in Hawaii in 1840; worked at Forts Stikine, Nisqually, Rupert, and Victoria before arriving at Belle Vue

Sheep Farm; engaged June 23, 1854; quit October 24, 1854 after being insulted over a forced search for stolen goods, left to work at Fort Victoria until 1857; from 1859-1862, a man named Nahor, who along with his wife and daughters was living on Kanaka Row, was charged with several morality-related offences (prostitution) (Barman and Watson 2006:357-8).

William Naukana (also *L'Gamine, Lacamin, Lackaman, Legamin, Lickamean*, and *Lucamene*, as well as *Nowkin, Noukin,* and even *Manton*) (1813-1909): Kanaka; HBC servant; joined the HBC from Oahu in 1845 and served at many posts; under the name *L'Gamine*, as a shepherd at Belle Vue Sheep Farm; after the boundary settlement moved to Canada, first pre-empting Portland Island and then to Salt Spring, where he and his wife *Cecile S-hal-tou-naught Thomas* (1825-1908), a Lummi, raised a large family (Barman and Watson 2006:364-365; Watson 2010:718-719).

William Newanna (also **William Kamo, Newanna,** or **Nuana/Nuanna, Joseph Tahouney, Cahoona)** (1826-1909): Kanaka, HBC servant, Belle Vue Sheep Farm; married *Mary Teseleachei* (1830-1916) and had many children; after the boundary settlement, moved to Salt Spring Island (Watson 2010 721-722). (They were probably the parents of *Joe Nuana*, also known as *Kanaka Joe*, who murdered *Mr. Fuller* and *James "Harry"* and *Selina Dwyer*.)

Joe Nuana [Kanaka Joe] (1865-1874): possibly the son of *Mary Teseleachei* (1830-1916), and *Joseph Nuana (Nuanna)* (1826-1909), who was also called *William Kamo, Newanna,* or *Tahouney Cahoona*; killed *Mr. Fuller* and *James "Harry"* and *Selina Dwyer* in 1872.

Pakee (ca.1819-?): Kanaka; HBC servant; first signed up for the HBC in 1840, and worked at several posts (Forts Vancouver, Nez Perce, Simpson, and Victoria), as well as on several ships (the *Vancouver, Mary Dare,* and *Beaver*), before his contract at Belle Vue Sheep Farm; engaged one year May 11, 1858; contract expired May 20, 1859; the last record of him is a sentencing for selling liquor to Indians in Nanaimo in 1865 (Barman and Watson 2006:380; Watson 2010:750-751).

Tamaree (1840-?): Kanaka; worked at Belle Vue Sheep Farm from 1858-1860, after which time he went to Victoria. (There are several incidents of arrest and sentencing there in 1869-1870.) (Barman and Watson 2006:408-9).

Belle Bue Sheep Farm Indian Employees
(Tribes are given in Griffin's spelling; dates are from *Post Journals*)

Ben's brother: Cowitchin; engaged July 25, 1858.
Bill: engaged July 25, 1858; re-engaged August 20 and September 18, 1858.
Charley: Cowitchin?; engaged April 1, 1858 .
Charley: Klalam.
Frank: Skatchet?; deserted May 8, 1858.
Harry: engaged July 25, 1858; re-engaged August 20 and September 18, 1858.
Harry: April 18, 1858.
Jack: Cowitchin; June 8, 1858.
Jim?: Cowitchin; June 21, 1858; Jack's brother.
Jim: Skatchet; deserted May 8, 1858.
Joe: Cowitchin; engaged April 1, 1858.
Johny: Chimsian; May 30, 1858.
Johny: Hyder; disengaged July 18, 1858, after 7 weeks.
Johny: Kilrooms; June 24, 1858.
Johnny: Klalam.
Loma; Millbank?; deserted August 14, 1858.
Polk: engaged December 7, 1858.
Slavie: April 1, 1854.
Stuart: engaged August 7, 1858.
Tom: Shatchet; boy; deserted May 8, 1858.

1 ***Burbank Bay***: July 24, 1858.
2 ***Chimsiams***: April 17, 1858.
1 ***Chimsian***: engaged August 1, 1858.
5 ***Cowitchins***: April 10, 1858; deserted June 22, 1858.
3 ***Cowitchins***: April 25, 1858.
2 ***Haidas***: June 8, 1858.
3 ***Iroquois***: engaged December 30, 1858.
20 ***Millbanks***: arrived April 20, 1858; engaged April 26, 1858; 13 departed May 3, 1858; 5 deserted August 7, 1858.

American Officials

Sherrif Ellis "Yankee" Barnes (1823-1858): born Plymouth, MA; sheriff of Whatcom County from 1854-1856; conducted "Sheep War" raid on Belle Vue Sheep Farm for alleged tax delinquency.

Lieutenant Thomas Lincoln Casey (1831-1896): son of *Silas Casey*; ordered to survey the U.S. military reservation on San Juan Island; as head of Office of Public Buildings and Grounds he oversaw the completion of the Washington Monument and the beginning of the Library of Congress.

Colonel Isaac N. Ebey (1818-1857): born Ohio; homesteaded and farmed on Whidbey Island; Collector of the Customs for the District of Puget Sound as well as Inspector of the Revenue for the Port of Olympia; bestowed the title "Colonel" for his involvement in the Indian Wars of 1855-1856; murdered at his Whidbey Island homestead by a party of Indians seeking vengeance for the death of their chief.

General William Selby Harney (1800-1899): commander of the U.S. Army's Department of Oregon; following the Civil War, he was brevetted to Major General.

Captain George Edward Pickett (1825-1875): born Virginia; stationed at Bellingham; in command of Company D, 9th U.S. Infantry, dispatched to San Juan Island during the Pig War crisis; later joined the Confederate Army during the Civil War, to gain infamy for Pickett's Charge.

Special Agent Charles E. Roblin (1870-1953): born Prince Edward, Ontario, Canada; special allotting agent for the U.S. Bureau of Indian Affairs; stationed in New Mexico, Montana, and Washington; worked from 1916-1919 to produce the *Roblin Report and Roll of Unenrolled Indians of Western Washington* (January 31, 1919).

General Winfield Scott (1786-1866): known as the "Great Pacificator" for his earlier efforts to resolve Canadian border disputes with the British, sent by President James Buchanan to quell the San Juan situation.

Governor Isaac I. Stevens (1818-1862): born North Andover, MA; appointed Governor of the new Territory of Washington (1853-1857); because Richard D. Gholson, appointed Governor of the Territory of Washington on March 5, 1859, but did not arrive to assume his duties until July 10th, Stephens acted in his stead during the Pig War crisis; known for his forced treaties with Washington tribes, including the Treaty of Medicine Creek, Treaty of Hellgate, Treaty of Neah Bay, Treaty of Point Elliott, Point No Point Treaty, and Quinault Treaty; killed in action during the Battle of Chantilly of Civil War.

Commanding Officers, American Camp

Capt. George E. Pickett July 1859-August 1859

Lt. Col. Silas Casey August 1859-October 1859

Capt. Granville O. Haller October 1859-November 1859

Capt. Louis C. Hunt November 1859-April 1860

Capt. George E. Pickett April 1860-July 1861

Capt. Thomas C. English July 1861-November 1861

1st Lt. Augustus Robinson November 1861-February 1862

Capt./Maj. Lyman Bissell February 1862-October 1865

Capt. Thomas Grey October 1865-June 1867

Maj. Harvey A. Allen June 1867-July 1868

Capt. Thomas Grey July 1868-September 1868

Capt. Azor H. Nickerson September 1868-November 1868

2nd Lt. John P. Peterson November 1868-January 1869

Capt. Joseph T. Haskell January 1869-January 1872

1st Lt. E. B. Hubbard January 1872-September 1872

1st Lt. James A. Haughey September 1872-July 1874

Commanding Officers, English Camp

Capt. George Bazalgette March 1860-June 1867

Capt. William Delacombe June 1867-October 1872

North West Boundary Survey
United States Commission

Archibald Campbell: *head of survey;* appointed by President Franklin Pierce on February 14, 1856; born in Albany, NY, in 1813; graduated West Point in 1835; civil engineer; appointed private secretary to Secretary of War in 1845.

Henry Heinrich Custer: *topographer;* born St. Gall, Switzerland, in 1825; engineer for Zurich-to-Bern Railroad; emigrated to California in 1849; worked as an assistant to Lt. Parke during railroad exploration; after North West Boundary Survey work with Clarence King on the Fortieth Parallel Survey (1867-1870).

George Clinton Gardner: *head of field survey;* born in 1832; assistant on the United States-Mexico Boundary Survey.

George Gibbs: *linguist, geologist, and ethnologist;* born Ravenwood (now Astoria, Queens), New York City in 1815; trained in law, travelled west, and participated in the Pacific Railroad Survey as well as Governor Isaac Stevens' Indian Treaty negotiations; known for his notes on the Indian Tribes of Washington Territory.

Joseph Smith Harris: *assistant surgeon and naturalist;* born in Pennsylvania in 1836; surveyor and civil engineer with experience as an astronomer.

Dr. Caleb B. R. Kennerly (1830-1861): born White Post, VA; surgeon and naturalist; married *Cecilia Che'ha'nook,* Semiahmoo, in 1858; died at sea of alcohol binge on the way home to the Civil War.

Lt. John Grubb Parke: *chief astronomer-surveyor;* born in 1827; enlisted U.S. Army Corps of Topographical Engineers in 1849; Pacific Railroad Survey 1833; after North West Boundary Survey served in Civil War, promoted to brevet major general.

William J. Warren: *secretary.*

North West Boundary Survey
British Commission

Hilary Bauerman: *geologist.*

Captain Robert Walsley Haig: *chief astronomer;* Royal Artillery.

Lt. Charles John Darrah: *astronomer.*

Captain John Summerfield Hawkins: *head of land survey;* Royal Engineers.

John Keast Lord: *naturalist and veterinary surgeon;* born Cornwall in 1818; author of *The Naturalist in Vancouver Island and British Columbia* (1866).

Dr. David Lyall: *medical officer and botanist;* born at Kinkairdineshire, Scotland, in 1817; studied medicine at Aberdeen and admitted a licentiate of the Royal College of Surgeons at Edinburgh; in 1839, he joined the Royal Navy as a medical officer and naturalist; served on the British Naval Expedition (1839-1843), Franklin Search Expedition (1852-1854), and a survey in the Pacific Ocean prior to joining the Land Boundary Commission.

James Charles Prevost: *commanding officer;* born Bedhampton, England, in 1810; Captain of the *HMS Satellite*; attained the rank of Admiral; Prevost Island in the Gulf Islands is named after him.

Lt. Charles William Wilson: *secretary and transport officer;* Royal Engineers.

Merchants to the Islands

Bowker and Tod. John Sylvester Bowker, a native of Massachusetts, first established a store in San Juan Town. (He was listed as a "bookkeeper" in the 1860 U.S. Census). However, after run-ins with the U.S. military authorities over supplying liquor, he was forced to close his store in 1865 when the U.S. commander decreed that only two stores could exist on the island. Bowker went into business with John Tod's son, John Jr., who had bought Hoffmeister's sheep, land, and improvements on Henry and Spieden Islands. In some cases, Bowker and Tod are listed as the principals, with D. C. H. Rothschild and Sigmund Waterman as sureties.

Rothschild & Co. D. C. H. (David Charles Henry) Rothschild (1824-1886) was born in Sultzback, Bavaria and moved to the United States in 1843. After working in Kentucky and California, he located in Port Townsend in 1858, where he ran a general merchandise shop under the name Kentucky Store. Later, with his sons Henry and Louis, he went into the "Shipping and Commission" business as Rothschild & Co.

Saunders Mercantile. Henry Saunders (1838-1904) was born in Stratford, England, and emigrated to New York City in 1862 at the age of 25. He probably moved to Victoria, BC, around 1874, for there is the record of a son born there to him and his wife, Elizabeth Jane Foster, in July of 1875. Both the 1881 and 1891 Canadian censuses enumerate him as a grocer. A historic photograph of his store on 561-563 Johnson Street, as well as several civil cases from that period confirm that his grocery store was an important source of goods for islanders.

Waterman and Katz. Begun in 1861 by Sigmund Waterman (1844-1888) and Solomon Katz (1837-1879), both German Jewish immigrants, Waterman and Katz later employed Katz's two nephews, Israel and William. Israel had emigrated in 1866 and two years later moved to Port Townsend. Solomon Katz died in 1879, and his interest in the Port Townsend store passed to Israel and his brother William. When William died by drowning in 1888, Israel moved back to Port Townsend and bought Waterman's entire interest. Waterman died later that year, but the firm continued under the old name.

References for Islanders

Jean Barman and Bruce McIntire Watson *Leaving Paradise: Indigenous Hawaiians in the Pacific Northwest, 1787-1898* (Honolulu: University of Hawaii Press, 2006).

Karen Jones-Lamb, *Native Wives of San Juan Settlers* (n.p.: Bryn Tirion Publishing, 1994).

Erwin N. Thompson, *Historic Resource Study San Juan Island, National Historic Park*, Washington (Denver: National Park Service, 1972).

Mike Vouri, *The Pig War: Standoff at Griffin Bay* (Pullman, WA: Basalt Books, 2022).

Bruce McIntire Watson, *Lives Lived West of the Divide: A Biographical Dictionary of Fur Traders Working West of the Rockies, 1793-1858* (Kelowna, BC: Centre for Social, Spatial and Economic Justice, University of British Columbia, 2010)

Charles Griffin to Governor James Douglas, June 15, 1859

I beg to report to your Excellency that an outrage was committed here today by a man of the name of Cutler[sic], an American, who has very recently established himself on a prairie occupied by me & close to my establishment, he has dug up about one third of an acre in which he planted potatoes & partly & very imperfectly enclosed, my cattle & pigs had free access to the patch, one of the pigs, a very valuable Boar, he shot this morning some distance outside this same patch & complains the animal was destroying his crop, he came to me this morning telling me what he had done & and offering a remuneration which was so insignificant it only added insult to injury, and likewise used the most insulting & threatening language & openly declared he would shoot my cattle if they trespassed near this place. Such outrages unless checked in the commencement will render my position here not only a dangerous one as far as I personally am concerned but also the position of my Herdsmen, as in protecting their flocks must inevitably in discharge of their duty come into collision with such lawless intruders, & the same man told me to my face that he would as soon shoot me as he would a hog if I trespassed on his claim. I distinctly gave him to understand he had not a shadow of a right to squat on the Island & much less in the centre of the most valuable sheep run I have on the Island, he replied he had received assurance from American authorities in Washington Territory that he had a right, that it was American soil & that he and all other Americans squatting or taking up claims would be protected & their claims recognized as being established on American soil. There are now upwards of sixteen squatters who have recently come & established themselves on various parts of the Island all claiming to be Citizens of the United States, & they have one & all taken up claims & making improvements / a log cabin & a potatoe patch / on the most important & valuable prairies I have in possession of my herdsmen & stock; one of them only a few days ago landed upwards of 20 head of cattle & a mare & has frequently said that the Surveyor General of Washington Territory had distinctly told him that as soon as a few American Citizens were once settled here on the Island he would have the place properly surveyed.

—Hunter Miller, San Juan Archipelago (1943), pp. 52-53.

Lyman Cutlar to Paul K. Hubbs, Jr., June 23, 1859

Pursuant to your request I hereat furnish you with my statement on honor of all the history of the late visit to my[sic] by the high functionaries of the Hudson Bay Co and of the cause that produced the visit. For some time passed I have been greatly annoyed by one of the Hudson Bay Co hogs (black Boar) entering my potatoe patch and destroying the crop, he was repeatedly driven off by myself back to the Hudson Bay Co premises (a distance of one and a half mile) and the Hudson Bay Co was aware of this fact. In the morning of the 15th inst I was aroused by some person riding by on horseback and upon going out the door found it to be Jacob, a colard man one of the Hudson Bay Co servants, I immediately glanced towards the potatoe patch (which is directly along side the road) and seen the Hudson Bay Co hog at his old game. I immediately became enraged by the independence of the negro knowing as he did my previous loss and upon the impulse of the moment seized my rifle and shot the hog. I then went immediately to Mr Griffin (the Superintendent of the Hudson Bay Co for the Island) and offered to pay for the hog. Or as I had some hogs on the Island would give one in the place of that, for the hog had annoyed me very much. Then Mr Griffin flew into a passion and said it is no more than I expected for you Americans are a nusance on the Island and you have no business here and I shall write Mr Douglas and have you removed. Then I said to Mr Griffin that is not what I came here for I came here to settle for shooting your hog not to argue the right of Americans on the Island for I consider it American soil. Then Mr. Griffin said the hog is worth one hundred Dollars and if you choose to pay that all right I said to him I think there is a better chance for lightning to strike you than for you to get a hundred dollars for that hog for I can buy a hog like that on the sound for ten dollars, Mr. Griffin for my part as we cannot settle this matter I am willing to leave it to an arbitration of our neighbors, no he said, I have my own opinion about this matter and I shall resort to other resorses to settle this matter with you. Then I left Mr. Griffin and returned to my house this was in the morning, in the evening Mr. Dallas (one of the Hudson Bay Co Directors) Mr. Fraser Dr Tallmil, Mr. Griffin (chief trader on the Island) and the niggar came to my place on horseback, they stopped in front of my house, Mr. Griffin said Mr Cutlar we wish to speak with you I walked out and asked what they wished Mr Dallas said are you the man that shot that hog this morning, I said to him I was the man, he wished to know my reasons for shooting the hog I said the hog had annoyed me very much for sometime past and this morning I was wakened by the footsteps of a horse when I amediately went to the door I saw this negro man going by on horseback then I took a glance at my potatoes and there was the hog at this old game, and knowing that the negro must have saw the hog in my potatoes (which I think he will not deny) and being aware as I suppose of my previous difficulty with the hog, I immediately became enrage and upon the impulse of the moment I seized my rifle and shot the hog, and then went to Mr Griffin to pay for the hog which he said was worth one hundred dollars, I told him I could buy the hog for ten dollars. Then Mr Dallas said if you do not wish to pay one hundred dollars for the hog we will take you to Victoria and see I then told Mr. Dallas I do not think you will take me to Victoria if I Know myself and I think I do, Mr Dallas, then said you had better be careful how you talk for the Steamer is here and a possy of men we can take you over with us, I then told Mr Dallas to Crack his whip and left them.

—Hunter Miller, San Juan Archipelago (1943), pp. 54-55.

Cutlar Affidavit September 7, 1859

That he has been a resident of San Juan Island since last April, at which time he located one hundred and sixty acres of land, agreeably to the preemption law, and upon which land he has ever since resided.

That on or about the 15th of last June he shot a hog belonging to the Hudson's Bay Company; that immediately after so doing he proceeded to the house of the agent of the Hudson's Bay Company on the island, Mr. Griffin, and informed him of the fact, stating that it was done in a moment of irritation, the animal having been at several times a great annoyance, and that morning destroyed a portion of his garden; he desired to replace it by another, or they could select three men, and whatever valuation they might place on the animal he would at once pay. Mr. Griffin, very much *enraged, said the only way it could be settled would be by him (Cutler) paying one hundred dollars. He replied he was astonished both at Griffin's conduct and his proposal, and left him. The same afternoon Mr. Griffin, in company with three other persons, came to his house. He afterwards learned they were Mr. Dallas, one of the directors of the Hudson's Bay Company; Dr. Tolmie, a chief factor, and a Mr. Fraser. Mr. Dallas asked him if he was the man that killed the hog; he answered, yes. Mr. Dallas then, in a very supercilious manner, asked him how he dared do it. He replied that was not the proper way of talking to him; that he dared do whatever he thought was justifiable, and that he had no cause to blame himself in the matter; as soon as he had killed the animal he went to Mr. Griffin and offered to make him a proper reparation—that he was ready to do it then; had he have chosen to have acted otherwise, he could have said nothing about it, and Mr. Griffin would never have known his loss; the animal was so worthless he would never have troubled himself about it. Mr. Dallas, in reply, stated this was British soil, and if he, Cutler, did not make the reparation demanded—one hundred dollars—he would take him to Victoria; their steamer (the Hudson's Bay Company steamer Beaver) was in port, and they had a posse at their command. He answered Mr. Dallas must be either crazy or deem him so, to pay one hundred dollars for an animal that was not worth ten; and as for taking him to Victoria for trial, that could not be done; when he brought their posse he would have his friends to resist them; this was American soil and not English; and whilst he was willing to answer before any American tribunal for what he had done, no English posse or authority should take him before an English tribunal. Mr. Fraser commenced speaking about its being British soil, &c.; he (Cutler) declined, however, having any conversation with him on the matter; he had said all he had to say about it. Dr. Tolmie said nothing. Griffin simply asked him if he ever knew him (Griffin) to disturb anyone of the settlers or insult them? He answered, never before that morning.*

As they rode off one of the party remarked, "You will have to answer for this hereafter," or words to that purport.

Their manner and language were both insulting and threatening.

—Hunter Miller, San Juan Archipelago (1943), pp. 53-54

Alexander Grant Dallas to General Harney, May 10, 1860

4. *I have never visited the island of San Juan in any man-of-war. My arrival there on the afternoon of the day upon which Cutler committed the trespass was purely accidental. I landed from the company's steamer Beaver, used solely for the purpose of trade, accompanied by two friends; next day accompanied in addition by chief trader Griffin, our agent upon the island, we took the opportunity in passing Cutler's hut or tent to call upon him. I remonstrated with him in regard to his offence, which he admitted, offering to pay the value of the animal killed, which was not accepted. No demand of one hundred dollars, or any sum of money was made upon him, nor did I threaten to apprehend him or take him to Victoria. On the contrary, I stated distinctly that I was a private individual and could not interfere with him. I have fortunately an unimpeachable witness to prove this. Cutler was perhaps alarmed at seeing four of us approach him on horseback, and conscious of being in the wrong, not unnaturally took it for granted we had come to seek reparation. After some further talk, in the course of which Cutler threatened to shoot any more of our animals that might interfere with him, we rode away, and the only other notice taken of the affair by me was in a conversation held with Governor Douglas, when I suggested to him an appeal to the authorities of Washington Territory, requesting them to restrain their citizens on San Juan Island from committing further trespasses. He declined to adopt my suggestion, and the matter dropped.*

5. *Cutler did not use any threat to me, and I gave him no cause to do so. What has been dignified by the name of his "farm" consisted of a very small patch of potatoes, partially fenced on three sides, and entirely open on the fourth. The boar was shot in the adjoining forest. With a stock of five thousand sheep and a number of horses, cattle, pigs, &c., it will be apparent to you that it would have been impossible for us to restrain any of these animals from committing depredations on such "farms" as Cutler's. The loss and annoyance occasioned to us by squatters in the midst of our sheep runs must also be equally apparent. Under circumstances of great provocation the utmost forbearance has been invariably exercised by the Hudson's Bay Company towards American squatters and others.*

—Hunter Miller, San Juan Archipelago (1943), pp. 55-56.

Indigenous People Listed In Censuses

The purpose of these lists is to identify Indigenous persons who are listed in the United States Federal and Washington Territorial censuses. Federal censuses were taken every decade, so the 1870 (even though "The Disputed Islands" were not yet officially part of the United States), 1880, and 1900 are listed here. Prior to statehood (1889), the Territory of Washington also took some censuses, in the years 1885, 1887, and 1889. The context of census-taking requires some explanation. Enumerators followed the instructions of their time; they listed residents by household, with a husband, where present, as "head," followed by his wife and children. Age, gender, race/ethnicity, occupation, relation, marital status, and country or state of origin are then enumerated (some also list country or state of origin of mother and father). Enumeration of "Race" differs: in the early (1790 on) Federal censuses, free "White" people were distinguished from other free and enslaved peoples; in 1850, "Color" was used for "Race" and the category "Mulatto" was introduced; and in 1870 the category "Chinese" was added. In the 1885 Washington Territorial census, the categories are White, [W] Black [B], Mulatto [M], Chinese [Ch], Indian/Half Breeds [I/1/2 I], and Kanakas [K].

In this listing, the data on adults are listed directly from the documents, with occasional bracketed corrections where known. "Indians" are indicated in italics and the following abbreviations are used: AK = Alaska; BC = British Columbia; CE = Canada English; WA = Washington; WT = Washington Territory

1870 Federal Census

Blakely Island
    Hubbs, Paul K.; Shepherd; *Susan (WT)*

Decatur Island
Reed, John T.; farmer; *Mary (BC)*

Lopez Island
Barlow, Arthur; farmer; *Lucy (AK)*
Brown, Charles; farmer; *Conna [K-naugh] (WT)*
Davis, Benjamin; farmer; *Jane (WT)*
Kingsbury, William; farmer; *Sophy (WT)*
Nelson, James; farmer; *Maria (BC)*
Wood, Robert; farmer; *Betsy (BC)*

Orcas Island
Adams, Michael; farmer; *Louisa (OR)*
Bradshaw, Michael; farmer; *Adel ¼ (WT)*
Bridges, Joseph; cooper; *Teresa (WT)*
Cayou, Louis; farmer; *Mary Ann (BC)*
Dickson [Dixon], Thomas; farmer; *Alice (WT)*
Gerard, Peter; farmer; *Mary (BC)*
Gibson, Joseph Y.; cooper; *Margaret (WT)*
Gordon, Isaac; laborer; *Kitty (BC)*
Hitching [Hitchens], Edward; shepherd; *Mary (WT)*
Howard, George; farmer; *Ann ½ (BC)*
Indian Dick; shepherd (WT)
Indian Jack; shepherd (WT)
Iott [Iotte], Joseph; farmer; *Lucy (WT)*
May, Enock [Enoch]; farmer; *Elizabeth (WT)*
McMillan, Charles; lime manufacturer; *Mary (AK)*
Moore, William; farmer; *Sally (BC)*
Oldham, John T.; farmer; *Elizabeth (BC)*
Robinson, John; farmer; *Louisa (WT)*
Shattuck, Chas W.; farmer; *Jeannie (WT)*
Shotter, George R.; lime manufacturer; *Lucy (AK)*
Stevens, John; laborer; *Annie (BC)*
Thurberg, Frederick; shepherd; *Lucy (BC)*
Trimblet, James; shepherd; *Jane (BC)*
Tunis, Bodina; farmer, *Mary (WT)*
Verick [Vierick], John G.; farmer; *Maria (WT)*
Williams, William; laborer; *Minnislaud (BC)*

Verick [Vierick], John G.; farmer; *Maria (WT)*
Williams, William; laborer; *Minnislaud (BC)*
Wood, Edwin; farmer; *Jeannie (BC)*

San Juan Island
Beigin, Patrick; farmer; *Lucy (AK)*
Brown, Martin; farmer; *Nellie (WT)*
Cahoona [Kanaka]; farmer; *Sally (WT)*
Fizzet, Pere [?]; farmer; *Catherine (WT)*
Handy, Kion [Kanaka]; farmer; *Cecilia (WT)*
Jewell, Peter; farmer; Fanny (BC)
Jones, Frederick; farmer; *Ellen (WT)*
Kami, Kam [Kanaka]; farmer; *Mary (BC)*
Kioni, Alum [Kanaka]; farmer; *Mary (WT)*
Low[e], Jacob [Black]; farmer; *Amelia (BC)*
McCarthy, John; shepherd; *Kitty (WT)*
McCoy (McKay?), Charles; farmer; *Mary (WT)*
Odin, George; cooper; *Mary (BC)*
Rosslynn [Rosler], Christoff [Christopher]; farmer; *Anna [Pike] (BC)*
Shambeau [Archambault], James [Jacques Cyprien]; farmer; *Mary (WT)*
Smith, William; farmer; *Catherine (BC)*
Verrier, Leissim [Lessim]; farmer; *Catherine (BC)*
Walker, George; farmer; *Cecilia (BC)*
Warno, William [Kanaka]; farmer; *{half breed children}*

1880 Federal Census

Blakely Island
    Whitener, H. W.; sheriff; *[Sarah] Dorse ["Lucy" Campbell] (BC)*

Decatur Island
    Reed, J. P.; farmer; *Mary (Alaska)*

Lopez Island
    Anderson, C. A.; farmer; *Mary ½ (WT)*
    Anderson, John; farmer; *Lucy [Ella] (BC)*
    Balam, John; sailor; *Mary (BC)*
    Barlow, William; farmer; *Lucey (Alaska)*
    Brown, John; farmer; *Mary (BC)*
    Chadwick, S. Z.; farmer; *Ideline [Adeline] ½ (WT)*
    Eizabeth Davis [O'Clair](BC)
    Grady, John; farmer; *Kitty (BC)*
    Hinton, Samuel; sailor; *Sophy (BC)*
    Langley; servant
    Smith, Thomas; farmer; *Kitty (BC)*

Orcas Island
    Basfeard [Batsford?], Charles; farmer; *Ella ½ (WT)*
    Bridges, J. H.; making barrels; *Betsy (WT)*
    Ball [Bull], Joseph ½ (WT); farmer; Mary (BC)
    Barke [Burke?], Alfred; farmer; *Annie (BC)*
    Cayou, Louis ½ [Kentucky]; farmer; Mary Ann (WT)
    Dingman, George; farmer; *Jenney (BC)*
    Dixon, Thomas; farmer; *Elizabeth ½* (WT)
    Fitzhugh, Mason ½ (WT); farmer; Mary ½ (WT)
    Fanchet [Frechette?], Peter; farmer; *Catherine ½ (WT)*
    Gray, John W.; farmer; *Lucy (BC)*
    Guthrie, James; farmer; *Ziermouth? (WT)*
    Hitchens, E.; farmer; *Nora ½ (WT)*
    Gotte [Iotte], Freeman; farmer; *Louise (WT)*
    Ladobaush [Ladebeauche], Jo (WT); farmer

LaPlant, Peter ½ (WT); farmer, *Idell ½ (BC)*
Lawrence, Lewis; farmer; *Matilda (BC)*
Maseat (BC); no occupation; *Adeline [niece] (BC)*
May, Erick [Enoch]; farmer; *Elizabeth (WT)*
McGee, James; farmer; *Emma (BC)*
Moore, William; farmer; *Sarah (BC)*
Nanancha, George (WT); farmer; Nani (WT)
Nickels [Nichols], M. W.; farmer; *Idell ½ (WT)*
Seward, David (BC); laborer; Mary (BC)
Shattuck, Charles; farmer; *Mary (BC)*
Sis Celam, Thomas (WT); farmer; Walwhets (BC)
Skecatin, John (BC); laborer; Lucy (BC)
Smith, William; farmer; *Kitty (BC)*
Stevens, John; farmer; *Emma (BC)*
Trudell, Louis; farmer; *Mary ½ (BC)*
Truworthy [Trueworthy], Jennie (BC) wd.
Vierick [Viereck], John; farmer; *Jennie (BC)*
Wan a cha, Debrick? (WT); farmer; Mary (WT)
Wekelet?, James (BC); laborer & fisherman; Ca…t (BC)

San Juan Island

Archambeau, J. C.; farmer; *Mary (WT)*
Beigin, Patrick; farmer; *Susan (Lucy?) (WT)*
Briggs, John; shoe & bootmaker; *Mary (WT)*
Brownfield, G.; farmer; *Jenney (WT)* "Consumption"
Clack, Le, Thomas (WT); laborer; Lalock (BC)
Friday, Peter [Kanaka]; *Mary (BC)*
Gross, Samuel H.; farmer; *Jennie (BC)*
Haras, W. (BC); laborer; Semalt (BC)
John (WT); Susan (WT)
Jones, Fred; farmer; *Ellen (BC)*
Lamie, Peter; fisherman; *Rosella (BC)*
Littleman, John (WT); laborer; Mary (WT)
Ma ma cha, John (WT); laborer; Jennie (WT)
Man Nacha, Thomas (WT); fisherman; Mary (BC)
McKay, Charles; farmer; *Mary (BC)*
Newton, W. H.; "boatman in Revenue Service"; *Lucey (Sitka Ty)*

Oakes, D. W.; farmer; *Maria (BC)*
Pappejon [Papillon], Elzi; farmer; *Ellen (Sitka)*
Peter (BC); [no occupation listed]; Colost (BC) "blind"
Peterson, Peter; farmer; "paralyzed"; *Caraline (BC)*
Rethlefsen, M. B.; farmer; *Nellie (WT)*
Rosler, Christopher; farmer; *Pike (BC)*
Selpannt (WT)
Semore (BC); laborer; Sequat (BC)
Senakin, Chaley (WT); fisherman; Jennie (BC)
Smith, William; farmer; *Adeline (WT)*
Statta'Mish (BC); laborer; Susan (BC)
Stowe, Sirus; [no occupation listed]; *Sallie (BC)*
Suke (WT); laborer
Tawk, Jennie (BC)
Taylor, John; farmer; *Victoria (WT)*
Thomas (WT); laborer; Caquade (BC)
Vernier, Catherine (widow) (WT)
Walker, Secellia (widow) (BC)
Wicham, Louis; laborer; *Manaeke (WT)*
William (BC); [no occupation listed]; ?(BC)

Shaw Island
Raider, H. R.; carpenter; *Kitty (BC)*

Stuart Island
Dechaw, John; fishing; *Betty (BC)*
Perkins, Henry; fishing; *Mary (BC)*
Smith, Robert; farmer; *Lucy (BC)*

Waldron Island
Gregory [Graignic], Edward [Edouard]; fishing; *Lina [Lena] (WT)*
Wiggins, Charles; fishing; *Mary (WT)*
Zeve, Jeffet; fisherman; *Louise (WT)*

1885 Territorial Census

Lopez Island
    Anderson, Chas.; farmer; E. F. (WT)
    Barlow, A.; farmer; Lucy (WT)
    Brown, Chas; farmer; Mary (BC)
    Chadwick, S. B.; farmer; D. [K-naugh] (WT)
    Dwyer, Nellie (WT)
    Reed, John; farmer; Mary (BC)
    Sery, Peter; farmer; Eliz. (BC)
    Swift, C. A.; farmer; Kitty (BC)
    Whitener, Sarah (WT)

Orcas Island
    Barnes, E. H.; farmer; Jennie (WT)
    Bull, Jo (WT); farmer; Mary (WT)
    Carle, John; farmer; Mary (WT)
    Cayou, Louis; farmer; Mary (BC)
    Clark, Wm.; farmer; Jenny? (BC)
    Coffelt, H.; farmer; Anna (WT)
    Dixon, Thos.; farmer; Lyzie (WT)
    Fitzhugh, Mason (WT); farmer; Mary (WT)
    Forchette [Frechette], Peter; farmer; Cath (WT)
    Forchette [Frechette], Peter
    Gray, J. W.; farmer; Lucy (Alaska)
    Guthrie, Jas.; farmer; Agnes (WT)
    Iotte, F.; farmer; Lou (BC)
    Iotte, F.; farmer; Jane (BC)
    Jarman, Wm.; fisherman; Alice (WT)
    Kittle, Robt.; cooper; (WT)
    LaPlant, Peter (WT); farmer
    Mason, Fitzhugh (WT); cooper; Mary (WT)
    Moore, Wm.; farmer; Sarah (BC)
    Muacha [Mana-at-cha], G. (WT); M. (BC)
    Manaatha [Mana-at-cha], Geo. (WT); Mary (WT)
    Sip Se Lam [Sit Ce Lum] (BC)
    Still, Walter; farmer; Sarah (WT)
    Verick [Vierrick], J. S.; farmer; Jennie (BC)
    Wiggins, Chas.; n.o.; Mary (WT)

San Juan Island
    Archambault, J. C.; farmer; Mary (WT)
    Beigin, P.; farmer; Lucy (WT)
    Briggs, John; farmer; Mary (WT)
    Dingman, George; fisherman; Mary (BC)
    French, Chas.; laborer; Mary (BC)
    Friday, Joe (WT); farmer
    Friday, Mary (WT)
    Grangnu [Graignic], Ed; fisherman; Lena (WA)
    Gross, S. H.; farmer; Jane (BC)
    Jones, Fred; farmer; Ellen (BC)
    Jones, Mary J. (WT)
    Knolson, Cecilia (WT)
    King, James; farmer; Adaline (WT)
    Lepree?, Louis; farmer; Laura (WT)
    Littleman, George (BC); farmer; Mary (BC)
    Lumi [Lamie], Peter; fisherman; Jane (CAN)
    McCape?, Wm.?; mason; Jenny? (WT)
    McKay, Charles; farmer; Mary (BC)
    Merrifield, S.; farmer; Hattie (WT)
    Knight, L.; n.o.; M. (BC)
    Nelson, Jo; farmer (WT)
    Oakes, D. W.; farmer; Mariah (Alaska)
    Papelion [Papillon], E. [Isaiah]; farmer; Ellen (BC)
    Perkins, H.; farmer; May (BC)
    Peterson, P.; farmer; C. (WT)
    Piten [Pappan], Semore [Seymore] (BC); n.o.; Emma (BC)
    Rethlefsen, M. P.; farmer; Nellie (WT)
    She Kla Malt (BC); farmer; Mary (WT)
    Skucum Tom (BC); n.o.
    Smith, Robert; farmer; Lucy (WT)
    Smith, W. P.; farmer; Ada (WT)
    Taylor, Nie (WT); n.o.; Mary (WT)
    Trudell, l.; farmer; Mary (BC)
    Vermouth, John; farmer; Kate (WT)
    Wiggins, Charles; fisherman; Mary (WT)
    Williams, Geo. (WT); n.o.; Mary (WT)
    Wilson, H.; cook; Emma (WT)

Shaw Island
Burke, A.; *farmer*; *Amy (BC)*
Rader, A. R.; *farmer*; *Kittie (BC)*

1887 Territorial Census

Lopez Island
Anderson, C. A.; farmer; *Ellie [Ella] (WT)*
Barlow, A.; farmer; *Lucy (Alaska)*
Brown, Chas; farmer; *Mary (BC)*
Chadwick, S. B.; farmer; *Adel [Adelia] (WT)*
Davis, E. *[Elizabeth] (BC)*
Lemaster, John; farmer; *Magee [Maggie] (WT)*
Reed, J. P.; farmer; *Mary (BC)*
Swift, Kitty (BC)

Orcas Island
Barnes, E.; farmer; *Jennie (WT)*
Bratton, Wm.; farmer; *Jane (WT)*
Bull, Jo (WT); farmer; *Mary (WT)*
Busford, Chas.; farmer; *Ella (WT)*
Cayou, Louis; farmer; *Mary (WT)*
Clark, Wm.; farmer; *Jane (WT)*
Coffelt, E.; sawyer; *Sarah (WT)*
Coffelt, W. H.; farmer; *Anna (WT)*
Dixon, Thos.; farmer; *Isabelle (WT)*
Frechette, Peter; farmer; *Catherine (WT)*
Gray, J. W.; farmer; *Lucy (Alaska)*
Guthrie, Jas.; farmer; *Agnes (WT)*
Iotte, F.; farmer; *Louise (WT)*
LaPlant, Peter (WT); farmer
Mason, Fitzhugh (WT); cooper; *Mary (WT)*
May, E.; farmer; *Fanny (WT)*
Moore, William; farmer; *Sarah (WT)*
Morris, Peter; farmer; *Mary (WT)*
Robinson, Thos.; farmer; *Julia (WT)*
Shattuck, Chas.; farmer; *Emma (WT)*
Still, Walter; farmer; *Sarah (WT)*
Sullivan, Jas.; farmer; *Emma (WT)*
Verick, J. S.; farmer; *Jennie (WT)*

San Juan Island
  Archambault, J. C.; farmer; *Mary (WT)*
  Beigin, P.; farmer; *Lucy (WT)*
  Briggs, John; farmer; *Mary (WT)*
  Dingman, Jane (BC)
  French, C.O.; cooper; *Mary (WT)*
  Gangu, E.; fisherman; *Lena (WT)*
  Geotz [Taylor], Victoria; farmer; (WT)
  Gross, S. H.; farmer; *June [Jane?] (WT)*
  Jewell, Norah (WT)
  Jones, Fred; farmer; *Ellen (BC)*
  Jones, Mary J. (WT)
  King, James; farmer; *Adelia (WT)*
  Littleman, George (WA); farmer; M. (BC)
  Lunnie [Lamie], Peter; n.o.; *Jane (CAN)*
  Mamancho, T. (WT); farmer; Louise (WT)
  McCarty, Charles (WT); n.o.
  McKay, Charles; farmer; *Mary (BC)*
  Merrilford [Merrifield?], S.; farmer; *Henrietta (WT)*
  Nelson, Jo; farmer (WT)
  Oakes, D. W.; farmer; *Mariah (Alaska)* [some children's surnames Burr and Smith]
  Papeom [Papillon], E.; n.o.; *Ellen (BC)*
  Perkins, H.; farmer; *Lucy (BC)*
  Peterson, Peter; farmer; *Caroline (WT)*
  Rethlefsen, M. P.; farmer; *[just children Indian?]*
  Ripen, Lemore; n.o.; *Jane (WT)*
  Rosler, C.; farmer; *Rike [Pike?] (WT)*
  Ruder [Rader?], A. R.; farmer; *Kittie (WT)*
  Smith, W. P.; farmer; A. (WT) [the children have the last name Burr]
  Wiggins, Charles; fisherman; *Mary (WT)*
  Wilson, Robert; farmer; *E. (WT)*

Shaw Island
  Burke, A.; farmer; *Anna (WT)*

1889 Territorial Census

Lopez Island
Anderson, Chs.; farmer; *E. A. (WT)*
Barlow, Arthur; farmer; *Lucy (WT)*
Brown, Chas.; farmer; *Mary (Alaska)*
Chadwick, S.G.; farmer; *A. (WT)*
Clark?, John; farmer; *Mary (WT)*
Coffelt, H.; farmer; *A. (WT)*
LeMaster, M. (WT); farmer; *Maggie (WT)*
Reed, J. P.; farmer; *Mary (Alaska)*

Orcas Island
Barnes, Edward; engineer; *Jennie (WT)*
Basford, Charles; farmer; *Ella (WT)*
Bratton, William; farmer; *Mary (BC)*
Bull, Joe (WT); farmer; *Mary (WT)*
Cayou, Louis; farmer; *Mary (WT)*
Clark, M. J.; farmer; *Jenny (WT)*
Coffelt, Ha[rrison?]; farmer; *Eliza (WT)*
Dixon, Thomas; farmer; *Isabelle (WT)*
Fitzhugh, Mason; farmer; *Mary (WT)*
Gray, John W.; farmer; *Lucy (Alaska)*
Guthrie, J. R.; farmer; *A. (Alaska)*
Iotte, Freeman; farmer; *Louisa (WT)*
May, Enoch; farmer; *F. J.? (WT)*
Nissell?, L.; farmer; *Lucy (WT)*
Olson, Chris; farmer; *Mary (WT)*
Robinson, Tho.; farmer; *May (Alaska)*
Still, Walter; farmer; *Sarah (WT)*
Still, Walter; farmer; *Mary (WT)*
Sullivan, J. R.; farmer; *Emeline (??)*
Trueworthy, William; farmer; *J. (WT)*
Viereck, J. W.; farmer; *Mary (WT)*
Wood, W.; farmer; *S. (WT)*

Waldron Island
Granguie [Graignic], E.; farmer; *L. (Alaska)*
LaPort, L.; farmer; *L. (WT)*
Wiggins, Ch-s.; fishing; *May [Mary?] (WT)*

1900 Federal Census

Blakely Island
Reed, Mary *(AK)*
Williams, Charles; farmer; *Sarah [Campbell] (AK)*

Lopez Island
Anderson, Charles A.; farmer; *Ella F. (Canada)*
Barlow, Arthur *(Alaska); farmer*
Brown, Charles; farmer; *Mary Jane (AK)*
Chadwick, Samson; farmer; *Adelia (WA)*
Davis, Elizabeth *(AK)*
Eaton, Erwin; farmer; *Mary Jane (AK)*
LeMaster, Charles Brown *(WA)*
Mitchell, Maggie *(AK)*
Thompson, Emily Matilda *(WA)*

Orcas Island
Bull, Alfred [Joseph] ½ *(WA); day laborer*
Bull, Joseph ½ *(BC); farmer; Mary ½ (WA)*
Colson, Charles; farmer; *Emma ½ (WA)*
Cayou, Louis; farmer; *Mary (BC)*
Cummings, C.; farmer; *Susie ½ (WA)*
Davis, N. [Nicholas] B.; farmer; *Annie [Moore] ½ (WA)*
Frechette, Catherine ½ *(WA)*
Clark, W.; farmer; *Jennie (WA)*
Gray, John; farmer; *Florence ½ (WA)*
Guthrie, James; farmer; *Agnis (WA)*
Iotte, Furman; farmer; *Louisa (WA)*
Kittles, John ½ *(WA);* farmer; *Isabelle ½ (WA)*
LaPlant, Peter ½ *(WA); day laborer*
LaPlant, William ½ *(WA); wood chopper*
Moore, Joseph ½ *(WA); farmer*
Person, [??]; fisherman; *Kate (BC CE) father Lummi mother Cowichan*
Robertson, Thomas; *farmer; Julia ½ (WA)*
Seymour, Sarah *(BC)*
Sluyler, Clem. [Clarence]; *farmer; Louise ½ (WA)*

Thompson, Henry; farmer; *Allie (CE)*
Verrier, Catherine *(WA)*
Verrier, Joseph ½ *(WA); stock raiser*
Wiggins, Charles; day laborer; *Mary (WA)*

San Juan Island
Archambault, James C.; farmer; *Mary (WA)*
Archambault, Peter ½ *(WA); day laborer; Mary J. ½ (CAN)*
Baalim, Henry ½ *(WA); ["Lodger" with Papillons]*
Beigin, Patrick; farmer; *Lucy (Alaska)*
Briggs, John; farmer; *Mary (WA)*
Churchill, Norman; merchant; *Sarah J. ½ (WA)*
French, Charles; farmer; *Mary (CAN)*
Gross, Samuel H.; prop fish trap; *Jane (WA)*
Houston, William J. ½ *(CAN); day laborer; Rose (1/2 CAN)*
Jones, William ½ *(WA); day laborer*
Knowlson, James; quarryman; *Cecilia CAN); stepchildren Walker*
McKay, Charles; quartz miner; *Mary (BC)*
McKay, James ½ *(WA); day laborer; Julia L. ½ (WA)*
Oakes, David[sic] W.; farmer; *Maria (Alaska)*
Ones, Ellen *(CAN)*
Papillon, Isaiah; farmer; *Ellen (CAN)*
Rethlefsen, Nellie *(WA); Widow*
Rosler, Christopher; farmer; *Mary (BC)*
Smith, William P.; farmer; *Adelaide (WA); Burrs listed as stepchildren*
Thomas, Mary *(Tsklouk); Saanich; f Saanich; m Cowichan [listed under "Indian Population"]*
Wiley, Meade; farmer; *Sara A. (BC)*

Stuart Island
Cayou, S General *(WA); farm laborer*
Cepas, Antone; farmer; *Emma J. F. (WA)*
Thomas, John *(WA); fisherman; Rose (CAN) stepchildren Smith*

Special Inquiries Relating to Indians:
    Lummi; f Lummi; m Cowichan
    Snohomish; f Victoria; m Snohomish
    Lummi; f Lummi; m Snohomish
    "Belfroymelt" Cowichan
    "Tahmewhat" Cowichan; f Snohomish; m Cowichan
    "Sholcelemn" Cowichan; f Victoria; m Cowichan

Waldron Island ["Indian Population"; *italics* Indian]
    Graignic, Edward; fisherman; *Lena (WA)*
    Laporte, *Louisa (WA); farmer; stepchildren Kertula*
    Lawson, John; farmer; *Jennie (CAN) stepchildren*
        Dingman and Johnson
    Percy, Richard *(CAN); Agatha (WA) stepchildren Thomas*

Special Inquiries Relating to Indians:
    Head ½ Cowichan through mother; Wife "Pathaote" tribe
        Skagit; f Skykomish; m Skagit; Children tribe
        Cowichan; f Cowichan; m Skagit
    "Salzelt" tribe Cowichan; f Cowichan; m Cowichan
    "Sebonetza" tribe Skagit; f Skagit; m Samish; children
        Skagit

NOTE: "Special Inquiries Relating to Indians" include:
    Other Name if any
    Tribe of this Indian
    Tribe of Father of this Indian
    Tribe of Mother of this Indian
    Has Indian any white blood; if so how much
    Is this Indian, if married, living in polygamy
    Is this Indian taxed
    Year of acquiring citizenship
    Citizenship acquired by allotment
    Is this Indian living in a fixed or movable dwelling

List of Petitioners For Naturalization, January 13, 1873

J. C. Archambault *Great Britain and Ireland*
J. L. Archambault *Great Britain and Ireland*
Patrick Beigen [Beigin] *Great Britain and Ireland*
William Bell *Great Britain and Ireland*
J. A. Bradshaw *Great Britain and Ireland*
Joseph Bull *Great Britain and Ireland*
Jno. [John] Crook *Great Britain and Ireland*
Henry Dirk *Great Britain and Ireland*
Robert Douglas *Great Britain and Ireland*
Edward Eustace *Great Britain and Ireland*
Robert Firth *Great Britain and Ireland*
William Frazer *Great Britain and Ireland*
Peter Frechette *Great Britain and Ireland*
Joseph Friday *Great Britain and Ireland*
Anton Gesselman *Germany*
John Gibson *Sweden*
Patrick Gorman *Great Britain and Ireland*
Ferman [Fermin] Yote [Iotte] *Great Britain and Ireland*
George Jackle *Great Britain and Ireland*
F. Jones *Germany*
P. [Patrick] Madden *Great Britain and Ireland*
Thomas McCarthy *Great Britain and Ireland*
Stafford Merrifield *Great Britain and Ireland*
Peter Nelson *Denmark*
A. Ofner *Austria*
Hugo Park *Great Britain and Ireland*
P. Peterson *Denmark*
Donald Ross *Great Britain and Ireland*
Alexander Ross *Great Britain and Ireland*
Isaac Sandwith *Great Britain and Ireland*
Joseph Sandwith *Great Britain and Ireland*
George Shotter *Great Britain and Ireland*
Thomas Smith *Norway & Sweden*
John Stevens *Great Britain and Ireland*
John Taylor *Great Britain and Ireland*
William F. Taylor *Great Britain and Ireland*
Lizincer [Lezim] Varrier [Verrier] *Great Britain and Ireland*
George Walker *Great Britain and Ireland*
Lawrence Welch *Great Britain and Ireland*

William Warner,
Description of a Passage between Spencer Spit and Frost Island off the East Shore of Lopez

Broke up camp at 9 o'clock a.m. and started for a small bay pulling into Lopez Id. about 7 or 8 miles to the north, and opposite to our camp on Blakely Id. When we first started there was a little wind blowing in flows. After getting a mile on our way the wind freshened and blew right after us. We put up the foresail which was as much as the boat could carry. After sailing about 3 miles (which distance we ran in about ?? minutes) the wind increased so that we took down the foresail and ran under the jib. The sea had now increased very much and occasionally a swell would wash over the stern of the boat, as the jib did not draw her through the water fast enough to keep ahead of the seas, and the foresail was more than we thought it prudent to carry. A new difficulty soon presented itself: what we took for a small island lying off of Lopez Id. we found was a part of Lopez, and connected with it by a long sand bar. It was as much as we could do to lay close enough up in the wind which was now blowing towards shore to clear this promontory; and when we came within about a mile of it we found that a sand bar ran out some distance beyond the promontory, and seemed to extend nearly across to Frost Id., leaving a narrow channel of about 20 yards to run through. Immense breakers were dashing upon this sand beach of Lopez Id. which would have swamped our boat instantly had we run into them. On the other hand, had one of the seas dashed us against the scragged rocks of Frost Id., our position would have been still more uncomfortable. Just before reaching the passage two men put out their oars and gave a few vigorous pulls, while I headed the boat as directly for Frost Id. as I dared without ?? the seas washing over the gunnels. We got under the protection of Frost Id. just in time to clear the breakers, and keeping just far enough from Frost Id. to clear the rocks, we ran safely between this Scylla and Charybdis. As soon as we rounded a point of Lopez Id. opposite Frost Id. we ran into a little bay where the water was as smooth as a mill pond.

—Geographical Memoir, Appendix F,
"Journal of William J. Warren"

Northwest Boundary Survey Storm Account, January 21, 1860

The wind increased during the day, and in the afternoon it blew a perfect gale. It blew the water from the tops of the waves, carrying the spray hundreds of feet like drifting snow. Every few minutes in the evening we would hear a sound as of distant thunder, followed by a trembling of the earth as the wind uprooted and leveled the giant fir trees. Occasionally a sound like the rattling of a volley of musketry warned us that tree had fallen so near us that we could hear the crashing of its branches. The wind blew in frightful gusts: first we would hear it howling near us; then a moaning sound would come to us from the distance as it swept over the island accompanied by the dull heavy sound of falling trees. We were fortunately protected in our position from the full force of the wind. Still as there were several trees standing near our tents, which bended and creaked in the blast, we did not feel entirely comfortable until the gale abated. The wind calmed down about 9 o'clock at night. This was one of the heaviest gales that I have ever known, even in this stormy region.

—*Geographical Memoir*, Appendix F, "Journal of William J. Warren"

Coast Salish Villages
(adapted from Suttles 1959 and Boxberger 1994)

San Juan
p'kweekh-EEL-wuhlh ('rotten-wood side'). Songish/Lummi. On point near entrance to Mitchell Bay.

SMUH-yuh. Songish/Lummi. On Garrison Bay at English Camp.

XWSuh?ngeng. Fish Creek.

WH'LEHL-kluh. Songish/Lummi. On Lonesome Cove, homestead in 1884 by She-Kla-Malt; "the Fitzhugh place" or "Pearl Little Estate".

Stuart
Kwuh-nuhs (Whale). Saanich. East shore of Reid Harbor near entrance.

Henry Island
lhuh-LHEE-ng'kwulh. Songish/Lummi. At head of Open Bay.

Orcas
EH-leh-luhng ('houses'). Lummi. At site of present town of West Sound.

tsuhl-WHEE'k-seeng. Lummi. At or near site of present town of East Sound.

muh-KWUHL-neech. Lummi. At Rosario on East Sound.

whuht'k-AW-ch'lh. Lummi. At Olga on East Sound.

Lopez
TLA W ALAMES (shortened to *Tlawalmes*), *Kalka'nip/ƛalƛa'lnip*" or *tluhl-TLUHL-neep* ('homesite'). Flat Point.

Lopez Village

Reef Net Locations
(adapted from Suttles 1959 and Boxberger 1994)

Henry
Lalionkwal. On the west shore of Open Bay.

John's
Xwciyaman. South shore

Lopez
Kseqan. Off Iceberg Point, near Iceberg Island (camp at Outer Bay).
Xweebjwabag. Watmough Head.
??. Langley Point.
Susuwalexan. Southwest corner of Lopez Island
Sxwglac. Off Fisherman's Bay.

Orcas
Xwlaqxai. Point south of Freeman Island near West Beach.
Kalaqs. Point Doughty ("Coal Point").

San Juan
Kexngineng. Eagle Point. Two sets of gear: one at flood tide and one at ebb tide.
Qoqcinathan. Off headland at the southeast of Kanaka Bay.
Sqwaenexw. Off west point of Kanaka Bay.
Sneu. Pile Point.
Qexemang. Northwest of Pile Point.
Citemas. Lime Kiln, off point north of lighthouse (with camp at Deadman's Bay).
Sqwehana. Andrews Bay, off the north side of Low Island (camp on beach south of Sunset Point).
?eketi?nas. Sunset Point.
?? Mosquito Pass.

Shaw
Xwitcosang. Off Reef Net Bay [formerly Squaw Bay].

Stuart
Qwanas. Off of the west shore of the mouth of Reid Harbor.

Waldron Island
Cxane. Fishery Point.

Joseph Banks' Instructions to Archibald Menzies

He was to investigate the whole of the natural history of the countries visited, paying attention to the nature of the soil, and in view of the prospect of sending out settlers from England, whether grains, fruits, etc., cultivated in Europe are likely to thrive. All trees, shrubs, plants, grasses, ferns, and mosses were to be enumerated by their scientific names as well as those used in the language of the natives. He was to dry specimens of all that were worthy of being brought home and all that could be procured, either living plants or seeds, so that their names and qualities could be ascertained at His Majesty's gardens at Kew. Any curious or valuable plants that could not be propagated from seeds were to be dug up and planted in the glass frame provided for the purpose. He was also to examine beds of brooks, sides of cliffs, and other places in search of ores or metals and mineral substances. He was also to note the sort of beasts, birds, and fishes likely to prove useful either of food or in commerce. Particular attention was to be paid to the natural history of the sea-otter and obtain information concerning the wild sheep, and note particularly all places where whales or seals are found in abundance. Inquiry was to be made into the manners, customs, language, and religion of the natives and information obtained concerning their manufactures, particularly the art of dyeing. He was to keep a regular journal of all occurrences, which journal, together with a complete collection of specimens of the animals, vegetables, and minerals obtained, as well as articles of the cloths, arms, implements and manufactures of the Indians, were to be delivered to H.M. Secretary of State or to such person as he shall appoint to receive them.

—J. Forsyth, "Biographical Note" pp. IX - X, C. F. Newcombe, "Menzies' Journal of Vancouver's Voyage" (1923)

Charles Wilkes

NAVY ARCHIPELAGO is a collection of 25 islands, having the straits of Fuca on the south, the Gulf of Georgia on the north, the Canal de Arro on the west, and Ringgold's Channel on the east. They have been named from distinguished officers late of the U.S. naval service, viz., Rodgers, Chauncey, Hull, Shaw, Decatur, Jones, Blakeley [sic], Perry, Sinclair, Lawrence, Gordon, Percival, and others. Most of them are of moderate elevation. Mount Constitution, on Hull's Island, rises to the height of 2356 feet. Hull's Island is the largest; it is indented by two deep bays, one of which has been called Ironsides, the other Guerriere [sic] Bay. It is composed of reddish granite and conglomerate; in some places the granite is seen to crop out. Both Rodgers and Chauncey Islands partake of the same character. On the north of Rodgers Island, and between it and Hull's, is President's Passage, 8 miles in length, but 1 or 2 in width. This passes into Ontario Roads, between Rodgers and Chauncey Islands, and Little Belt Passage; on the north, the waters flow through Frolic Straits, into Ironsides Bay, and around the Macedonian Crescent, between Blakely and Obstruction, Decatur and Blakely, again into Ringgolds Channel. The soundings throughout these waters are very deep, seldom less than 30 fathoms.

—Charles Wilkes, United States Exploration Expedition Volume IV, Chapter XVI

John S. Lawson
Description of Survey Methods

In this work the steamer was run at a slow speed, and as close to shore as was safe; the courses were taken by compass, and distances by patent log, and the shores sketched as we progressed. Prominent hills, points, and outlying rocks were determined by cross bearings and sextant angles. We came to anchor each afternoon, in time to permit the erection of the observatory, a small portable house, made in panels, and quickly erected, set up the instrument block &c. In this way observations for a time and latitude were obtained about every 40 miles, between which the running of the steamer could be readily reduced and plotted. As soon as we came to anchor at any place, it was my duty to locate the observatory and get the instrument on the ground. Mr. Davidson made the observations, and I recorded. Whenever desirable, sketches were made of our anchorages, I making or assisting in the topography, and the officers of the steamer executing the hydrography. In the sketching of the coast both Mr. D. and I assisted the hydrographic part.

—John S. Lawson, Autobiography of John S. Lawson *(NOAA 2000), p. 24*

George Davidson
Description of San Juan Islands

Bellevue island (San Juan) is the resort of great numbers of Indians, with an extensive fishery near Henry Island, and an old fishing station on the inside of the southeastern extremity...
The Soil of the islands forming the straits is scarce and poor, and very dry during the summer. The islands generally are covered with a thick growth of Oregon Pine, other kinds of wood being exceptional. The highest mountains are Constitution on Orcas, Lake on Cypress, Erie on Fidalgo, and Lummi Peak on Lummi, ranging from 1,200 to 2,500 feet in height. The top of Mount Constitution is destitute of trees. Most of the islands abound in deer, and elk are found in great number on Orcas.
All the islands present the same general geological features; sandstone and conglomerate prevail, in some cases to a thickness of several thousand feet, with a very great dip, which in some instances is almost perpendicular.
There are indications of coal on Patos, Lucia, Orcas, and Lopez. On Orcas (N.W. point) there is said to be a seam thirty-two feet thick...
The straits are navigated only by fishing-vessels. Those arriving from Bellingham coal and vessels of the Hudson's Bay Company invariably pass through Rosario Strait. All traffic in these waters will eventually be carried on by small steamers or tow-boats. A steamer now runs regularly between Olympia and Victoria, and last year made trips to the Columbia River.

—George Davidson, Appendix, Report of the Superintendent of the United States Coast Survey (1855), p.177

North West Boundary Survey
Descriptions of Agricultural Land

In an agricultural point of view San Juan assumes a decidedly prominent place among the rest of the islands of the Sound. Its soil is almost thoroughly good and productive, and in low situated places even rich. In the lower portion of Oak prairie, where in

Winter ponds of water collect, and render the ground sufficiently moist during the Summer season, the soil is very rich and productive, its depth being from 2 ½ to 3 feet. The same can be said of some of the lower portions of the timber land where also grain of every variety could be cultivated with rich returns. According to reliable information, obtained from persons who know the island will [sic], about 50 to 60 claims of 160 acres each of good and valuable land could be laid out. Of the prairie land, about one and one half square miles is situated on the hill sides, the soil is thin and rocky, and only productive of good grass. Some portions also, those lying on the south west side of the island, are so exposed to the sweep of the southern gales that no grain or fruit could be grown there. The violence of these gales is sufficiently shown by the appearance of the trees, whose tops are bent almost at right angles to the remainder of the trunk. All land not fit for cultivation is nevertheless perfectly adapted to grazing purposes. Mr. Griffin estimates one third of the area of the island to be good arable soil, the rest only productive of grass.

—Henry Custer, Geographical Memoir, Appendix D (1859)

W. F. Tolmie
Letter on Hudson's Bay Company Claims on San Juan Island

Victoria V.I. British Columbia
11th November 1867

William G. Smith, Esquire
Secretary

Sir

1. We have now the honor of addressing you on the subject of the losses sustained by the Company at the Island of San Juan since its occupation by use, through damage by State or Federal Acts.
2. Until the occupation of San Juan Island by the Military Forces of the United States in 1859, the whole island was in the possession of the Hudson's Bay Company and was pastured by their flocks of sheep and herds of cattle, horses, and pigs. The Company also carried on farming operations there, hav-

ing had in different localities farm buildings, inclosed fields, sheep stations a wharf and fisheries, particulars of several of which as they existed in 1859 is given below.

3. The arrival of the Military, and of numerous American settlers following in their train, made it impracticable for the Company to continue in the operation for their live stock was dispossessed and deprived of their usual range. The Military and those who supplied them, imported Beef Cattle which were herded on the open lands, and the settlers squatted upon the lands inclosed and unenclosed, taking possession thereof and of the buildings. These aggressions may be considered as consequent on the act of the Federal Government in placing troops on the Island etc and testimony in proof of the same can, if needed, we believe obtained.
4. Thus, interfered with the Company operations had to be gradually discontinued, and their livestock reduced and ultimately withdrawn.
5. In 1858 & 59 the Company owned, and occupied the following amongst other buildings and improvements in the localities now known as

1st Stubbs Point viz   A Fishing Station having thereupon a large log building, and strong Cattle Pens for shipping stock.
2nd Main Station or "Bellevue Farm"
Consisting of several squared log dwelling houses, a Granary, large Barn, and enclosed fields, &c. The United States Military Post is built on part of this Station. A portion of it is leased to an old employé of the Company, named Robert Firth, for a minimal rent, in order to retain possession.
3rd "Frasers Farm" viz Sheep Station, Pens, &c.
4th "Droyen [Dwyer?] do" "   Log dwelling House, Garden and Pens, enclosed fields.
 5th "Blakes   do" " Log House and Pens
 6th "Longacres do" "   Two Log Houses " do.
 7th "Chandlers Prairie" "   Dwelling house " do.
 8th "New Station" "Do.   " do.
 9th "Limestone Station" "   Sheep pens
 10th " John Bull do"   Dwelling house and sheep pen
also a cultivated field.

On the Main Station, Dwyon [Dwyer?] Farm, and Bulls Station land was cultivated by the Company, and the Stations as a whole gave complete command of all the pastures on the Island.

6. In paragraph 4 of Mr Dallas's letter of 20th February 1860 to Mr Secretary Fraser to which we would beg to draw particular attention, the balance of Account against the San Juan Establishment as on 31st May 1859, say for Outfits 1854 to 1858 inclusive – is stated at ₤ 6633.15/5 besides the least of many services of steamers &c rendered to the Island, but for which no charge has ever been made. We now beg to inclose an abstract Statement of the Account thus referred to, exhibiting apart from the Steamboat – and other service rendered as abovementioned, the Company's Outlay in Establishing and stocking the Farms &c on the Island, after crediting proceeds or Returns therefrom each year, and to be regarded as expenses incurred by the Company, with the other uncharged items aforementioned up to that time, in retaining possession of San Juan Island, as a dependency of Vancouver Island. It amounts to ₤ 6633 " 15 " 5 exclusive of interest, which at 5% per annum come to ₤ 3920 " 1 " 20 making all a sum of ₤ 10553 " 16 " 7 as shown in the statements.

7. The above includes a sum of ₤ 1450 13/" transferred in Outfit 1855 to the debit of the United States Government for that Outfit on account of loss sustained, as shown by the Accounts that year transmitted to London – with L 870 " 7 " 10 Interest thereon at 5% per annum for the (12) twelve years from 1855 to 1867, being together ₤ 2321 " 0 " 10 and which we presume is still unpaid in London. In this connexion we beg to refer to Chief Trader Douglas's letter of 28th September 1855 to the Secretary, on the subject of the losses inflicted on the Company by the unlawful proceedings on San Juan Island of certain American citizens, residing in Washington Territory, and pretending to act under authority of its laws. The damages in consequences as claimed against the United States amounted to ₤ 2990 " 13/ " and were by Mr Douglas represented as a moderate estimated of the losses sustained. The details of the same were set forth in a Report and Statement from Mr Griffin the Company's Officer in 1855 and till 1859 and subsequently in charge at San Juan.

We trust that the documents are to be found in the London Office, as we have not been able to find them here. Copy of Mr Douglas's letter therein referred to is enclosed.

8. This aggression which is clearly chargeable against the Territorial Government of Washington Territory is the first on record, although for some time prior to the year 1855, the Legislative Assembly of that Territory pretended to include the Aro Islands in the County of Whatcom, and San Juan is the principle of these. The next aggression recorded is the killing in June or July 1859 of a Boar Pig belonging to the Company at San Juan by a recently arrived Squatter there named Cutler, and this is also to be regarded as a consequence of the Territorial Act of claiming these Islands as United States Territory, although it was ostensibly the immediate cause of the Establishing of troops there by the U. S. General Harney.

9. We also enclose an abstract Statement of Account for Outfit 1859 to 1864 inclusive, showing by amount realized from the Sale of Stock &c. after deducting Wages and Interest as shown in the Statement:

£ 4247.8.2
@ 5% per annum 1147.5.6
£ 5394.13.8

The Company have now no stock on any part of the Island. We have given the above mentioned Accounts in separate Statements, and have calculated the Interest in the particular manner, shown on the documents, as being the most desirable course in our ignorance of the present position of the case, as well as of the manner in which the Governor and Committee purpose dealing with it.

10. The particulars of the Accounts in the two Statements will be found in the detailed Accounts for the several Outfits in London.   I have the honor to be &c &c &c

—W. F. Tolmie
Mike Vouri, The Pig War, (2022), pp. 321-324

Homestead Implements

August Bjork 1889 Shaw	2 axes, 1 maul, oxen, have borrowed other tools of my neighbors
Anthony Buckner 1880 Shaw	2 scythes, 3 rakes, 1 fork, 3 hoes, 1 ax, 1 maul, 1 cross cut saw, 1 hand saw and small tools
Hans Christiansen 1882 Shaw	2 plows. Harrow. 2 Mattox. 3 hoes. 2 spades. Shovel. 2 Potatoe hoes. 2 hay forks. 3 axes. Cross cut saw. Maul & wedges etc.
David A. Gailey 1890	3 Axes, 1 Crosscut Saw, 1 Brush Hook, 1 Grind Stone, 1 Sledge & 2 Wedges, 2 Spades, 1 Garden Hoe.
William Hambly 1888 Orcas	Wagon, Cultivator, Plow, Harrow, 2 axes, Shovel, Brush hook, Scythe, Hoe, Cross cut Saw, Steel Maul & wedges, Flaw[?] & small tools.
Newton Jones 1888 Shaw	1 shovel 1 mattock 2 axes 1 cross cut saw
Alex McDonald 1884 Shaw	Shovel, Spade, 2 hay forks & rake, Mattox, Cross cut saw, Maul & 3 steel wedges, Steel Sledge 2 axes Brush hook Grass scythe & small tools & Hay Drag.
Antoni Marino 1883 Shaw	3 axes, 1 maul, 2 wedges, 2 hatchets(?), 2 saws, 1 shovel, 1 brush hook, 1 grub hoe, 1 potatoe digger
Thomas Mulno 1882 San Juan	Cultivator, Harrow, 2 hoes, 2 spades, Shovel, Pick, 2 Mattox, Brushhook + Scythe, Crosscut Saw, Maul + wedges, Hay Scythes + rakes
John L. Murray 1889 Shaw	1 hoe 1 rake 1 shovel 2 axes 1 maul & 4 wedges 1 cross cut saw
Archibald Rader 1880 Shaw	Plow harrow 4 hoes 2 mattox 1 Pick 3 pitch forks timothy syth[sic] and grain cradle. 2 rakes cross cut saw full chest of carpenters tools
Theodore Tharald 1888 Shaw	4 axes 1 mattock 1 shovel 1 spade 1 hoe 1 hay rake 1 scythe 1 pitch fork
Bert Tift 1883 Shaw	Plow. Harrow. Seed drill & cultivator. Spade. Shovel. 4 hoes. 3 axes. 3 Mattox. 3 scythes complete. Grain cradle, 2 cross cut saws, Steel Maul & Wedges

Lila Hannah Firth
San Juan Island Range Wars

...after the Hudson Bay Co.'s sheep were moved off Mount Dallas, my father in some way got a bunch of Goats, & put up there on the mountain, & it was not many years before there were hundreds of them, they multiplied so rapidly! At times, the mountain was just spotted with Goats, at times Father, & Mother, would go out on Horseback & herd a bunch of them in for killing, marking & etc. Finally there came in from the north side of the mountain some sheepmen, who wanted the range for their sheep so they started shooting the goats. Dead goats were found lying all over the mountain. There seemed nothing could be done about it, as the property was no-mans-land, & the men & boys would go out in droves it seemed, as, hundreds of goats were found there dead,

scattered all over the mountains sides. Father did not want to kill their sheep so, in time the sheep men got the range. My Father was a good honest straight-forward Christian man, & detested such treachery as that & he knew well, who these parties were, & some of their offsprings are running about the Island yet.

—Lila Hannah Firth, Early Life on San Juan Island *(1943), p. 9*

An Act to Regulate the Running of Sheep at Large in San Juan County

Section 1. *Be it enacted by the Legislative Assembly of the Territory of Washington, That it shall be unlawful for sheep to run at large in the county of San Juan, until the actual legal owner thereof has obtained a permit therefore form the board of commissioners of said county.*

Sec. 2. Permits shall be granted only to citizens of the United States, or those who have declared on oath their intention to become such, in accordance with the naturalization laws of the United States, and who are also actual residents of said county...

—Local and Private Laws, Laws of Washington Territory *1875*

Tools and Building Materials

Tools

3 crosscut saws	12 pick helves
1 pit saw	1 frow
12 spades	12 whitewash brushes
6 shovels	1 water brush
1 chest carpenter's tools	12 sweeping brushes
12 iron wedges	12 scrubbing brushes
24 felling axes	1 hand trowel
6 timber dogs	2 plastering trowels
2 cold chisels	20 pointing trowels
2 hammers	1 solder iron
24 ax handles	4 sticks of solder

Lumber

"A small quantity of lumber for cooking a building house"
5,000 feet of planking
  800 feet of scantling
  300 feet of scantling 2 X 3
  300 feet of scantling 2 x 5
    4 sashes
10,000 shingles
4,000 shingles
3,000 feet of boarding
  500 feet of batten

Hardware

80 lbs. 3½-inch nails	6 locks, complete
150 lbs. 3-inch nails	1 [lb.?] 1-inch brads
155 lbs. 2½-inch nails	6 iron bars, 5-ft., each
130 lbs. 2-inch nails	14 ft. bar iron
115 lbs. shingle nails	6 meat hooks
6 cant hooks	12 doz. packets of tin tacks
6 hinges	

Paint

1½ gal. turpentine	For a boat
2 gal. raw oil	12 lbs. white lead
2 gal. boiled oil	6 lbs. black paint
1 "Dryers Patent"	1 gal. linseed oil
25 lbs. white lead	1 gal. boiled oil
25 lbs. black paint	

Miscellaneous Items

2 knives for sharpening	3 horses
6 oars	2 bridles & saddles
4 oarlocks	4,560 lbs. hay
12 [?] glue	3,800 lbs. oats
6 meat hooks	3,040 lbs. straw
96 rolls paper	1 curry comb
692 yards calico	1 mane comb
1 stove for guardhouse	1 horse brush
12 mops	2 leathers [?]
2 doors	3 lbs. leather
1 iron back piece, officers stove	2 pitchforks

—Erwin N. Thompson, Historic Resource Study (1972), pp. 201-202

Homestead Houses

Joe Friday 1877 San Juan	Hewed Log House 18 by 24 ft. square with Doors & Windows
David A. Gailey 1890 Orcas	Log house 14 x 26, 2 rooms, I Door, 3 Windows, Val $175.
Jeremiah N. Griswold 1885 Shaw	"There was a house, barn and out buildings. I bought these of Louis Julian." Witness: Log & Lumber House with Doors 3 Rooms and Windows
Samuel H. Gross 1882 San Juan	A hewed log house 14 by 20 feet, 3 windows, 3 doors, fireplace
James Guard 1892 San Juan	Log house 12 x 14 1 door 1 window roofed and floored
William Hambly 1888 Orcas	House 20x20 5 rooms 5 doors 4 windows Ceiled over head and papered inside Val. $100
James M. Hannah 1882 San Juan	Dwelling 16 by 32 feet, 5 rooms, 5 windows, 8 doors, 2 brick fireplaces
Charles Hawkins 1877 San Juan	Lumber house 20 x 30 feet square with 4 rooms windows doors chimney
Jennie Hellen 1889 Shaw	A lumber house about 28 x 24 ft 1½ story 5 rooms 4 doors 9 windows, floor ceiled. Witness says "a frame house 18 x 24 ft 1½ story floored, roofed and ceiled. 3 rooms 4 doors 4 windows an addition to the main building 12 x 16 feet with panty and porch"
William H. Higgins 1881 San Juan	A dwelling 12 x 24 (log house) 3 rooms, 4 doors, 3 windows
Claus Sax Hinrichs 1881 San Juan	House...15 x 22 feet having a shake roof lumber floor one door two windows one room fire place & chimney is all furnished and comfortable to live in
Harvey Hudson 1883 Shaw	Built a house of lumber
Alfred Jones 1892 San Juan	A hewed cedar log house 14 x 18 ft. 1½ story 3 windows 2 rooms 1 door
Newton Jones 1888 Shaw	1 lumber house 16 x 24 3 rooms 3 doors 4 windows Val. $150
Pierre Lami 1883 San Juan	Dwelling 17 by 25 feet, 6 windows, 2 doors, fireplace
Alex N. McDonald 1884 Shaw	Hewed cedar log house 12 x 14, 1 door, 1 window cedar shakes roof planed cedar floor Val $50. Witnesses called it "split cedar log house" and "a cedar log house hewed inside"
Antoni Marino 1883 Shaw	10 x 12 ten feet high built of lumber tongued & grooved floor. Planed lumber ceiling, 1 door, 1 window, shingle roof Val $100. Witness said house had a porch.
Christian V. Mork 1903 Lopez	Frame House 20 x 24 feet, 4 rooms.
John L. Morrison 1879 Shaw	Hewed log house with a lumber addition with Doors, Windows & Chimney 1½ story high ("log part of house was there when I bought it")

John L. Murray 1884 Shaw	The main building is built of logs 12 x 16 has 1 door 1 window has an addition built of lumber 8 x 16 has another addition 8 x 10 built of logs val. $150. Witness says 2 additions and 3 rooms.
Thomas Mulno 1882 San Juan	Frame Lumber house 22X30, 1 ½ stories, 7 rooms, 8 doors + 10 windows house ceiled throughout—Value $500.00
Oliver O'Hara 1872 Shaw	Dwelling 16 by 26 feet, 2 rooms, 4 windows, 3 doors, fireplace
Hugh Park 1872 Shaw	Log house 12 x 14 feet, 1 door, 1 window, fireplace
Archibald Rader 1880 Shaw	A lumber house L shape 24 by 48 feet. 7 rooms and shed. 7 doors & 8 windows wood shingled roof good floor val. $500. Witness says "well finished for country" and adds "weatherboarded."
Matthias Paul Rethlefsen 1879 San Juan	A one-room log house, 20 x 24 feet, with a shingle roof, lumber floor, two doors, five windows, and household and kitchen furniture
James Ross 1883 Shaw	There was a house built by Martin Thomas and I purchased the same from him.
George R. Shaw 1881 Shaw	A log house 14 x 16 ft 1 room 1 door 1 window. Witness adds "1 story" and "1 room"
Timothy G. Stewart 1890 Shaw	A good house 14 x 16
Charles Stillman 1889 Shaw	Log house 16 x 18 with lean to 12 x 18 frame. One witness says 15 x 20.
Henry Stuve 1889 San Juan	Lumber house 10 x 22 two rooms, 2 doors, 3 windows, food cedar shake roof, tongue and grooved floor Val. $150
John Sweeney 1888 Orcas	Log house 14 x 22 3 rooms 3 doors ceiled overhead well furnished inside good roof & floor $50-75
Theodore Tharald 1888 Shaw	Log house 14 X 16 1 door 2 windows $60 New house partly built—24 X 32 $300
Bert Tift 1883 Shaw	Hewn cedar log house 16½ x 16½ feet 1½ stories high. Porch one end & side, 2 rooms 2 doors & 3 windows, good roof and floor bal. $75.00. Frame wood house 12 x 14 val $25.00
Charles Tift 1889 Shaw	Wood house 12 x 14. One witness says "lumber house 16 x 18 2 rooms 3 doors 3 windows floored roofed and ceiled. Other witness says "16 x 20 house 2 rooms 2 doors 4 windows."
W.D. Tift 1889 Shaw	House 24 x 26 little house 14 x 16. Witness calls them "new house" and "old house."
Thomas Wakefield 1890 Shaw	House 14 x 16
William Wright 1885 Orcas	Log house there (1874); built lumber house 24 by 36 5 rooms doors windows chimney

Homestead Furnishings

August Bjork 1889 Shaw	1 cookstove & fixtures, 1 bed, 2 tables, 3 chairs 1 rocking chair & 1 lounge
Anthony Buckner 1880 Shaw	2 beds, 3 chairs, 2 tables, 1 cooking stove complete
Hans Christiansen 1882 Shaw	Cooking stove complete, tables, 4 chairs, 2 beds, Clock, Tableware, Milk pans, etc.
David A. Gailey 1890	1 Cook Stove, 2 Beds, 2 tables, 1 Writing Desk.
William Hambly 1888 Orcas	Cooking Stove complete, heating Stove, 2 beds, 5 chairs, Sewing machine, Clock, Lounge, 2 lamps, 2 tables & table ware. Cloths wringer, &c.
Newton Jones 1888 Shaw	2 beds 2 stoves(?) 6 chairs 1 table 1 clock 1 cubboard 2 trunks Dishes of all kinds
Alex McDonald 1884 Shaw	Cooking stove and utensils, Table & Table ware for three. Bed & bedding, chair & 2 stools, Clock, looking glass, Lamp
Antoni Marino 1883 Shaw	1 bed & bedstead, 1 table, 1 chair, 1 stove, and cooking utensils 21 pieces
Thomas Mulno 1882 San Juan	Working Range & utensils, 3 tables and tableware, 13 chairs 2 lounges, 3 beds, cubboard, 5 lamps, 4 clocks, one bedroom set
John L. Murray 1889 Shaw	2 beds 6 chairs 1 table 1 cubboard 1 cook stove & fixtures
Archibald Rader 1880 Shaw	4 beds 6 chairs 4 tables cooking stove complete Clock looking glass etc.
Theodore Tharald 1888 Shaw	1 cooking stove & fixtures, 2 Beds, 1 table 3 chairs
Bert Tift 1883 Shaw	Cooking stove & utensils 2 tables and tableware 12 chairs 2 stands Cubbard 4 beds & bedding 3 clocks 4 lamps

Homestead Improvements

Charley Anderson 1891 Shaw	6 ½ acres clear and cultivated and fenced. 315(?) fruit trees four strawberries
August Bjork 1889 Shaw	1 chicken house 12 x 12 $25 1 acre cleared & fenced $125 3 acres slashed $45
Anthony Buckner 1880 Shaw	Lumber barn shingle roof 18 x 21 val $100. 40 acres cleared, picket fence, 3 acres in orchard val. $300.00 4 acres slashed picket fence in pasture $150.00 100 acres fenced val $100.00.
Alfred Burke 1886 Shaw	Barn Out house Well Fencing Orchard Ditching Value of same $1200.00
Sampson G. Chadwick 1884 Lopez	Out Buildings. Sheep sheds & Hay sheds. One mile fencing. Fruit Trees. Four acres under cultivation 20 acres cleared. Value $500.
Christian Christensen 1890 Shaw	Barn [$25]; store house [$15]; 5 acres cleared & under cultivation [$100] 1 acre slashed [$7] & fenced [$50]– ditching [$50] well [$10]
Hans Christiansen 1882 Shaw	Cedar post barn 57 x 60, good cedar shake roof $150. Chicken house, Smoke house, wood shed, pig hose val $600. 150 acres about of land fenced and under good cultivation 125 fruit trees val $600. Between 25 & 30 acres slashed & partly cleared & fenced val $175.

Elihu Fowler 1888 Shaw	Barn, 4 chicken houses, wool shed, 225 fruit trees, small fruit, 6 ac. Cultivated 5 or 6 ac slashed & seeded, fencing 30 rods ditching, 2 wells, 2 ac. slashed
Joe Friday 1877 San Juan	Barn & chicken house. About Fifty acres enclosed with a Rail Fence
David A. Gailey 1890	1¼ under cultivation Val $150. 4 acres Slashed and partly Cleared, Val $200. 100 Rods of fencing Val $50.
Jeremiah N. Griswold 1885 Shaw	Barn. Work Shop. Orchard. Fencing. Ten acres cleared & fenced. 40 acres enclosed. Value of the same $700.00
William Hambly 1889 Orcas	Cedar Post Barn 32x42 Val. $100. Chicken house, wood house, smoke house and outbuilding Val. $45.$\underline{00}$ 17½ acres cleared fenced with cedar rails under cultivation & pickets, 293 fruit trees ⅓ bearing Val. $775. 5 acres slashed Val $50. 215 rods of ditching Val. 90
Jennie Hellen 1889 Shaw	Chicken house, wood house, root house & cellar, 2 ac. cleared & cultivated 5 ac. slashed 135 fruit trees fencing 1400 feet picket fence some draining small fruits well
Harvey Hudson 1883 Shaw	Enclosed two acres with picket fence Planted 40 fruit trees and enclosed about five acres with a rail fence. Witness says "Well dug. Road & Trails cut."
Newton Jones 1888 Shaw	1 chicken house 10 x 12 $15 1 cow shed $20 1 acre cleared fenced & under cultivation $150 1 ac slashed & burned off and seed in clover 80 rods of Rail Fence $100 2 wells $25
Alex N. McDonald 1884 Shaw	Cedar log 2 chicken houses 10 x 16 [&] 10 x 11 cedar log root house 9 x 12 feet, 7 acres under cultivation & 2 ac. slashed and seeded down in Timothy and Clover, 40 rods ditching 35 fruit trees set out val. $300
Antoni Marino 1883 Shaw	12 ac. plowed val $50 5 ac. cleared, excepting for stumps all sown in grass $250 9 ac. fenced $150 16 fruit trees total val $550
Christian V. Mork 1903 Lopez	Frame Barn 18 x 28 ft., chicken house 17 x 21 root house 10 x 12, well, picket fence around 2 acres. Value $900.
John L. Morrison 1879 Shaw	Well, Barn, Ditching, Fruit Trees, Wood Shed, Fencing, Val. $1500; Witness said: "1½ story high Barn of lumber 30 by 86 feet square with a shed. Fencing. Well. Value $1200."
Thomas Mulno 1882 San Juan	Post Barn with sheds, Lumber Chicken house, and a root house and hog house. Val. $150. 60 acres fenced with rails and balance with brush fence. 50 acres slashed 7 acres under Cultivation, an orchard 60 trees 40 bearing, bal. 1000.
John L. Murray 1884 Shaw	1 chicken house 10 x 12 val $20 Barn started but not finished val $10 1¼ acre under cultivation 88 fruit trees planted val $250 4 ac. of slashing $40
Oliver O'Hara 1872 Shaw	shed, fenced and ditched about 40 acres val $500
Christian Olsen 1888 Shaw	2 acres cleared 5 or 6 acres slashed some fencing value $450
Hugh Park 1872 Shaw	Barn and outbuilding, orchard, 16 acres fenced [8 acres cultivated], and ditches
Archibald Rader 1880 Shaw	Chicken house & hog house val $25 Orchard of 100 bearing trees of different kinds val $100 clearing 2 acre and picket fence $100 40 acres slashed, burnt off and seeded val $300 fencing claim $100

James Ross 1883 Shaw	Slashed 12 acres preparatory to burning
George R. Shaw 1881 Shaw	1½ ac cleared & under cultivation 4 slashed 2 ac. fenced ["good cedar rail"]well
Timothy G. Stewart 1890 Shaw	Cleared 3½ ac. [Witness says "several acres of slashing, partly burned"]
Charles Stillman 1889 Shaw	Barn, Root house, about 15 acres in good fences An Orchard of 300 trees in bearing. A good well #500 ["6 or 7 acres meadow']
Theodore Tharald 1888 Shaw	Barn 24 x 30 $100 Chicken house 10 x10 $20 75 Rods Picket Fence $100 150 Rod Rail Fence $140 12 Acres cleared $900
Bert Tift 1883 Shaw	Two cedar log barns val. $75.00 30 acres under rail and picket fence. About 20 acres cleared and mostly in grass. 4 acres under cultivation. An orchard of over 100 trees and half bearing. Smallfruit & berries val $1,000. [One witness adds "Hewed cedar log Root & Milk houses & Privy val $300"; Another ""Chicken house"]
Charles Tift 1889 Shaw	Stable 16 x 16 feet [$30]; wood house 12 x 14 feet [$25]root house 14 x 16 feet [$25] chicken house 12 x 14 feet [$20] cleared 1½ acres [$150] slashed 2 acres [$16] 45 fruit trees [$20] some small fruits [$5] 6 acres fenced [$50] 30 rods ditching [$25] well [$10]
W.D. Tift 1889 Shaw	Barn 16 x 24 3 hen houses 4 sheds 12 acres cultivated 300 fruit trees well, fencing, small fruit
Thomas Wakefield 1890 Shaw	Barn 20 x 36, wood shed, chicken house, well, picket and rail fencing, 200 fruit trees, 5 acres cleared [Witness adds "hog pens"]

Edible Marine Invertebrates
(adapted from Suttles 1951: 65-69,505)

Echinoderms
- Green Sea Urchin (*Stongylocentrotus droebachiensis*)
- Purple Sea Urchin (*S. purpuratus*)
- Giant Red Sea Urchin (*S. franciscanus*)
- Giant Sea Cucumber (*Parastichopus califonrnicus*)

Mollusks
- Giant Pacific Chiton (*Cryptonchiton stelleri*)
- Black Chiton (*Katharina tunicate*)
- Lined Chiton (*Tonicela lineata*)
- Mossy Chiton (*Mopalia muscosa*)
- Purple Whelk (*Nucella [Thais] lamellose*)
- Native [Olympia] Oyster (*Ostrea lurida*)
- Edible [Blue] Mussel (*Mytilus edulus*)
- Heart Cockle (*Clinocardium nuttallii*)
- Bent-Nosed Clam (*Macoma nasuta*)
- Butter Clam (*Saxidomus giganteus*)
- Horse Clam (*Tresus capax*)
- Littleneck Clam (*Protothaca staminea*)
- Sand Clam (*Macoma secta*)
- Soft-Shell Clam (*Mya arenaria*)

Crustaceans
- Acorn Barnacle (*Balanus glandula*)
- Thatched Barnacle (*Semibalanus cariosus*)
- Dungeness Crab (*Cancer magister*)
- Red Rock Crab (*C. productus*)

Edible Plants
(adapted from Suttles 1951:57-65,503)

Berries and Fruits
- Blackberry (*Rubus ursinus*)
- Blackcap (*Rubus leucodermis*)
- Native Cranberry (*Oxycoccos oxycoccos*)
- Crabapple (*Malus fusca*)

Blueberry, Blue Elderberry (*Sambucus nigra sssp. Cerulea*)
Red Elderberry (*Sambucus racemose*)
Gooseberry, Currant (*Ribes spp.*)
Huckleberry (*Vaccinium parvifolium*)
Black Hawthorn (*Crataegus douglasii*)
Indian Plum (*Oemlaria cerasiformis*)
Kinnikinic, Bearberry (*Arctostaphylos uva-ursi*)
Oregon Grape (*Berberis aquiflolium & B. nervosa [formerly Mahonia]*)
Salal berries (*Gaultheria shallon*)
Salmonberry (*Rubus spectabilis*)
Serviceberry (*Amelanchier alnifolia [ssp. florida not accepted]*)
Soapberry (*Shepherdia canadensis*)
Little or Dwarf Rose (*Rosa gymnocarpa*)
Woodland Strawberry (*Fragaria vesca*)
Thimbleberry (*Rubus parviflorus*)

Bulbs and Roots
Great Camas (*Camassia leichtlinii*)
Small or Purple Camas (*C. quamash*)
"American Carrot" (*Daucus pusillus?*)
"Carrot" (*?*)
Brake Fern, Bracken (*Pteridium aquilinum*)
Tiger Lily (*Lilium colombianum*)
Hooker's Onion (*Allium acuminatum*)
Nodding Onion (*Allium cernuum*)
Rice-Root, Chocolate Lily (*Fritillaria lanceolota*)
Wapato (*Sagittaia latifolia*)

Sprouts and Stems
Cow Parsnip (*Heracleum lanatum*)
Dock   (*Rumex occidentalis*)
Common Horsetail (*Equisetum arvense*)
Salmonberry (*Rubus spectabilis*)
Thimbleberry (*Rubus parviflorus*)

Fishes And Other Seafood
(adapted from Suttles 1951: 114-132,506)

Salmon
    Spring, King, Chinook (*Oncorhynchus tschawytscha*)
    Sockeye, Red, Blueback (*O. nerka*)
    Humpback, Pink (*O. gorbuscha*)
    Silver, Coho (*O. kisutch*)
    Dog, Chum (*O. keta*)
    Steelhead (*Salmo gairdnerii*)

Flounder and Halibut
    Starry Flounder (*Platichthys stellatus*)
    Pacific Halibut (*Hippoglossus stenolepis*)

Sturgeon
    White (*Acinenser tansitinanus*)
    Green (*A. mediostris*)

Rock Fish

Herring
    Pacific Herring (*Clupea harengus pallasi*)

Smelt
    Surf Smelt (*Hypomesus pretiosus*)
    Euchalon, Candlefish (*Thaleichthys pacificus*)

Dogfish
    Spiny Dogfish (*Squalus acanthias*)

Octopus
    Giant Pacific Octopus (*Octopus dofleini*)

Seal and Porpoise
    Harbor Seal (*Phoca vitulina*)
    Dall's Porpoise (*Phocoenoides dalli*)
    Harbor Porpoise (*Phocoena Phocoena*)

Homestead Livestock

August Bjork 1889 Shaw	Oxen
Anthony Buckner 1880 Shaw	3 cows and 4 calves
Hans Christiansen 1882 Shaw	19 head of cattle 25 sheep 7 hogs 5 doz. poultry
William Hambly 1888 Orcas	3 Horses, 2 Cows, 2 young Cattle, 12 sheep, 3 hogs, 4 doz chickens
Newton Jones 1888 Shaw	60 chickens
Alex McDonald 1884 Shaw	2 cows & a calf & about 100 chickens
Thomas Mulno 1882 San Juan	6 head of Cattle, 18 sheep, 4 hogs, 40 chickens
John L. Murray 1889 Shaw	40 chickens
Archibald Rader 1880 Shaw	100 head Cotswold sheep 3 hogs and 1 cow 2 doz chickens
Theodore Tharald 1888 Shaw	1 Cow and Calf. 12 sheep. Mink took chickens.
Bert Tift 1883 Shaw	Two milch cows, pair of work oxen, 10 sheep, 3 hogs, 4 doz poultry (7 head cattle that's not his)

Appraisal of Property, Augustin Hibbard Probate, January 30, 1871

Wooden Dwelling House $1,000.00

Store Room
6 kegs nails.. 15.00
2 sets block & tackle 30.00
9 hammers, 5 shovels, 16 drills, crowbars, & picks for quarry purposes... 50.00
1 large crosscut saw & wedges 7.50

Kitchen
Cook stove & furniture 30.00
Crockery & cutlery for 16... 20.00
Tables & cupboards 10.00

Dining Room
Tables, benches, scales, & bell 15.00

Sleeping Apartment
8 iron cots and wood bedstead	30.00
14 straw mattresses	30.00
9 blankets	18.00

Parlor and Bedroom
1 bedstead	4.00
4 mattresses	8.00
10 blankets	20.00
1 feather bed, 2 bedspreads	7.00
8 arm chairs @ $10; 3 tables	15.00
1 map; 1 wash stand & bowl	4.00

Cooper Shop
1 wood building	100.00
1 set cooper's tools	30.00
Bunches of stave horses	10.00
1 ? stove	5.00
Lb stock on hand	10.00

Black Smith Shop
One wooden shed	10.00
Anvil, bellows, tongs, hammer, and vice	15.00

One stone lime drawer kiln lined/brick in good order	1750.00
4 Outside log houses	40.00
Blasted and broken rock	45.00
45 cords firewood not hauled	69.50
24 cords firewood at kiln	60.00
1230 empty barrels	615.00
One two-horse wagon	175.00
One wharf	60.00
Land claims	2500.00

—*Washington State North West Regional Archives,
San Juan County Probate Files*

List of Property of William F. Taylor
Sold at Sheriffs sale.
San Juan January 28, 1874

One House San Juan hotel	$52.50
One House	155.00
One Billiard Table	51.00
One show case	17.00
One carpenters chest of tools	31.50
One stove	12.50
One iron safe	15.00
One lot of furniture	10.00
One box of tools	7.50
One book case	6.00
" ox yoke	5.50
" Howe's scale	6.00
Chairs bedsteads & mattresses	4.25
Remnants of grocery stores	<u>74.00</u>
Total	$447.50

—Irwin N. Thompson, *Historic Resource Study (1972)*

Inventory of Goods
J. K. Bowken Store San Juan Town
November 1865

50 gal. rum	8 lbs coffee	3 ax handles
50 " sherry wine	8 cans oysters	50 lbs. tobacco
30 " whiskey	20 ½-pints champagne	5 bottles pepper
3 " syrup	½ box starch	5 tins sardines
1 bbl. vinegar	2 axes	2 lbs. coffee
½ " cider	9 lbs tea	6 bags salt
1 sack oats	4 bottles pepper	1 case Scotch
5 " potatoes	6 doz. tins sardines	1 case claret
23 bottles cloves	39 cases gins	130 gal. port
22 " mustard	12 cases brandy	6 boxes "Segars"
21 " allspice	7 " Old Tom gin	5 cases champagne
23 " sage	25 gal. porter	5 doz. pipes
27 boxes bleaching	17 " ale	20 gal. coal oil
20 lbs sugar	12 brooms	1 doz. lamps
3 chests tea	1 box Castile soap	205 yds. Alpaca
6 mats sugar	1 ream paper	1½ doz. gloves
6 " rice	1 box yeast powder	4 coats
1 box coffee	10 sacks oatmeal	30 shirts
1 sack coffee	10 " cornmeal	24 Crimea shirts
½ bbl. sugar	10 " buckwheat flour	24 shirts
1 " w. sugar	10 gross clay pipes	3 doz Scotch rubber combs
2 doz. English pickles	1 box pepper sauce	1 box Windsor soap
*2 doz. peaches	2 gross matches	1 doz. brushes
*2 " turkey	5 bbl. flour	½ doz. guitar strings
*2 " chicken	4 boxes soap	1 case boots
*2 " goose	3 doz. green peas	1 " shoes
*2 " corn	1 sack beans	3 doz. socks
*2 doz. lobster	25 " salt	10 pr. pants
3 boxes raisins	2 doz neckties	
1 box tacks	2 " suspenders	
* In tins.		

—Irwin N. Thompson, Historic Resource Study (1972), p. 186.

Mortgages And Loans

Date	Borrower	Lender	Amount	Terms	Security
1871	John Little	William Taylor	$159.00	2%/month	34 lambs
1873	Peter Person	Waterman & Katz	$48.10	1%/month	12 ac oats 2 ac peas 9 ac barley
1873	Peter Person	Waterman & Katz	$126.51	1%/month	12 ac oats 2 ac peas 9 ac barley
1874	Stephen Boyce	Henry Saunders	$609.25	?	?
1873	John Briggs Paul K. Hubbs, Jr.	Rothschild & Company	$300.00	1½%/month	Goods and livestock
1874	Ebin Watson	Augustus Hoffmeister	$533.50	?	?
1874	William Smith	Bowker & Tod	$100.00	2%/month	sheep
1874	William Smith	Bowker & Tod	$259.88.	2%/month	sheep
1874	William Taylor	Rothschild & Company	$685.05	1½%/month	Possessions @ Wells Fargo
1877	John Anderson James Peers	Israel Katz	$66.38	1%/month	Sheep?
1877	John Anderson James Peers	Israel Katz	$50.38	2%/month	Sheep?

Washington State Northwest Regional Archives, Samuel H. Gross Insolvency

Petition of Samuel H. Gross for Insolvency

In the District Court for the 3rd Judicial District of Washington Territory holding terms at Port Townsend, Jefferson County

In the matter of the application of Samuel H. Gross an insolvent debtor.

To the Hon. Roger S. Green Justice of the Supreme Court of Washington Territory and Judge of the 3rd Judicial District therein.

The petition of Samuel H. Gross respectfully shows.

That he is now and has been continuously since the month of May A.D. 1868 a resident of what is now the County of San Juan in Washington Territory, and has been during all of said time and is now a citizen of the United States and has a wife and four children.

That he owes debts amounting to about twenty six hundred dollars.

That he is unable to pay the same in full.

That he desires to be discharged from his said debts, and that he is willing to execute an assignment of all of his property for the benefit of all his creditors, and that he desires to obtain the benefit of an Act of the Legislative Assembly of Washington Territory approved Jan 31st 1864 entitled "An Act in Relation to Insolvent Debtors".

That the following is a statement of the circumstances, which compel him to surrender his property to his creditors, to wit:

That in the year 1868 he settled on San Juan Island, in said San Juan County, upon a land claim. That at that time he had two thousand five hundred dollars in money. That he invested in cattle and sheep, about twelve hundred dollars. That in the year 1869, he, thinking to obtain a better claim moved to another part of the Island and took another piece of land, and expended the remainder of his money in ditching, ~~and~~ clearing, ~~and~~ fencing and erecting necessary buildings upon said claim, and contracted debts to the amount of about five hundred dollars. That after said land was improved and had raised one crop the land would not yield enough to pay the labor of cultivation, and was worthless. That it became necessary for him to obtain other lands in order to support his family. That he was required to pay interest on the debts as contracted at about 2 per ct per month and interest accumulated upon the unpaid interest. In the fall of 1874 he moved upon the ~~farm~~ claim where he now resides and has taken the same as a Homestead, under the laws of the United States.

That the cattle and sheep first purchased by him have many of them been lost by unavoidable accident. Fifty sheep were poisoned in two days by eating poisonous weeds in a swamp nearby and many others lost in the same way at other times. A number of cattle was lost by missing, and some by hard weather in the winter. In the year 1874 he lost his winter crop except of the value of sixteen dollars, by a frost in the month of June.

That debts have increased since 1874 and payment of high rates of interest have eaten up his property and made it impossible for him ever to pay his debts in full.

Your petitioner respectfully refers as a part of his petition to a schedule herewith annexed, containing a summary statement of his affairs with a list of his creditors with the amount due each; also a full and complete inventory of all his property with its true cash value as near as the same can be ascertained.

Wherefore your petitioner prays that he may be adjudged an insolvent debtor, that he be allowed to make an exception of his estate, and that he be discharged from his debts in pursuance of the said Act of the Legislative Assembly of said Territory.

And your petitioner as in duty bound will ever pray.
Samuel H. Gross

Washington State Northwest Regional Archives,
Samuel H. Gross Insolvency

Samuel H. Gross, Exhibit One, Account of Sales

Description	Purchaser	Price	
368 lbs Wool @ 18 cts per lb	I. Katz	66.	24
2 Chisels	Mr. Ross		75
1 Cradle	I. Katz	1.	00
1 Broad Ax	I. Katz		75
1 Bundle Hayrake	I. Katz		25
1 Horse Collar	I. Katz	1.	50
1 Ox Chain	I. Katz		25
1 Rasp	Mr Douglas		25
2 Pr. Sheep Shears	I. Katz		25
1 Auger	I. Katz		25
2 Scythes & Snaths	I. Katz		75
1 Brush Hook	I. Katz		75
Harness and Chain	I. Katz		50
1 Scythe & Snath	Mr Fleming	1.	50
1 Scythe & Snath	Mr Sandwith		87½
1 Shovel	I. Katz		12½
3 Rakes	I. Katz		87½
1 Brush Hook	Mr Smith		75
1 Spade	Mr Fleming		62½
1 Pick	Mr Sandwith		25
1 Lot of Sacks	I. Katz		12½
3 Pitchforks	I. Katz		87½
3 Hoes	Black Jack		37½
1 Grindstone	Mr French		62½
3 Axes	I. Katz		25
2 Plows	I. Katz	3.	00
1 Harrow	I. Katz	1.	25
2 Handsaws	I. Katz		62½
1 Monkeywrench	Mr Ross		75
2 Planes	Cash		75
1 Roller	---		00
1 Ox Cart	I. Katz	20.	00
1 Haypress	I. Katz	4.	50
1 Yoke of Oxen	Mr McCurdy	80.	00
40 Chickens	I. Katz	10.	50
1 Lot of Timothy Seed	Mr Larson	1.	25
3 Steers	I. Katz	17.	00
1 Cow	I. Katz	7.	00
158 Sheep @ $1.75	Mr Smith	276.	50
1 lot of Sheep	I. Katz	7.	00
23 Hogs @ $2.50	I. Katz	57.	50
		$572.	86

Washington State Northwest Regional Archives,
Samuel H. Gross Insolvency

Creditors of Samuel H. Gross

Name of Creditor	Nature of Securities	Amount
John Keddy	Promissory note, dated Nov. 17th 1876 for $120. Borrowed money at 2 percent per month secured by chattel mortgage on Forty (40) head of sheep, and one yoke of oxen	120.00
Charles O. French	Promissory note dated Dec. 14th 1878 for $120.00 borrowed money, with interest at the rate of 6 per cent per annum, secured by chattel mortgage on one hundred and twenty head of sheep and thirty head of hogs.	120.00
Israel Katz	Mortgage dated July 1878 on growing crop on my farm in San Juan Island W.T. to secure pay of said five hundred dollars. Paid on said mortgage Two Hundred & Seventy ($270) dollars, leaving balance of	230.00
Charles Ostergard	Promissory note date Dec. 1877 at 1 per cent per month, given for goods wares and merchandise	85.00
John Anderson	Note dated Dec. 1877 at 1 per cent per month, given for cattle	30.00
James Fleming	Note for $50. dated July 19th 1876 at 2 per cent per month for borrowed money -- $24 paid Dec. 1878	50.00
Charles O. French	Note for cash, labor and grain date Dec. 1878	120.00
John Brown	Note dated April 1876 with int. at 2 per cent per month	20.00
Adam Neighbor	Note date Nov 30th 1874	50.00
Israel Katz	Account for goods wares merchandise growing 2 per cent per month since Dec. 1877	1315.00
Israel Katz	Account for goods wares & merchandise	400.00
James McCurdy	Account for goods Feb. 1877	16.00
Charles O. French	Account for cash loaned	20.00
Charles O. French	Account for work & labor	12.00

Washington State Northwest Regional Archives,
Samuel H. Gross Insolvency

The Excursion to San Juan

The steamer enterprise with the San Juan excursionists, numbering about 180 ladies and gentlemen, returned to the Hudson[sic] Bay Company's wharf last evening at 9 o'clock, having been absent about 11 hours. We learn that the affair was successful... Bellevue was reach about noon, and a landing effected in open boats, which occupied over an hour. A shady spot was selected close to American camp [where they ate]... The officers of the American and English garrison partook of a luncheon with the pic-nic party... After the cloth was cleared, dancing was commenced on the grass, but the sun's rays proving too powerful for terpsichorean indulgence, an invitation was given by the medical officer in charge to adjourn to his quarters, which they accordingly did, and continued dancing until six o'clock, when the steamer's whistle summoned them...

The British Colonist August 28, 1863

School House No. 1
Minutes

San Juan Island, July 1, 1865—At a meeting of the settlers of San Juan Island, Mr. Boyce in the chair, stating the object of the meeting being for the purpose of selecting a suitable locality for the erection of a schoolhouse, of what material, also to choose and appoint a building committee.

Moved by Mr. Murray, seconded by G. Mickle, that the location be selected a little north of the Hudson's Bay Company bridge. Moved by Captain Valpey, seconded by I. Dwyer, as an amendment, that the location be south of the Hudson's Bay Company's bridge on Portland Fair Hill. Amendment carried, 20; motion amended, 14.

Move by Mr. Murray, seconded by Mr. Hamblet, that a committee of three men be appointed to stake off the ground and superintend the building of the house; motion carried. Committee elected by ballot consisting of Messrs. Boyce, Whity and Keddy.

Moved by Mr. McCoy, seconded by Mr. Fleming that a hewn log house be erected, 20x30 feet. Carried.

Moved by Mr. Mickle, seconded by Mr. Murray, that Captain William Smith be collector and treasurer for the committee. Carried.

Moved by Mr. Murray, seconded by Mr. McCoy, that the house be built by subscription, to be paid by either labor, material, or money, as the committee may require. A day's work for a man to count as $2.00, a day's work for a yoke of oxen, $1.00. Carried.

Moved by Mr. McCoy, seconded by Mr. M.R. Mickle, that a subscription list be placed in the hands of the treasurer at once, carried; after which the meeting was adjourned.

Signed, J. K. [John Keddy], secretary pro tem

—Angie Burt Bowden, Early Schools of Washington Territory
(Seattle: Lowman and Hanford Company, 1935), p. 412.

Subscribers to Portland Fair School House

William Anawana
I. C. Archambault
P. Beigin
Joseph Billard
R. Blake
S. V. Boyce
Joseph Bradley
Henry Dirk
James Dwyer
Louis Farado
Thomas Fleming
John Frazer
Joe Friday
E.T. Hamblet
John Kahana
Johan Kamiah
John Kearney
John Keddy
John Lakamin
John and T. C. Little

M.R. Lundbland
Charles McCoy
Angus McDonald
Edward McGeary
George Mercer
George A Mickle
S.F. Murray
P. Nelson
Joseph Nickenou
John Pelamce
John Roberts
Henry Quinlan
Christopher Rosler
William Smith
? Tahana
I. Valpey
George Walker
John Whity
Robert and I.L. Wilie

—*Angie Burt Bowden,* Early Schools of Washington Territory *(Seattle: Lowman and Hanford Company, 1935), p. 412.*

July 1, 1865
Assessment of Property on San Juan Island
Henry R. Crosbie, Whatcom County Assessor
May 20TH, 1859

Hudson Bay Company

80 acres of land fenced and under cultivation planted in peas, oats & potatoes

Stock
- 4000 Sheep
- 40 Head of Cattle
- 5 Yoke of Oxen
- 35 Horses
- 40 Hogs

Implements
- 10 Frame Houses of which 8 are habitable or dwelling houses
- 2 Barns
- 1 Sheep House

Employees
- C.J. Griffin Chief Trader Hudson Bay Company
- 18 Servants of whom
- 3 are whites viz 2 Scotchmen—one the head shepherd & the other the dairyman—the third a Canadian
- 4 half breeds
- 6 Kanakas
- 4 Chim-zi-an Indians

—*National Archives, Record Group 76, Envelope 5A.*

ACKNOWLEDGEMENTS

- Lovel Pratt: fellow disputant, helpmate, true friend, and the love of my life
- My family, who despite rolling their eyes and groaning whenever I mention The Pig, practice mutual forbearance striving to be love
- Lynn Weber Roochvarg, excellent editor—but all mistakes remain my own, despite her best efforts!
- Mike Vouri, for our many adventures in Bells Vue Sheep Farm land
- In memory of Robin Jacobson, genealogist extrodinaire
- Readers: Bill Engle, Robin Donnelly, Cyrus Forman, and Nancy McCoy
- Washington State Archives Northwest Regional Branch
- Lopez Island Historical Museum: Amy Frost and Breton Carter
- Orcas Island Historical Museum: Nancy Stillger, Edrie Vinson, and Terri Vinson
- San Juan Historical Museum: Kevin Loftus and Andy Zall
- Shaw Island Historical Museum: Cherie Christiansen
- San Juan Island Library
- Kris DayVincent, Bob Guard, Eliza Habegger, Thor Hanson, Beth Helstein, Shaun Hubbard, Doug McCutchen, and Candace Wellman
- W. Bruce Conway, book design services

Detail of Kanaka Bay Villagers and Visitors ca. 1873
(courtesy of San Juan Historical Museum)

PHOTO AND ILLUSTRATION CREDITS

Graphs and Maps
    Graphs and Maps by Lovel and Boyd C. Pratt

General Land Office, Bureau of Land Management
    Township and Range Survey Map of San Juan Valley, San Juan Island
    Telegraph Line on 1874 Township and Range Survey

Northwest Regional Branch, Washington State Archives
    Map of Brown's [Grindstone) Bay
    Sketch of County Road, Keddy [Cady] Mountain to Friday Harbor
    Map of Road Dispute in San Juan Valley, 1887
    Israel Katz Invoice for Samuel H. Gross
    Witness Transportation Costs

Orcas Island Historical Museum
    Children of Catherine Delaunais LePlante
    Louis Cayou with His Yoke of Oxen
    Orchards in Eastsound, Orcas Island, ca. 1900

Royal British Columbia Museum and Archives
    Robert Frazer Land Claim

San Juan Island Historical Museum
    San Juan Valley with Fences
    View of San Juan Valley from Bailer Hill
    Reef Net Fishing in Mitchell Bay
    Gillnetting on Salmon Bank
    Coast Salish Fishermen Reef Netting off Stuart Island
    Graignic Family in the *City of Paris*
    Kanaka Bay Camp ca. 1873
    San Juan Lime Company (Lime Kiln)
    Lime Kiln and Quarry Crew, Cowell's, San Juan Island
    North Kiln and Boarding House, Lime Kiln, San Juan Island

Coopers Displaying the Tools of Their Trade, Roche Harbor, San Juan Island
Hauling Cordwood, San Juan Island
Woodcutters with Springboards and a Misery Whip
Reef Netters off Stuart Island
Canoes and Columbia River Gillnetters at Kanaka Bay
Alfred and Annie Burke and Family, Shaw Island
No. 1 Schoolhouse, Portland Fair, San Juan Island
Earliest Photo of Friday Harbor
Jessie Douglas, Pioneer Cabin, San Juan County Fairgrounds

San Juan Island National Historic Park
Firth Farm (formerly Belle Vue Sheep Farm and American Camp)
1854 U.S. Coast Survey of West Side of San Juan Island
Captain G. H. Richards Survey of Roche Harbor and Its Approaches
James Madison Alden, Sketch of Belle Vue Sheep Farm
Belle Vue Sheep Farm, Photo by North West Boundary Survey, ca. 1859
Belle Vue Sheep Farm Structure with *Piece sur Piece* Construction
Sibley Tents at American Camp
English Camp 1860 with Garden and Tents
American Camp from the Redoubt
Brig. Gen. Nathaniel Michler, Map of English Camp
Sheep Station on North End of San Juan Island
James Madison Alden, View of Griffin Bay and San Juan Town

SeaDoc Society, UC Davis and Tombolo Maps
Bathymetry of the San Juan Islands

Washington State University, Washington Digital Archives
Salish Woman Digging Bulbs
Squamish Woman Spinning Woolly Dog Wool

A

Adams, Mike L., 368
alcohol, 26, 234, 306
Alden, Lt. Com. James, 83–84, 160, 228, 350, 361, 390
Alden, James Madison, 84, 116, 316
Allen, Maj. Harvey A., 240, 402
American Camp, 28, 35, 43, 77, 99–100, 117, 137, 139–141, 143, 145, 160, 166, 168, 174, 178, 184, 233–234, 240, 243, 261, 264, 268–269, 273, 277, 279–280, 282, 290, 297, 304, 306–309, 311, 315, 326–327, 333, 355–356, 369, 381, 384, 387, 389, 402
Anderson, John, 110, 288, 368, 378, 383
apples, 212–213, 274, 283
Archambault, Jacques Cyprien, 44, 96, 426

B

Bailer, E. P., and Gregory 266, 363, 368
Bailey, N. C., 215, 275
Banne, Antoine, 30, 392
Barlow, Arthur "Billy", 41, 369
barn, 118, 130–132, 136, 141–142, 145, 162–164, 166, 204, 209–210, 292, 356, 395, 435
Barnes, Ellis "Yankee", 255, 331, 400
Bauerman, Hilary, 86, 404
Bazalgette, Capt. George, 144, 326
Beaver [HBC Steamer], 14, 160, 232, 258-259, 380, 393, 398, 410-411
beavers, 190, 276
Beaverton Valley, 166, 190, 229, 356, 384
Beigin, Patrick, 37, 43, 48, 170, 252, 265, 301, 310, 369
Bell, William, 38, 312, 314, 369, 426
Belle Vue Sheep Farm, 2, 14–15, 17, 21, 25, 27, 29–32, 77, 86, 91, 99, 103, 110, 115–118, 127–128, 130, 133, 143, 148, 164–166, 173, 184, 203–204, 208, 229, 235–236, 243, 254–255, 260, 277, 290, 295, 307, 324, 331, 334, 343, 346, 359, 374–375, 389, 391–400
Berdillon, Mary Jane "Jennie", 46, 369
Berishe, George, 30, 393
Bissell, Capt. Lyman, 326, 402
Bohn, Baptiste, 30, 392
Bowker, John Sylvester, 280, 369, 387, 405
Bowman, John H., 330, 369
Boyce, Stephen, 34, 318, 369
Bradshaw, James, 42, 44–45, 151, 188, 320, 369
Briggs, John Wesley, 42, 370
Brown, Charles, 41, 370, 423
Brown, John Collins, 370–371
Brown, Lars, 151, 234, 370, 377
Bull, Catherine, 33, 370
Bull, John, 31, 33, 91, 108, 370, 386, 395–396, 435
Bull, Joseph, 38, 320, 370, 386, 426
bulrushes, 125

burial, 99, 295, 303–305, 309
Burr, Smith, 46, 76, 256, 370, 372

C

Caines, Robert Marshall, 370
camas, 7–8, 17–18, 26, 49, 72, 75, 78, 107, 115, 173, 176, 181–184, 207, 241, 274, 306, 447
Campbell, Archibald, 86, 89, 350, 403
Campbell, Sarah Dorse "Lucy", 371, 389
canoe, 14, 24, 34, 43, 72, 116–117, 119–120, 122, 124–125, 130, 149–150, 171, 178, 186, 188, 191–192, 196–198, 200, 210, 227, 240, 243–255, 260, 276, 280, 293, 296, 303–304, 316, 325, 349, 362
Captain George, 77, 374
Casey, Lt. Col. Silas, 136, 143, 400, 402
Casey, Lt. Thomas Lincoln, 400
cattle, 70, 106, 110–111, 165, 175, 184, 203–204, 206–207, 210–211, 260, 277, 279, 286–288, 304, 313, 315, 325–326, 335, 407, 411, 434–435
Cayou, Louis, 42, 106, 114, 151, 188, 320, 383
cedar, 66–67, 84, 109–110, 116, 120–121, 124–126, 134–135, 141, 146, 149, 153–155, 161, 163–165, 167–169, 176, 179, 196–199, 227–229, 231, 244–245, 248, 251–252, 311, 317, 361–362
cemetery, 7, 51, 96, 99, 303–305, 340, 366, 371
Cha-owa-thoit, Mary Min-a-cla-it, 371
Chadwick, Sampson, 43, 75, 210, 371
Chanique, Jane "Cecilia", 46, 370–371
Chapuis, 30, 393
Charboneau, Joseph, 30, 393
Chinese, 4, 29, 60, 217, 240, 292, 333, 412
Christensen, Hans Lee, 372
church, 1, 7, 32, 37, 296–297, 305, 309–312, 330, 334, 340, 389
civil cases, 266, 281, 332–334, 405
Colony of Vancouver Island, 13, 29, 130, 391
Columbia River Salmon Boat, 252, 256
cooper, 174, 201, 217, 224–225, 326, 413, 417, 420–421, 450
cord wood, 231–232
Courcy, John Fitzroy de, 391
Cowichan, 18, 21, 25, 41–42, 52, 91, 163, 209, 325, 329, 344, 380, 382, 385, 423–425
Cowlitz, 32, 45, 54, 79, 107, 131, 204, 241, 270, 368, 372–374, 395–397
criminal cases, 332–336, 367
Crook, John, 38, 372
Crook, William, 101, 372
cross-cultural, 3, 5, 10, 21, 31, 33, 39–41, 45–48, 50, 60, 115, 147, 150, 152, 163, 172, 297–298, 300–301, 305, 311, 344, 347
Crow Valley, 33, 47, 65–66, 98, 100, 283, 370, 373–374, 379, 384
Cussans, Richard W., 228, 372
Custer, Henry, 71, 87, 350, 403, 434
custom of the country [à la façon du pays], 295, 297-301
customs, 101, 174, 256, 274, 289–292, 331, 365, 376–377, 388–389, 392, 400
Cutlar, Lyman A., 14–18, 21, 63, 115, 173, 243, 295, 372

D

Dallas, Alexander, 17, 29, 391
Darrah, Lt. Charles John, 86, 404
Dease, Napoleon, 30, 393
deer, 7, 18, 41, 45, 47, 55, 65–66, 72, 75, 100, 109–110, 151, 169, 185–190, 206, 260, 262, 270, 320, 369, 371, 373, 378–379, 381, 385, 433
Deer Harbor, 41, 45, 47, 65–66, 75, 151, 186, 188, 270, 320, 369, 371, 373, 378–379, 381, 385
Delacombe, Capt. William, 146, 402
Delaunais, Catherine, 42, 44–45, 369, 372–374, 379, 388
Delaunais, Louis Henry, 370, 372–373
Delaunais, Mary Adelaide, 370, 372
Delaunais, Mary Agnes, 46, 373
Denman, C. L., 373
District Court, 56, 101, 286–287, 298, 327, 332, 339, 351, 365
ditches, 165–166
divorce, 302, 334, 367
Dixon, Thomas, 46, 373, 379
Douglas fir, 66, 106, 155, 228, 231, 256, 361
Douglas Treaties, 4, 49, 328
Douglas, James, 4, 14, 17, 24, 29, 40, 42, 49, 90, 92, 127, 130–131, 199, 203, 205, 228, 233, 236–237, 260, 328, 346, 351, 354, 359–360, 391–392, 407
Douglas, Robert, 101, 373, 426
Duwamish et al v. United States, 2, 55, 76, 126, 350, 353, 357
Dwyer, James "Harry", 28, 118, 373

E

East Sound, 21, 51–52, 73–74, 77, 98–100, 152, 217, 270, 283, 304, 311, 314, 317, 319, 330, 348, 380, 382, 386, 429
Eastsound, 47, 51, 64–65, 110, 188, 212–213, 270, 283, 292, 314, 319, 348, 350, 368, 383, 385, 388
Ebey, Col. Isaac N., 389, 400
Eliza, Capt. Francisco de, 390
elk, 55, 187, 190, 199, 227, 433
English Camp, 43, 76, 101, 117, 119, 138, 144–145, 151, 160, 177, 180, 182, 206, 210, 214, 217, 228–229, 233, 235, 239, 243, 263–264, 272–274, 277–279, 290, 304, 309–310, 314, 324–326, 339, 353, 355–356, 372, 376–377, 389, 402, 429
English, Thomas C., 402
Exstine, Moses, 373

F

Faito, George, 396
fences, 97, 109–110, 114, 128, 166–169, 204, 210, 229, 271, 277, 307, 356–357
Finlayson, Roderick, 391
Firth, Lila Hannah, 34, 111, 118, 147, 164, 169, 190, 211, 240, 256, 277, 307, 312–313, 335, 348, 438–439
Firth, Robert, 30, 38, 374–375, 426, 435

fishing camp, 74, 122, 124, 171, 196, 200, 309
Fitzhugh, Edmund C., 374
Fleming, Thomas, 73, 108, 168, 175, 190, 206, 255, 265, 305, 330, 335, 349, 357, 374
Fort Nisqually, 72, 108, 135, 204, 259, 354, 394
Fort Vancouver, 25, 29, 35, 40, 94, 105, 107–108, 128, 131, 160, 203–209, 212, 237, 254, 258, 347, 354, 359, 361, 391, 393–394, 396–397
Fort Victoria, 14, 24, 26, 29, 40, 117, 128, 130, 188, 201, 206, 208, 233, 237, 254, 277, 359, 361, 391, 395–396, 398
Fourth of July, 307–308
frame construction, 116, 134, 144, 146, 152, 156–157, 159–165, 171, 209, 222, 256, 310, 314–315, 317, 356, 431
Fraser River Gold Rush, 35, 42, 152, 375, 379, 382
Fraser, Donald, 392
Frazer, Robert, 92, 374
Frazer, William, 426
Frechette, Peter, 44–45, 374, 379, 426
Freizie, "King Freezie", 26, 31, 396
French Canadians, 4, 14, 16, 29–30, 37, 60, 188, 344
Friday Harbor, 7, 31–32, 45–46, 55, 58, 85–86, 103, 110, 144, 230, 234–235, 261–262, 264, 267, 269–270, 279, 284, 291, 314–315, 319–322, 339, 342, 349, 353, 360–361, 365, 367, 369, 378, 380, 383, 388
Friday, Joe, 27, 31-32, 374
Friday, Pierre (Peter), 31-32, 396
Fuller, William M., 335, 374

G

Galiano, Lt. Dionisio Alcalá, 390
Gardner, George Clinton, 86, 403
Garrison Bay, 73, 76, 98, 118–119, 125, 144, 177, 180, 260, 279, 304, 429
Garry oak, 7, 18, 72, 106, 128
gathering, 19, 26–27, 49, 55, 78, 114–116, 119, 124, 173, 175–179, 181–183, 240, 242, 296, 306, 353
General Allotment Act [Dawes Severability Act], 53
Geographical Memoir, 67, 89, 93, 108, 206, 214, 248, 347, 350, 360, 362–363, 434
Gibbs, George, 22, 24, 29, 49, 86, 91, 93, 202, 204, 236, 329, 347, 350–351, 403
Gillette, E. C., 214, 265, 314, 330, 366, 372–373, 376, 382
Gorman, Patrick, 37, 310, 375, 426
Graignic, Edouard, 43, 203, 375
granary, 130, 134–135, 142, 164, 209–210, 435
Grey, Thomas, 327, 402
Griffin Bay, 8, 77, 85, 99, 117, 126, 132, 136, 178–179, 200, 257, 268–269, 278, 282, 316–317, 346, 406
Griffin, Charles John, 2, 21, 29, 392
Gross, Samuel H., 42, 282, 285–286, 298

H

Haida, 16, 21, 23–25, 27–28, 41, 54, 198, 243, 245, 247, 276, 304, 344, 373, 378, 399
Haller, Capt. Granville O., 402

Hannah, James Madison, 375
Harney, Gen. William Selby, 400
Haro Strait, 1, 14, 63, 81, 86, 117–118, 136, 243, 274–275, 323, 328
Harris, Joseph Smith, 403
Haskell, Capt. Joseph T., 402
Haughey, 1st Lt. James A., 402
Hawkins, Capt. John Summerfield, 86, 404
Henry Island, 41, 73, 79, 186, 211, 279, 387, 429, 433
Hibbard, Augustin, 215, 218, 326, 335, 368, 376, 386, 388, 449
Higgins, Isaac E., 268, 376
Hoffmeister, Augustus, 210, 277, 376
Holland, Thomas, 393
homestead, 2, 7, 19, 30, 33-34, 37, 42, 51–52, 91–92, 98–105, 114, 125, 152–156, 158, 160–165, 168–171, 189, 211–212, 231, 279, 283–284, 319, 335, 337, 339, 351–352, 356, 369–370, 372, 380, 382–383, 386–388, 400, 429, 438, 441, 443, 449
homesteaders, 1, 99, 103–105, 109, 115, 152, 156, 158–159, 165, 211, 274, 284
Hon-Hontoo, 376
Hubbard, 1st Lt. E. B., 402
Hubbs,, Jr., Paul K., 16, 325, 334, 346, 408
Hudson's Bay Company, 2, 4, 7–8, 14–18, 21, 24–27, 29–30, 33, 35, 37, 40–42, 45, 63, 71–72, 84–85, 90, 94, 101, 105, 107–108, 110, 115, 117, 125, 127–128, 130, 134, 136, 140–141, 147, 159–160, 164, 171, 173, 183–185, 188, 190, 199, 203, 210–212, 214, 235, 241, 243, 254, 258–260, 262, 264, 268, 273, 276–278, 280, 282, 295, 297, 309, 317–320, 327–328, 331, 341, 343, 346–347, 351, 354, 359, 361, 368, 391–392, 395, 409–411, 433–434
Hunt, Capt. Louis C., 402
hunting, 18–19, 26–27, 55, 57, 75, 78, 109, 114–116, 119, 124, 173, 175, 183, 185, 187–190, 242, 260, 296
Hutchinson, Jr., Hiram E., 269, 314, 376
Hyland, Rachel Morris "Daisy", 189, 314-315, 377

I

Ignace, Jean, 30, 393
Indian Homestead Act, 51–53
Indigenous seasons, 175
Iotte, Fermin, 38, 370
Irish, 4, 14, 37–38, 60, 309, 344, 369, 381, 384, 386, 391
Izett, John M., 290

J

Jack, Lucy Ontonna, 377
Jaffrett, Yves, 151, 377
Jefferson County, 256, 339, 351, 362
Jewell, Nora, 336-337, 377
Jewell, Peter, 265–266, 313, 336–337, 339, 377
Jones, Frederick Albert, 337, 378

K

Kahahopa, 31, 396
Kahaliopua, 31, 396
Kahana, John, 33, 386, 395–396
Kama Kamai, 148, 396
Kamaka, 31, 397
Kanaka, 4–5, 10, 16, 21, 28–34, 38, 60, 77, 79, 85, 91, 98, 108, 118, 126, 147–148, 150, 207, 237, 250, 252, 256–258, 265, 297, 335, 344, 348, 354, 370, 373–374, 386, 395–399, 412, 416, 430
Kanaka Bay, 31-34, 77, 147-150, 252, 354
Kanaka Joe, 34, 118, 335, 373–374, 398
Katona, Mary Lucy, 378
Katz, Israel, 101, 103, 269, 282, 284, 286, 288, 319, 322, 331, 333, 337, 364–365, 378
Kaukana, 31, 397
Kauna, 397
Kay, John, 110, 114, 368, 378
Keaini, William, 33, 397
Keddy, John, 210, 266, 313, 330, 371
Keddy, William, 335, 378
Kennerly, Dr. C. B. R., 88, 109, 187, 318, 350, 352, 359
King, James F., 44, 46, 388
Kitchené, Georgius, 273, 378
Kittles, John Taylor, 47, 378–379
Konea, 397

L

La Laima, 31, 397
Ladebauche, Isabel, 46, 379
Ladebauche, Joseph, 379
Lamane, 14, 31, 393
Lami, Pierre, 256, 379
Land Ordinance Act, 92
LaPlante, Catherine, 44–45, 374, 379
LaPlante, Pierre, 45, 379
LaPlante, Victoria Frances, 44-46, 379
La Porte, Louis 379
Laurence, Julien, 42, 379–380
Lawson, Peter, 77, 114, 156, 263, 268, 284, 296, 380
lime, 35, 64, 75, 79, 99–100, 134, 145, 155, 161, 173–174, 214–224, 226–227, 231, 233, 240, 257, 270–271, 275, 284, 290, 295, 308, 325–326, 335–336, 360, 368, 372, 375–376, 380–382, 384–386, 388, 413, 430, 450
liquor, 234–235, 280, 290, 317, 325, 328, 331, 333, 335, 369, 398, 405
Littleman, George and Mary, 51–52, 380
loan, 285–286, 288
log cabin, 15, 115, 152–154, 156, 159, 162, 301, 309, 319, 343, 407
longhouse, 50, 77, 115–116, 119–124, 126–127, 148–149, 164, 177, 251–252, 309, 316
Lopez Island, 21–22, 28, 41, 43, 62, 65, 67, 75, 78, 84, 89, 96, 100, 108, 179, 188–189, 194, 228, 231, 269–270, 272, 274, 314, 319, 330, 367–368, 370–372, 376–378, 383–385, 389, 413–414, 417, 419, 422–423, 430

Lopez Village, 74, 166, 189, 283, 317, 319, 376, 428
Lord, John Keast, 86, 350, 404
Low, Jacob, 33, 380
Lummi, 2, 4, 16, 21–23, 33, 41, 46, 49–51, 54–56, 73–75, 81, 83, 119, 122, 125, 127, 151, 178, 188, 194, 202, 298, 325, 329, 344, 346, 349–350, 353, 370–371, 377, 382, 386, 395–396, 398, 423, 425, 429, 433
Lyall, Dr. David, 86, 404

M

Madden, Daniel and Patrick, 37, 310, 381
marks and brands, 111, 352
marriage, 2–3, 5, 10, 19, 26, 30–31, 33, 40–41, 45, 47–48, 50, 54, 150, 183, 217–218, 273–274, 295–303, 309, 337, 344, 347, 365, 367, 376–377, 381, 387
May, Enoch, 151, 381
Mayne, Lt. Richard Charles, 85, 390
McDonald, Alexander, 393
McDonald, Angus, 394
McDonald, William John, 394
McKay, Charles A., 43, 46, 380
McLachlan, Daniel and Robert 217, 380–381, 386
McLachlan, William, 217, 381
McLeod, Jr., Murdoch, 394
McLeod,, Sr., Murdoch (Murdo), 394
McMillin John S., 384–385
Menzies, Archibald, 74, 82, 121, 124, 350, 390, 431
Mercer, George I., 381
merchant, 35, 174, 270, 278, 286, 405, 424
Merrifield, Stafford, 38, 342, 381, 426
Métis, 14, 16, 344, 354, 393, 395
Meyerbeck, Solomon, 239, 381
Meyers, Hanna and Henry, 381–382
mink, 109
Mitchell Bay, 28, 41–43, 46, 50, 53–58, 73, 75–77, 101, 126, 148, 151, 218, 256, 286, 296–297, 314, 329, 369–372, 375–376, 378–380, 383, 385, 387, 393, 429
Mitchell Bay Band, 41–42, 54–56, 58, 286, 296–297, 329, 370–371, 393
Michler, Brig. Gen., Nathaniel, 144, 147
Montigny, Leroux, 394
Moore, William, 42, 188, 233, 280, 297, 320, 382, 385
Mordhorst, Bernhardt, 382
Morrill Tariff, 291
mortgage, 104, 215, 234, 285–287, 351
Mulno, Thomas, 103, 382

N

Na-ME-At-Cha, George, 52-53, 382
Nahouree, 397
Nahua, 31, 397

naturalization, 37–38, 113, 332, 339, 426, 439
Naukana, William, 31, 33–34, 148, 398
Newanna, William, 33–34, 398
Newsome, Frank, 214, 372, 375, 382
newspaper, 1–2, 48, 57, 267–268, 270–271, 275, 309
Nickerson, Capt. Azor H., 402
North West Boundary Survey, 24, 29, 46, 71, 80, 88, 93, 109, 119, 130, 142, 206, 214, 229, 231, 240, 255, 258, 262, 318, 350–352, 359–360, 375, 403–404, 427, 433
Nuana, Joe, 34, 335, 398

O

O'Bryan, Ella Elizabeth B., 383
O'Clain, Mary Elizabeth "Lizzie", 41, 383
Oakes, Daniel W., 267, 382
Olga, 42, 65, 70, 73, 96, 100, 187–188, 213, 230, 270, 320, 382, 429
open range, 110–111, 113–114, 368, 383
Orcas Island, 21, 33, 41–42, 45–47, 51–52, 62, 64–66, 70, 72, 74–75, 77–79, 96, 100, 106, 112, 150–151, 180, 186, 189–190, 199, 211–213, 217–218, 224, 230, 233, 258, 262, 269–270, 283, 288–290, 292, 297, 305, 314, 320, 330, 348, 360, 363, 368–371, 373–374, 376–388, 413–414, 417, 419, 422–423
orchard, 109–110, 160, 165, 169–170, 189–190, 212–213, 279, 301, 388
oxen, 104–106, 160, 203, 206, 208–209, 239, 258, 278, 285, 287
oysters, 75, 79, 178–179

P

Page, William "Old Man", 394
Page, Young, 394
Pakee, 31, 398
Park, Hugh, 105, 351, 383
Parke, Lt. John Grubb, 86, 403
Pattle, William, 383
Pe-el, 371, 383
pears, 212–213
Peers, James, 113, 288, 365, 368, 383
Pender, Capt. Daniel, 85, 390
pest, 107, 109, 190
Peterson, 2nd Lt. John P., 402
Pickett, Capt. George Edward, 400
pig, 1, 3, 8, 13–17, 21, 25, 33, 35, 43, 60, 63, 71, 107, 110, 185, 204, 206–207, 211, 257–258, 278, 290, 295, 307, 317, 324, 341, 346, 350, 372, 374, 380, 400–401, 406–407, 411, 434, 437
Port Townsend, 18, 34, 37, 157, 187, 213, 215, 231, 243, 257, 260, 268–270, 275, 279–283, 286, 289–291, 298, 307, 319, 327, 331–334, 336–337, 339, 355, 361, 366, 371, 376, 378, 384, 388–389, 405
Portland Fair, 85, 190, 305, 312–314, 339
potato, 8, 14–18, 33, 37, 63, 84, 103, 110, 131, 158, 164, 165, 173, 175, 182, 183, 185, 189, 204, 208-210, 237, 238, 243, 276, 277, 280, 284, 285, 287, 292, 380, 407, 409,

Powell, Richard K., 394
preemption, 33, 91, 93–94, 99–101, 373, 375, 409
Prevost, Capt. James Charles, 144, 404
prices, 256, 276–278, 284–285
probate, 2, 33, 52, 91, 105, 211, 215, 279, 330, 332, 338–339, 351, 376, 388, 449–450
prostitution, 19, 26, 126, 235, 274, 317, 398

Q

Quimican, Mary, 383
Quimper, Ens. Manuel, 81, 390
Quinlan, Henry, 384

R

rancheria, 126
rape, 333, 335–337, 367, 377
rations, 207, 236–239, 361
redoubt, 117, 139
Reed, John P., 41, 389
reef net, 49, 52, 74, 79, 122–123, 195–196, 202, 249–250, 252, 273, 350, 380, 385, 430
Rethlefsen, Matthias Paul, 166, 384
Richards, Capt. George Henry, 85-87, 391
Richardson, George Stillman, 384
roads, 72, 85, 97, 117, 136, 211, 260–262, 264–268, 314, 317, 331, 334, 363, 432
Robillard, Joseph, 30, 394
Robinson, 1st Lt. Augustus, 402
Robinson, Allen Y. and John B., 384
Roblin, Charles E., 53, 400
Roche Harbor, 64, 70, 77, 85–87, 103, 145, 218, 223, 225, 270, 291, 314, 325, 360, 381, 384–385
root houses, 131, 135, 164, 209–210
Rosario Strait, 3, 63, 73, 81, 84, 86, 175, 182, 193, 347, 390, 433
Rosler, Christopher, 41, 43, 118, 126, 285, 297, 330, 384
Ross, Alexander, Colin and Donald, 38, 218, 381, 426
Ross, John, 395
Rothschild, D. C. H., 280–281, 289, 405

S

Saanich, 4, 16, 21, 23, 41, 49, 51, 54, 73, 175–176, 182, 191, 199, 298, 309, 329, 344, 349, 377, 393, 424, 429
Sacom-Dack, Jennie Bee-osh, 385
salary, 236, 238, 315
salmon, 26, 49, 56, 75, 78, 84, 86, 89, 122–124, 176, 180, 183, 191–202, 205, 237–238, 252, 256, 273–274, 287, 309, 358–359, 394, 448
Samish, 4–5, 16, 21–23, 41, 49, 52, 54–56, 74–75, 77, 126, 175, 179, 199, 299, 309, 329, 344, 349, 366, 374, 385, 388, 425

Samish, Harry, 385
San Juan Island, 1, 3, 5–8, 10, 12–13, 15, 21–26, 28–35, 37, 39–43, 45, 49–51, 53–57,
    60, 62–64, 66–68, 70–71, 73–79, 82–92, 94, 96, 98–100, 103, 107–108, 110–111,
    114–117, 119, 125, 127, 131, 133, 136–139, 143–144, 166–167, 169, 173, 177,
    179–180, 182–184, 190, 193, 199–200, 214, 217–218, 220–221, 225, 229–231,
    238, 240, 243, 249, 257–258, 260–263, 265, 270, 272–275, 280, 284–286, 290,
    293, 295–298, 302, 304, 307, 310–311, 314–316, 323–333, 335–337, 339–342,
    346–353, 355, 359–361, 363–365, 368–370, 372–382, 384–392, 394–397, 400,
    406, 409, 411, 415, 418, 421, 424, 434, 436, 438
San Juan Islander, 47, 77, 179, 274, 348, 350
San Juan Valley, 32–33, 37, 66, 70, 91, 98, 101, 107, 168, 188, 229, 261–263, 266, 272,
    284, 305, 309–310, 314, 337, 368–375, 377–381, 384, 386, 388, 396
Sandwith, Isaac, 211, 279, 385, 426
Sangster, James, 392
Saunders, Henry, 280, 333, 405
saw pit, 229
school, 1–2, 8–9, 47–48, 145, 189, 197, 267, 279, 310–315, 329–330, 332, 340, 349, 358,
    366, 369, 375, 377, 389
Scots, 4, 14, 16, 21, 29, 38, 60, 344, 387
Scott, Gen. Winfield, 327, 400
scows, 257–258
Scudder, Robert, 395
Scurr, Richard and Robert, 381, 385
seals, 176, 193, 199, 431
Seymour, Thomas Robinson, 42, 385
Shattuck, Charles W., 152, 330
Shaw Island, 3, 42, 79, 96, 105, 160, 163, 171, 188, 270, 328, 351–352, 356, 372,
    379–380, 383, 385, 387, 417, 420–421
sheep, 2, 7, 14–15, 17–18, 21, 25, 27–32, 40, 63, 72, 77, 86, 91, 97–99, 103, 106, 108,
    110–113, 115–118, 127–128, 130, 132–133, 135–136, 143, 148, 164–166,
    173–175, 183–185, 203–206, 208, 210–211, 229, 235–237, 243, 254–255,
    257, 260–262, 266–267, 277–280, 285–286, 288–290, 295, 303, 307, 324, 331,
    334–335, 343, 346, 359, 368, 371, 374–375, 378, 383, 387–389, 391–400, 405, 407,
    411, 431, 434–435, 438–439
shellfish, 177–179, 228
shingles, 120, 131, 134, 143, 149, 152, 155, 160, 229, 231, 317
Shotter, George R., 215, 217–218, 376, 380, 386
Sit-Sa-Lum, Thomas, 52, 386
Skagit, 16, 25, 41, 54–55, 73, 155, 192, 249, 299, 323, 325, 332, 372, 376, 394, 425
Skomiax, Chief Jim, 32, 386, 396
Skqulap, Fu-hue-wut Mary, 33, 370, 386, 395–396
slavery, 16, 240–241, 274, 362
sloops, 149, 243, 253, 255–256, 275
smallpox, 23–24
smuggling, 283, 289–291, 293, 335, 365
Songhees [Songish], 4, 16, 21–23, 25–26, 31–32, 34, 41, 49, 54, 73, 122, 148, 199, 249,
    257, 329, 344, 346, 386, 396, 429
Sooke, 4, 22–23, 41, 54, 329, 344
steamers, 231–233, 243, 258, 260, 268, 433, 436

Stevens, Gov. Isaac I., 401
stores, 237, 243, 248, 268, 280, 282–285, 293, 318–319, 378, 405, 451
Strait of Georgia, 63, 67, 69
Stuart Island, 3, 23, 51, 79, 96, 98, 182, 249, 377, 382, 387, 416, 424
sutlers, 277–280, 293, 328
Sweeney, John and Joseph, 33, 101, 269, 284, 310, 322, 386

T

Tamaree, 399
taxes, 2, 52, 255, 265, 278, 313, 329, 331, 335, 339
Taylor, William F., 364, 387, 426, 451
telegraph, 174, 256, 268, 271–273, 328, 378
tents, 88, 117, 132–133, 136–139, 144, 152–153, 262, 317, 428
Tharald, Theodore and Thomas, 109, 169, 387
The British Colonist, 270–271, 278
Thomas, John "Johnny Tom," 387
Thomas, She-Kla-Malt, 387
Thornton, Thomas, 275, 387
timothy, 105, 162, 165, 203, 211
Tod, Jr, John, 40, 211, 279
Tolmie, Dr. William Fraser, 14, 392
Town of San Juan, 263, 317, 319
Township and Range, 9, 75, 95, 112, 114, 180, 241, 263, 272, 350, 357, 366
trails, 34, 109, 260, 262, 268
trapping, 27, 108, 185, 190, 242, 287
Treaty of Oregon, 89
Trudelle, Louis, 387
Trueworthy, Samuel James, 371, 388
Tsimshian, 16, 21, 23, 25, 41, 43, 54, 247, 297, 344, 353, 370–371, 383–384, 388–389
tules, 122, 125
Tulloch, James Francis, 2, 47–48, 72, 112, 297, 348, 388

V

Vancouver, Capt. George, 80–81, 187, 390–391
Verrier, Adeline, 44, 46, 378, 388
Viereck, Johann Gottlieb, 388
Von Gohren, E. L., 213

W

wages, 217, 236–237, 239, 333, 361, 436
Waldron Island, 3, 75, 79, 97, 202, 213, 330, 352, 370–371, 375, 379, 385, 417, 422, 425, 430
Warbass, Edward D., 111, 270, 279, 281, 318, 330, 333–334, 337
Warren, William J., 86, 119, 240, 352, 403
Waterman, Sigmund, 280–281, 289, 405
Watts, Charles, 215, 335–337, 368, 376, 388

Webber, Henry, 99, 290, 389
weeds, 107–108, 183, 207
Weeks, Thomas J., 310, 389
Weldon, Tacee "Little Bird", 384, 389
wells, 170–171
West Sound, 21, 66–67, 73, 77, 96, 178, 186, 211, 213, 270, 320, 378, 429
Whatcom County, 153, 157, 204, 255, 263, 278, 298, 323–324, 326, 328–329, 331–332, 339, 352, 363, 365, 374, 383, 400
Whitener, Wesley Henry, 371, 389
Whitlock, Charles, 109–110, 153, 239, 352, 356, 389
Wilkes, Capt. Charles, 82, 391, 431–432
Williams, John, 395
Williams, Richard, 395
Williamson, James, 395
Wilson, Lt. Charles William, 86, 404
Witty, John Frederick, 389
wolves, 108–109, 352
woolly dog, 113, 183–184

www.ingramcontent.com/pod-product-compliance
Lightning Source LLC
Chambersburg PA
061732070526

LPB00024B/2644